PEOPLE
WHO CHANGED
THE WORLD

for Chrissie

PEOPLE
WHO CHANGED
THE WORLD

by Rodney Castleden

First published in Great Britain in 2005
This trade paperback edition published in 2006
by Time Warner Books

ISBN-13: 978-0-316-02715-1
ISBN-10: 0-316-02715-4

Produced by Omnipress Limited

Printed in India

Time Warner Books
An imprint of Little, Brown Book Group
Brettenham House
Lancaster Place
London WC2E 7EN
A member of the Hachette Livre Group of companies

www.littlebrown.co.uk

Photo credits
Cover images: Alamy
Inner photos: Getty Images

CONTENTS

. . . .

I: THE ANCIENT WORLD

II: THE MEDIEVAL AND RENAISSANCE WORLD

III: THE ENLIGHTENED WORLD

IV: THE NINETEENTH CENTURY WORLD

V: THE MODERN WORLD

INTRODUCTION

· · · · · · · · ·

SOME PEOPLE IN history seem to have been born to transform the world. In the hey-day of monarchy, now long gone, people were born into royal dynasties, and that placed them in a position where they were able to change things. An old-style absolute monarch had the power to declare war or make peace, and that decision in turn could change the course of history, not only for the nations directly concerned but for a whole continent. Enthroned by an accident of birth, power handed to them on a plate, hereditary monarchs have always been in a position to order change. As the crown prince of Macedonia, Alexander the Great was in a strong position to do great things. Others have been born to inherited wealth and that has given them the ability to do great things. Tolstoy was one of these.

But there are many among the people featured in this book who were at the other end of the social scale, people who started with no advantage of birth and who had no family fortune to support them. Sometimes they were lucky with their teachers, as Shakespeare seems to have been, sometimes just lucky in having the right idea at the right moment. Many of these people who came out of nowhere had origins that were unbelievably humble and it looks as if some-times it was the sheer hardship of their childhood that gave them the drive to escape poverty and powerlessness. Newton, Rousseau, Robespierre, Dickens, Stanley, Schliemann and Lomonosov are all members of this category.

Above all, it is the qualities of determination, drive and tenacity that mark out the world-changers from the rest of humanity – Leibniz, Wilberforce, Pasteur and Edison stand out as prime examples of people who achieved things through sheer hard work. Sometimes the drive and self-confidence amounted to monomania or even egomania, and I sense that some of the world-changers were pyschologically abnormal. Some probably 'suffered' from narcissistic personality disorder, a greatly inflated sense of their own importance. Alexander, Ivan the Terrible, Wagner and Hitler were of this type.

This book has a fixed length and there is only room to fit in a finite number of world-changers – about 175 of them in all. It is very obvious that as many names again could easily have been included in the list, and some readers may disagree about who has been included and who has not. Plato is in, Socrates is out. Richard Trevithick is in, George Stephenson is out. Elvis Presley and the Beatles are in, Igor Stravinsky and Michael Tippett are out. These are not finely calculated snubs or rejections, and it should not be assumed that the people who have not been included in this book are second rate. I have simply targetted people whose original or seminal influence on others or impact on events is obvious. Plato is in because he left behind writings that can still be read; Socrates did not. Trevithick was the original inventor of the steam locomotive; the better-known Stephenson was the self-promoting entrepreneur who made money from Trevithick's invention. I have also tried to balance up different areas of endeavour; it would be possible to find 175 inventors, or 175 writers, so only a representative selection is possible.

Possibly we would all come up with different lists, though I suspect a fair number of the names would crop up in list after list – and there could in any case be a second volume containing another 175 people of generally equal importance. All the people I have selected altered the world in some significant way, through having an idea, inventing something, discovering something, doing something, or in some cases simply by being something. People such as Oscar Wilde and Marilyn Monroe changed the world by being in themselves symbols or icons, heroes or anti-heroes, role models or anti-role models. Some changed the world for the better, like Pasteur and Lister, some for the worse, like Hitler, Mao and bin Laden. Some people have been included because they changed other people's perception of the world; and changing people's perception of the world is in effect to make the world a different place. Newton and Einstein did that.

During the course of writing this book it struck me again and again that one world-changer has very often been influenced or inspired by another. Lister was inspired by Pasteur. Jung was inspired by Freud. John F. Kennedy was inspired by Martin Luther King; Martin Luther King was inspired by Gandhi; Gandhi was inspired by Tolstoy; Tolstoy was inspired by Jesus. There is a kind of invisible chain of influences connecting them one to another.

I have often wondered about the existence of such a chain since the first time I met Michael Tippett, probably the greatest creative force I have encountered and a great influence on my own creative life, not that I count myself as a world-changer. As we talked, I understood that he was in a similar way greatly influenced by meeting T. S. Eliot. Tippett did not actually meet Yeats or Shaw, though he wanted to, and admitted that he tried very hard to meet Shaw; the nearest he got was seeing Shaw coming out of a house, climbing into a car and being driven off. I had a youthful fantasy of having lunch with Wagner, and imagined the things Wagner would have said. When I met Tippett for the first time, and listened to him telling me over lunch about his own creative relationship with Beethoven, I had the strange sensation that this was the fantasy realized, that here was Wagner, as Wagner related his own achievement back to Beethoven's in just the same way. It was only recently I discovered that in 1840 Wagner wrote a short story, *A Pilgrimage to Beethoven*, in which he, Wagner, fantasized about his visit to meet Beethoven, which seemed somehow to close the circle.

Such meetings, and meetings of minds, are crucially important to the creative process and to the development of civilization. The network of inspiration spreads endlessly outwards and backwards in time, through Wagner to Schopenhauer and Beethoven, through Beethoven to Mozart, through Eliot to Bertrand Russell, through Shaw to Marx and Dickens, through Galileo to Copernicus and Pythagoras. The movers and shakers move and shake one another, just as much as they move and shake the world around them. Sometimes the world-changers are very agreeable and friendly people – Sophocles, Leonardo, Nelson and Lincoln stand out as the friendliest of men – but often they are competitive, demanding, abrasive, striking sparks off one another. The great quarrel between Freud and Jung is just one well-known example; there were fierce intellectual quarrels between Hume and Rousseau, D. H. Lawrence and Bertrand Russell, Wagner and Nietzsche. People of heightened talent are often drawn together by the attractions of genius but ultimately divided from each other by having their own original and incompatible views. Often the relationship is strained by excessive idealization on the part of one or both parties. Nietzsche started off idolizing Wagner. Then he got to know him really well, saw Wagner's personality flaws and disillusionment led to bitterness and fierce hostility. Freud and Jung started off by idolizing one another, and that certainly couldn't last.

Sometimes the influence of one world-changer on another is unconscious. We often forget where we heard or read an idea, and re-invent or re-discover it later. Napoleon based his invasion of Egypt on an anonymous strategic plan that had been devised long before and lay in an archive store in Paris. It was only during his later conquest of Europe, when he took Hanover in 1803, that he stumbled on the original manuscript of the strategic plan; it had been written by Leibniz. Jung thought his animus/ anima theory of the unconscious mind was totally original. Then someone pointed out a passage in *Tristram Shandy*, the novel by the eighteenth century English writer Laurence Sterne. Sterne wrote of 'the two souls in every man living, the one being called the ANIMUS, the other, the ANIMA.' Far from being disconcerted by this discovery, Jung looked further and found that Sterne had recycled the idea from the Rosicrucians; the idea was an archetype. Mrs Thatcher once famously said, 'There is no such thing as society.' Did she think that up for herself? No, she got it from her guru Laurens van der Post, and he in his turn got it from his guru – Carl Gustav Jung. We can never be quite sure where our ideas have come from.

To highlight some of these connections, where the story of one world-changer connects with another entry in the book, the name is highlighted in bold. In some entries it becomes obvious that there is a lot of interaction among great minds, and that influences in many directions are at work. Just to take one example, in the entry on Sophocles, the reader will find references both backwards and forwards in time – to Homer, Aeschylus, Euripides, Agamemnon, Pericles, Aristotle and Freud.

Even though the list of people who have changed the world could be lengthened, doubled or even trebled, I am left with the overriding impression that the human race owes a very great deal to a surprisingly small number of people in total, and conversely that enormous suffering has been inflicted on the human race by a relatively small number of different people.

I
THE ANCIENT WORLD

IMHOTEP

Lived about 2970 BC, in the reign of King Zoser.
The earliest architect whose name we know.

ACHIEVEMENTS:
Designed and built the very first Egyptian pyramid.
The first individual person to have designed a monument.
Created a lasting memorial to one of the early kings of Egypt.
Revered by ancient Egyptians for his wisdom.
Awarded the status of a cult-hero and god in later centuries.

IMHOTEP WAS AN ancient Egyptian, a physician and adviser to King Zoser. It was Imhotep who designed the unique Step Pyramid at Saqqara, overlooking the city of Memphis. Not surprisingly, in time Imhotep came to be revered as a great guru. By 500 BC, over two thousand years after his death, he was regarded as a minor god, the life-giving son of Ptah, the god of Memphis. Scribes poured out libations to him before beginning their work. The Greeks saw him as the Egyptian equivalent of their god of healing, Asclepius. Many bronze figurines of Imhotep as a god of healing have been found.

When Herodotus saw and described the pyramids in 450 BC, Imhotep was as far removed from him as the life of Herodotus is from us. One poet wrote:

> *I have heard the discourses of Imhotep and Hardedef*
> *With whose words men speak everywhere.*
> *What are their habitations now?*

Their walls are destroyed, their habitations are no more,
As if they had never been.

This feeling is common in ancient Egyptian poetry – keening over the infinite poignancy of the transience of man. Human life is short and human achievements crumble and vanish. But as far as Imhotep was concerned, they were wrong. We not only remember Imhotep, thousands of years later, we can see the buildings he created. They are still standing.

Imhotep's particular achievement was the development of the pyramid, an ambitious new type of monument. Until Imhotep's time, royal burial monuments in Egypt were single-storey structures, massive rectangular buildings called mastabas. These monuments were at first built with inward-sloping walls of brick encasing rubble interiors, and only later made of more durable stone. They were raised for the kings of the early dynastic period. The mastabas were almost certainly built in imitation of the palaces of kings and nobles, houses for the dead imitating houses for the living. It was Imhotep, they said, who invented the use of stone for building.

Imhotep's Step Pyramid was built in an enclosure that imitates the plan of King Zoser's palace in Memphis. It features blind doorways carved in solid stone, doorways that stand tantalizingly ajar; they give mortals no hope of access to the interior.

The Step Pyramid, which was a revolutionary design, started off as a limestone-faced square mastaba 8 metres high, covering a maze of underground royal burial chambers. Then Imhotep had the inspired idea of building another, slightly smaller, mastaba on top and then two further mastabas, each smaller than the last, stacked on top of that. At this point, he realised that he had created an imposing monument that could very easily be made even more imposing by increasing the area of the base and adding a further two storeys. The final version of the Step Pyramid had six tiers.

Imhotep's new building was higher, more complex, more impressive than anything that had previously been built in Egypt. It was also very luxuriously fitted out with stone carvings and beautiful vessels of alabaster, porphyry and serpentine. Although many of the fittings have been plundered, a surprising number still lie in place at the site – and the pyramid itself still stands intact.

Later pyramids were built on an even grander scale, but it was Imhotep who showed the way by inventing the pyramid design, and in effect became the designer of the oldest wonder of the ancient world. Expert opinion has it that Imhotep achieved this remarkable design in one go, actually thinking it out during the course of building the Step Pyramid. He can also be credited with being the first royal servant to give his patron, King Zoser, the immortality he craved. In 3000 BC, kingship was itself in its infancy. With the new phenomenon of kingship came personality cults, and with those came the desire to make a visible impact on the landscape, the desire to be forever remembered. Imhotep was the first person to fulfil those desires.

HAMMURABI

Born about 2087 BC, died about 2025 BC.
King of Babylon, empire-builder, pioneer law-giver.

ACHIEVEMENTS:
Created the great Mesopotamian empire of Babylonia.
Turned Babylon from a village into a great city.
Established Babylon as the political and intellectual centre
  of western Asia.
Compiled the earliest known comprehensive code of laws.

HAMMURABI WAS BORN in about 2087 BC and became the sixth king of the Amorite dynasty of Babylonia. He is believed to make an appearance in the Old Testament disguised as 'Amraphel, king of Shinar', who invaded Canaan in the time of Abraham. He extended the Babylonian empire during his 43-year reign, making his home town of Babylon into a great metropolis, first rivalling then surpassing the neighbouring city of Kish, just 12km away to the east. Under his rule Babylon became the political, cultural and intellectual centre of western Asia, and then remained so right through to the time of Christ; the famous 'wise men from the east' probably came from Babylon.

During Hammurabi's time, and presumably with his encouragement, the priests of Babylon raised the status of the local deity, Marduk, to the status of a great god. In the later Akkadian epic of creation, Marduk is made to supplant Ninurta, the older god who features in the Sumerian creation epic.

A letter to his governors has survived, and this shows that he had set up a remarkably efficient government administration. The unification of the kingdoms of Sumer and Akkad was achieved by his father, Sinmuballit, and Hammurabi built on this legacy by extending the empire northward to take in the valleys of the Tigris and Euphrates. This proved to be one of the most far-reaching and momentous events in ancient history.

Hammurabi is remembered today chiefly as a great law-giver. He compiled one of the earliest known codes of law. Evidently monumental pillars were set up, probably one in each town, for reference by courts throughout the empire. A nearly complete tablet inscribed with his laws in the Sumerian language was found at Susa, a diorite slab 2.5m high. It now resides in the Louvre Museum in Paris. The text of the laws is inscribed below a bas-relief showing the king praying to the sun god Shamash, who is giving the laws to Hammurabi in person. This concept was probably a common one throughout the Middle and Near East, and it was later incorporated in the story of Moses acquiring the Ten Commandments directly from Yahweh on Mount Sinai.

Hammurabi had something approaching 300 laws inscribed on the slab found at Susa. Not all copies of the laws were as comprehensive. A set of tablets carrying extracts from the law code have been found at Nippur.

Hammurabi's 43-year reign was the most momentous in the ancient history of the Middle East. He established a huge Mesopotamian empire with an efficient centralized administration. He established Babylon as the greatest city in western Asia. He presided over wide-reaching religious reforms, including a reconstruction of the Sumerian pantheon; in effect he reorganized the gods. He set up a comprehensive code of laws and ensured that it was enforced throughout his empire.

MOSES

Lived in the 14th and 13th centuries BC.
Prophet, law-giver, leader of the people of Israel, creator of the nation of Israel, creator of Judaism.

ACHIEVEMENTS:
Uniting the Israelite tribes into an embryonic nation.
Leading the Israelites out of captivity in Egypt.
Supplying the Israelites with a god, Yahweh, and mediating between the two.
Receiving the Ten Commandments.
Creating the new religion of Judaism.
Leading the Israelites to a God-given 'Promised Land'.

MOSES WAS AN Old Testament Hebrew prophet and lawgiver. He was born in Egypt of Levite parents, at a time when the people of Israel were slave workers in Egypt. As a baby, Moses (Hebrew 'Mosheh') was saved from a general slaughter of male Jewish children, ordered by Pharaoh, by being concealed by his mother in a chest in bulrushes by the bank of the River Nile. He was found there and brought up by one of Pharaoh's daughters. When he grew up he killed an Egyptian who was bullying an Israelite, and had to take flight to avoid retribution.

As a young man he lived in Midian with the priest Jethro, marrying one of Jethro's daughters and becoming the father of Gershom and Eliezer. At the holy mount, Moses had a momentous encounter with God. Disclosing his name to Moses as 'Yahweh' (Jehovah), God told him to bring the people of Israel out of Egypt. The newly named god showed his displeasure at the Egyptians' behaviour by afflicting them with a series of plagues, culminating in the death of the first-born.

Moses had by this stage become the leader of the people of Israel. In about 1270 BC he led them out of captivity, east into the Sinai peninsula, and from there into Kadesh and Moab. The Egyptians who pursued them were drowned in the Red Sea.

While on Mount Sinai, Moses had another encounter with Yahweh, who gave him the Ten Commandments, a very brief and simplified law code. In presenting the Israelites with this law code and mediating with Yahweh, Moses in effect became the founder of the Jewish religion.

After a long period of 'wandering', during which the Israelites were tested and proved by their new god, Moses led them towards the borders of what was seen as 'the promised land', the land of Israel that ever afterwards was claimed by them as God-given. This continuing belief lies behind many of the territorial struggles that have gone on in Israel/Palestine over the last half century.

At Mount Nebo, to the north-west of the Dead Sea, Moses died. It was left to his successor, Joshua, to lead the Israelites across the River Jordan into the Promised Land of Canaan.

Later stories were invented round the life of Moses, such as his initiating the worship of snakes and bulls, and it is impossible to know which stories are historically true and which are not. There is no doubt, though, that Moses was the founder of Israelite nationhood. It was Moses who welded together the many tribes into one nation. He was also, in a quite extra-ordinary way, the founder of the Israelites' religion; he introduced the Israelites to their new god, Yahweh, and acted as the sole mediator between people and god. He was clearly a great charismatic leader, central to the events surrounding the Israelites' escape from Egypt.

The receiving of the Ten Commandments was perhaps less of an achievement, representing a simplified and incomplete code of ethical conduct. Even so, in its simplicity and brevity, it became a memorable banner for the new religion – and has remained so. The Ten Command-ments have all the power of a corporate logo. Moses unquestionably stands out as one of the greatest and most significant figures in human history.

MUWATALLIS

Born about 1335 BC, died about 1282 BC.
Great king of the Hittites, military commander, strategist.

ACHIEVEMENTS:
Defeated the Egyptians at the Battle of Kadesh.
Established the Hittite Empire as equal in power to Egypt.

MUWATALLIS WAS THE Great King, or over-king, of the Hittite empire in the run-up to the Trojan War. He ruled a huge sprawling empire that was sometimes called Hatti, covering most of what is now Turkey. Along the western coast there were problems with incursions by the Mycenaean Greeks, who attacked and ransacked several towns before finally attacking Troy in the north-west. The Hittite Great Kings frequently tried diplomacy in dealing with these incursions in the west, because there were larger-scale problems in the east, where there was a clash of interests with the Assyrians and Egyptians.

Muwattallis was the son of Mursilis II, who had preserved the empire his father had left him, intact, for 30 years. Muwatallis was a fat, good-natured man who led a life of action rather than contemplation. It was he who avenged the humiliation of Suppiluliuma, and defeated Ramesses II at the Battle of Kadesh. Kadesh transformed the Hittite Empire and Egypt into rivals of equal status and strength.

Unfortunately, though there are extensive Hittite archives, very little is written by Muwatallis, and nothing at all about the Battle of Kadesh, has been found. This may be because Muwatallis moved his capital from

Hattusa, which has been both identified and excavated, to a place called Dattassa, and that site has yet to be found. When it is, we may find out more about this remarkable king. One theory is that Dattassa was near Adana, because that is where a monumental carved relief of Muwatallis was discovered. It is not known why Muwatallis moved his capital, but maybe he wanted to be closer to the Syrian border so that he could react more quickly when the border was challenged.

Another possibility is that it represented a division of responsibility; Muwatallis ruled the south, while his brother Hattusilis acted as a kind of self-appointed viceroy on the northern border. What Hattusilis was doing was unconstitutional, but the effect was that Hatti had two kings, collaborating to control internal conflict. Hattusilis was able to ensure that contingents came from 'his' region of Hatti to swell the Hittite army Muwatallis led to confront the Egyptian Pharaoh.

The shared responsibility was not easily managed though. On two occasions, Muwatallis launched formal legal action against his brother for offences that are now obscure but probably involved conspiracy of some kind.

Muwatallis left little information about himself and his deeds. We have to turn to Ramesses, his enemy, to read a full account of what Muwatallis did at Kadesh. Ramesses ordered that a full description of the origins and development of the conflict should be carved on the walls of the Ramesseum – and also at Karnak, Luxor, Abydos and Abu Simbel. Temples doubled as museums and libraries in those days. The specific cause of the fighting was the defection to Egypt of the Hittite kingdom of Amurru, roughly corresponding to modern Lebanon. This small kingdom was unimportant, except for its location at the junction of three spheres of influence – Hittite, Assyrian and Egyptian. On the strength of this defection, Ramesses, then an impulsive and energetic man in his early twenties, led an army out of Egypt in the hope of conquering the whole of Syria. Muwatallis was informed and gathered an army to prevent Ramesses from achieving his goal.

A problem is that we usually hear of the Battle of Kadesh from the Egyptian side, which is inevitably biased. An Egyptian poem empathized with the Pharaoh:

When the earth became light, then did I join battle, armed for the fray like a lustful bull. . . I thrust my way into the tumult and fought as a falcon stoops . . . I was like Ra at his appearance in the morning; my rays scorched the face of my foes . . . Then did the Wretched One of Hatti send forth and revere the great name of His Majesty: 'You are a ruler, the likeness of Ra . . . There is a dread of you in the land of Hatti, for you have broken the back of Hatti for ever.'

The 'Wretched One of Hatti' was King Muwatallis, but it is unlikely that he spoke in such terms to or about Ramesses. It was, in fact, Ramesses who was defeated at the great battle. Some information comes from the Hittite archives, which reveal that they used clever subterfuge and skilled military strategy to trick and outwit Ramesses. Probably it was only nightfall that saved Ramesses from complete annihilation. Ramesses escaped from the battlefield only because the Hittites did not pursue him.

This colossal battle between empires took place in 1285 BC. Muwatallis lay in wait for Ramesses and his huge army, in effect setting up an elaborate trap. Ramesses took the bait – false information supplied by two Bedouin posing as Hittite deserters – and suddenly found his camp surrounded. One of the Egyptian divisions was massacred.

Even from Ramesses' description of the battle, which is biased in favour of the Egyptians, it is clear that Muwatallis and his generals were master strategists unparalleled in history. Ramesses escaped, lived to fight another day, and was able to portray the event as a victory, but he was in reality defeated. Muwatallis had shown sufficient military might to show the Egyptians that they would never encroach any further to the north.

Muwatallis did not live long after his great victory. In the treaty with Egypt concluded by his successor, Hattusilis, we learn only that 'Muwatallis, the Great Prince of Hatti, my brother, passed away according to his destiny.'

RAMESSES II

Born 1304 BC, died 1237 BC.
Pharaoh, monument builder, master propagandist and self-publicist.

ACHIEVEMENTS:
Reigned over Egypt for 67 years.
Great self-publicist, ensuring his lasting place in history.
Commissioned the Abu Simbel temples.
Completed the colonnaded hall of the temple at Karnak.
Created the definitive 'look' of the ancient Egyptian civilization.

RAMESSES THE GREAT was the third king of the 19th dynasty, and perhaps the greatest of the Egyptian pharaohs in terms of historic reputation.

As a young man, he tried to extend the borders of his empire north of what is now Lebanon, which brought him into direct confrontation with the Hittite Empire. In the decisive Battle of Kadesh, he was defeated by Muwatallis, although he presented the battle as an Egyptian victory in his account of it. Ramesses had outstanding gifts as a self-publicist, using his scribes and artists to create an image of him as a god-like figure. In the accounts of the Battle of Kadesh his scribes credited him with killing thousands of the enemy. In practice, Ramesses can have done little other than act as a battle standard, giving orders that were often unhelpful. Ramesses' leadership was the weakest link in the Egyptian military machine; his ideas of strategy – at Kadesh – were conspicuously naïve compared with those of Muwatallis. Ramesses lost the battle, and the territory round Kadesh that his predecessors had acquired, yet he succeeded in convincing his own and subsequent generations that he had won a great victory. It was a masterpiece of spin.

Some time after the battle, a treaty was negotiated with the Hittite Great King, establishing peace and mutual recognition between them. Ramesses married a Hittite princess.

Ramesses ruled Egypt for 67 years. During this incredibly long reign, he built a whole series of magnificent stone monuments, completing the mortuary temple of his father, Seti I, at Luxor and the colonnaded hall of the temple at Karnak. It was Ramesses too who ordered the creation of the rock-cut temple at Abu Simbel. The architectural style, with its massive outsized statues, is typical of 'great dictator' art; it is a rigid, hieratic and showy style that gives the ancient Egyptian civilization its distinctive and instantly recognizable look.

Ramesses also spent a great deal of time fathering children – 150 of them. His self-promotional activities diverted attention from the failing health of the Egyptian empire. The mummy of the 90-year-old Ramesses was found at Deir-el-Bahari in 1881. His face was well preserved, with flowing hair still attached to the back and sides of his head.

Ramesses II is believed to have been the Pharaoh of the Oppression, in other words the pharaoh who took the people of Israel into captivity, using them in Egypt as slave labour. Merenptah or Ramesses III are traditionally identified with the Pharaoh of the Exodus, but these identifications are not at all certain. One problem in interpreting the scriptures as straight history is that different sections of the Old Testament text were written at different times; one writer, for instance, was well informed about Egyptian geography and constructed a detailed route for the Exodus. Even so, given the length of Ramesses' reign and the scale of his building projects, it is reasonable to assume he absorbed a significant quantity of forced labour – and the Israelites could easily have been part of that. If he was the pharaoh of either the Oppression or the Exodus, Ramesses played a crucial, if entirely unintentional, role in the generation of the nation of Israel and the shaping of Judaism. Many of the most momentous changes in history have been unintended. Without Pharaoh there could have been no Moses.

AGAMEMNON

Lived in the 13th century BC.
King of Mycenae 1250–1220 BC, King of Achaea, victor of the
  Trojan War.

ACHIEVEMENTS:
Made Mycenae into one of the leading cities in Greece.
United bronze age southern and central Greece into a
  confederation.
Piloted Greek nationhood.
Became High King of the Mycenaean Greeks.
Led the Greeks against Troy and won the Trojan War.
Became an icon of military glory.

AGAMEMNON FEATURES AS one of the leading figures in Homer's epic poem, the *Iliad*. Some scholars still believe the *Iliad* was a work of fiction written in the eighth century, but most now think that at least some of the story is true. It seems likely from the archaeological evidence that there really were Bronze Age kings ruling from urban centres like Pylos, Therapne and Mycenae, and there is no reason why they may not have been called Nestor, Menelaus and Agamemnon.

On the whole, it is more likely that Agamemnon was an historical figure than not. We know from contemporary documents that the Hittite Great Kings knew and respected the Greek commander-in-chief. Letters survive that are addressed to 'the King of Ahhiyawa' (Achaea) and refer to him as a Great King, in other words of equal stature to the Hittite Great King, who ruled most of Anatolia. There are also references in the Hittite archives to another King of Ahhiyawa who raided the Anatolian coast further south. He was called Attarissyas, which may be the Hittite version of 'Atreus', the name of Agamemnon's father.

After the murder of Atreus, Agamemnon and his brother Menelaus took refuge with Tyndareus, the King of Sparta, and they married his troublesome daughters, Clytemnestra and Helen. Agamemnon had three daughters, Iphigeneia, Electra and Chrysothemis, and a son called Orestes. When Tyndareus died, Menelaus succeeded to the throne of Lacedaimon (Sparta). Agamemnon enlisted his brother's help in ousting his uncle Thyestes from Mycenae, so that he could claim the throne of Mycenae for himself.

Agamemnon was an aggressive warrior and soon established himself as the most powerful warlord in Greece. He naturally emerged as commander-in-chief of the combined Greek forces that sailed against Troy to avenge the abduction of the wife of Menelaus, Helen. According to Homer the punitive expedition was organized solely to avenge the abduction of Helen. Helen was taken by Paris, a Trojan prince and the son of King Priam of Troy, while Paris was staying as a guest at the palace of Menelaus. It may well be that the Greeks wanted to annexe the important port of Troy, which stood at the entrance to the Dardanelles, and so occupied a location that had great strategic importance.

The Greeks had been interfering along the west coast of Anatolia for a hundred years. This coastline was so far from Hattusa, the Hittite capital, that the Hittite Great King was unable to oppose the Greek raids. The Greeks succeeded in capturing several coastal towns, notably Miletos, and they also established bases on Aegean islands close to Troy. In fact just before the Trojan War it seems that the Hittites regained control over Miletos, so Agamemnon would have had an additional reason for trying to capture a major trading base in the north – to replace it.

Agamemnon organized a colossal fleet contributed by kingdoms all over Greece, a total of 1,200 ships, and well over 100,000 warriors. Many scholars have doubted that the fleet and army could have been that big, but accounts of the Battle of Kadesh, which happened a few decades earlier, show that battles were certainly fought on a grand scale.

After the fall of Troy, the spoils were shared out. Agamemnon was given Cassandra, the daughter of King Priam, as his share.

When Agamemnon eventually returned home after a difficult storm-ridden voyage, he was spotted approaching the port of Nauplion from a watchtower and the news was signalled by way of Argos to Mycenae. While Agamemnon had been away fighting, his place was usurped by Aigisthos, the son of Thyestes, who had become the lover of Agamemnon's queen Clytemnestra. Agamemnon knew nothing of this, rode inland to Mycenae, where he was welcomed. While he was dressing after bathing, Clytemnestra and her lover Aigisthos murdered him. Aigisthos wanted his throne. Clytemnestra wanted revenge for the death of her daughter; Agamemnon had sacrificed Iphigeneia at Aulis in Boeotia in order to placate the goddess Artemis, whom he had offended and who was controlling the winds to prevent the Greek fleet from sailing to Troy. Clytemnestra blamed Agamemnon for her daughter's death, but the sacrifice took place at the insistence of the priest Calchas. After Agamemnon's assassination there was a bloodbath in which Cassandra perished along with many of Agamemnon's supporters.

It is likely that Agamemnon was buried in the beehive tomb immediately outside the Lion Gate of Mycenae, the tomb ironically known by the name 'Tomb of Clytemnestra'. It was the last in the series of royal tombs at Mycenae, built at about the right time, 1250–1220 BC, and it was conspicuous for its position by the entrance to the citadel and its coating of white plaster. The murder of Agamemnon was eventually avenged by his son Orestes, who returned to Mycenae in about 1212 BC, killed both Aigisthos and his mother, and succeeded to his father's throne.

The extraordinary life and death of King Agamemnon were given immortality by successive generations of poets and dramatists. The poems of the Epic Cycle contained a summary of events; this was elaborated into a cycle of tragedies by Aeschylus called the Oresteia. The first play in this cycle, called the *Agamemnon*, opens with the news arriving, by the lighting of a beacon on the mountain top, at Argos. By the time Aeschylus wrote his play, Argos had become a far more important place than Mycenae, so the play had to have Argos as its setting. This kind of spin has made it very difficult to disentangle the historical reality from the later embellishments.

But it is at least clear that Agamemnon's career has been a major inspiration to artists, writers and composers across many centuries, from Homer, Aeschylus and Euripides to Berlioz and Richard Strauss.

Agamemnon succeeded in uniting, for a time, perhaps as many as twenty separate bronze age kingdoms in Greece, in a common cause, the destruction of Troy. Maybe, as with many later wars, the cause was not much more than a pretext. The war itself was the main thing: a kind of bonding exercise that gave Greece an embryonic nationhood. Even Homer tells us that the heroes gloried in their killing, and no greater title could be awarded to a king than 'sacker of cities'.

HOMER

Lived in the eighth century BC.
Legendary author of the Iliad *and* Odyssey.

ACHIEVEMENTS:
Committed to writing, and so preserved, an oral tradition
dating back 500 years.
Recorded an episode in bronze age history that would otherwise
have been lost.
Passed on to later generations the names and exploits of warrior
heroes of the Bronze Age.
Set a standard for story-telling – for ever after.

HOMER WAS A Greek epic poet who is believed to have written down the Iliad and the Odyssey, two long poems telling the story of the Trojan War and Odysseus's journey home after the war was over.

Considering Homer's unusually high profile in Greek literature – he was in many ways its founding father – we know very little about him. Some scholars have suggested that he did not exist, and there are good grounds for believing that the *Iliad* and the *Odyssey* were written by two different poets. Evidence from the text of the *Iliad* suggests that its author lived in Ionia, in a Greek colony on the west Anatolian coast. This means that the *Iliad* was written by a Greek ex-patriot, probably for an ex-pat audience. Four different city-states along the Anatolian coast have been claimed as his birthplace – Smyrna, Ciolophon, Ephesus and the island of Chios.

How the great poems came into being has been discussed endlessly by scholars. So many details embedded in the *Iliad* have been verified by archaeology that it seems very unlikely that the poem was composed from scratch in 750 BC. Homer must have used pre-existing material, some of it at least handed down by word of mouth from the Bronze Age. At one time that seemed unlikely, but story-tellers and bards in Ireland and eastern Europe were reciting epic sagas of a similar length to the *Iliad* – from memory – until quite recently. In the days before writing, far more must have been committed to memory than now.

The *Iliad* and the *Odyssey* are just two parts of a sequence of eight long poems known as the Epic Cycle. The other six parts, including the story of the wooden horse, have been lost; luckily an ancient scholar named Proklos thoughtfully made a summary of them, and that at least has survived.

It looks as if a huge body of historical and poetic material was available to the poets of the eighth and seventh centuries, who selected and re-assembled it as they wrote their versions down. Homer was one of the first of these, but there is no way, now, of knowing whether he was the best. Homer and the other epic poets were working at the time when writing was being re-invented. The tradition that he was blind and had to dictate his poems to an amanuensis has no historical basis; it is itself a piece of story-telling. On Chios there is an open-air sanctuary originally dedicated to the goddess Cybele, but now called 'The Stone of Homer'; a late and probably fictitious tradition developed that this was where the great poet sat and dictated the *Iliad*.

Homer's main achievement was accidental – the preservation of a fragment of late bronze age history, a record of a Greek attack on Troy. What was not accidental was the high quality of the epic poetry, which is among the most vivid, striking and monumentally grand ever written. He set a standard that no others have been able to reach. Since Homer's day, poets, historians and story-tellers – especially the writers of sagas – have always written with his work as the most inspiring model to follow. He wrote lines and phrases that once heard are unforgettable, such as 'rosy-fingered Dawn' and 'the wine-dark sea'.

NEBUCHADNEZZAR II

Born about 635 BC, died about 562 BC.
King of Babylon, aggressive conqueror, oppressor of the
   Israelites.

ACHIEVEMENTS:
Restored the Babylonian Empire.
Rebuilt the city of Babylon.
Took the Israelites into captivity.
Helped create the Israelites' sense of national identity.
Built the Hanging Gardens of Babylon.
Generated the Babylonian civilization.

NEBUCHADNEZZAR II WAS King of Babylon, succeeding his father Nabopolassar in 604 BC. He was a Chaldean by birth, and he married Amuhia, daughter of the Median king.

He reigned for 43 years, during which time he recovered provinces of the kingdom that had been lost. He restored Babylon to the high status it had formerly achieved during the time of Hammurabi. He also rebuilt or restored virtually every temple in the kingdom. In Babylon he ordered the building of the famous Hanging Gardens, which became one of the Wonders of the World, although nothing of it survives today. The new palace he had built was completed in an astonishing 15 days. The city was surrounded by a defensive wall and moat. The Euphrates, flowing right through the city, was lined with brick. A startling feature of the new city was its use of blue-glazed bricks, which, used on a large scale, must have been dazzlingly impressive. It also had spectacular stepped pyramids or ziggurats.

His works became part of the fabric of history because his administrators carefully recorded everything. Archaeologists continually unearth tablets, cylinder seals or bricks inscribed with his name. In this way he ensured his own immortality. Ironically, we usually remember him as Nebuchadnezzar, but his name as it appears in cuneiform, the script of his time, is Nabu-kudurri-usur, which means 'Nebo, defend the landmark'.

He was, like all successful kings of his age, an aggressive military dictator, though the archives of his conquests are incomplete. In 605 BC, he defeated Necho at Carchemish, driving the Egyptians out of Asia, annexing Syria to the Babylonian Empire – and that was the year before he succeeded to his father's throne. In a foray to the west he and his army laid siege to Tyre to quell a revolt there. Once Tyre had fallen and was safely back under Babylonian control, Nebuchadnezzar marched on Jerusalem, which he captured in 597 BC. When Jerusalem fell, he had King Jehoiakim put to death, replacing him with a puppet king. Three months afterwards the puppet king was deposed and Zedekiah was made king instead. When Zedekiah led a new revolt against Babylon in 588 BC, Nebuchadnezzar laid siege to Jerusalem a second time, destroying the city's temple in 586 BC. Nebuchadnezzar took the surviving citizens back to Babylon, where they remained in captivity. Like Ramesses, Nebuchadnezzar played a role in creating the Israelites' sense of identity, and their historic sensitivity to oppression.

Nebuchadnezzar later asserted his regional dominance by waging another campaign against the Egyptians. In 567 BC, he mobilized his army to defeat the army of the Pharaoh Amasis (or Ahmose).

He was a great warrior and commander, but there was another dimension to Nebuchadnezzar. He was also unusually devout, committing enormous resources to the restoration of temples throughout his lands. He is remembered as a kind of grand impresario, presiding over the creation of a civilization of barbaric splendour and originality, and in particular over the creation one of the most enigmatic Wonders of the World, the Hanging Gardens of Babylon.

PYTHAGORAS

Born on Samos 582 BC, died at Metapontium 497 BC.
Ancient Greek philosopher, sage and mathematician.

ACHIEVEMENTS:
Founded a community of philosophers and mathematicians.
Laid the foundations of modern mathematics.
Discovered the properties of right-angled triangles.

PYTHAGORAS WAS BORN on the island of Samos in 582 BC and became a pupil of Pherecydes. In 529 BC he settled in Croton, which was a Greek colony in southern Italy. There he founded a religious community or brotherhood. It seems he suffered some kind of persecution and was driven out under the tyranny of Polycrates. He acquired a reputation as a learned, inquisitive and universally informed man.

Pythagoras did not write anything, and his life is shrouded in legends, which included extensive travels in foreign lands. Pythagoreanism was more a way of life than a system of philosophy, with an emphasis on asceticism, moral reform and purification; it was more religious than philosophical. The Pythagorean way of life had much in common with that of the Orphic communities. He observed various kinds of ritual self-denial; one of his rules was 'do not eat beans'. He believed in the transmigration of souls and the kinship of all living things. Pythagoreanism established a short-lived supremacy in Greece, but entanglement with politics led to its downfall. The movement against the Pythagoreans happened within Pythagoras's lifetime, under the leadership of Cylon, in about 510 BC.

Cylon was able to force Pythagoras to retire, and after that the great man went to Metapontium, where he died in 497 BC. The Pythagorean order continued for several more decades, until it was violently suppressed. The meeting-houses of the order were sacked and burned. The 'House of Milo' in Croton was attacked without warning and 50 or 60 Pythagoreans who were living there were killed. The survivors took refuge at Thebes, later returning to Italy, where Taras (Tarentum) became their headquarters. Archytas, the friend of Plato, ruled Taras and was never defeated in battle. The Pythagorean school eventually died out in around 350 BC.

It is not for any of these things that Pythagoras is remembered, but for his mathematical discoveries. He arrived at a mathematical analysis of musical intervals, and daringly proposed that those musical intervals lay behind the structure of the universe. It seems Pythagoras thought of the universe as a series of concentric spheres; although the model has the earth at the centre it is an important first step towards the sun-centred model Copernicus put forward hundreds of years later, and we know that Copernicus consciously built on the system proposed by Pythagoras.

Pythagoras said that numbers lay behind space itself; 'one' was a point, 'two' was a line, 'three' was a surface, 'four' was a solid. He also famously stated the properties of the right-angled triangle. Oddly enough it was not the right-angled triangle that became an object of veneration among the Pythagoreans, but the equilateral triangle made up of ten points, arranged 4 + 3 + 2 + 1.

Because Pythagoras did not produce any written works, it is difficult to be sure what he himself discovered and what was discovered by his disciples. He can nevertheless be credited with initiating a school of thought within which many remarkable discoveries were made. His followers recognized the profound implications of these discoveries too. The Pythagorean oath shows this; 'Nay, by him who gave us the tetracys (equilateral triangle) which contains the fount and root of ever-flowing nature.'

Pythagoras started an analytical approach to numbers and trigonometry which inspired, fed and stimulated scholars, laying the foundations of all later mathematics. The thinking of the Pythagoreans also had a profound influence on many later philosophers, astronomers and mathematicians, most notably the philosophers Aristotle and Plato. It was Pythagoras's theory of the immortality and transmigration of the soul that had the greatest effect on them, because it underlined the kinship between people and animals.

BUDDHA

Born about 563 BC, died at Kusinagara about 483 BC.
Founder of Buddhism.

ACHIEVEMENT:
Founded a major new world religion.

PRINCE GAUTAMA SIDDHARTHA, the founder of Buddhism, was born in about 563 BC, the son of the rajah of the Sakya, a warrior tribe in Nepal, 150km north of Benares. To begin with, he lived the conventional life of a prince. When he was 29 years old he put the luxurious court life behind him. He abandoned his wife and all his possessions to lead the life of an ascetic. For six years he led an extremely austere existence, amounting to self-torture; at the end of this he achieved self-enlightenment.

According to tradition, he achieved enlightenment while sitting under a banyan tree near Buddh Gaya in Bihar. After this he became known as Buddha, 'the enlightened one'. He formed an order of monks and spent the next 40 years as a wandering teacher, gaining many followers. During his lifetime an order of nuns was also created. He died at the age of about 80 at Kusinagara in Oudh.

At one time it was thought that the life of the Buddha was purely mythological, but now it seems likely that it represents an historic reality, although the miracles belong to a still earlier period. Monuments put up by Asoka after his conversion can still be seen. There was great excitement in the nineteenth century when a monument containing five vessels was discovered in Nepal. One of them contained some bones and carried the inscription, 'Of the brothers Sukiti, jointly with their sisters, this is the receptacle of the relics of Buddha, the holy one of the Sakyas.' But it seems that the bones belong to the time of Asoka, 200 years after Buddha's death, and therefore are unlikely to have belonged to Buddha himself.

It is debatable whether Buddha invented a completely new religion; probably he was promoting a revolutionary transformation of an existing Brahmin faith. The key ideas of Buddhism are that human existence is miserable, that non-existence or 'nirvana' is the ideal state, and that nirvana can be achieved by devotion to the rules of Buddhism. Death does not bring nirvana, because souls transmigrate after death. The unholy are condemned to transmigrate through many existences.

Buddhism became a very popular faith, spreading rapidly through India, especially after the conversion of King Asoka. By the third century BC it dominated the whole of the Indian subcontinent. Later it went into decline, especially during persecutions by Brahmanism in the seventh and eighth centuries AD and the ensuing invasion by Islam. Buddhism has nevertheless flourished by spreading to China, Sri Lanka, Burma, Thailand and Japan.

Buddha founded one of the great religions of the world. Because of the distinct beliefs involved, he also had a major effect on the cultural development of south-east and eastern Asia. It is hard to imagine what the cultures of the east would have been like without Buddhism.

CONFUCIUS
(K'UNG FU-TZU)

Born in Shantung 551 BC, died 479 BC.
Chinese philosopher, conservative force in Chinese culture.

ACHIEVEMENTS:
Created an ethical philosophy.
Created a secular teaching that replaced religious observance.
Crafted moral sayings that guided the development of the
    Chinese character.
Became an icon of conservatism in Chinese culture.

CONFUCIUS (LATIN FOR 'the Master K'ung') was born into a family of poor aristocrats in the state of Lu, now the province of Shantung. His father, Heih, died when he was only a year old. It was noticed that when he was five or six Confucius liked to play with his friends at setting out sacrifices and practising ceremonial postures. At 15 he decided on a life of learning. At 19 he married and became a government official in Lu. When he was 22 he set up a school for young men who wanted to be instructed in principles of right conduct and government; he was in effect training them for government service. He was promoted to ministerial rank, and had a very successful career as a civil servant.

In 517 BC, Confucius visited the capital of the kingdom, where he was able to study the works in the royal library. There he also met and conversed with Lao-tsze, the founder of Taoism. Lao-tsze, a transcendental dreamer, thought little of his visitor, while Confucius, an openminded and inquiring thinker, thought highly of Lao-tsze.

Confucius was very popular, attracting first jealousy then hostility. In 497 BC, amid general disorder, he left Lu with the ruler he had served and became a wandering sage. He went from one court to another, looking for a sympathetic patron. The ruler of Ts'i did not know how to treat him. He sensed that Confucius was a man who should be honoured, yet he held no conventional rank to justify that. The ruler proposed to give him money, but Confucius was unwilling to accept money if his political advice was going to be ignored. After the development of further unsatisfactory situations, Confucius decided to go back to Lu. He was accompanied in his travels by a group of his disciples. In 485 BC, he returned to Lu and spent his last years teaching.

In 482 BC, his son died, though this did not affect him unduly. In 481 his favourite disciple, Yen Hwui, died. At this Confucius was distraught, mourning with an intensity well beyond what his disciples thought was appropriate. A further blow was the death of his next favourite disciple, Tze-lu. He was seen wandering up and down outside his door, chanting:

The great mountain must crumble,

The strong beam must break,

The wise man must wither away like a plant.

Confucius sensed that no worthy ruler wanted his advice, so he might as well be dead. He took to his bed and died a week later.

His disciples buried him with great ceremony, many of them building their huts near his grave. The grave of Confucius still exists, in a large rectangle separated from the rest of the K'ung cemetery outside the city of K'iuh-fow. The grave is a large mound with a marble statue in front of it.

After Confucius died in 479 BC, his disciples wrote the Analects, a disjointed compilation of their master's sayings and doings. Most of the other writings attributed to Confucius were compiled later and were probably written by other people. The philosophy of 'Confucianism' is therefore only partly the work of Confucius himself. *The Doctrine of the Mean*, by his grandson, and *The Great Learning*, by his disciple Tsang Sin, probably give a good idea of his teachings.

The one book Confucius himself wrote, and referred to as his own book,

Spring and Autumn, is a big problem. It is full of inconsistencies between facts and conclusions, and scarcely seems like the work of a great mind. Confucius said, 'by the Spring and Autumn men would know him and men would condemn him.' Over the centuries Chinese scholars have invested enormous efforts on it, attempting to find alternative readings in specific sentences or words, in order to create consistency, but their efforts seem futile. It has been commented that it would help the reputation of Confucius if it could be shown that he was after all not the author of *Spring and Autumn*!

Confucius was nevertheless a great moral teacher who tried to replace the old traditional religious observances with moral values as the basis for social and political order. In *The Way* (tao), Confucius emphasized the practical virtues of benevolence, reciprocity, respect and personal effort, which were to be developed pragmatically, according to circumstances. His Golden Rule is admirable in its simplicity and common sense; 'What you do not like when done to yourself do not do to others.'

Confucius was also conscious that the literature of the past had to be conserved, respected and handed on if the culture was to survive. Without the links to the past that books created, China would drift from its moorings. The ancient book that he prized most highly was the *I-Ching* or *Book of Changes*, which dated back to 3000 BC. Confucius is said to have worn out three successive bindings of his copy. There are some ideas in common between the *Book of Changes* and the ideas of Pythagoras, who was a contemporary of Confucius, but it is difficult to see how Pythagoras could have had access to the ancient Chinese book.

The Qin emperor swept away many aspects of the old feudal system, and tried to wipe out all memory of Confucius, burying alive many scholars who remained loyal to his memory. The emperors of the next dynasty, the Han, made great efforts to restore Confucianism.

Confucius was in some ways intensely conservative, but in others way ahead of his time. His attempt – his very successful attempt – to replace a religion-based society with secular values was not emulated in Europe until the twentieth century. Confucius was treated with great reverence by later generations of Chinese, and Confucianism became the state religion of China – remaining so until recently. The sayings and ideas have done much to create the character of Chinese people. A typical Confucian saying is, 'Extravagance leads to insubordination, and parsimony to meanness. It is better to be mean than insubordinate.' Many Chinese know the sayings by heart and they have seeped deep into the Chinese way of life.

AESCHYLUS

> *Born in Eleusis about 525 BC, died about 456 BC.*
> *Greek dramatist and tragedian, icon of Greek literature.*
>
> ACHIEVEMENTS:
> *Wrote several powerful tragedies that influenced many later*
>   *writers.*
> *Established tragedy as an art form.*
> *Vividly re-presented several ancient Greek legends and gave*
>   *them new life.*
> *Set high standards in writing poetry.*

AESCHYLUS WAS BORN at Eleusis, the town of the Mysteries just to the west of Athens. His father Euphorion was a member of the old Athenian nobility. As a young man, Aeschylus served in the Athenian army during the Persian Wars and was wounded at the Battle of Marathon in 490 BC. At this historic battle he fought alongside his brother Cynaegirus, who was killed while attempting a conspicuous act of bravery. The two brothers were featured in the national picture of the battle which the Athenians later set up in the 'Picture Porch' in the city of Athens. Aeschylus probably also fought at the Battles of Artemisium, Salamis and Plataea, so he was no ivory-tower writer who had to imagine what great battles might be like; he knew from first-hand experience what high politics led to and what the realities of warfare were. His personal involvement in these historic and heroic battles as part of a great national enterprise contributed enormously to the vigorous and lofty tone of his writing – and to its intense seriousness.

The playwright's brooding meditations on the power of the gods and the dark mysteries of fate may have much to do with his boyhood, with growing up in Eleusis, the town of Mysteries associated with the worship of Demeter. As an impressionable child, he would have seen many processions, ceremonies, awe-inspiring dramatic spectacles – all wrapped up in ancient beliefs about the human soul and its relationship with the underworld. All of this must have helped to give his dramas their quite extraordinary gravity.

A typically weighty yet vivid passage is the chorus that accompanies a funeral procession in *Seven Against Thebes*:

> *Nay, with the wafting gale of your sighs, my sisters,*
> *Beat on your heads with your hands the stroke as of oars,*
> *Speeding on its way the black-robed sacred bark –*
> *The bark Apollo comes not near,*
> *The bark that is hidden from the sunlight –*
> *To the shore of darkness that welcomes all!*

It is dark, grave and profoundly tragic in tone, yet also lyrical and full of arresting images.

Aeschylus had his first work performed in Athens in 499 BC, when he was just 25 years old; his was a very long career spanning 40 years. Athens ran formal drama competitions and Aeschylus' first triumph in these came in 484 BC. After winning the first prize for tragedy thirteen times, he was profoundly hurt on being defeated in 468 BC, when Sophocles was declared the winner, possibly for political rather than artistic reasons.

This defeat may have been the spur that made Aeschylus leave Athens for Sicily, where he produced a new version of his Persians, originally performed in 472 BC. Another likely reason for his departure from Athens was his trial on a charge of divulging the Mysteries of Eleusis, which he would have felt as a further humiliation. The charge was brought against him when Aeschylus was himself acting in one of his plays, and a moment came where he referred to the goddess Demeter. The audience suspected him of revealing secrets of the Mysteries, and rose in anger. Aeschylus had to run to the altar of Dionysus in the orchestra; even the angry Athenian crowd respected the sanctuary of the altar. At his trial, his defence was 'that he did not know that what he said was secret', and this was accepted by the court. It was said later that his war record was the real reason for the court's leniency.

His last great victory came in 458 BC. This time the prize was for his trilogy of tragedies, the *Oresteia*.

Aeschylus died at Gela in Sicily. Aeschylus is known to have written over 60 plays, and it was said in antiquity that there were 90; only seven of them have survived; *Persians, Seven Against Thebes, Prometheus Bound, Suppliants* and the three plays that make up the *Oresteia*. Aeschylus was a regular entrant in the drama competitions, and a requirement was the submission of four plays per entry, so it looks as if he entered the competition every second year, or twenty times in all.

Aeschylus is known as the father of Greek tragedy. His style and subject matter are entirely individual, and his plays stand apart from the rest of Greek literature. The gravity of his themes and the grandeur of his theological conceptions give his plays a profoundly religious quality; he believed in the rule of providence, the inheritance of sin and the ultimate sadness of the human condition. He was recognized in his own time, and ever since, as a playwright without equal.

XERXES

> Born about 510 BC, died about 465 BC.
> King of Persia, conqueror of Egypt and Babylon, ruthless
>   military dictator.
>
> ACHIEVEMENTS:
> Conquered the civilizations of ancient Egypt and Babylon.
> Led an invasion of Greece and was defeated.
> Decisively cleared the way for the supremacy of the ancient
>   Greek civilization.

'XERXES' IS THE Greek form of the Persian name 'Khshayarsha', but the Persian king is always remembered now by the name the Greeks gave him. Xerxes was the son of Darius I and Atossa, the daughter of Cyrus the Great. He succeeded as king of Persia in 486 BC, when Darius died while preparing to launch a second expedition against Greece.

Xerxes' first act was to subdue the Egyptians, who had mounted a rebellion. His predecessors, his father included, had been unable to bring Egypt, or any of the other older civilizations, under control. Xerxes succeeded by being more brutal, more extreme. In 484 BC, made a similarly vigorous onslaught on Babylon, abolishing the 'kingdom of Babel'. He took away the golden statue of Bel (or Marduk), which the legitimate king of Babel was supposed to touch on the first day of each year; he also killed the priest who tried to stop him. This provocative act prompted two rebellions by the Babylonians, both suppressed.

Darius left to his son the considerable task of punishing the Greeks for interfering in the Ionian rebellion and for their victory at Marathon.

From 483 BC on, Xerxes prepared his expedition with great care, planning some major engineering works as part of the overall strategy. Xerxes also took the precaution of concluding an alliance with Carthage, to ensure that the Greeks could not call on Carthage for support.

He gathered a vast army drawn from every part of the Persian empire and advanced with a fleet provided by the Phoenicians. He had a floating bridge constructed across the Hellespont, the channel separating Europe from Asia Minor; this was made out of a double line of boats carrying a walkway. He also caused a canal to be cut through the peninsula of Mount Athos.

In 482 BC Xerxes' army began its march towards the Hellespont, and from there crossed into Greece. At first Xerxes was successful, winning the Battle of Artemisium. When his huge army reached Thermopylae, it was halted for a time by the heroic resistance of Leonidas. After Leonidas and his men had been killed, Xerxes and his army resumed their march towards Athens.

When Xerxes reached Athens, he found it deserted, and he destroyed the city. The fleet meanwhile had sailed round Attica from the island of Euboea to the waters in front of Piraeus, the port of Athens. There, on 28 September 480 BC, Xerxes witnessed a great sea battle in the strait between Salamis and Attica, the historic Battle of Salamis in which he saw his fleet defeated, and which decided the outcome of the entire expedition. Following this setback, which cut off his sea route back to Asia, Xerxes withdrew to Sardis. When his general Mardonius was killed leading his land army on the battlefield of Plataea in 479 BC, Xerxes gave up the enterprise of the conquest of Greece and retreated.

Little is known of the later years of Xerxes. His ambition was undiminished, but found new directions. He sent Sataspes off to attempt to circumnavigate Africa. He built a new palace at Persepolis. But the resounding defeat of his great army and navy by the Greeks stung the Persian Empire into a kind of torpor. Xerxes became bogged down in the politics of the palace and harem, and came to depend on courtiers and eunuchs. In the end, in 465, Xerxes was murdered by Artabanus, his vizier.

This great military dictator failed, ultimately, to conquer Greece. He made a huge impression on the Athenians and Spartans, frightening the Athenians enough to make them desert their city. He also made a huge impression on every other nation in the region. It is thought that 'Ahasuerus' in the biblical books of Ezra and Esther was really Xerxes.

PHEIDIAS

Born 500 BC, died 432 BC.
Ancient Greek sculptor, designed the Parthenon and statues of
   Athena and Zeus.

ACHIEVEMENTS:
Became known as the greatest sculptor of ancient Greece.
Created the statue of Athena in the Parthenon.
Created the statue of Zeus at Olympia.
Created, in Zeus, the enduring image of God the Father.

PHEIDIAS, THE SON of Charmides, was born in Athens in 500 BC. He was taught by Hegias of Athens and became known as the best sculptor of his time. Among his early works were a chryselephantine (gold and ivory) statue of Athena that he made for Pellene and a memorial for the Battle of Marathon, commissioned to stand at Delphi. He also made the large bronze statue of Athena that soared above the Acropolis buildings in Athens; its glinting helmet and spear-point could be seen even from the sea. The head of a statue of Apollo was found in the River Tiber, and it bears so many of the hall-marks of his work that it is possible that this too was made by Pheidias.

It was natural that he should be commissioned by Pericles to create the most important statues for the city of Athens as part of a major rebuilding programme. Pericles also made Pheidias the superintendent for all public works, which meant that he controlled the architecture which would be a setting for his sculptures. He had under him a substantial team of designers and craftsmen including architects, masons, stone carvers, bronze-workers and so on.

Pericles wanted to reshape the monuments on the Acropolis at Athens so that they made a more imposing and unified whole. Pheidias designed and created the Propylaea (the gateway buildings through which people were to enter the Acropolis). He also created the Parthenon, the huge and stately temple to Athena which still dominates Athens and which to many has come to symbolize western civilization. The layout appears informal, but is governed by elaborate trigonometry which makes the buildings more imposing.

Pheidias designed, but probably did not carve, the marble sculptures that fitted on the walls of the Parthenon, including the remarkable processional frieze that ran round the temple under the eaves - and now known as the Elgin Marbles. Pheidias was not known for marble statues; the works he was known for were made of bronze, gold and ivory. It is likely that the marble statuary on the Parthenon was the work of his pupils, very likely Alcamenes and Agoracritus.

Pheidias also designed and oversaw the construction of the phenomenal gigantic statue of Athena that stood inside the Parthenon. It was a hollow structure made of timber-framing, and its surface was sheathed in ivory and gold. The individual pieces of ivory were necessarily small, but they were individually crafted and tacked onto the wooden frame to create an illusion of vast expanses of pale skin. The statue, known as Athena Parthenos, the Virgin Athena, was dedicated in 438 BC. Although the statue itself was destroyed long ago, we know what it looked like because small-scale marble copies of it were made; two have been found in Athens. The statue showed the goddess Athena as the protectress of the city, wearing a helmet and carrying a shield and a huge spear. The concept was borrowed or recycled later on by the Romans for their goddess Fortuna, and by the British for their patron goddess Britannia. So Pheidias produced what Jung would one day call an archetype, an enduring icon of the protecting goddess.

The great sculptor became known throughout the ancient world for this one awe-inspiring sculpture. There was one more gigantic commission to come, though. He was asked to create a similar sculpture of Zeus for the Temple of Zeus at Olympia. This was a seated, enthroned figure of a majestic male, again made of timber, ivory and gold. The drapes were made of gold and ivory was used to represent the flesh. Although this statue was a masterpiece, and became one of the Wonders of the World, it was too large for the temple. The top of its head very nearly touched the roof, so it would have been impossible for the statue, if living, to have stood up inside the temple. Indeed, to get into the temple, Zeus would have had to crawl in on all fours, like dog going into his kennel. Because of its excessive size, it was oppressive and aesthetically unsatisfactory by comparison with the Athena. Yet it was profoundly awe-inspiring and, for the many who saw it, it became the defining image of god the father – majestic, mature, bearded, benign, impassive and commanding. It has been the world's image of God ever since.

The statue of Zeus has gone, though there are small copies of it on surviving coins which at least give an idea of the pose. Zeus was seated on a throne, every part of which was elaborately decorated.

Pheidias was accused of two improprieties while working on the Zeus. It was inevitable that Pheidias had rivals who were jealous of his success and wanted to bring him down. It was alleged that he had used his own likeness for an ornamental detail, which he may have done as a kind of covert signature, and at the time this was regarded as irreligious. He was also accused of taking for himself some of the gold intended for the statue. It is not known whether either of the accusations is true, but they brought his career to an end. Disgraced, he disappeared from Athens. Archaeologists exploring the site of his workshop at Olympia found a cup with the name 'Pheidias' marked on it.

Pheidias was the greatest sculptor that ancient Greece produced. His statues no longer exist, but they were copied and widely imitated and had enormous influence on later artists. It was fundamentally his concept of heightened naturalism that was picked up by Renaissance artists like Michelangelo and is a living presence with us still. Pheidias created noble images of the assertive protecting goddess and the majestic god the father, images that have become universal archetypes.

SOPHOCLES

Born at Colonus Hippius 496 BC, died 406 BC.
Greek dramatist and tragedian.

ACHIEVEMENTS:
Wrote several classic tragedies.
Invented the heroic 'tragic flaw' as a dramatic device.
Was the inspiration for Aristotle's principles of aesthetics.

SOPHOCLES WAS AN Athenian, the son of Sophillus, born at Colonus Hippius, a suburb of Athens. As a boy of 15 and a pupil of the musician Lamprus, Sophocles was chosen to lead the chorus of boys in the celebration after the great victory at the Battle of Salamis. He evidently loved the stage and nursed an ambition to be an actor, but his voice was not strong enough and he had to give up the idea of a career on the stage. Instead he became a dramatist, writing more than a hundred plays. It was unusual for a dramatist not to take part in his own plays, and Sophocles is thought to have been the first dramatist to have taken this step.

Most of Sophocles' plays were conventional light satirical plays, though only one of these has survived, called the *Ichneutae*. Of his major plays, seven survive - all written after the spectacular turning-point in his writing career, his victory over Aeschylus in the drama contest of 468 BC. This momentous event was in effect the end of Aeschylus' career and the start of Sophocles'.

Sophocles won the first prize at the Great Dionysia 18 times in all. The peculiar preoccupations of the ancient Greeks are very evident from their dramas. Sophocles wrote two great plays, *Ajax* and *Antigone*, highlighting the ethical and religious problems connected with burial, which would not seem a major issue to most modern people. Aeschylus, Euripides and Sophocles each wrote their own versions of *Electra*, which again may seem a strange preoccupation with a gruesome matricide, the murder of Clytemnestra by her son Orestes for the murder of his father Agamemnon – by her lover.

Sophocles' masterpiece is the *Oedipus Tyrannus*. This was profoundly influential in the ancient world, in that it formed the basis for the aesthetic theory put forward by Aristotle in his Poetica. It was influential in the modern world too, in that Sigmund Freud used it as the basis for the name and function of the Oedipus complex. Sophocles' play shows how a relatively minor character flaw, in combination with the cruel workings of a fate designed by the gods, can bring a person to a tragic end. Aristotle discussed this 'tragic flaw', which arouses the emotions of pity and fear in the audience and allows these emotions to be exercised in a way that entails no real risks. This is very different from the tragedy of Aeschylus, which is essentially static: in Aeschylus the hero is fundamentally doomed from the start and there is no real plot development.

The diction Sophocles uses is reminiscent of Homer's *Odyssey*, but his subject matter was mainly drawn from later epics – and chosen for its tragic potential.

He was appointed at the age of 55 to be one of the generals who would serve with Pericles in the Samian War of 440–439 BC. This appointment is typical of Sophocles' life; he took his civic duties as an Athenian citizen very seriously and was ready to serve as a foreign ambassador when required. The travel involved increased his knowledge of the world and informed his writing considerably.

Sophocles was known for his affability. Unlike many other great artists, he seems to have been extremely likeable. Everybody liked Sophocles. Many stories were told about Sophocles that are no better than gossip, which his celebrity status naturally attracted. The story told by Satyrus about the nature of Sophocles' death is typical of these absurdities - that he just ran out of breath when failing to pause while reading his play *Antigone*.

The date of Sophocles' death, 406 BC, is inferred from a reference to it in *The Frogs* by Aristophanes, which was written in 405 BC.

Sophocles wrote several great masterpieces of tragic drama and, by seeing human destiny as an interaction between a tragic human flaw and the cruel machinations of the gods, he developed the concept of tragedy several steps beyond Aeschylus. He was a profound influence on Aristotle's theory of aesthetics and an influence through Aristotle on many later writers. He also influenced the thinking of Sigmund Freud and contributed to the Oedipus complex, one of the most controversial ideas in modern psychology.

PERICLES

Born in Athens 490 BC, died in Athens 429 BC.
Athenian statesman, ruler of Athens, art patron, friend of
   Sophocles and Herodotus.

ACHIEVEMENTS:
Ruled Athens as general-in-command for 14 years.
Expanded the Athenian empire.
Provoked the Peloponnesian War with Sparta.
Commissioned great buildings such as the Parthenon.
Commissioned great art works such as the statue of Athena.
Presided over the peak of ancient Greek civilization.
Created a more inclusive society that looked forward to the
   welfare state.

PERICLES WAS THE son of Athenian aristocrats, Xanthippus and Agariste. Xanthippus had taken a prominent role in Athenian politics and it was natural that he should educate his son with care towards a great career in public service. He chose the most progressive teachers of the day: Damon for music, Zeno for the power of dialectic and Anaxagoras for philosophy. Anaxagoras lived side by side with Pericles in friendship and it is to him that Pericles owed most, a calm undaunted attitude that he maintained even in adversity. Pericles' political rise was swift and he quickly became the leader of the dominant democracy.

Pericles was often compared to Olympian Zeus because he was always serene and dignified, and because he was so eloquent that he hypnotized both friends and enemies alike. He was strikingly good-looking, except for one peculiarity – his tall pointed skull, which the Athenian comedians exploited to the full. The famous portrait of Pericles wearing a helmet deliberately conceals this deformity.

In around 463 BC Pericles joined in dealing a blow at the oligarchy by depriving the Areopagus of it political power. Shortly after this, Pericles emerged as Athens' pre-eminent leader, holding from 443–429 BC the office of general-in-command. His power was exerted through direct charisma, and for the rest of his life he remained the most influential speaker in the popular assembly.

The rise of Pericles was associated with an expansion of Athenian power. He launched successful naval expeditions to Thrace and Sinope and, by skilful use of numerous colonies, he increased Athenian sea power. Pericles' major setback came in 447 BC, with the defeat of the Athenians at the Battle of Coroneia. The entire Athenian army had surrendered to the Boeotians and held to ransom; the price of the army's release was the Athenian evacuation of Boeotia. News of this encouraged other dissident states to rebel; the Megarians slaughtered their Athenian garrison and a Spartan army penetrated Attica as far as Eleusis.

Pericles' most ambitious project was the formation of a grand Hellenic confederation, with the intention of putting an end to wars that were mutually destructive. The Spartan aristocracy sabotaged the scheme, and unfortunately the enmity between Athens and Sparta was so strong that a Peloponnesian war was virtually inevitable. Even so, a peace was concluded with Sparta in 445 BC, which delayed the outbreak of war for 30 years. The price was Pericles' renunciation of Athens' claim to supremacy in Greece.

The aristocratic party tried to overthrow the supremacy of Pericles by attacking him in the popular assembly for wasting money on buildings like the Parthenon and on festivals and amusements. After surviving this onslaught, Pericles reigned as undisputed master of Athens. It was a time when Athenians were achieving incredible things. Aeschylus, Sophocles and Euripides were writing some of the greatest dramas ever to be written, Pheidias and his pupils and assistants were designing and creating some of the finest buildings and sculptures ever to be made. Pericles was in effect the patron of artists like Pheidias, Callicrates and Ictinus. It was also the age of

Socrates and Herodotus. This was the city-state that Pericles presided over.

The negative side of Pericles' supremacy was that enemies who could not strike at Pericles himself were reduced to sniping at his friends, Aspasia, Anaxagoras and Pheidias.

Under the rule of Pericles Athens reached a peak of civilization that would never be surpassed. It was Pericles who commissioned the Parthenon, the Erechtheum, the Propylaea and many other buildings besides. It was Pericles who encouraged and sponsored music and drama. It was Pericles who stimulated the industry and commerce that paid for the art and architecture.

In the end, the Peloponnesian War between Athens and Sparta broke out, in 431 BC. Plague swept through Athens in 430 BC. In the autumn of 429 BC the plague claimed Pericles himself, and the greatest phase of achievement in one of the greatest civilizations in the world came to an end.

One of the greatest achievements of Pericles was in making Athens more truly self-governing and in some ways more democratic. Public service was paid for, and this opened the door to poorer citizens to participate in government. Jury service was rewarded with cash payment. He set up a fund to enable poor citizens to attend the religious dramas of the Dionysia. Pericles was not a modern socialist by a long way. He was an old-style aristocrat, but he wanted the state of Athens to become more inclusive, to involve more of its citizens in active service, and established practical methods for them to do so.

PLATO

Born in Athens about 428 BC, died about 348 BC.
Greek philosopher, friend of Socrates, teacher of Aristotle.

ACHIEVEMENTS:
Recognized as one of the greatest philosophers of all time.
Founder of the Athenian Academy, the first university.
Influenced many later political theorists.
Perpetuated or invented the story of the lost land of Atlantis.

PLATO WAS BORN in Athens of a distinguished aristocratic family, the son of Ariston and Perictione. Plato is thought to have been brought up mainly in the house of Perictione's second husband, Pyrilampes, who was a prominent supporter of Pericles, the ruler of Athens. He was related to Critias and Charmides, who were old friends of Socrates; probably Plato knew Socrates from boyhood. Although Socrates was not Plato's formal teacher, he clearly had a more profound influence on him than anyone else.

Growing up in a political family, Plato inevitably, at first, had ambitions to go into public life. These political ambitions had withered a few years before Socrates was condemned to death in 399 BC. Plato had sympathies with the reactionary party, of which Critias and Charmides were prominent members. Plato held back from joining them, and was later very glad that he had not involved himself when he saw the excesses of the violent reactionary terror of 404 BC. Plato was not one of the group of disciples who stayed with Socrates while he took poison, possibly because he was a family friend rather than a pupil. He was also probably fearful of the consequences of being too obviously associated with Socrates. Later he was to make up for his cowardice by immortalizing the death of Socrates in three 'dialogues'.

After the death of Socrates, Plato and the other disciples of Socrates took refuge in Megara. Plato then became a wanderer, travelling widely in Egypt, Greece and the Greek colonies in southern Italy. In Sicily, Plato made friends with Dion, the brother-in-law of Dionysius I, ruler of Syracuse.

In 387 BC he thought it was safe to return to Athens, where he founded the Academy. This became a renowned centre for learning, for research into philosophy, mathematics and science, and Plato presided over it for the rest of his life. In 367 BC, he revisited Sicily at the request of Dion, to tutor Dionysius II in statecraft. The idea was to turn the new young ruler into a philosopher-king. The scheme failed. Plato made another visit to Sicily in 361 BC. This put him in considerable danger, and the scheme was given up. Plato died in about 348 BC at the age of over 80.

Plato's writings often took the form of dramatized 'dialogues', featuring Socrates as one of the speakers. They give a vivid impression of the way the ancient Greeks sought after truth by way of discussion. One group of dialogues shows Socrates expressing his views, and it is assumed that these are in reality the views of Plato rather than Socrates, but it is difficult to tell.

The *Timaeus* and *Critias* are curiosities, claiming to tell the true story of the fall of Atlantis. Readers are divided between those who see the description as a complete fiction invented from scratch by Plato, and those who believe that Plato was passing on a genuinely historical tradition. Plato insisted repeatedly that the story of Atlantis was 'certainly true' and explained that he had got hold of the story by way of his ancestor Solon (six generations before), who picked up an account from temple-priests in Sais in Egypt. Those who want to argue that Plato invented Atlantis seem to forget that an obscure writer called Hellanicus is known to have written a work called *Atlantis* a century before Plato. Unfortunately only a few lines from Hellanicus's book have survived.

Plato is probably best known for the Republic, which describes his political utopia, an ideal state ruled by philosopher-kings and with a rigid social hierarchy. Almost as important is his *Laws*, a long book containing Plato's maturest judgements on ethics, education and jurisprudence. It is in effect a model for constitution-making and legislation for those members of the Academy who might be called upon to act as advisers in the founding or re-founding of cities. There was a genuine practical need to think radically about the construction of constitutions.

Plato was a pupil of Socrates and the teacher of Aristotle; these three wise men were undoubtedly the greatest figures in ancient philosophy. Through the window of Plato's dialogues we have an insight into the way Socrates lived and thought. Taken as a whole Plato's philosophy has had a pervasive and profound effect on political and social thinkers of every period, right through to the present day.

ARISTOTLE

Born at Stagira 384 BC, died at Chalcis 322 BC.
Ancient Greek philosopher, moralist, psychologist, political
thinker; tutor of Alexander the Great.

ACHIEVEMENTS:
Stimulated Alexander's curiosity about the world, accelerated his
drive to the east.
Invented the syllogism.
Created the modern Western approach to learning by subjects.
Created empiricism, the modern Western intellectual tradition
of learning by observation.
Guided the development of scientific thought in the Middle Ages.
The Renaissance and the Reformation were in part a rejection
of Aristotle.

ARISTOTLE WAS BORN at Stagira, a Greek colony on the Chalcidice peninsula in the north-west Aegean, the son of Nicomachus, physician to the King of Macedon. This king, Amyntas II, was the father of Philip of Macedon and the grandfather of Alexander; Aristotle was of the same generation as Alexander's father. He was, racially, an Ionian; Stagira had been colonized by Ionians from the island of Euboea. Aristotle's mother was from Euboea and it was natural that in the final year of his life he should retire to her home on Euboea. The Ionian philosophers were particularly interested in studying nature and it may be that Aristotle's profound interest in studying all aspects of nature was rooted in that tradition.

In 367 BC he went to Athens to study at Plato's Academy. He stayed there, as a teacher, until Plato died in 348 BC. Then Speusippus became head of the Academy and Aristotle left Athens for 12 years. He went to Atarneus in Asia Minor, where he married, and then went to Mitylene.

In 342 BC he was appointed by King Philip of Macedon to be his son's tutor. Aristotle duly went to Pella to teach the boy Alexander, who was then 13. At the end of this remarkable episode, when Philip of Macedon was assassinated and Alexander became king, there was no further reason for Aristotle to stay in Macedonia. Aristotle seems to have had little influence in Macedonia, though he probably developed a circle of friends there, which included Theophrastus. He returned to Athens in 335 BC to found his own academy, a formal college which was called the Lyceum after the Temple of Apollo Lyceus which was close to it. Aristotle taught at the Lyceum for 12 years, and his relationship with Alexander, off conquering the world, naturally petered out. Some arrangement was made with Alexander's staff to send back scientific information to Aristotle from the east. Aristotle also wrote a piece called *Alexander*, or *on Colonies*. The deeds of Alexander himself show little influence by his great teacher, though Aristotle may be credited with stimulating Alexander's curiosity about the world, and so accelerating Alexander's drive to the east.

Aristotle's followers became known as peripatetics, because of their quaint habit of wandering up and down while lecturing. To begin with, Aristotle's thinking followed Plato's, but after Plato's death he inevitably followed a distinctive path of his own. While Plato had studied reality as a whole, and then mainly as an intellectual concept, Aristotle divided his reality into several spheres, such as physics, biology, politics and psychology. Aristotle's is much more recognizably our modern Western approach to study, with enquiry and learning broken up into many different subjects. Western education is based on this principle; it is how we are all taught at school.

Aristotle invented the syllogism, the now-familiar three-part argument: 'All men are animals; all animals die; therefore all men must die.'

When Alexander died in 323 BC there was a vigorous anti-Macedonian reaction in Athens; Alexander had been a great oppressor of his neighbours and they were glad to see the back of him. Aristotle suffered in this backlash. He was accused of impiety. Remembering what happened to

Socrates in a somewhat similar situation, Aristotle fled to his mother's home at Chalcis on Euboea, where he died the following year.

Little is known of Aristotle as a person, except through his works. The portrait busts show firm lips and intent inquisitive eyes. Tradition gives him a lisp and a concern for his dress. He was a courtier, but with the insatiable and relentless curiosity of the Greek mind.

Aristotle would have a small place in history as the teacher of Alexander, but he is a far more significant figure because of his huge output of writing on a huge range of subjects, from ethics, politics and rhetoric to biology, physics and psychology. In reality, most of the writings are lecture notes written down by his students, edited and published by Andronicus of Rhodes in the first century BC. The body of work is evidently not complete, but shows the extraordinary range of Aristotle's mind. Aristotle's most widely read works are the *Metaphysics*, *Politics* and *Poetics*. It is a great loss that his work *On Justice*, an answer to Plato's *Republic*, has not survived.

As well as being wide-ranging, Aristotle was original, systematic and sophisticated in his thinking. He is particularly important in having a huge influence on later thinkers, especially in the Middle Ages, through Thomas Aquinas. Dante was strongly influenced by Aristotle, referring to him as 'the Philosopher'. Aristotle has had a profound effect on the whole Western scientific and intellectual tradition.

ALEXANDER THE GREAT

---

*Born at Pella in Macedonia in 356 BC; died at Babylon in
  323 BC.*

*Charismatic general, king of Macedonia, military dictator,
  conqueror, creator of a great empire, icon of warrior-kingship.*

ACHIEVEMENTS:

*338 BC - Commanded an army at 18 at the Battle of
  Chaeronea.*

334 BC - Battle of the Granicus: defeated the Persian army.

333 BC - Battle of Issus: defeated the Persians under Darius.

332 BC - Besieged and took Tyre.

331 BC - Founded the city of Alexandria.

331 BC - Battle of Arbela: defeated the Persians under Darius.

*331 BC - Took Babylon, Sousa and Persepolis. Destroyed
  Persepolis.*

*330 BC - Pursued Darius to Media, where Darius was
  murdered.*

326-5 BC - Attempted to conquer India.

Became a role-model for later conquerors.

ALEXANDER 'THE GREAT' was the son of King Philip of Macedon, a first-rate general and administrator, and Queen Olympias, who was brilliant, impulsive and hot-tempered. Alexander inherited to a high degree the qualities of both his parents. The most striking difference was that Alexander was more ambitious than his father; he was in fact one of the most ambitious people of all time. His mother Olympias taught him that

Achilles was his ancestor, and he became so fixated with this idea that his tutor, Aristotle, actually called him Achilles. As part of this obsession, Alexander learnt the Iliad by heart, always carried a copy of Homer's epic poem with him, and consciously acted out the dangerous fantasy that he was one of Homer's heroes.

As a boy, the strong and fearless Alexander famously succeeded in taming Bucephalus, a spirited horse that nobody else dared to mount. It was when he was 13 that Alexander became Aristotle's pupil, and Aristotle taught him a great love of literature, geography and ethnology, all of which fed and informed his military career. When he was 18, Alexander commanded a section of his father's cavalry at the Battle of Chaeronea. He was also entrusted with acting as his father's ambassador to Athens. He was a youth carefully groomed for kingship.

When Alexander was 20, Philip of Macedon was assassinated. It is not known whether Alexander was involved in the conspiracy to kill his father, but the assassination looks like a well-orchestrated palace coup, and the timing suited Alexander perfectly. There is a suspicion that Olympias played a part in it. While Alexander was away making war on a tribe in the north, the people of Thebes, to the south, heard a rumour that he was dead and revolted against Macedonian domination, inviting Athens to join them in a rebellion. Alexander stormed Thebes with his army and destroyed every building except the temples and the house of the poet Pindar. The incident shows several aspects of the nature of Alexander: the well-judged reverence for certain things, the poignant sentimentality, the grand gesture, the brutality and the wanton destructiveness. Alexander's fans weaken at the knees at the thought that he spared the house of the poet, sliding over the fact that he sold 30,000 non-combatant Theban citizens into slavery.

The father had dreamed of conquering Persia; now the son wanted to outdo the father by achieving it. In 334 BC, Alexander crossed the Hellespont with an army 35,000 strong. He was met by the Persian army on the banks of the Granicus River. He won the battle, and all Asia Minor opened before him. Halicarnassus withstood a siege, but the other towns gave in easily. In 333 BC, after a serious bout of illness, he marched along the south coast of Anatolia into Syria. Darius III, the Persian king, raised a huge army to stop him, but Alexander captured Darius's camp, taking Darius's wife and mother prisoner. Once again, Alexander won credit by behaving gallantly towards them.

After a seven-month siege, he captured Tyre by building a causeway out to the island. He killed 8,000 citizens of Tyre, selling 30,000 more into slavery. This operation is considered Alexander's greatest military achievement. He went on to do the same to Gaza. After that came Egypt, where Alexander was welcomed as a deliverer; the Egyptians hated their harsh Persian rulers. On the Nile Delta, Alexander founded a new city, naming it after himself - Alexandria.

In 331 BC, Alexander turned back to deal with the Persian army. Darius had gathered an enormous host, including the heavy cavalry and many chariots with scythe-like blades protruding from the wheel-axles. The Persians cleared and smoothed a huge level plain at Arbela, east of the River Tigris, to make an arena where their chariots could be effectively deployed. In the Battle of Arbela (or Gaugamela) which followed, Alexander's army routed Darius's and the Persian army retreated. It was one of the most decisive battles in history. Babylon surrendered, and Alexander took the Persian cities of Susa and Persepolis, yielding him vast treasures in gold and silver.

At Persepolis, Alexander committed some of his worst atrocities. All the inhabitants of the city were either killed or sold as slaves and the great and beautiful city was burned to the ground. It was a terrible act of vandalism.

In 330 BC Alexander crossed the Zagros Mountains to reach Media. Darius had fled there, and shortly afterwards he was killed by his own nobles. With Darius dead, Alexander effectively became king of a huge empire, stretching from Greece right across Anatolia and the Near and Middle East. Not content with this, Alexander took his army on to the southern shore of the Caspian Sea, hammering local tribes as he went, and setting up Persian nobles as local governors, though many of these rebelled against his overlordship after he had moved on. The march continued through Bactria and Sogdiana, where Alexander married Roxane, the daughter of a Sogdian lord. It was in Sogdiana that the violence in

Alexander broke out on a personal level. He lost his temper when drunk and killed a close friend, Clitus. For this single act, amongst all the acts of mass cruelty, his Macedonian troops never forgave him. They remembered him as the murderer of Clitus.

In 326 BC, Alexander reached northern Pakistan, where he defeated Porus, one of the local princes. He had planned to go on to conquer the Ganges valley, but his army mutinied. They were too far from home. It is interesting to speculate just how far Alexander would have gone if the troops had been willing. Would he have gone on to China? The huge sprawling military campaign had reached its furthest point though, and he turned to sail down the Indus River to its mouth, then led the army west in a terrible westward march across the desert of southern Iran. The army and the fleet returned to Susa.

Alexander then busied himself with an insane plan to turn Europe and western Asia into a single country with Babylon as its capital. Intermarriage would bond the different regions together, and he placed soldiers from all the provinces of this empire in his army. He introduced a common currency system throughout the empire. He encouraged the spread of Greek ideas, customs and laws into Asia, regarding them as more enlightened than the existing local laws. It sounds progressive and enlightened, looking forward to the era of the European Union. But the scale was hopelessly grandiose, given the communications systems of the time, and there was, underlying all of it, the megalomania of the mad dictator. In order to command recognition as the supreme ruler everywhere in his empire, Alexander required all the provinces to acknowledge him as a god.

Alexander's plan expanded, and at the time of his death he was planning a new expedition to Arabia. In Babylon he was taken ill with what may have been malaria, dying there in June 323 BC. His body was put into a gold coffin and transported to Alexandria where it was placed in a beautiful tomb. The tomb of Alexander has, rather surprisingly, been lost. Alexander left no successor either, and a successor was essential for the survival of his empire. For all the brilliance and dash of Alexander's career, much of it was to do with personal vanity and egotism, and the manner of his conquest was invariably cruel. As always, a multitude had to die to fulfil one man's dream.

There are today, just as there always have been, varying views of Alexander. He was very conscious of his image, and worked hard to project an image of himself as a reckless, energetic, romantic super-hero ready to take on the world. He even got his architect Deinocrates to prepare a plan to sculpt the Greek peninsula of Mount Athos into a vast sculpture of himself, Alexander the Great, reclining; this astonishingly egotistical scheme was revived in the seventeenth century, when the idealized (sanitized) image of Alexander seemed to represent a great human ideal. The idea was presented to his namesake Pope Alexander VII in about 1655, but fortunately came to nothing.

Alexander very deliberately followed his role models, the warrior-heroes of Homer's Iliad, and it was not at all by chance that he crossed the Hellespont to visit Achilles' tomb at Troy before going to meet the Persian army. He needed his army and his biographers to see him doing that. He was a brilliantly successful propagandist for his own self-image, which lived on as a powerful role-model for many generations of warriors and military dictators. That role model is the principal way in which Alexander changed the world. For many of us today, the horrific death toll involved in his conquests speaks far louder than the personal glamour. Alexander's actions were those of the mass-killer and, whatever glamour the distance of history may have lent his name, he brought immeasurable misery and suffering on tens of thousands of his contemporaries, across a swathe of Eurasia from Greece to the Indus valley.

HEROSTRATUS

THE TEMPLE OF Artemis was one of the Wonders of the World known as the Artemisium. It was one of the greatest classical temples ever built, a colossal, over-sized building made of gleaming white marble, dazzling and awe-inspiring to behold. It was raised on a stepped platform nearly 80m wide by over 130m long, and its roof was supported on a forest of giant fluted columns, 127 of them and 20m high. At the climax of major ceremonies in her honour, the goddess Artemis appeared in a square window high up in the pediment. Because Artemis (actually a priestess disguised as the goddess) was so high up, to see her properly, people needed to stand a long way in front of the temple, so the altar court where the sacrifices took place was located 60m away. It was an incredibly impressive building, and few doubted that the goddess actually lived there, presiding over events. The fall of the temple was a great shock to the Ephesians, who had assumed that Artemis was guarding it.

It was in 356 BC that the disaster came. A man called Herostratus set fire to the temple and burnt it to the ground. We know nothing else about Herostratus except that he committed the crime in order to be immortal, and in a sense he succeeded as his name is remembered.

Plutarch improved the story. He said the goddess Artemis was too busy taking care of the birth of Alexander the Great to send help to her threatened temple. Alexander was born, according to Plutarch, on the very same night that the Temple of Artemis burnt down; it may be true, but if so it seems a remarkable coincidence.

Alexander visited Ephesus to see the partially restored temple when he was 22. He knew that a few years earlier a statue to his father had been put up in the temple. He also knew that the name of Croesus had been inscribed on the columns of the destroyed temple. He knew that contributions to a building entitled the donor to a plaque. He tried to please the Ephesians by paying for a sacrifice and a procession for a festival to honour Artemis. He offered to pay for the completion of the temple if he could have his name on it. The Ephesians declined this offer with great diplomacy, saying that it was not fitting for one god to make gifts to another.

The rebuilt Temple of Artemis stood until AD 262, when it was destroyed again, this time by the Goths. There was some rebuilding before the final destruction came in AD 401. This time the villain was St John Chrysostom, intent on wiping out pagan worship, though his destructive act was not entirely successful. The building was regarded as so holy that stones from it became objects of worship.

Herostratus is one of those people who cling to the edges of the pages of history, desperate to get in, and who succeed in changing the course of events by destroying or killing. He stands for all of those people who change history just for the sake of it, in order to be remembered for having done something.

EUCLID

Lived about 300 BC.
Greek mathematician.

ACHIEVEMENTS:
Set rigorous standards for mathematical argument.
Founder of geometry.
Wrote the standard textbook on geometry.

EUCLID WAS AN ancient Greek mathematician who lived in Alexandria. He was probably trained as a mathematician in Athens by pupils of Plato, but little is known of his life. It was in Alexandria that he founded his mathematical school at the time of Ptolemy I.

Euclid is remembered for just one work, called *Elements*, but often referred to as *Elements of Geometry*. He wrote Elements, in 13 books, which make up the most substantial treatise on mathematics to have survived from ancient Greece. Euclid wrote other books about geometry, astronomy, optics and music, but unfortunately most of these have been lost. The *Elements of Music* may have been by Euclid originally but it appears to have been edited by others. His *Elements of Geometry* is the best-known mathematics textbook of all time. It has been printed in countless editions, with modifications and simplifications, and was still in use as a school textbook in the early part of the twentieth century. Only then did rival textbooks start to appear.

King Ptolemy asked Euclid whether there was any shorter way in geometry than that of his book. Euclid answered, 'There is no royal road to geometry.' A student of Euclid learnt the first proposition and then asked what he would get by learning it. Euclid called his slave and said, 'Give him threepence, as he needs to profit by what he learns.'

Euclid's book was a landmark in the development of Western civilization. It was the first book on mathematics to be printed, and so acquired a major importance in the post-medieval world. It also stood as a model of rigorous mathematical argument for hundreds of years, though the manner of exposition was criticized by Bertrand Russell.

ARCHIMEDES

Born in Syracuse about 287 BC, died in Syracuse 212 BC.
Greek mathematician and inventor.

ACHIEVEMENTS:
Invented the Archimedean screw.
Designed and constructed the first orrery (model of the solar system).
Discovered the principle of displacement.
Discovered formulae for the areas and volumes of planes and solids.
Became the most influential mathematician of all time.

ARCHIMEDES WAS BORN in Syracuse in around 287 BC. He was the son of an astronomer called Pheidias. Archimedes moved in the upper circles of Syracusan society and was on very friendly terms with the king, Hieron, and his son Gelon. Archimedes travelled to Egypt and studied mathematics at Alexandria. It is probable that in Alexandria he met Conon of Samos, a mathematician he greatly admired; they became friends. When he returned to Syracuse he devoted himself to the lifelong study of mathematics.

Archimedes has a central importance in the study of mathematics for his discovery of simple and workable formulae for calculating the areas and volumes of parabolas, cylinders, spheres and other plane and solid figures. The methods he used looked forward to theories of integration that were to be developed nearly 2,000 years later.

He founded the science of hydrostatics, making a study of floating bodies of various shapes. His work on astronomy has unfortunately been lost.

He is most famous for his inventions, which he himself set no value on, regarding applied mathematics as a very inferior pursuit. For King Hieron, he designed and constructed siege engines which were so formidable that even the Romans found them intimidating. It was probably while he was in Egypt that he invented the Archimedean screw that is still in use there for raising water for irrigation. There is a story that he constructed a burning mirror which set on fire the Roman ships in the harbour at Syracuse when they came within a bow-shot of the city wall.

He is also remembered for his shout of 'Eureka!' ('I have found it!') when, in the bath, he discovered the principle of displacement. This was connected with a question from Hieron about a crown that had been made for him. It was supposed to be made of solid gold, but Hieron wondered whether it was a silver alloy. Could Archimedes find a way of testing it? The crown and equal weights of gold and silver could be put separately into a vessel filled with water and the differences in overflow noted.

In his lost work *On Sphere-making*, Archimedes explained how to construct a sphere that would imitate the movements of the sun, moon and five known planets across the sky. In effect, Archimedes described how he built the first orrery, or model of the solar system. When Cicero was in Sicily in 75 BC, the model still existed; Cicero saw it and described it.

His pioneering work in mechanics has found many modern applications. He is supposed to have said, 'Give me a place to stand, and I will move the earth.' Hieron asked Archimedes to demonstrate his contention that a very great weight could be moved by a small force. Archimedes devised a method by which Hieron himself was able to move a large and fully-laden ship.

Archimedes was one of the most original and influential mathematicians of all time. His work combines an incredible freedom of approach with enormous technical skill in the working out of detailed proofs. Much of his work only survived through to the medieval period in Arabic translation. There are ten surviving works by Archimedes.

In 212 BC Archimedes was in Syracuse when it was besieged and attacked by a Roman force under Marcellus. Following the fall of Syracuse, there was a general massacre of citizens, in which Archimedes perished. A Roman soldier challenged him while he was drawing a mathematical figure in the sand. Archimedes was so lost in thought that he took no notice; the soldier ran him through with his sword. Marcellus had given specific orders that Archimedes' house was to be left alone and that no harm must come to Archimedes himself, who was an illustrious figure, an international celebrity. Marcellus was horrified when he heard that Archimedes had been killed, ordered that he should be given an honourable burial, and went out of his way to befriend the dead man's family.

Following his own wish, Archimedes' tomb was marked by a sphere drawn within a cylinder. He regarded his work in discovering the relationship between the surface and the volume of a sphere and its circumscribing cylinder as his greatest achievement. When Cicero was posted to Sicily as a Roman administrator in 75 BC, he found the tomb of Archimedes overgrown with thorns and briers. Syracuse had forgotten the tomb of one of its greatest citizens.

Archimedes was the most original, the most wide-ranging and most inventive of the ancient Greek mathematicians. His pioneering work on geometry and mechanics are major foundations of all later mathematics.

QIN SHI HUANG TI
(THE QIN EMPEROR)

Born 259 BC, died 210 BC.
The first emperor of China.

ACHIEVEMENTS:
Achieved a temporary unification of China.
Established a model for a future unified state.
Tried, by the Burning of the Books, to eradicate history –
* and failed.*
Tried to eradicate Confucianism – and failed.

BEFORE THE POWERFUL and war-like Qin dynasty, China was divided. The 250 years of the Chou emperors were known as 'The Contending States'. The Chou dynasty faded out in a general anarchy and disintegration. The end of the Chou and the unification of the states into a single empire were achieved by the rulers of the state of Qin, on the north-west frontier. The last Chou emperor was deposed in 249 BC.

The Qin emperor who ascended the throne in 246 BC styled himself Shi Huang Ti. This emperor was ably supported and advised by his minister Li Ssu. First, they abolished the political system of the Chou, with its many small states and principalities, and set up a single state with 36 provinces. Over each province, the emperor set officials and administrators appointed directly by himself, and responsible directly to him. It was a straightforward hierarchical system, but created at a single stroke rather than evolving. It was a major achievement.

Power was centralized, and to symbolize that centralization the Qin emperor built a new capital close to Hsi-an in Shensi province. He also introduced a uniform system of weights and measures, a single currency, even standardizing the size of wagon wheels, aiding commerce and unity. The infrastructure was improved by building roads and canals; food production was increased by digging irrigation and drainage channels. He also extended the empire by conquest, incorporating several new provinces. By the year 221 BC what is recognizable as China, which takes its name from this dynasty, had been created. To defend the new empire from the north and north-west, the most frequent direction of attack by barbarians, the emperor ordered the building of the Great Wall of China. This probably already existed in sections, but the Qin emperor completed and strengthened it.

One of the most destructive and controversial actions of the Qin emperor was the suppression of free speech, which included the suppression of Confucianism, which he associated with the previous era. The attempt to wipe out all memory of the previous era was extremely unpopular at the time – and has been condemned by subsequent generations of Chinese too. The scholars who remained loyal to Confucius were buried alive. The existing literature on philosophy and politics were collected and destroyed. This infamous 'Burning of the Books' happened in 212 BC. The only books to be exempt were on divination, pharmacy, medicine and agriculture. He ordered scholars not to discuss the past.

Qin Shih Huang Ti died in 210 BC and was buried in great pomp in a magnificent burial mound. It was guarded by an army of life-sized clay warriors – the famous Terracotta Army. Almost as soon as his strong arm was removed, China disintegrated again. Insurrection broke out and the feeble 'second emperor' was assassinated. Within four years of the Qin emperor's death fighting had once again broken out among the chieftains. The Qin emperor probably tried to achieve too much too quickly and with too much violence. How can you stop people discussing the past? It is in defiance of human nature. It may be significant that the most extreme, impractical and violently destructive actions came close to end of the Qin emperor's regime. Even though the Qin emperor's pioneering attempt at a unification of China had failed, it was not forgotten, but remained in the minds of the Chinese people as a model for the future, an empire that might be achieved again one day.

Meanwhile we are left with the Terracotta Army, which ensure that the Qin emperor impresses new generations afresh. His tomb will not be opened for another hundred years, but when it is it will doubtless add to the long-dead emperor's legacy.

JULIUS CAESAR

Born 102 BC, died 44 BC.

Roman general and dictator, conqueror of Gaul, invader of Britain.

ACHIEVEMENTS:

Conquered Gaul and made it part of the Roman Empire.

Initiated the conquest of Britain, preparing to make it a Roman province.

Cut across the Roman class system.

His apparently limitless ambition created fear in the senate and led to his assassination.

Tacitly named Octavian as his heir, and was therefore responsible for the reign of Augustus.

GAIUS JULIUS CAESAR was born in 102 BC to an old patrician family. In 83 BC Caesar married Cornelia, the daughter of Cinna. Caesar went and fought against the pirates and was elected pontifex in 73 BC. He supported Pompey in 67–66 BC. In 65 BC as curule aedile he spent lavishly on games and public buildings. He was elected pontifex maximus in 63 BC and praetor in 62 BC. It is not clear whether he was involved in the Catiline conspiracy of 63 BC. In 61 BC he was governor of Hispania Ulterior and on his return was elected consul in 59 BC. He negotiated a reconciliation between Pompey and Crassus and then established the informal alliance called 'the First Triumvirate'.

Thus far, Julius Caesar was building a conventional political career, building an impressive portfolio of offices and positions, establishing his position at the forefront of Roman public life. Then he engineered his military career, spending nine years extending the Roman Empire to the west. He first defeated the Helvetii tribe, then went on to defeat the Belgic confederacy. By 56 BC, he was tackling the tribes of Brittany and Normandy. In 54 BC, he forced a nominal surrender of south-east England. Caesar went back to northern Italy, but then had to return to Gaul to put down a rebellion led by Vercingetorix. At Alesia in 53 BC, Caesar decisively crushed the united armies of the Gauls.

Meanwhile Crassus had been killed and Pompey was moving away from Caesar. The senate called for Caesar to resign his command and disband his army, at the same time entrusting large-scale power to Pompey. Caesar made the critical, dangerous decision to defy the senate. He marched his army into Italy, chased Pompey to Brundisium and from there to Greece. Julius Caesar was in control in Italy and appointed dictator for a year. At the Battle of Pharsalia in 48 BC, the senatorial army was defeated and Pompey fled to Egypt, where he was murdered. Julius Caesar's dictatorship was renewed. After further expeditions, Caesar had to go to Spain to put down a rebellion led by Pompey's sons.

By 45 BC, when he returned to Rome from Spain, Julius Caesar was at the height of his success, the most powerful figure in the Roman world. A problem was that some people, both common people and courtiers, wanted to shower him with ever higher honours, while others were alarmed at the emergence of a personal dictatorship. It is unclear whether Julius Caesar himself really wanted any further aggrandizement. He certainly claimed that he didn't, on more than one occasion. Once, while travelling from Alba to Rome, some people saluted him, calling him king. The word had a resonance then that it does not have today; in ancient Rome, 'king' could also mean 'tyrant'.

He could see that the rest of the crowd did not like it and seemed not to like the word himself. He called out that his name was Caesar, not king. Another time, when he was in the Senate, he made a point of behaving towards the others present as if they were all equals together, and he said that he should have honours taken away from him rather than added as he had too much already.

But the idea of making Julius Caesar king was put about, perhaps by Caesar's friends, perhaps even by his enemies, who wanted to see him fall. He was in a sense caught in a well-established tradition, the cursus honorum, the honours race, in which men of noble birth competed for honours and gradually climbed up the hierarchy of honours. It was naturally assumed that men who had reached a certain level in the honours race would seek to climb to the next rung. This may be why so many republicans feared Julius Caesar. He could reach up to the next rung, so he certainly would. He in fact accepted some honours and offices without using them. For instance he accepted the power of the magistracies without actually wielding it; by doing this, he enabled other aristocrats to develop their careers without hindering them.

Julius Caesar spent the last few months of his life planning a huge military campaign against Parthia. The idea was to avenge the defeat of Crassus. It may be that, to him, being away from Rome on campaign was actually preferable to staying there and dealing with the possibly insoluble problem of his precise personal status. It may also be that a war against foreign enemies would unite Rome and make her forget all these petty quarrels.

Although he had said to the Senate that he had too many honours already, he went on accepting them, so as not to appear ungrateful. He was appointed 'perpetual dictator' and he started wearing the knee-high red boots of the kings of Alba Longa, from whom he was descended. Antony publicly offered him a diadem, a white linen band worn across the forehead; this was the Greek symbol of monarchy. Caesar refused the offered diadem, but it is not clear whether he was feigning modesty; he may have intended to accept it if offered it again.

Then the plotting began. The instigator of the plot to assassinate Caesar seems to have been Gaius Cassius Longinus. Cassius was aggrieved because although Caesar had pardoned him for earlier disloyalty, he felt he had been slighted by not being offered a command in the forthcoming war against Parthia. Cassius persuaded his brother-in-law Marcus Junius Brutus to join the plot.

Brutus was fanatical and merciless. He had fought on Pompey's side at Pharsalia, like Cassius, and also been pardoned by Casear. Julius Caesar had in effect been more than generous to both of them and they owed him a debt of gratitude. Perhaps that was one of the reasons why they hated him – the sense of obligation. Brutus was well-known as a descendant of Lucius Junius Brutus, who lived in about 500 BC and who was thought to have founded Republican government in Rome. It was that earlier Brutus who drove an earlier king, Tarquinius, out of Rome for misrule. The later Brutus came to think of himself as re-enacting that early cleansing of Rome. In killing Julius Caesar, he was destroying the monarchy in Rome for a second time. The idea appealed to his ego.

Neither Brutus nor Cassius had any real reason to assassinate Julius Caesar, but Cassius's minor feeling of slight combined with Brutus's tendency to fanaticism was enough to do it. It became an obsession.

Caesar knew of the plot to assassinate him, but disregarded the warnings. He was attacked and stabbed to death at a senate meeting in the Theatrum Pompeium by a group of conspirators, most of whom had been pardoned by Caesar and had their careers advanced by him; the attack was a monstrous act of ingratitude.

The immediate aftermath of Caesar's death was a kind of paralyzed shock. The sheer pointlessness of the assassination was underlined by the assassins total failure to create an alternative government in the days and weeks that followed. Caesar had not nominated a political heir, but he had left a huge amount of money to one man. He had left three-quarters of his estate to the 18-year-old Gaius Octavius, who was the son of his niece Atia. Octavius had been sent to Greece to serve with the Legions in the preparations for the war with Parthia. Now, of course, he returned at the head of Caesar's legions to claim his inheritance. With that huge fortune, and Julius Caesar's evident blessing behind him, he was bound to wield enormous power.

Perhaps Caesar's greatest legacy was creating Augustus.

MARK ANTONY

Born 83 BC, died 30 BC.
Roman statesman and soldier, member of the triumvirate with
Octavian and Lepidus.

ACHIEVEMENTS:
Avenged the assassination of Julius Caesar.
Prevented the founding of a republic after Julius Caesar's
murder.
Inadvertently paved the way for the reign of Augustus.

MARCUS ANTONIUS WAS born in 83 BC. An upper class Roman youth related to Julius Caesar, he at first led a life of dissipation. He made a career for himself in the army, making himself useful to Julius Caesar in Gaul in 54 BC. He went to Rome and with Caesar's support and sponsorship he became tribune of the plebs. He defended Caesar's cause in 49 BC. He was expelled from the senate when civil war broke out and fled to Caesar. Caesar in turn made Mark Antony's expulsion the pretext for declaring war on Pompey. Caesar left him in charge in Italy. In 47 BC he was made Master of the Horse and left to govern Italy while Caesar was away in Africa. In 44 BC he was consul together with Caesar.

When Caesar was assassinated, Antony skilfully won the people of Rome round. The conspirators fled, leaving Antony in complete control in Rome. He was unfortunate in having Octavian (later Augustus) to contend with. Octavian was an even more astute political operator than Antony. Antony found himself besieged and then defeated at Mutina in 43 BC. He fled across the Alps to Gaul, where he visited Lepidus, gained favour with the army and took command. As a result of this manoeuvre, Antony was able to return to Rome at the head of a colossal army consisting of 17 legions and 10,000 cavalry.

Octavian, up to now apparently a Republican, changed sides, negotiated with Antony and Lepidus and the three men agreed to share the Roman empire between them as a 'triumvirate'. This new regime began with a reign of terror in which Cicero and 300 other senators were executed or summarily killed, in order to secure control and raise money. After this the main conspirators in the assassination of Caesar were hunted down. Brutus and Cassius were defeated at the Battle of Philippi in 42 BC. This battle in effect wiped out any chance of the republican and senatorial parties gaining power in Rome. The empire was shared among the three men, with Octavian controlling Africa, Antony Gaul and Lepidus Spain.

Antony next visited Egypt where in 41 BC he fatefully met Cleopatra, the queen of Egypt. From the beginning he was infatuated with her. While he was away in the east, a new division of the empire was arranged, with Octavian taking the west, Antony the east and Lepidus Africa. Antony's dalliance in the east was exploited and to an extent misrepresented by Octavian in Rome. A propaganda war developed. Octavian (Augustus) declared open war on Cleopatra, defeating her and Antony in a sea-battle at Actium in 31 BC.

After this crushing defeat Antony was deserted by his troops; Cleopatra escaped from the battle with 60 ships. Antony realised he was finished. When he heard a false rumour that Cleopatra had committed suicide, he believed it, fell on his sword and killed himself. When Cleopatra heard the news, and feared that she would be exposed to the indignities of a Roman triumph, Cleopatra committed suicide too. Antony had been married in succession to Fadia, Antonia, Fulvia and Octavia and left several children.

Antony contributed to the development of the Roman empire in several ways. He turned Rome against the murderers of Julius Caesar; if he had not, a Republic might have followed, perhaps led by Brutus. His head-strong and impulsive adventure in the east enabled Augustus to pick off both him and Lepidus, preparing the way for Augustus' own reign as emperor. In his love for Cleopatra, Antony was the classic 'flawed hero'. The idea of a man with the world at his feet sacrificing it all for love has appealed over many generations, as a real-life tragedy that *might* have been written by Sophocles, and eventually was written by Shakespeare.

AUGUSTUS

Born 63 BC, died 14 BC.
The first Roman emperor.

ACHIEVEMENTS:
Became the first Roman emperor.
Reconstructed Roman society.
Renovated and beautified Rome.
Guaranteed the peaceful survival of the Roman Empire for
    200 years.

GAIUS OCTAVIUS, OR Octavian, was born in September 63 BC, the year of
the Catiline conspiracy. His family was well connected; his father Gaius
Octavius was a senator and his mother Atia was the niece of Julius Caesar.
When Octavian was five his father died and his mother remarried; after that
his guardian was his stepfather, Lucius Marcius Philippus. When Octavian
was 16 he assumed his manly gown and was elected to the pontifical college,
a premature honour that he undoubtedly owed to his family connection; his
great-uncle, Julius Caesar, was dictator and master of Rome. With a family
tie like that, anything was possible for young Octavian.

In 45 BC, he was made a patrician by the senate and designated Master
of Horse for the next year. Caesar was planning a Parthian campaign, and
sent Octavian to study at the Greek colony of Apollonia in Illyria. It was
there that he heard of Caesar's murder, and he set sail at once to return to
Italy. When he landed he discovered that Caesar had made him his heir
and posthumously adopted him into his family; his name was to change to
Gaius Julius Caesar Octavianus. The legacy was a dangerous one and

family members tried to dissuade him from accepting it. Octavian decided to take the risk and gravely assumed his role as Caesar's executor.

Meanwhile Mark Antony, an older and more experienced man, had already got hold of Caesar's papers and made light of Octavian's pretensions. Brutus and Cassius, Caesar's murderers, similarly paid little regard to the young man. Cicero flattered Octavian, hoping to make use of him and get rid of him later. But Octavian handled the situation cleverly, using those around him for his own ends without helping any of them. He gained support, not least in the senate. When the senate armed the consuls against Antony, who was refusing to surrender Caesar's property, it was Octavian they asked to take the leading role. When Antony was defeated at the Battle of Mutina in 43 BC, Octavian's capabilities became clear. Suddenly Octavian became much more powerful; his soldiers demanded the consulship for him and, though unwilling, the senate was unable to refuse. Octavian formed a coalition with Lepidus and Antony; the three would rule the empire jointly for five years. Then they drew up a list of proscribed citizens and organized the assassination of 300 senators.

Octavian and Antony crossed the Adriatic to deal with Brutus and Cassius, Caesar's murderers, along with the republicans who had taken refuge with them. Lepidus was ineffectual, and Antony lost his position by lingering too long in Egypt with Cleopatra. Octavian found it relatively easy to turn Rome against Antony and assume power for himself, becoming, in his own words, 'master of all things'. With Antony out of the way after the Battle of Actium in 31 BC, Octavian was legally invested for ten years with the government of the frontier provinces, and sole command of army and navy. In Rome, he was to be elected consul year by year. Octavian's formal power increased in stages. He was finally awarded the title Augustus by the senate on 17 January 27 BC, when he became the first Roman emperor. Now there was no question of reinstating the republic.

The reign of Augustus was not only the beginning, it was the golden age of the Roman Empire. In achieving this transformation he was ably supported by his wife Livia, whom he married in 38 BC. Augustus was far from charismatic himself, but he surrounded himself with talented administrators – as well as poets and historians. The writings of Horace, Virgil, Ovid, Propertius and Livy were seen at the time and still are seen as the glories of the Augustan Age. Augustus himself was a writer; he wrote an autobiography.

His greatest public setback came in AD 9 with the loss in Germany of three entire legions under Varus. His domestic life was continually beset by problems and tragedies. He named worthy successors and heirs, who then died prematurely. He eventually achieved a succession by adopting his stepson Tiberius and naming him as his heir in AD 4.

In AD 14 Augustus left Rome for Naples. At Nola, his father's old home, he stopped to rest on his journey and died there on 19 August.

The reputation of Augustus has been severely damaged by the unscrupulous and devious methods he used to gain power, his cruelty and deceit, and the use he made of power when he had achieved it. Some see him as an astute and successful intriguer and an accomplished political actor. But the magnitude of what he achieved as emperor cannot be ignored. He was unquestionably one of the world's great men, a statesman who carried through an ambitious scheme of political reconstruction which completed the transformation of Rome from republic to empire, kept the empire together and guaranteed a period of peace in which Roman civilization could continue to develop for more than 200 years.

JESUS CHRIST

Born about 6 BC, died AD 33.
Teacher, prophet, healer, miracle-worker, founder of
* Christianity, believed by his followers to be the Messiah.*

ACHIEVEMENTS:
Preached that there are higher loyalties than to the state.
Preached an inclusive religion favouring the weak and the poor.
Subverted existing socio-political orders.
Persuaded his followers of his divinity.
Founded one of the major world religions.
Emphasized the Fatherhood of God.

ACCORDING TO THE surviving accounts in the Gospel of St Matthew and St Luke, Jesus was the first-born son of Mary, the wife of Joseph, a carpenter. Jesus was born, they say, in a stable in Bethlehem because Mary and Joseph were on their way to Nazareth, Joseph's home town, for a Roman population census and there was no room for them at the inn. The date is difficult to verify. According to Matthew, Jesus was born just before the death of Herod, which is known to have taken place in 4 BC; the Roman census referred to in Luke is known from other sources to have taken place after AD 6. The various astronomical explanations for the 'star' that led the wise men to Bethlehem suggest 6, 7 or 8 BC.

The information in the four canonical ('approved') gospels and the Acts of the Apostles is strictly limited, covering a total of only 50 days in the life of Jesus, and contains little in the way of personal detail. We are not told what Jesus looked like, or even whether he was married, though there is circumstantial evidence that Mary Magdalene was his wife. There is insufficient material to write a 'Life of Christ', although that has not deterred countless well-meaning authors from trying, inevitably fleshing the story out with their own projections.

It is evident from the gospels that Jesus made a profound impression on his followers. The particular personal quality that was responsible for this impression was described as his grace. This seems to have entailed a ready sympathy, an understanding tenderness, and a way of meeting people as if they were already of importance to him. The grace of Jesus has been described as 'a deep-seated adequacy, bestowing itself on others and enriching them'. Another quality was his enormous power or authority. This gave him the ability to interpret scriptures, and even to forgive sins.

The circumstances of Jesus's birth, familiar from Nativity plays, Christmas carols and cards, are surrounded by mythological detail that probably bear no relation to what actually happened. Many of the details have been shown to be disingenuous references back to Old Testament scriptures, added in an attempt to show Jesus fulfilling a whole raft of prophecies for the coming of the Messiah.

As a boy, it is likely that Jesus followed his father's trade as a carpenter. At the age of 12 he was found, by his astonished mother, knowledgeably discussing serious religious issues with priests. When he was 18 he was baptized by his cousin John the Baptist, and this experience seems to have given him an intimation of his mission.

Jesus spent 40 days in the wilderness, wrestling with all kinds of temptations. After this rite of passage, he gathered 12 disciples and organized two missionary journeys round Galilee, which culminated in a huge rally where it was said he miraculously fed 5,000 people.

A particular characteristic of Jesus's missionary journeys was his willingness to flout the social conventions of the time. He did not mind mixing with socially unacceptable people such as publicans, tax collectors and sinners; he was prepared to perform miracles on the Sabbath; he drove the money-lenders out of the temple; the Sermon on the Mount favoured the lowly and the disadvantaged. The emphasis of his mission was always on inclusiveness – he was happy to preach to non-Jewish people – and on love, humility and charity. It was while on these travels that Jesus revealed himself to his disciples as the Messiah, the promised saviour who would release the Jews, but also hinted at his impending suffering, death and resurrection. It is a great puzzle that Jesus never claimed to be the Messiah, never claimed to be the Son of God; these claims were made on his behalf. He allowed Peter to call him the Messiah, and he is alleged to have admitted it to the High Priest at his trial, though the account of the trial is suspect. He nevertheless made it clear that people needed to respond to him in an appropriate way if they were to be spiritually saved. 'Blessed are the eyes which see what you see' can only mean, 'You are exceptionally privileged to be in my company.' And he was right.

Jesus referred to God in a conventional way and seemed on the face of things to have no special original view of God; he was the Jewish God who had been worshipped for the previous six or eight centuries and Jesus did not make a point of preaching about him in particular. But the ancient Hebrew God, Yahweh, Jehovah, had distinct archetypal roles incorporated into his image that appear not to have interested Jesus. The ancient God was the lord of the animals, the lord of harvest, the lord of wisdom, the lord of war. What Jesus did was unusual. Instead of overtly re-interpreting the ancient Hebrew God, or appearing to re-cast him in a new role, Jesus repeatedly referred obliquely to God in his own idiosyncratic way, almost off-handedly, emphasizing the Fatherhood of God. Jesus in fact used the word Father as a substitute for God almost all the time. This evidently sprang from his knowledge that he was in some sense the *Son* to this *Father*, and his desire that others should see their lives in terms of *Sonship* to the *Father-god*.

According to the Gospel of St Mark, Jesus entered Jerusalem in triumph, but it is likely that he arrived in the run-up to a religious festival, the Passover, along with a lot of other pilgrims in a joyous holiday mood – and that the 'Hosannas' were not for him. At his famous Last Supper with the disciples, the Passover meal, Jesus hinted that he would be betrayed by one of them. Judas Iscariot, one of the disciples, immediately afterwards went to the authorities and that betrayal led to the arrest of Jesus within a few hours in the Garden of Gethsemane.

Jesus was subjected to a hurried trial and condemned to death for blasphemy by a Jewish council. He was then taken before the Roman procurator for confirmation of the sentence. According to the gospels, Pilate could find no grounds for convicting Jesus of treason because he had not claimed to be the king of a territory, only the King of the Jews. The suspicion among scholars is that the narrative has been tampered with in order to vindicate the Romans and put the blame for Jesus's death squarely onto the Jews. It is likely that Pilate would have found Jesus guilty for causing a civil disturbance, and if the Sanhedrin had found him guilty of blasphemy the sentence should have been stoning.

Jesus was crucified on the Passover, the day when Jews by custom sacrificed the Passover lamb, hence the references in Christian mythology to the 'Lamb of God': Jesus was the sacrificial lamb. Pilate was surprised when he was told that Jesus was dead after hanging on the cross for only a few hours, but gave permission for the body to be taken down for burial. Joseph of Arimathea provided his own tomb.

Three days later the disciples had various indications that Jesus had 'risen from the dead'. A great deal of discussion over the centuries has failed to resolve the question of what really happened that first Easter Morning, but the gospel accounts invite us to believe that Jesus physically came back to life in the tomb, and walked out into the garden to greet Mary Magdalene, who had arrived to anoint his body. Some Christians believe that Jesus remained physically dead, but the disciples were overwhelmed by his spiritual presence. Another possibility is that Jesus was not actually dead but unconscious when taken down from the cross, and revived later, maybe even that the crucifixion was somehow stage-managed so that Jesus would survive the ordeal. A problem with this explanation is that the disciples saw virtually nothing of Jesus after those first few days following the crucifixion. The suggestion that he just wandered off and started a new life somewhere else, taking no further interest in the new religion that he had launched, leaves too many questions unanswered.

Whatever happened, followers who had scattered in dismay immediately after his shameful execution as a common criminal were reunited in Jerusalem a few weeks later. There were about 120 of them and for some reason they were fired with a common conviction that Jesus was alive, had been seen by several people, and would shortly return as the Messiah. They adopted an attitude that had been gradually evolving during Jesus's lifetime, an attitude of religious faith.

What is certain is that the disciples were sufficiently convinced that the spiritual presence of Jesus was still with them that they committed the rest of their lives, and risked martyrdom, to preach the Christian message. They did so with enthusiasm and success. Within a few centuries it became the official religion of the Roman Empire, and went on from there to become one of the major world religions.

PTOLEMY

Born about 90, died about 168.
Egyptian mathematician, astronomer and geographer.

ACHIEVEMENTS:
Refined the Hipparchan model of the universe – the Ptolemaic
*   System.*
Devised a scientific method for making maps.
Devised the latitude-longitude grid system for fixing
*   geographical locations.*
Produced the first scientifically-based world map.
Invented the atlas.

CLAUDIUS PTOLEMAEUS WAS born at Ptolemais Hermii, a Greek colony town in Egypt. Very little else is known about his life, except that he was an astronomer, and made his astronomical observations at Alexandria during the reigns of Hadrian and Antoninus Pius. Shortly after his lifetime it was said that he lived in the Temple of Serapis at Canopus, near Alexandria. This is quite possible, as Egyptian temples also functioned as libraries and centres of learning. At the temple they raised pillars with the results of his observations inscribed on them.

Ptolemy wrote on many mathematical subjects, including refraction. Ptolemy's mathematical and astronomical work included major contributions on trigonometry, and his exposition of the table of chords (equivalent to the modern table of sines) by Hipparchus was in use by astronomers for more than a thousand years. Ptolemy's Hipparchan model for the motion of the heavenly bodies, known as the Ptolemaic system, was the prevailing model for the same length of time. It assumes that the Earth is at the centre of the universe and that the heavenly bodies revolve round it. Beyond and in the ether surrounding the Earth's atmosphere were eight concentric spherical shells. To seven of these one heavenly body was attached, and the fixed stars were attached to the eighth.

Ptolemy's Almagest was to have a great influence on astronomy during the Renaissance, when many key classical works were rediscovered and re-evaluated. The Ptolemaic System was nevertheless to be shaken vigorously by the likes of Copernicus and Galileo.

His 'great compendium of astronomy' was described by the Greeks as megiste, meaning 'the greatest'. This led to its being called the Almagest in Arabic, and it is still generally known by this Arabic name.

In some ways, Ptolemy's work as a geographer had further-reaching effects, and by the same route. A lot of Ptolemy's work was not original or innovative; he was largely a compiler and corrector of other people's work, but no less useful for that. In astronomy he was very dependent on the work of Hipparchus. In geography he was similarly dependent on Marinus of Tyre, for whom he became a corrector, editor and updater. Ptolemy's great work was the *Guide to Geography*. This, along with a lot of other classical learning, was forgotten or even lost in Europe, and only kept alive by Arabic scholars. It was the rediscovery by Europeans of those Arabic copies that fuelled the Renaissance. The astronomer Hipparchus pointed out that the only way to construct a reliable and trustworthy map of the world was to use astronomical observations to fix the latitude and longitude of all the principal points on its surface. This was good in principle, but the means of acquiring this sort of information were lacking. Then, just before Ptolemy's time, Marinus of Tyre started to collect determinations of latitude and longitude from itineraries. It is not clear how far Marinus got, but Ptolemy evidently used Marinus' work and started where he left off. Ptolemy borrowed the system Hipparchus invented for dividing up the equator into 360 parts, and these became our modern degrees. Ptolemy drew lines through these points, connecting them to the North and South Poles to make lines of longitude. He drew another set of lines parallel to the equator to mark the latitude. Then he located his known points on this grid.

So far, so good. Then Ptolemy made an odd mistake. Eratosthenes had correctly calculated the circumference of the earth as 25,000 miles. Posidonius had wrongly reduced this to 18,000 miles, and both Marinus and Ptolemy unfortunately followed Posidonius instead of Eratosthenes. Significant errors were built into his map from the start. Ptolemy was also working on relatively little data on longitude. Given the flaws in his approach, Ptolemy made an honest attempt at a world map, and Europe, Asia and Africa are recognizable. He also produced regional maps, and in effect invented the atlas. He established regional and world maps as a way of looking at the world – and that was a major step in changing people's perception. In remote antiquity, long before Ptolemy, people never thought in cartographic terms; after Ptolemy, most educated people did think in cartographic terms.

It is easy to find fault with the result – its lack of geographical information such as climate, inhabitants, resources, vegetation, relief, drainage. However, Ptolemy was primarily an astronomer and he was constructing a map of the world in much the same spirit as he might have made a map of the moon. Even so it was odd that he was ready to leave so much out. Strabo had, after all, shown that he was well aware of the need to include the rivers and mountains that, to use Strabo's own word, 'geographize' a country. In Gaul, Ptolemy included a stream that happened to be the boundary between two Roman provinces, yet left out the major tributaries of the Rhine.

The *Guide to Geography* included tables of places and their locations, showing an admirable scientific rigour of approach, one that would be a model to the Renaissance world. Ptolemy's maps, for all their faults, were better than most of the maps constructed in medieval Europe. The rediscovery of a copy of Ptolemy's maps, together with the statistical tables that had led to their construction, was a turning point in the European Renaissance.

ALARIC I

Born on Peuce in Dacia 370, died 410.
King of the Visigoths, conqueror of Athens and Rome.

ACHIEVEMENTS:
395–96 Almost conquered the eastern empire.
396 Captured Athens, Corinth, Argos and Sparta.
410 Conquered and pillaged Rome.
Gave an early warning that the Roman empire was doomed.

ALARIC I WAS born in Dacia, on an island called Peuce at the mouth of the Danube, in about 370. He was born into a noble Visigothic (western Gothic) family which had taken refuge in the Danube valley after fleeing from their enemies the Huns. In the year 394 he served as leader of the Gothic auxiliaries of the eastern Roman emperor Theodosius I, in a campaign against the usurper Eugenius. The battle that brought this campaign to a close, the Battle of the Frigidus, was fought near the Alpine passes, and it was here that Alaric discovered how easy it would be to penetrate Italy's natural defences on the north-east side.

In the general reshuffling of offices that took place at he beginning of the reigns of Arcadius and Honorius, the sons of Theodosius, Alaric hoped to gain significant military power. He hoped for one of the great war ministries, giving him the formal command of several legions. For some reason this was denied him; he was instead left as commander of Gothic auxiliaries. Alaric was thwarted, frustrated and angry. The Visigoth soldiers were also frustrated, for a different reason; their customary prize money was withdrawn.

The Visigoths responded by electing Alaric as their king in 395. He was only 25, but made king of the Visigoths on merit. Alaric decided to strike first at the eastern empire. He marched on Constantinople, but found that besieging that city would be too great an undertaking and retraced his steps, using the unguarded Pass of Thermopylae to invade Greece. He ravaged Attica but spared the great city of Athens. Then he went on into the Peloponnese (southern Greece) and took its most famous cities, Corinth, Argos and Sparta. Alaric was stopped by Flavius Stilicho, leading troops from the western empire, and eventually driven out of the Peloponnese.

Then came an extraordinary development. The eastern emperor Arcadius appointed Alaric governor of the prefecture of Illyria as a kind of bribe, hoping this would pacify him. But from this position of strength Alaric was able to set off on the warpath again and he invaded Italy. Once again he was stopped by Stilicho, at Pollentia on the Tanarus on Easter Day in 402. The Battle of Pollentia was a military victory for the Romans, but an expensive one. It was a propaganda victory for Alaric as he had trusted that the sanctity of the religious festival would give him immunity to attack on that day. There were large numbers of Visigoth women and children present, which hampered the fighting; it seems that Alaric was turning his military invasion into a national migration.

Stilicho's enemies accused him of unfair tactics in exploiting a religious festival and he switched to diplomacy. Through his mediation Alaric was persuaded to join the western emperor, Honorius, in an attack on the eastern emperor, Arcadius. A large sum of money was promised, in effect to compensate for the cost of mobilization and Honorius foolishly failed to pay. Stilicho brought pressure to bear on the Roman senate to pay the agreed sum. Shortly afterwards Stilicho himself was treacherously killed with connivance from the timid and jealous Honorius. Alaric turned from ally to enemy and laid siege to Rome, arriving outside the walls of the city in September 408 and starting a blockade.

The famine-stricken citizens of Rome agreed to pay a huge ransom to end the siege and Alaric lifted it. He had no wish to destroy Rome or its empire – he wanted them for himself. His condition on lifting his first siege of Rome was the grant of an eastern empire for himself, between the Danube and the Gulf of Venice and the title commander-in-chief of the imperial army. But the terms were not agreed by Rome. In the end, all the diplomatic efforts to save Rome failed. Alaric breached Rome's defences on 24 August, 410 and entered the city by the Salarian Gate. For six days Alaric's Visigoths pillaged and looted the city that for many centuries had represented the pinnacle of western civilization.

Alaric was not a stereotypical barbarian king at all. He was in fact a Christian, an Arian Christian. He gave specific orders to his men not to dishonour women or to destroy any religious buildings. In this he was more enlightened and civilized than the Romans.

Later in the same year, he set off to invade Sicily with a view to extending his rule over the whole of Italy, and then Africa too, for its corn crops, but he died at Cosenza. His body was buried in the bed of the River Busento. The river was temporarily diverted, a grave was dug and the king and some of his most precious spoils were buried, then the river was allowed to flow back over the grave. The prisoners who had done the work were put to death so that no-one would learn where the grave of Alaric was – or what it contained. It has never been found.

ATTILA THE HUN

Born 406, died 453.
Leader of the barbarian hordes, threatened to destroy the
  Roman Empire.

ACHIEVEMENTS:
Became legendary as the hero Atli of the Edda poems and Etzel
  in the Nibelungenlied.
434 – Became king of the Huns.
440 – Became commander in chief of a huge army of Vandals,
  Ostrogoths, Gepids and Franks.
447 – Laid waste eastern Europe, three times defeating the
  emperor Theodosius.
451 – Invaded Gaul, besieged Orleans.
452 – Threatened to take the city of Rome.

THE ROMANS ENCROACHED on other people's possessions and interests in the process of creating their empire. Inevitably, their neighbours resisted and counter-attacked, though the Romans often seem to have been surprised by this. They saw the people of central and northern Europe as 'barbarians', troublesome subversive people who threatened the stability of the empire. These barbarians were simply trying to defend their homelands, and they repeatedly attacked Rome. Often they were demonized by the Romans for doing so, and it is sometimes hard to evaluate the Roman accounts of what happened. The Greek historian Herodotus, writing in around 480 BC, was in the same mindset when he described the Scythians skinning their enemies to make coats. There were, even so, several tribes who were astonishingly aggressive and bloodthirsty, and who relentlessly harried the Romans, to the extent that within a few decades they caused the Roman Empire to collapse under the strain.

Goths from Sweden moved south, reaching Rome in 410. The city was sacked in a week-long orgy of killing and destruction. The Vandals arrived from Germany a few decades later, after raiding Gaul, Spain and North Africa, leaving a trail of destruction behind them. Then the Huns arrived to harry Rome.

The Huns originally came from the windswept steppes of central Asia, driven out of their homeland by the Chinese in the second century. This push from the Far East had a domino effect, displacing people westwards until they impacted on Rome. The Huns massacred their way through, eventually settling north of the Danube, where they came to an arrangement with Rome, buying acceptance by agreeing to subdue troublesome neighbours. Rome paid an annual tribute of 350 pounds of gold to King Ruas, but also took hostages as a guarantee of loyalty. King Ruas had a nephew called Attila, who went to Rome as one of the hostages. This proved to be a useful experience for Attila, as it enabled him to learn the customs and geography of Italy.

King Ruas died when Attila was 27 years old. Attila inherited the Hunnish throne jointly with his brother Bleda, and they worked together to strengthen their kingdom by fighting neighbouring Teutonic tribes like the Gepidae and the Ostrogoths. By 444 Attila had consolidated his control over the lands that are today Romania and Hungary. He had also made himself sole ruler by the simple, age-old technique of murdering his brother. Now he was ready to take on Rome.

Attila looked for a pretext to attack Rome, and soon found one. Honoria, the sister of the Roman Emperor Valentinian III, had a scandalous affair with a courtier. She became pregnant. Valentinian had her removed to Constantinople, where she was kept a virtual prisoner. Bored and frustrated by events, she smuggled a plea for help to Attila, who was at Budapest, offering to marry him if he would rescue her. Attila already had many wives and did not need another, especially one as troublesome as this, but saw the proposal as a major political opportunity. He wrote to Valentinian asking for permission to marry Honoria – and as a dowry half the Roman Empire. It was an impudent request, which he knew would be refused, but the snub gave him his excuse to release a ferocious attack on the Empire.

In 447 Attila led his warriors south into Macedonia (northern Greece) to Constantinople. The Romans bought him off with a massively increased annual tribute and paying a huge indemnity for Attila's withdrawal. Attila went home with his plunder.

Four years later, Attila was on the move again, leading a huge army of Franks, Vandals and Huns westwards across the Rhine into Gaul. Several Gaulish towns were ruthlessly destroyed. As Attila was about to attack and destroy Orleans in the same way, Roman legions arrived together with a Visigoth army. Attila withdrew to the plain near Chalons-sur-Marne, ready to fight. The battle lasted all day, with huge loss of life on both sides. One person who was there described the fighting as 'ruthless, immense, obstinate'. Among the thousands who died that day was the king of the Visigoths. Attila was forced to retreat, back across the Rhine. The battle was crucial in European history. If Attila, with his Mongol background, had won the battle, not only would subsequent history have been different, but the ethnicity and culture of Europe would have been different.

The defeat at Chalons did not deter Attila from trying again. The next year he led his warriors south into Italy, completely destroying Aquileia, the main city in Venetia, and inflicting appalling atrocities on its inhabitants. The Huns went on to the Adriatic Sea, killing the innocent citizens of the towns of Altinum, Concordia and Padua and burning their houses. Refugees fled to islands in the coastal lagoon, where they founded a new settlement that would one day become the city of Venice. As the Huns rampaged across the Plain of Lombardy, Rome itself was clearly in danger. Pope Leo I made the incredibly brave decision to travel to meet Attila, who was so struck by Pope Leo's boldness that he agreed to end the blood-letting and take his men home, though he still talked of coming back if Honoria was not treated better. But he did not return.

On 15 March 453, Attila gave a great banquet to celebrate his marriage to yet another wife, the beautiful Ildico. In bed with Ildico that night, Attila burst an artery and died of the resulting haemorrhage.

Attila's achievement was the mobilization of a great anti-Roman army that shook the bars of the Roman Empire. He did not succeed in bringing Rome down, but he did succeed in showing that it could be done – and how it could be done. Attila's campaign against Rome was a dress rehearsal for the fall of the Roman Empire.

II
THE MEDIEVAL AND RENAISSANCE WORLD

CLOVIS

Born 465, died in Paris 511.
King of the Franks, creator of France.

ACHIEVEMENTS:
Founder of the Frankish monarchy.
First true king of all the Franks.
Creator of the Salic law.
Founder of France.
Established a strongly centralized administration in France.
Established Paris as the capital of France.

CLOVIS, OR CHLODWIG (Old German), was born in 465, the grandson of Merovech, from whom the Merovingian dynasty took it name, and the son of Childeric I, king of the Salian Franks. Childeric's Frankish kingdom extended only as far west as the River Somme in what is now northern France and his capital was at Tournai.

In 481, at the age of only 15, Clovis succeeded his father as king. Nothing is known of his activities until, five years later, he overthrew the last Roman governor in Gaul, Syagrius, who had carved out a principality for himself on the west of the Somme. Through this victory, which took place near the city of Soissons, Clovis took control of the whole region of what is now France between the Somme and the Loire. Clovis established a new capital at Soissons. Syagrius took refuge with the Visigoth king Alaric II, who handed him over to Clovis. From then on, Clovis worked to conquer more and more of France, capturing city after city.

In 493 Clovis married Clotilda of Burgundy, who was later to be St Clotilda. Through her he was to be converted to Christianity following his great military victory over the Alemanni near Cologne in 496. At Rheims, on Christmas Day 496, there was a mass baptism at which Clovis and 2000 of his soldiers were baptized; it was conducted by Remigius, the Bishop of Rheims. The baptism of Clovis was an event of historic importance. From that moment on, the orthodox Christians throughout the neighbouring kingdoms of the Burgundians and Visigoths looked to Clovis to deliver them from their kings, who were Arian Christians. Clovis became a champion of orthodox Christianity against the Arians, who were perceived as 'heretics'.

Clovis was unsuccessful in his struggle against the Burgundians, but fared better against the Visigoths. In 507 he defeated the Arian Visigoths under their leader, Alaric II. This took place at the Battle of Vouille, not far from Poitiers, and it enabled Clovis to take possession of the whole country as far to the south-west as Bordeaux and Toulouse. In the great battle, Clovis killed Alaric with his own hand. To the south-east he was stopped at Arles by an Ostrogoth army under Theodoric the Great, but at least, following the death of Alaric, the whole Visigoth kingdom stretching as far the Pyrenees was added to his kingdom. In 508, Clovis was awarded the insignia of the consulship from the eastern emperor, Anastasius, at Tours. The title was merely honorific, but nevertheless a mark of Clovis's high status and profile in Europe generally.

Clovis thus became the creator of France and as such he occupies a unique, almost legendary position in French history. Not only that, he set up his new capital at Paris, which would from that time on remain the country's capital. Clovis was not only king of the Franks by hereditary right, he was the choice of the army too. Clovis spent his final years in Paris, where he built the church of the Holy Apostles, later known as St Genevieve. He had the petty kings ruling at Cambrai, Cologne and other centres murdered, in order to become sole king of all the Frankish peoples. He replaced each of the petty kings and princes he removed with an entirely new type of provincial official, called the graf or count. Enormous numbers of decisions were to be made by Clovis himself, creating the model for strongly centralized government that was followed in France down through the centuries to the present day.

When Clovis died in 511, his Frankish kingdom was divided among his four sons, who used military conquest to enlarged their father's empire even further.

COSMAS INDICOPLEUSTES

Lived in the sixth century.
Merchant, traveller, cosmographer.

ACHIEVEMENTS:
Devised a flat earth theory of the universe that was acceptable
  to the medieval Christian Church.
Drew the first known maps of the Christian era.
Created the shape that would be used for the Sistine Chapel.

COSMAS OF ALEXANDRIA was a sixth century merchant. His nickname, 'Indicopleustes', means 'Indian Traveller'. When young he was indeed a great traveller, his journeys taking him through Ethiopia and parts of western Asia, including the Persian Gulf, India and Ceylon (Sri Lanka). He returned to Egypt in about 550 and retired to the seclusion of a Sinai monastery, where he wrote a work on *Christian Topography*.

In this work his intention was to prove the authenticity of the Biblical account of the world. According to Cosmas the earth is not in any sense round – not a sphere and not even a disc – but a flat rectangular plane. The heavens are a vaulted roof covering the earth like the lid and sides of a chest. In the centre of the plane is the inhabited earth, surrounded by ocean, and beyond that lies the paradise of Adam. The sun revolves round a conical mountain to the north, round the summit in summer, round the base in winter, accounting for the seasonal difference in day length.

Cosmas proposed a simple model for the universe which kept the earth as its focus, which made it consistent with biblical teaching. The work of Cosmas contains the first maps of the Christian era. Cosmas's flat earth model was one that found favour with the Christian authorities in the middle ages. The Sistine Chapel in the Vatican was based on the Cosmas model, with its rectangular floor representing this world and the barrel-vaulted ceiling bearing Michelangelo's fresco representing heaven. The fresco scheme commissioned by Pope Julius spelt out the late medieval cosmology, but the basic form of the chapel as commissioned by Pope Sixtus was itself already a model of the universe. And it was Cosmas who designed it.

MOHAMMED

Born 567 or 569, died 632.
Caravan conductor, prophet, founder of Islam.

ACHIEVEMENTS:
Founded Islam, a major new world religion.
Responsible for the creation of the Muslim world.

MOHAMMED WAS BORN in 567 or 569, the posthumous son of Abdullah and Aminah and the nephew of the chief of a small tribe. His mother died when he was still very young and he was brought up first by his grandfather, then by a poor uncle, Abu Talib.

In his youth, Mohammed seems to have visited the desert to acquire the customs of the Bedouins, and also accompanied traders from Mecca to Syria, south Arabia and possibly Egypt and Mesopotamia. He gradually became drawn to a life of religious contemplation. His life as a caravan conductor probably ended when he married Khadija, a wealthy 40-year-old widow who was 15 years older than him. With Khadija, Mohammed had six children including their daughters Fatima and Umm Kulthum, who married the third caliph. After his marriage, Mohammed seems to have been part-owner of a shop selling farm produce.

He also acquired a reputation for practical wisdom, though his education was not exceptional. At the time when Mohammed decided to become the legislator or mouthpiece of God, the paganism of northern Arabia had fallen under the Christianizing influence of the Byzantine empire. The south had fallen under successive influences – Jewish, Abyssinian, Persian. There is a story of Mohammed going off in search of 'the religion of Abraham'.

Claiming to be God's mouthpiece was a claim to autocracy, but Mohammed was extremely cautious in the way he asserted the claim. For three years his followers formed a secret society, and before that there was a period of preparation which involved a revelation on Mount Hirah near Mecca. The earliest revelations took the form of pages which were to be revealed only to his nearest relatives; the solemn utterances were in the form of rhymes. Early on the production of written communication was dropped in favour of oral; the prophet would speak in a trance and followers would write down the utterances. The revelations would eventually make up the Koran.

This early work was done very much in private, within the family but, by the time Mohammed made his first appearance as a public preacher in Mecca in 616, he was already the head of a united community of followers. As he became more successful, some of his followers were persecuted and he found a refuge for them in Axum. The Abyssinian king and his advisers took the side of the refugees, apparently regarding them as persecuted Christians – completely misunderstanding who and what they were. They were nevertheless being supported and this diplomatic victory infuriated the Meccan leaders, who blockaded Mohammed in one quarter of the city.

Mohammed responded with a conciliatory 'revelation', to the effect that the Meccan goddesses should be recognized as well as Allah. Mohammed later declared this revelation to be a fabrication of the Devil.

Shortly after this both Abu Talib and Khadija died, leaving Mohammed unprotected. He fled to the oasis of Taif and from there negotiated with various wealthy Meccans for protection. Mohammed was glad to have an invitation to go to Yathrib (later named Medina) as dictator; the citizens at Yathrib suffered from feuding and wanted an outsider to come and act as arbitrator. Accordingly, he went into exile or hejira ('flight') and the date, 16 July, 622, is taken as the start of the Mohammedan era. The Meccan authorities were alarmed at the prospect of a hostile regime in control at Medina, which lay on an important caravan route, and plans were laid to have Mohammed killed. The Prophet, as he came to be known, took temporary refuge in a cave, delaying his arrival at Medina until 20 September, 622 (the Jewish Day of Atonement).

From this point on, Mohammed's power grew. He bound his followers to himself and then to one another by a range of ties, instituting brotherhoods. At first, Mohammed seems to have courted an alliance with the Jews, but found no possibility of compromise with them on religious questions. Islam began to evolve its distinct practices and customs, to distinguish it clearly from other sects. The prohibition of wine, enacted in 625, was prompted by the drunken misbehaviour of one of his followers. The spread of Islam was swift and proof of conversion was reduced to a simple test, the expression of belief in Allah and Mohammed.

Mohammed and his followers needed a source of income. Attacking Meccan caravans was the only option open to them. Early on, Mohammed gave his permission for followers to go to war to fight the enemies of Islam. A state of open warfare soon developed, and the Meccans were defeated in the Battle of Badr in 624. In 627, He repelled an attempt by the Meccans to capture Medina. Mecca itself fell to Mohammed and his Islamic warriors in 629; the Meccans then recognized him as chief and prophet. Remarkably, in 630 Mohammed had control over the whole of Arabia.

Much interest has been shown in Mohammed's domestic life. Some decisions were taken for political reasons. The royal harem he set up, for instance, was probably instigated because he needed to demonstrate conquest, and it was customary for the victor to take possession of the former monarch's wife or daughter. The only prominent member of the harem was A'isha, the daughter of one of his first followers, Abu Bakr. It was in A'isha's arms that the Prophet died on 8 June 632, in his sixties, and it was she who left an account of his last hours.

Mohammed was a physically and mentally active man of medium height with greyish hair that was neither straight nor curly. He had a large head, large reddish eyes, a thick beard, broad shoulders and thick hands and feet. He was strongly emotional, and his expressions of both mirth and anger were fierce.

Mohammed was buried in a tomb in the mosque at Medina, having founded one of the world's major religions.

CHARLEMAGNE

Born 742, died 814.
King of the Franks, Christian emperor of the West.

ACHIEVEMENTS:
Created a huge Frankish Empire.
Consolidated the Christianization of Europe.
Encouraged the arts.
Presided over a Carolingian renaissance.
Worked towards creating a Europe-wide empire that looked
  forward to the European Union.

CHARLEMAGNE WAS THE eldest son of Pepin III (Pepin the Short) and the grandson of Charles Martel. When Pepin died in 768 the Frankish kingdom was divided between Charlemagne and his brother Carloman. Three years later Carloman died and Charlemagne became sole ruler.

His early reign was spent strenuously trying to subdue and convert to Christianity the Saxon kingdoms to the north-east and the Lombards of northern Italy. He was crowned King of Lombardy. In 778 Charlemagne led a crusading expedition against the Moors in Spain, but withdrew when he was needed elsewhere. In 782 the Saxons rebelled and destroyed a Frankish army at Suntelberg; Charlemagne avenged this by executing 4,500 Saxons. Eventually, in 785, the Saxon leader Widukind, submitted and accepted baptism; he became a loyal vassal to Charlemagne.

In 788, Charlemagne absorbed Bohemia into his realm, deposing its ruler. Advancing still further east, he conquered the Avars in the middle Danube valley, creating an eastern buffer zone. He created a similar buffer zone to the west, on the Spanish side of the Pyrenees.

In 800, Charlemagne entered Italy to support Pope Leo III against the Romans and in gratitude, on Christmas Day, the Pope crowned Charlemagne Emperor of the Romans under the name 'Carolus Augustus'. Charlemagne spent the rest of his reign consolidating his huge empire, which now stretched from the River Ebro in northern Spain to the River Elbe in Germany. The process of Christianization was reinforced by establishing bishoprics in the Saxon kingdoms.

Charlemagne had his court and capital at Aachen, where he had a splendid palace built and founded an academy to which many scholars and churchmen were invited. Charlemagne himself could read Greek and speak Latin; he was a great promoter of education, architecture and the arts. In spite of his zeal in Christianizing the Saxon lands, he was keen to establish good relations with the east, and in this he succeeded. The caliph of Baghdad, Haroun al-Raschid, sent ambassadors to Charlemagne's court, along with a gift of a white elephant.

Charlemagne was a great king with noble ambitions. He wanted to establish secular order and peace across Europe; he wanted to establish Christianity across Europe; he wanted to rescue the Roman civilization and bring it alive again; he wanted to be the Roman emperor that he was, in the end, at least in name. Charlemagne was truly 'Carolus Magnus', Charles the Great; he changed the face of Europe. In many ways his was a continent-wide vision that not only looked back towards the Roman Empire but also forward towards the ideals of the European Union – but with Christianity and monarchy added.

WILLIAM THE CONQUEROR

Born at Falaise 1023, died at Rouen 1087.
Duke of Normandy, King of England, conqueror of England.

ACHIEVEMENTS:
Conquered England in 1066.
Carried out the first national census and survey of resources.
Set new standards for atrocities committed against innocent
    civilian populations.
Introduced Norman French to England, greatly enriching the
    English language.
Inadvertently prepared the way for the eventual emergence of
    English as the world language.

ENGLAND WAS CONQUERED, in 1066, by a Norman Duke who had no hereditary right to the English crown; nor did he have an invitation or a welcome from the people of England. The invasion was an unwarranted and gratuitous act of aggression on a country that had its own highly developed culture, its own customs and laws, and these were savagely overridden and suppressed by the invader. The invader, William the Conqueror, was no less than a thief on the grand scale, a thief who stole a nation.

William the Conqueror was born in Falaise in Normandy, the illegitimate son of Robert Duke of Normandy by a tanner's daughter called Arlette. Edward the Confessor died childless and William, a cousin of Edward's, claimed that the dead king had promised him the throne of England during a visit in 1051. He may have received such a promise, and the pope approved William's claim to the English throne, but it still does not amount to an entitlement. William assembled a fleet, crossed the Channel and defeated Harold Godwinson, the rightful English king, on 14 October, 1066.

At the Battle of Hastings, the English King Harold made a courageous last stand with his house-carls as they gathered round the English standard. The Normans broke through their shield wall and butchered Harold and most of his house-carls. The last Saxon King of England was murdered. The following day, Harold's mother, Gytha, sent a request to William offering him the weight of the dead King's body in gold if he would hand it over for burial. William shabbily refused, insisting on giving the King an anonymous, unmarked grave on the beach he had tried to defend. Duke William added dishonourable behaviour to the crime of murder.

Duke William marched on Dover, where he stayed for a week before setting off for London by way of Canterbury, using the old Roman road. It was only in Southwark, on the southern edge of London, that William began to meet significant resistance. London did not give in so easily. Out of spite, William set fire to the area, turned away to the south and marched through Surrey, Hampshire and Berkshire, ravaging the countryside as he went. By the end of the year, William and his army had slashed and scythed a great curving swathe of destruction right round London. He then approached London again, this time from the north, via Berkhamsted. Demoralized by the reports coming in of the devastation all round London, the Londoners knew they had to give in. On Christmas Day 1066 William was crowned king of England – king by usurpation – in Westminster Abbey by Aldred, Archbishop of York. The Abbey was almost completely deserted, emptied for security reasons. A disturbance outside the abbey was wrongly interpreted as an attempt to attack the new king and houses in the neighbourhood were gratuitously put to the torch.

On the strength of the one battle, William now claimed all of England, though the claim was not really supported by right or by military conquest. He had in truth only conquered those parts of England he had marched through. William saw that one way of avoiding further pitched battles was to allow the powerful lords of the north, such as Morcar, Earl of Northumbria, to hold their lands as a grant from him as their new lord. But most of the English landowners were robbed of their lands. William needed to reward the Norman knights and barons who had helped him win Hastings, and giving them lands in England was the only way he could do that. Some of the leading supporters were granted huge estates.

In 1067, King William I led his army on a tour of England. He organized the confiscation of land from English landowners and built wooden castles to keep the rebellious English under control. There seems to have been no major opposition to this intimidating behaviour, as William had by now acquired a reputation for being harsh and merciless, and he felt secure enough to leave Odo of Bayeux in charge of England while he returned to Normandy in the spring of 1067. While he was away, rebellions broke out in Kent, Herefordshire and the North, and in December William had to come back to put down the rebellions. In a few months William had stamped them out, but in 1068 another insurrection broke out, this time in the West Country. This too he put down. Castles were shortly afterwards raised at Exeter and other key towns. A similar rebellion in Durham in 1069 was put down and a castle was built there too.

The English had not welcomed William as a saviour or rescuer, nor did they quickly come round to the idea that his presence in England was acceptable, desirable or necessary. There was resistance to Norman rule in one county after another. William was simply not wanted. The only way he could hold onto this kingdom was by force, and he did not flinch from using it. The spate of castle-building was a clear indication that the populace would be kept in order by military force.

Raids on the North led by King Sweyn of Denmark created further problems. In September 1069, Sweyn sailed a fleet into the Humber and up the Yorkshire Ouse – and burnt York down. William managed to beat the Danes into retreat, crushed a rebellion in Staffordshire, and then burnt houses and crops across the whole area between York and Durham. This devastation of the North was one of the most barbaric acts William carried out – on a totally undeserving population. The chroniclers described the area as a desert after he had ravaged it. The ordinary people died of starvation. The Northern rebellion came to an end in 1070 when William took Chester.

William also dismantled the English Church, sacking all but two of the

English bishops and replacing them with Normans. Lanfranc became the new Archbishop of Canterbury. All this was with extraordinary speed by the end of 1070.

Then, in 1071, came one final revolt against the Norman invasion and usurpation. Under the leadership of the Saxon nobleman Hereward the Wake, the rebels occupied the Isle of Ely in the Fens. William led the Norman army in person against Hereward and his men. The rebels were savagely punished, with mutilation and life imprisonment. The English resistance was over.

After the series of rebellions, William thought it was safe to return to Normandy in 1073, but while he was away two English earls, Waltheof and Ralph, Earl of Norfolk, conspired against him. Geoffrey of Coutances dealt with the rising and afterwards ordered that every rebel should have his right foot cut off. William returned in 1076 and had Waltheof executed; Ralph had already escaped to Brittany.

William's rule was neither secure nor welcome in Normandy. In 1077, William's eldest son Robert Curthose proposed that he should rule Normandy instead of his father. When William refused, Robert rebelled and tried to seize Rouen; he failed and had to flee to Gerberoi. William laid siege to his son, but his wife Matilda persuaded him to end it and come to terms with his son. When William returned to England in 1082 he was dissatisfied with the way Odo had been running England in his absence and, after a trial, threw him into prison for five years.

Then William launched his famous Domesday Survey of England. This was partly to assess people for tax, and partly to sort out exactly who owned some of the land. Today people look back on the *Domesday Book* as a valuable historical document, and are grateful to William the Conqueror for making it available to them, but at the time when it was compiled it was a culture shock, a phenomenon that was culturally alien to the way England was organized.

As he aged, William the Conqueror became very fat. In 1087, he was told that the French King Philip had described him as looking like a pregnant woman. William was incensed by this insult and consequently launched an attack on the French King's lands. On 15 August he captured the town of Mantes and set fire to it. While he was riding round the burning town, gloating over the destruction, his horse was startled by the flames and stumbled. William was thrown forward onto the pommel of his saddle. He sustained severe abdominal injuries, from which he died a lingering death in Rouen on 9 September. His doctors left him the moment he died; his sons had already left him; his servants stole his weapons, robes and other belongings and left the Conqueror's body half-naked on the floor.

The motive for the Norman invasion of England was very clear to the English. They wrote in 1087,

'King William and his chief men loved gold and silver and did not care how sinfully it was obtained provided it came to them. He [King William] did not care how wrongfully his men got possession of land or how many illegal acts they did.'

As for the killing and the atrocities, William himself was directly involved and directly responsible. A Norman chronicler boasted that William dominated battles, always leading from the front. He must therefore take full responsibility for the scale of the killing. The Devastation of the North was a terrible and completely unjustified criminal act, a deliberate democide. There would be no further rebellions in the North for the simple reason that the North would be empty.

Pope Gregory VII had reservations about William the Conqueror. In a letter to a friend he wrote, 'The King of England is not as religious as we would wish.' William showed contempt for the lives and well-being of ordinary English people. He created large deer forests for his own amusement, but if any ordinary man dared to kill a deer he was to be blinded.

On his deathbed, William seems to have had belated qualms about his actions. Here, written right at the end, is his confession:

'I tremble, my friends, when I reflect on the grievous sins which burden my conscience . . . It is out of my power to count all the injuries which I have caused during the sixty-four years of my troubled life.'

William is most remembered for conquering England and imposing a Norman elite on the English. The Norman invasion had the positive effect of introducing many new words to the English language and greatly increasing its versatility and flexibility as a language for literature. William thus inadvertently paved the way for English to become the second language of choice for the world as a whole.

SALADIN

Born at Tigrit 1138, died 1193.
First Ayyubite Sultan of Egypt.

ACHIEVEMENTS:
Stemmed the tide of Christian European incursion in the Near
    East.
Blocked the Crusades, ending the Kingdom of Jerusalem.
Became an icon of Muslim resistance to Christian incursion.
Became a glamorous model of Muslim heroism.

BY A STRANGE coincidence, Saladin was born in the same place as Saddam Hussein, the town of Tigrit in what is now Iraq. Saladin's father was Ayyub (Job), an Armenian Kurd. Saladin grew up in a Muslim world that was severely disunited and therefore powerless. The Seljuk Empire had been divided since 1104. The Latin kingdom of Jerusalem had managed to survive only because it was an organized force in a disorganized world. Inevitably, the Christian zeal that supported Jerusalem eventually aroused an equal and opposite zeal among Muslims. The situation gave Saladin his great opportunity; there was a conscious demand for political unity in the Muslim world to defend Islam against the incomers, and the period of this demand coincided with his lifetime. Saladin was the right man in the right place at the right time.

Muslims had already begun raising armies and attacking occupying Christians. Zengi, the atabeg of Mosul, had already initiated the holy war in Syria in 1135–46. When Zengi died in 1146, Ayyub moved to his court at Damascus, and it was his influence that secured the succession of Zengi's son Nureddin, who continued the to promote the holy war. It was in these

PEOPLE WHO CHANGED THE WORLD

influential circles, in one of the great centres of Muslim learning, that Ayyub's son Saladin grew up.

The first part of Saladin's career is the story of his conquest of Egypt, which took ten years from 1164. The conquest of Egypt was an essential part of Nureddin's plan because it menaced his empire to the south. The struggle for Egypt was protracted, with interventions from the Christians under King Amalric of Jerusalem.

The second phase of Saladin's career was the annexation of Syria and Mesopotamia (1174–86). When Nureddin died in 1174, his vassals rebelled against his young heir, as-Salih. Saladin went north, pretending to go in order to help as-Salih recover the situation, but actually to take over. In 1177, Saladin returned to Cairo, which he enriched with colleges, an aqueduct and a citadel. The episode in the north was not a random sortie. Saladin had in effect, by consolidating Muslim power to south and north, achieved a complete encirclement of the Crusaders and the Kingdom of Jerusalem.

The final phase of Saladin's brilliantly successful career involved the destruction of the kingdom of Jerusalem and the series of campaigns against the invading European Christians, from 1187 until 1192. The breach in the truce by the brigand Raynald of Chatillon prompted Saladin's series of attacks. In May 1187 a small force of Crusader knights, Hospitallers and Templars, was massacred at Tiberias. Two months later Saladin inflicted a crushing defeat on the combined Christian army at Hittin. He overran Palestine, besieged Jerusalem in September, entering and 'purifying' the city in October.

Saladin made one of biggest mistakes in holding back at this point. The only remaining Christian stronghold in the Holy Land was Tyre, and he could have taken Tyre if he had attacked at once. Instead he waited, and the Christians were able to use it as a base from which to attack Acre. In June 1191, Acre surrendered to Richard I, who then organized an orderly march along the coast to Jaffa, to win another great victory at Arsuf.

Even so, as far as Jerusalem was concerned, Saladin remained master of the situation. The combined Muslim forces annihilated the Kingdom of Jerusalem. Richard returned to Europe. Saladin returned to Damascus where, after a few days' illness, he died on 4 March 1193.

Saladin was an extraordinary character. He was a Muslim of his age, fiercely hostile to the unbelievers who were occupying the region, but at the same time he was tolerant towards the Christians among his own subjects. He was very proud of his race – 'God reserved this triumph for the Ayyubites before all others.' He was also generous and hospitable; he proved this through his gifts to Richard I and in his treatment of captives. He was physically and emotionally strong, but had another side to his nature too. He was extremely gentle and kind, and he loved children. Above all he was ready to surrender himself to the greater cause of Islam.

Saladin was a key figure as the conqueror who stemmed the tide of western conquest in the Near East and pushed the Europeans back. He established a Muslim Near East. He was also an iconic figure, the Muslim hero who incorporated in his personality and actions all that was best in the ideals of Islam.

GENGHIS KHAN

Born at Deligun Bulduk 1162, died at Ninghsia 1227.
Mongol conqueror, ruler over a huge Mongol Empire.

ACHIEVEMENTS:
Ruthlessly conquered a huge part of Asia.
Great administrator.
Created a Mongol Empire stretching from the Black Sea to the
   Pacific.
Created states within this empire that were viable and durable.
Leading the Israelites to a God-given 'Promised Land'.

IT WAS ALMOST a millennium after the time of Attila that a very similar Mongol war-leader emerged. Temuchin, or Temujin, as he was called, after a tribal chief his father Yesukai had recently defeated, was born in 1162 at Deligun Bulduk on the River Onon, the son of a Mongol chief. Thirteen years later, Yesukai was killed in an ambush, leaving the boy Temuchin deep in tribal in-fighting. He had to fight for years against hostile tribes. He proved more than equal to the dangerous situation he found himself in, killing one of his brothers in a petty dispute over a fish, and massacring an entire tribe who dared to kidnap his wife.

He spent six years subjugating the Naiman tribe, between Lake Balkhash and the Irtysh, and conquering the land of Tangut, which lay to the south of the Gobi Desert. The Turkish Uigurs surrendered to Temuchin's overlordship without fighting, and it was from them that the Mongols developed most of their culture, including an alphabet and laws.

Temuchin was cruel and ruthless, but it could be argued that he needed to be in order to survive in a cruel and ruthless world. One of his rivals boiled 70 of his followers alive in cooking pots. But by being more cruel and more ruthless than any of them, he rose to supremacy. By 1206 Temuchin was strong enough to impose his will on all of the Mongol tribes. He courageously called together the leaders of many warring factions to a gathering by the River Onon, where he proclaimed himself their overlord. He took a new name, Genghis Khan, 'Universal Ruler'.

The Chinese were the first to feel Temuchin's new power. In 1211, the Mongol hordes poured across the Great Wall, sacking cities, trampling down and setting fire to the crops. By 1214, Genghis Khan had control of most of China north of the Yellow River. In 1217, he conquered and annexed the Kara-Khitai Khanate, which stretched from Lake Balkhash to Tibet.

Next, in 1218, he looked to the south-west, to the lands of the Khwarizms (Turkestan, Iran, Iraq, Afghanistan, Pakistan, northern India). Genghis Khan sent messengers to Shah Mohammed promising peace and suggesting a trading treaty. This met with a favourable reply, but the first caravan of Mongol traders was massacred by the local governor, Inaljuk, at the border town of Otrar. Genghis understandably demanded the extradition of the governor. Shah Mohammed responded by beheading the leading envoy and sending the others home without their beards. This dangerous insult resulted in a ferociously bloodthirsty response from Genghis Khan.

The 400,000 Khwarizm warriors posted along the border river, the Syr Daria, were not enough to stop the invasion of the Mongol hordes. Inaljuk was captured and executed by having molten metal poured into his eyes and ears. The Shah fled, leaving his subjects to be raped or slaughtered. One technique Genghis Khan used on this campaign was the human shield. He herded crowds of prisoners in front of his army, as many as 30,000 at a time, as he moved into the new territory. A terrible catalogue of cruelty unfolded as one town after another was taken. At one, all the women were raped in front of their families. At another, the inhabitants were tied up and shot with arrows. At another, the poor were decapitated, while the rich were tortured to find out where their treasure was. All of this happened at great speed.

Shah Mohammed fled to a village on the Caspian Sea, where he died of pleurisy. Meanwhile Genghis Khan followed his son and successor,

Jelaleddin, in the conquest of the huge new territory. At Herat, where the governor he had installed was deposed, Genghis Khan put the city under siege for six months. When Herat fell, it took a week for all the inhabitants to be killed.

Remarkably, and undeservedly, Genghis Khan died of natural causes at the age of 65. He set out to chastise the king of Tangut, and thoroughly subdued the territory in the usual way. It was while laying siege to the Tangut capital of Ninghsia in 1227 that he fell ill and died. He has been described as the 'mightiest and most bloodthirsty conqueror of all time'. The final victims were in a way the most pitiful of all. They were innocent bystanders who accidentally saw the funeral procession making its way to the burial ground in the valley of Kilien. They were all killed. They had seen too much.

Genghis Khan was the great Mongol conqueror. But he was more than a mere warrior: he was a skilled ruler and administrator. He conquered a huge empire stretching from the Pacific to the Black Sea, but he also organized them into viable states that outlived him.

MARCO POLO

Born in Venice 1254, died in Venice 1324.
Traveller, merchant, adventurer.

ACHIEVEMENTS:
Travelled widely in southern and eastern Asia.
Wrote an account of his travels.
*Raised Western awareness of the greatness of Chinese
  civilization.*
Prepared the way for later voyages of discovery.

MARCO POLO WAS born into a noble family in Venice in 1254, the grandson of Andrea Polo and the son of Nicolo Polo. He was born while his father and uncle were away on an expedition to Bokhara and Cathay (China). The two brothers, Nicolo and Maffeo, had been engaged in ambitious trading for a long time. Their trading took them to Constantinople, then on to the Crimea and eventually to Bokhara. There they met some envoys returning from Kublai Khan, and they travelled with them into Cathay.

Nicolo and Maffeo Polo were well-received there by the great emperor, Kublai Khan, who it seems had never seen Europeans before. He was delighted with them and commissioned them to act as his ambassadors to the Pope. He wanted them to ask the Pope to send 100 well-educated Europeans who were learned in the arts and sciences. The Polos had every intention of carrying out this potentially epoch-making mission in 1269, but they found when they returned to the West and reached Acre that no new pope had been elected following the death of Clement IV the previous year. With, no doubt, an acute sense of failure, they returned to Venice, resolving to go back to Cathay.

The Polo family set off again in 1271, this time taking with them the young Marco, who was then 17. They travelled through Mosul, Baghdad, Khorassan, the Pamirs, Kashgar, Yarkand, Khoton, Lob Nor, the Gobi Desert, Tangut and Shangtu, arriving at the court of Kublai Khan in 1275. The places they passed through on the second half of their journey were almost totally unknown to Europeans, though they were familiar stopping-places for Asian traders. The Khan was once again very pleased to see them and specially interested in the young Marco Polo, who was soon sent off as an envoy to Yunnan, Burma, Karakorum, Cochin China and Southern India. Marco was taught the languages of the Khan's subjects. For three years he served as governor of Yang Chow.

The Khan was very reluctant to let these useful Westerners leave his court, but they were apprehensive about what might happen to them in the wake of the old khan's death, which was surely not far away. For their own safety, they needed to be out of Cathay before he died. Eventually an opportunity arose by chance. They were commissioned to escort a young noblewoman on a long sea voyage. After long delays on the coasts of Sumatra and India, they managed to sail to Persia. The Polos finally returned to Venice in 1295, bringing with them the great wealth they had acquired along the way. But on arrival at their family mansion they were at first rejected and ridiculed as unrecognizable, as they were wearing worn and outlandish clothes; nobody believed they really were the Polos.

In 1298, Marco Polo commanded a galley at the Battle of Curzola, in which the Venetians were defeated by the Genoese. He was taken prisoner and kept in Genoa for a year. He had his notes, which he had originally written for the khan, sent across from Venice and another prisoner in Genoa, Rusticiano of Pisa, helped him to make a continuous prose record from them. It was called *Divisament dou Monde*.

After Polo was released, he returned from Genoa to Venice, where he died in 1324.

Map-makers tried to incorporate Marco Polo's geographical information into their maps. This was not done with any great accuracy, but hitherto empty areas of maps were now filled in. Marco Polo did not introduce the idea of block printing from China. Indeed he rather oddly did not mention the distinctive Chinese printing method at all. Discrepancies and omissions like this have led some modern commentators to dismiss Marco Polo's book as a traveller's tale in the worst sense of the phrase – a tall story with little truth in it. Indeed it is hard to understand why the great khan would have wanted to use as envoys foreigners with little or no understanding of the languages spoken in China. Perhaps the Polos exaggerated their importance in Cathay to make a good story better, but it cannot be seriously doubted that they travelled there.

The impact of their travels was profound. Europeans had to come to terms with the fact that there was a great civilization in eastern Asia, that was in many ways more advanced than the great European civilization. It encouraged a mental outreach that would bear fruit in the physical outreach of the Columbus voyages and other major European voyages of discovery.

DANTE ALIGHIERI

Born in Florence 1265, died in Ravenna 1321.
Italian poet, author of The Divine Comedy.

ACHIEVEMENTS:
The national poet of Italy.
One of the half-dozen greatest writers of all time.
Wrote The Divine Comedy, *one of the greatest works of*
  literature.
Expressed a fully developed medieval view of the universe and
  gave a uniquely full view of the medieval mind and spirit.
Forged Italian into a language of literature.

DANTE (DURANTE ALIGHIERI) was born in Florence in 1265, the son of a
lawyer and a member of the noble Guelph family. All that is known of his
boyhood is his singular, intense love of a girl. He first saw this lifelong love,
'Beatrice' (assumed to be Bice Portinari), when they were both nine in
1274. She was married at an early age to Simone de' Bardi, but Dante's
devotion continued, and even intensified after her death in 1290. Dante
tells the story of this unfulfilled passion with great pathos in his Vita
Nuova. He was 'pierced with sadness'. Dante was to marry Gemma Donati.

As a youth, he was a hard-working student and wrote poetry assidu-
ously, like most cultivated young men of his period. He was a friend of the
painter Giotto, who painted his youthful portrait.

Like a good Florentine citizen, Dante played a full part in the city's
social and political life. In 1289 he fought in the front rank at the Battle of
Campaldino, at which Florence defeated the Ghibellines. In Florence he
was recognized as a poet. In 1300, after occupying various minor public

posts, he became one of the six priors of Florence; these were elected from the arts. In this two-month role, he banished members of various families and interest groups with impartiality. In 1301, there was alarm at the prospect of intervention by Charles of Valois at the instigation of the Pope, and Dante was sent on a diplomatic mission to Pope Boniface VIII in Rome.

Dante never returned from Rome, and never set foot in Florence again. He was banished and sentenced to death in absentia, along with many others. He wandered from city to city, possibly including Paris, finally settling in Ravenna in 1318. When he died there in 1321, he was buried with great pomp.

Dante's great work, *The Divine Comedy*, was begun in 1307. The work puts Dante himself among the half-dozen greatest writers of all time. It consists of an extraordinary, dramatized mystical journey through the various levels of Hell, Purgatory and Heaven. It has sometimes been described as an epic poem, but is quite unlike any other epic; it is completely unique, partly because the author is the hero, partly because its intention is not to entertain but to improve and morally educate, 'to put into verse things difficult to think.' The three-part poem shows a fully developed medieval view of the universe and gives a uniquely full view of the medieval mind and spirit.

Before the writing of *The Divine Comedy*, the Italian language was so rough and ready, so unformed, that Dante wondered whether it could be employed on such an ambitious project; he is said to have made a start on it in Latin. Dante's skill in handling Italian in his poem did much to forge Italian into a language of literature.

WILLIAM OF OCCAM

Born at Ockham about 1285, died in Munich about 1349.
English philosopher.

ACHIEVEMENTS:
The greatest late-medieval philosopher.
Challenged the authority of the Pope 200 years before the
    Reformation.
Devised Occam's razor, which underpins modern science.

WILLIAM OF OCCAM was born at Ockham in Surrey in around 1285.
He entered the Franciscan order when young and studied theology at
Oxford. Because of his controversial views he never graduated and became
known as 'the Venerable inceptor' (undergraduate). For the same reason he
was never allowed to take up a formal teaching post.

Pope John XXII summoned him to Avignon to answer a charge of heresy.
He then became involved in the dispute about Franciscan poverty, which the
pope had denounced. Realising he was in some danger, in 1328 he fled to
Bavaria, where he lived under the protection of Emperor Louis of Bavaria for
20 years and it was at this time that the Pope excommunicated him. William
of Occam was an unusually forward-looking thinker, and was ready to
challenge the authority of the Pope – and this was 200 years before the
Reformation. He also challenged the unjustified speculations of many other
medieval philosophers and theologians. He was the greatest late-medieval
philosopher. He wrote several works on logic and a commentary on Aristotle.
He wrote on politics, in particular attacking the pope's claims to civil authority.
William of Occam is best known for his rule of ontological economy; 'entities
are not to be multiplied beyond necessity.' This has been applied more widely,
to mean opting for the simplest explanation that the facts will support. It is
known as Occam's razor, and it underpins most of modern science.

JOHANNES GUTENBERG

Born in Mainz 1400, died in Mainz 1468.
German printer, inventor of printing, instigated the first
 printed Bible.

ACHIEVEMENTS:
Invented printing.
Manufactured the first mass-produced Bible.
Democratized Christianity, reduced the power of the clergy.
Prepared the way to the Reformation.
Opened the way to an information revolution and mass
 education.

JOHANNES GUTENBERG WAS born in Mainz in 1400, the son of well-to-do citizens. His father was Friele zum Gensfleisch and his mother was Elsgen Wyrich (or Gutenberg, after her birthplace). It was Gutenberg himself who decided to call himself Gutenberg rather than Gensfleisch. The family seems to have been expelled from Mainz and settled in Strasbourg. Gutenberg was there between 1430 and 1444, where he was possibly making a living as a goldsmith.

Probably he had begun work as a printer in Strasbourg by 1439. By 1448 he was back in Mainz again, and by 1450 he was working in partnership with Johannes Fust, who financed Gutenberg's printing press with 800 guilders. This was not a happy partnership. It ended after 5 years with Fust suing Gutenberg for the 800 guilders and receiving the printing equipment in lieu of payment. It is not known whether in amongst all the quarrelling they produced any books during this period, but Gutenberg must have devoted a lot of time to the preparation of the plates for his great project, the first printed Latin Bible.

Fust then carried on the business with the help of Peter Schoffer, his son-in-law, the two of them completing the famous 'Gutenberg Bible' which Gutenberg had begun. This historic and extremely ambitious feat was accomplished in August 1456. It involved the printing of 1282 pages in two columns with gaps left for hand-painted illuminated initials. Meanwhile Gutenberg himself set up another press in Mainz with Konrad Humery. Archive evidence shows that Gutenberg went on struggling with debt repayments.

In 1465, Johannes Gutenberg accepted a post as a salaried courtier from the Archbishop Adolf. In this capacity he received a suit of livery and an allowance of corn and wine. He seems to have died in Mainz early in 1468. According to tradition he was buried in the Franciscan church in Mainz.

Gutenberg has for a long time been credited with the invention of printing, but inevitably some scholars have challenged this claim, suggesting that printing must already have existed in a rudimentary form. Gutenberg nevertheless takes the credit for refining and using the new technology for a highly significant and ambitious project. Apart from anything else, the Bible is a very long book. He remains the best claimant to the title 'inventor of printing', even though no books bear his name as printer. No portrait of him is known. Until his time, bibles were handmade, scarce and expensive. Producing them, whole pages at a time, on a press, made bibles cheaper and more accessible. Gutenberg's activity led to the democratization of Christianity, the reduction of the power of the priests who recited and interpreted the Bible, and the consequent reduction of the power of the Church. Gutenberg's work led in short order to the Reformation itself.

CHRISTOPHER COLUMBUS

Born in Genoa 1451, died in Valladolid 1506.
Genoese navigator, discoverer of the New World.

ACHIEVEMENTS:
Discovered the West Indies, North America and South America.
Opened the New World to European colonization, which
*   started at once.*
Opened the New World as an arena of European political
*   activity.*
Opened the minds of Europeans to the idea of a much larger
*   world.*

CHRISTOPHER COLUMBUS WAS born in Genoa, Italy, the son of Domenico Colombo, a weaver, and Suzanna Fontanarossa. The events of his early life are uncertain. His son later recorded that he went to the University of Pavia, where he studied astronomy, geometry and cosmography; Columbus himself told a significantly different story – that he went to sea at the age of 14. In 1470 he was shipwrecked off Cape St Vincent, and reached the Portuguese coast on a plank. In 1474, after consulting the Florentine cosmographer Paolo Toscanelli, he arrived at the idea of reaching India by sailing west instead of east. The success of such a voyage depended on the now-widely-accepted idea that the earth was a sphere, and quite a small sphere. Thanks to an error of Ptolemy, Columbus under-estimated the size of the earth and overestimated the size of Asia; the two miscalculations put China where eastern North America actually lies, and the East Indies where the West Indies are. Was all of this by chance, as we are led to believe, or was it arrived at by a process of reasoning back from reports of secret landfalls already reported from across the Atlantic? Certainly Columbus knew about reports of driftwood picked up 400 leagues west of Cape St Vincent, which implied that there was land not far off in that direction.

In 1477 he sailed '100 leagues beyond Thule', which may mean he reached Iceland. He needed a patron for his planned voyage west, and negotiated for seven years with Ferdinand and Isabella of Castile before they agreed to sponsor him.

It is not clear to what extent Columbus 'prepared' the discovery of the New World or had it prepared for him. The possible lying about his education suggests that there was some concealment. Recent research strongly suggests that the existence of a landmass across the Atlantic was already known, and the Columbus voyage was a kind of 'show discovery'.

Columbus set sail on his historic voyage across the Atlantic on 3 August, 1492, in command of the Santa Maria, accompanied by two even smaller ships, the Pinta and the Niña. He took 87 men with him. After reaching the Canaries, morale fell. The Pinta had already lost her rudder and they had put in dock at Tenerife to refit. There was talk of Portuguese caravels on the prowl with orders to intercept the voyage of discovery. The sailors saw a meteor fall into the sea, and were unnerved by the vast plains of seaweed known as the Sargasso Sea. It was a frightening experience.

Then on 11 October bits of driftwood were seen and a branch covered with berries; land could not be far away. Land was sighted the next day. Columbus called it San Salvador, but it was probably Watling Island in the Bahamas. Columbus put on his Sunday best clothes for the formal landing, and went ashore as if in a historical pageant, which in a way it was, bearing the royal banner of Spain. The Pinzon brothers carried banners of the Green Cross (Columbus's device). Many members of the crew went with them. It was a tableau made for the painters of historical scenes, and designed to be just that. Columbus visited Cuba and Haiti, founding a small colony there before setting sail for home.

A second voyage with a larger squadron set sail in September 1493, reaching Dominica in the West Indies in November. This time Columbus was directed specifically to deal kindly with the inhabitants of any new lands and to try to convert them to Christianity. The third voyage in 1498, this time with six ships, led to the discovery, on 1 August 1498, of the mainland of South America. Columbus had for a long time believed that a landmass existed there, and once again it must be suspected that earlier travellers, perhaps blown a long way off their intended courses, had reported the existence of such a continent. Columbus's voyages of discovery have an air of having been planned. It is almost as if he was following some sort of itinerary. A comparison between Columbus's voyages and Cook's is revealing in this respect; Cook's zig-zagging exploration of the South Pacific really does look like groping in the dark.

A final, fourth, voyage in 1502–4 explored the south coast of the Gulf of Mexico. Columbus was stranded for a whole year in Jamaica, where his crew behaved badly and he himself suffered badly from disease. The lawless behaviour alienated the natives, who had initially been friendly and hospitable, and they were often short of food. He finally set sail for Spain again in September 1504, arriving at San Lucar in November. After many years of hardship and ill treatment, Columbus died at Valladolid in Spain on 20 May 1506.

Opinion is still divided about Christopher Columbus. Some scholars still believe that Columbus was the first European navigator to cross the Atlantic, that he really was the first European to visit the New World. Others think Columbus knew the width of the Atlantic before he set sail because Portuguese ships had already crossed it unofficially, accidentally blown across by the trade winds. If so, the Columbus voyages were in effect a publicity stunt, a formal grand opening of the New World to Spanish and Portuguese colonization. His ill-concealed formal education in astronomy, cosmography and geometry certainly point to a level of navigational expertise that might be required to duplicate voyages that had already been undertaken, perhaps by Portuguese sailors. Either way, Columbus's voyages expanded the horizons of Europeans in an instant and opened the way to European colonization of North and South America.

The native Americans would come to regret the voyages of discovery, which led to their humiliation and disinheritance, the destruction of the Aztec and Inca civilizations, and the wholesale destruction of the ancient ways of life of the first peoples of the New World.

LEONARDO DA VINCI

Born 1452, died 1519.
Italian painter, scientist, engineer and polymath.

ACHIEVEMENTS:
Produced a series of great paintings, including the Mona Lisa.
Relied on observation and anatomical dissection for models.
*One of the first 'modern men', a humanist free of conditioning
    by earlier ages.*
Became the fullest development of 'the Renaissance man'.
*Redefined for following generations what it means to be
    human.*

LEONARDO WAS THE illegitimate son of a Florentine lawyer, and entered
the studio of the painter Verocchio in 1470. His first great work, the mural
of *The Last Supper* (about 1494), was technically unsatisfactory, a painting
on damp plaster which started deteriorating immediately, yet this ghost of
a picture is still regarded as one of the world's masterpieces. The painting
that has intrigued people with its secretive smile ever since it was painted
in 1504 is the *Mona Lisa*.

Leonardo's pre-eminent reputation as one of the greatest artists in one
of the greatest periods in art history rests on a surprisingly small number
of finished paintings. The many artists who have been influenced by him
have resorted to the collections of his fine drawings in Milan, Paris,
Florence, Vienna, London and Windsor.

He was exceptional in many ways. He was a Renaissance painter who
was influenced hardly at all by Greek or Roman models; he based his art
on a searching observation of what he saw. In relying on his own senses he

was one of the first 'modern men', a humanist free of conditioning by earlier ages.

In 1516 the French king awarded him a yearly allowance and gave him the Chateau Cloux, where he lived until his death in 1519. Leonardo was good-looking, charming and well-mannered but under the amiable surface he was driven by boundless intellectual energy and curiosity.

Leonardo filled his notebooks with drawings that show an astonishing range of scientific observations. He used looking and drawing as a medium for understanding. He had an advanced knowledge of the sciences, including biology, anatomy and hydrology, and was able to apply his understanding in the design of a variety of machines. He was secretive, using mirror writing so that no-one else could read his notes. He deliberately incorporated mistakes in his designs for war engines, so that the machines would not work if the designs fell into the wrong hands.

Leonardo represents the fullest development of what has come to be known as 'the Renaissance man', accomplished in the arts and sciences, embodying all existing knowledge and striving to extend its boundaries. His life and work redefined for following generations what it means to be human.

VASCO DA GAMA

> Born at Sines 1469, died at Cochin 1525.
> Portuguese explorer, discoverer of the sea route to India.
>
> ACHIEVEMENTS:
> First European to sail to Asia round Africa.
> First European to find a sea route to India.
> Opened a more reliable trade route to the Far East.
> Opened a new phase of European colonization.
> Founded Mozambique, the second European colony in southern
>   Africa.
> Began the European domination of India.

VASCO DA GAMA was born at the small seaport of Sines in Portugal in 1469, the same year that Prince Henry the Navigator died. Vasco da Gama's voyages were in a real sense the ultimate fulfilment of Prince Henry's brilliant programme of exploration and discovery. Prince Henry's main aim was to find a sea route round Africa, and da Gama was the first to find it and sail it. He distinguished himself as a fearless navigator and adventurer at an early age, fighting in the wars against Castile. Da Gama was chosen by King Emanuel I of Portugal to find a sea route to India via the Cape of Good Hope, then thought to be the southernmost tip of Africa.

Vasco da Gama set sail from Lisbon on 9 July 1497 with three ships. It took him four months just to reach St Helena Bay in southern Africa. The voyage round the Cape was a difficult one because of storms and mutinies, but he managed to reach Malindi on the east coast of Africa early in 1498. From this point on, da Gama's voyage was on known waters and therefore much easier. From Indian merchants at Malindi he acquired a skilled pilot to help him cross the Indian Ocean to Calicut on the Malabar coast.

The Muslim traders in Calicut were hostile as they sensed that significant new commercial competition had arrived – as indeed it had – and they stirred up the local Hindus against da Gama. Da Gama had to fight his way out of the harbour.

In 1499, Vasco da Gama returned to Lisbon in triumph. The king was delighted with this totally successful enterprise and ennobled da Gama. The little chapel at Belem on the Tagus estuary where da Gama and his crew had prayed before setting off was demolished and a grandiose church was raised on the spot in commemoration of the historic voyage.

Then came news that all forty of the unfortunate Portuguese left behind in Calicut had been murdered. The king sought revenge and fitted out a squadron of ten ships, again under da Gama's leadership, which sailed in 1502. Da Gama was now sailing with the significant title 'Admiral of India', showing that the Portuguese were making a territorial claim. This expedition founded the colony of Mozambique, bombarded Calicut, and treated the inhabitants of Calicut with brutal savagery in retaliation for the murders.

Vasco da Gama returned to Lisbon in September the following year with his ships richly laden. Once again there were great celebrations in Lisbon and further honours and rewards were showered on him. Soon after his return, da Gama retired to his home in Evora, though he continued to advise Emanuel I on matters relating to India and maritime strategy until 1505 and remained in favour with the monarch for the rest of his life. In 1519, he was created Count of Vidigueira.

Indian affairs were overseen by a series of viceroys. The fifth of these viceroys was such a failure that he had to be dismissed and, in 1524, da Gama was called out of retirement to become the sixth viceroy of India. He accordingly arrived in the new Portuguese colony of Goa in September 1524 and immediately set about correcting abuses there. He died three months later, in Cochin in the south-west of India, and it is a mark of his celebrity status that his body was taken home to Lisbon for burial.

Vasco da Gama is justly famous as the first European to find a sea route to India, the first European to sail to Asia round Africa. His landmark voyage opened a more reliable trade route to the Far East. It also opened, immediately, a new phase of European colonization. Da Gama himself founded Mozambique, the second European colony in southern Africa; Angola on the South Atlantic coast, was the first, founded by the Portuguese a few years earlier. On his final voyage he oversaw the first European colony in India – Goa – which was founded, or rather taken over, in 1510. Vasco da Gama must take the doubtful credit for beginning the controversial domination of India by Europeans.

NICOLAS COPERNICUS

Born at Torun 1473, died at Frauenburg 1543.
Polish astronomer who proved that the sun is the centre of the
  solar system.

ACHIEVEMENTS:
Proved that the Earth is not at the centre of the universe.
Devised the heliocentric (sun-centred) model for the universe.
The first modern scientist.
Established scientific observation as the prime basis for
  interpreting reality.
1530 – Commentariolus.
1543 – De Revolutionibus Orbium Coelestium.

NICOLAS COPERNICUS WAS born at Torun in Poland in 1473. His father was a native of Cracow and his mother was German, so Copernicus is claimed as a national genius by both Germany and Poland. Copernicus was virtually adopted and brought up by his uncle, Lucas Watzelrode, who was the bishop of Ermeland from 1489 onwards. From 1491, he studied mathematics, perspective and optics under Albert Brudzewski at Cracow University. In 1496 he studied law at Bologna, where he also attended lectures in astronomy by Domenico Novara. The following year he was appointed canon of Frauenburg, the cathedral city of Ermeland. He spent the year 1500 in Rome, gave some very warmly received lectures on astronomy, and it was there that he observed an eclipse of the moon.

Not content with his mastery of astronomy, Copernicus next went off to Padua to study medicine in 1501. Two years later he was made doctor of canon law at Ferrara. Although he was canon of Frauenburg, Copernicus never became a priest. Instead he became medical attendant and secretary to his uncle the bishop, living with him in the castle at Heilsberg. After his uncle Lucas's death in 1512, Copernicus moved to Frauenburg, where he continued his methodical observations of the stars from 1513 onwards. While he was pursuing this ground-breaking astronomical study, he was at the same time busying himself with the duties of bailiff, military governor, judge, tax collector, vicar-general and doctor. He even put forward a scheme for the reform of currency.

His life as a civic administrator and public servant was made difficult by the political intrigues and wars leading to West Prussia's restoration to the Teutonic Knights and its assimilation into Brandenburg. He always made his medical expertise available to the poor, but found that his time was in demand by the rich. His life was not easy.

His astronomical thinking was driven by a profound dissatisfaction with existing models of the universe. He was dissatisfied with Ptolemy's model from early on and in Italy picked up what were called 'Pythagorean' theories of a sun-centred universe. His developing ideas on the structure of the universe were not published, but instead circulated in draft form in manuscript.

In 1530, he completed his major work, the work for which he is now famous, *De Revolutionibus Orbium Coelestium*, in which he proved that the sun, not the earth, is the centre of the universe. Copernicus delayed its full publication until just before his death in 1543. In 1530, he released only a popular summary of his findings which was circulated in manuscript form; this was called *Commentariolus*. This was well received in certain quarters. Widmanstadt lectured on the theory of Copernicus in Rome. Rather surprisingly, Pope Clement VII approved and Cardinal Schonberg pressed Copernicus to publish the theory in full. Copernicus was for some reason reluctant to do this, and it was only after he was badgered by his friends and supporters that in 1540 he agreed to publication. The first printed copy arrived at Frauenburg shortly before Copernicus died. He had a stroke, was paralyzed at the end of 1542 and died in May the following year. Mercifully, he was unable to read the anonymous preface that had been surreptitiously slipped into his book during the publication process by

Andreas Osiander; this was intended to defuse potential hostile responses by insisting that the work was merely hypothetical in nature. The whole point of Copernicus' work was that it was based on scientific observation and inference – it was emphatically not hypothetical. However, Copernicus was beyond noticing any of this. His great idea was launched.

Copernicus supplied one of the central ideas of the Renaissance, one of the ideas that marked the age as fundamentally different from the preceding Middle Ages. The Middle Ages were dominated by a bible-based earth-centred model for the universe, the sort of thing that Cosmas created. The Renaissance and the Enlightenment that followed were dominated by a sun-centred model based on observation. Both Copernicus's idea and his scientific approach were absolutely revolutionary, in every sense, and they proved to be key issues that would create friction between men of science and the church for centuries to come.

FRANCISCO PIZARRO

Born at Trujillo 1475, died 1541.
Spanish conquistador, conqueror of Peru.

ACHIEVEMENTS:
Conquered Peru.
Murdered the Inca emperor Atahualpa.
Destroyed the Inca empire and civilization.

FRANCISCO PIZARRO WAS born at Trujillo in Extremadura in Spain in around 1475. He was the illegitimate son of Gonzalo Pizarro. Very little is known of Pizarro's early years, except that he was neglected. He appears to have been poorly cared for and had little or no education. He entered military service, serving under Gonsalvo di Cordova in Italy. He was in the town of Seville at the time when news came that the New World had been discovered. A rootless man with few prospects in Spain, Pizarro not surprisingly decided to take his chance and travel to this New World to see what he could make of his life there.

He became one of a dangerous, heedless band of emigrants to the Caribbean, the Spanish conquistadors. He is known to have taken part in an expedition from Hispaniola to Uraba in 1510, under the command of Alonzo de Ojeda, who entrusted him with the supervision of the settlement of San Sebastian. Pizarro also accompanied Balbao when the latter discovered the Pacific Ocean. Later he was to betray Balbao and play a part in having him executed.

In 1522, Pizarro formed a partnership with a priest called Hernando de Luque and a soldier called Diego de Almagro, with a view to organizing exploratory journeys to the south. He also had a secretary called Xerxes. Conquest was in his mind and he went off exploring along the west coast of South America, feeling his way southwards. At one point he was left stranded for several months on the island of Gallo, with thirteen men and no stores. It was there that he showed great courage and leadership skills for the first time. Pizarro pushed on until he reached 9 degrees south of the Equator, all the time gathering detailed accounts of the nature of the Inca empire.

The governor of Panama showed no inclination to encourage Pizarro, so Pizarro decided to appeal to the King of Spain in person. He sailed back to Spain early in 1518 with this request in mind. Charles V was won over by what Pizarro told him, decorated Pizarro with the Order of Santiago, and granted him a coat of arms. On 29 July, 1529 at Toledo, Pizarro was given a formal official title deed to his new personal empire. He was to be governor and captain general of the 'province of New Castile' which was to extend along 200 leagues of the newly discovered coast of South America.

Pizarro sailed from San Lucar in January 1530, shortly afterwards followed by his brother Hernando. Pizarro invaded Peru with the intention of conquering the Inca empire. The Inca empire extended from Peru into northern Chile and it reached its zenith under its eleventh ruler, or Sapa Inca, Huayna Capac (1493–1525), On Huayna Capac's death in 1525, the Inca empire was divided in two between his sons Huascar and Atahualpa, which led to a debilitating civil war. Atahualpa succeeded in killing his brother Huascar, but then Pizarro captured the Inca capital, Cuzco, and imprisoned Atahualpa.

The Inca emperor tried to buy his freedom by filling a room with gold as a ransom. Pizarro had him cruelly strangled anyway. From that moment, Pizarro held the Inca empire for himself, but he did not enjoy his conquest for very long. After the Incas' final effort to get Cuzco back again in 1536–37 had been quashed by Diego de Almagro, a power struggle broke out between Almagro and Pizarro. They would not agree on the boundary separating their jurisdiction. There was a battle. Almagro was defeated and

Pizarro had him executed, but Almagro's supporters in their turn conspired against Pizarro and assassinated him on 6 June 1541.

Pizarro is remembered as the man who conquered Peru for Spain. He did rather more than that. He murdered the Inca emperor, Atahualpa; he destroyed the Inca empire; he destroyed the Inca civilization. We remember Pizarro as one of the great destroyers of history.

FERDINAND MAGELLAN

Born at Sabrosa about 1480, died at Mactan 1521.
Portuguese navigator, leader of the first expedition to
* circumnavigate the world.*

ACHIEVEMENTS:
Organized and led the first voyage round the world.
Became the first person to visit every line of longitude.
Led the first Pacific crossing.
Finally proved that the world is a sphere.
Gave Patagonia and the Pacific Ocean their names.
Supplied information leading to the demarcation of Portuguese
* and Spanish interests in the New World.*

MAGELLAN WAS BORN at Sabrosa in the Tras os Montes province of Portugal. He was a fourth-order nobleman, the son of Pedro de Magalhaes, and was brought up as a page of Queen Leonor, consort of King John the Perfect. He enlisted in 1504 as a volunteer for the voyage to India of the first Portuguese viceroy, Francisco de Almeida. He served in India again in 1508 and was wounded at the Battle of Diu in 1509. Later that year he embarked from Cochin on a voyage intended to reach the Spice Islands, but the expedition was waylaid at Malacca. By 1510 he had been rewarded for his service, in which he had been wounded several times, with the rank of captain. He distinguished himself again at the capture of Malacca under Albuquerque. He was then given the task of sailing from Malacca to explore the Spice Islands; he returned with reports of abundant spices.

Magellan returned to Portugal in 1512 and the following year he accompanied an expedition to capture the town of Azamor in Morocco. Magellan was wounded during the action and lamed for life. He was accused of trading with the Moors and consequently fell out of favour with the Portuguese king, Manuel, who led him to understand that Portugal would have no further use for his services.

Magellan responded to this doubly crippling adversity with great spirit. He was always the man of action and resolve, and curiously never the man of letters; he left no written record of any of his remarkable exploits. He rode the King of Portugal's snub by formally renouncing his Portuguese nationality and offering his services as a navigator to the court of Spain. In particular he offered Charles V an ambitious scheme, in effect an extension of the Columbus scheme, to reach the Moluccas by the westerly route. Columbus had sailed west apparently under the impression that there was but one ocean between Europe and the Spice Islands; Magellan knew there were two. He would have to cross the Atlantic and the Pacific. What Magellan set out to do was therefore far more ambitious and daring than Columbus's Atlantic crossing just 20 years before.

He hoped to find a sea passage to the south of South America, even though none had been discovered. He is said to have declared that he was ready to sail as far as latitude 750 South in search of the sea passage through to the Pacific. It was a terrific gamble.

Magellan had help from Faleiro, an astronomer, in planning his expedition, and from Christopher de Haro, a financial backer who had a grudge against the King of Portugal. On 22 March, 1518 Magellan and Faleiro, as joint captains general, signed an agreement with Charles V by which they would receive one-twentieth of the profits of the expedition. The government of any lands conquered would rest in their hands and those of their heirs.

Magellan set sail from Seville on 10 August, 1519 with 5 ships and 270 men. Faleiro stayed behind; he had cast his horoscope and found that the expedition would be fatal to him. Statistically, he was probably right. Only one of the five ships, the Vittoria, was to return to Spain. While sailing south along the coast of Argentina Magellan dealt with a formidable mutiny and met the natives, whom he named 'Patagonians' (Big Feet). Magellan therefore inadvertently named the region of Patagonia. He found his way through the winding strait which still bears his name, the Magellan Straits separating the mainland of South America from Tierra del Fuego. At that time it was assumed that Tierra del Fuego (the Land of Fire) was the northernmost tip of a huge southern continent, though it eventually proved to be an island. In November 1519, the tiny Spanish fleet entered Balboa's 'Great South Sea', which Magellan flatteringly named the Pacific Ocean.

By this time, one ship had been wrecked, one had turned and headed back to Spain. A third ship had later to be burned and scuttled in the Pacific because so many men had died that only two ships could be properly manned. Then these two ships became separated. One was captured by the Portuguese.

The huge expanse of the Pacific came as a great shock and nearly killed everyone on the expedition. It took Magellan 98 days to cross it. In all that distance he only discovered two islands, both small, uninhabited and sterile. His crews had to do without fresh provisions, including fresh water, and the ravages of scurvy became terrible. They ended up eating sawdust, oxhides and rats. At last they made landfall in some inhabited islands, which Magellan unflatteringly named the Ladrones, after the thieving nature of the inhabitants. This was Guam.

Magellan himself was killed in a skirmish with natives in the Philippines. His ship nevertheless returned home to Spain, complete with a heavy cargo of cloves, taken by the last surviving Spanish captain, Juan del Cano. Del Cano reached Spain on 6 September 1522, the first man to sail right round the world in a single expedition. Of the 270 men who had started the voyage, only 18 made it back to Spain after this epic tour of the earth. Magellan did not make it back to Spain, but, falling at Mactan, he died at a point further west than the longitude of his earlier furthest east in the Moluccas. In that sense, Magellan did go right round the world.

Magellan's achievement was enormous. The circumnavigation showed for the first time that the earth was a sphere, and demonstrated the true size of that sphere. He gave Patagonia, the Straits of Magellan and the Pacific Ocean their lasting names.

MARTIN LUTHER

Born at Eisleben 1483, died at Eisleben 1546.
Religious reformer, leader of the Reformation.

ACHIEVEMENTS:
Challenged corrupt practices in the Catholic Church.
Led the Reformation.
Was largely responsible for the creation of the Protestant
  Church.
Wrote hymns.
Wrote an influential translation of the Bible.

MARTIN LUTHER WAS born at Eisleben, the son of Margaret Ziegler and Hans Luther, an iron ore miner. The family belonged to the peasant class, but Luther's father seems to have been a man of drive and initiative, qualities which Martin inherited. Within a short time of arriving in Mansfeld, a centre of iron ore mining and smelting, Hans Luther had become the lessee of several smelting furnaces and one of four elected members on the town council – so he was no ordinary miner.

Martin Luther was brought up harshly; his parents were disciplinarians and though Martin knew they meant well, he later complained about their unnecessary severity. From the age of 14 he went to school at Magdeburg, where he was taught Latin, singing and religion. He was a good, diligent pupil, though he later complained about the teaching. When he finished school he went to Eisenach, where he was received into the home of a rich burgher, Kuntz Cotta, and his wife; they felt sorry for the boy who had to earn his living by singing in the street. At Eisenach, Luther took higher courses in Latin grammar, composition, rhetoric and poetry. Here he easily outshone his fellow-pupils and was full of praise for his teachers, Rector Trebonius and his assistant Wigand. In 1501 he went to the prestigious University of Erfurt and took his Bachelor of Arts degree the following year. Then he spent a further two years studying for a master's degree

The result of this intensive study was a firm grasp of scholastic philosophy and a well-developed dialectic skill. He belonged to a group of students who met to discuss philosophy – and he was its star. Luther developed a loyalty to the 'modern' school of philosophy propounded by William of Occam, the 14th century English Franciscan. He spoke of Occam as his master, and infinitely preferred his way of thinking to the philosophy of Thomas Aquinas. Luther was also drawn to Aristotle, whose logic and philosophy dominated even Occam.

He was led via philosophy to scripture study and, in May 1505, Luther abruptly dropped the law course his father had decided on and entered the Augustinian monastery at Erfurt. The decision seems to have been unpremeditated. Probably a variety of influences, religious, psychological and philosophical, played on his highly-strung and impulsive temperament to produce this result. Luther described it vividly. It came to him as suddenly as Paul's conversion. He was on the open road and overtaken by a thunderstorm. A flash of lightning earthed close to him and he fell, scared to death – scared of death. Entering the monastery was involuntary, and he regarded it as a direct call from God.

In 1507 he was ordained a priest, and the following year he lectured on philosophy at the University of Wittenberg. As a preacher he had even more power and influence. He went on a mission to Rome in 1510–11, and was shocked by what he found there. Money was needed in Rome; selling indulgences was seen as an easy way to generate revenue. An indulgence was in effect a paid forgiveness for sins. When he returned to Germany his epoch-making career as a religious reformer began.

Luther was very indignant at the shamelessness with which indulgences were sold, and could not contain his anger. He was Professor of Biblical exegesis at Wittenberg from 1512 –1546, and he began to preach a doctrine of salvation through faith rather than by works. Suddenly he emerged from an academic world into a world of decisive and committed action.

On 31 October, 1517, Luther drew up a list of 95 theses (assertions or beliefs) regarding indulgences, and nailed them onto the door of the church at Wittenberg. The practice of indulgence had grown out of the Church's system of penances. To punish sins, the Church had temporarily excluded people from the fellowship. To mitigate this punishment, the sinner might pay a sum of money to be readmitted. It was a practice that had become big business in the Catholic Church since 1300. The Wittenberg Dominican Johann Tetzel, who had been freely selling indulgences, withdrew to Frenkfurt as der Oder, where he published a set of counter-theses and burnt Luther's. Luther's students responded by burning Tetzel's.

In 1518, Luther was joined by Melancthon. At first Pope Leo X took little notice of Luther and the disturbance he was causing, thinking it was no more than a quarrel among monks, but in 1518 the summons to Rome came. Luther's university and the elector intervened and there were some negotiations. At Leipzig, in the following year, there was a memorable debate between Luther and Eck, the Pope's envoy to the Saxon court. The attempt to silence him made Luther even bolder. He went on to attack the papal system as a whole. Erasmus joined in. Eck went to Rome to raise the Curia against Luther. This resulted in a formal Bull of Condemnation, but it only made Luther more aggressive than ever.

In 1520, Luther published his famous address to the *Christian Nobles in Germany,* followed by another reforming tract, *On the Babylonian Captivity of the Church of God.* A papal bull was issued containing 41 theses levelled against him; he publicly burned these in front of a crowd in Wittenberg. A frenzy of excitement was building up in Germany. Charles V convened his first diet (government) at Worms in 1521, and an order was issued for the destruction of Luther's books. Luther himself was ordered to appear at Worms. Finally he was put under a ban, and on his return home he was arrested and confined, mainly for his own protection, in the Wartburg.

During his year in captivity, Luther did a great deal of writing and translated the Bible. In 1522 he had to return to Wittenberg because of the mounting unrest there. He rebuked those who were creating the disorder. He also published a bitter reply to Henry VIII's piece on the seven sacraments. A rift opened between Luther and Erasmus. In 1525, Martin Luther married Katherine von Bora, an ex-nun.

In 1529, Luther engaged in a conference on religious reforms with Zwingli and other Swiss theologians. Luther stood by his conviction regarding the consubstantiation: that Christ was actually present in the bread and wine of the Eucharist. The drawing up in 1530 of the Augsburg Confession, at which Melancthon represented Luther, marks the climax of the German Reformation. Luther was unable to attend the meeting at Augsburg because he was now an outlaw. For Melancthon, Luther was a truly great figure on a level with the great prophets of the Bible, the prophets who drew their inspiration directly from God.

During his last ten years, Luther suffered increasing ill-health. He visited his birthplace, Eisleben, to arbitrate in a dispute between two counts. He preached several times to huge congregations, but exposure to bad weather while travelling and the effort of the negotiation wore him out. As he lay dying he was asked if he remained steadfast to the doctrine he had taught. He answered with an emphatic 'Yes!', which was his last word. Luther was buried at Wittenberg.

Melancthon sometimes suffered under Luther's excessive masterfulness and vehemence. Melancthon idolized Luther, but admitted that he was too hard and rough, even in his writings. Even so, 'His heart was true and without falseness, his utterance friendly and kindly.' He was, as the final attempt at arbitration showed, always ready to conciliate and resolve quarrels. He hated intrigue. He was a man with massive energy, huge intelligence, manly and affectionate simplicity, with a coarse sense of humour. He was also a determined and courageous spiritual visionary; he put in motion a movement that would in a very short time create a sparer alternative to the Roman Catholic Church – Protestantism – which quickly came to dominate northern Europe. Luther was also a great innovator in religious music; he wrote several hymns of monolithic power, which gave great character to what had every appearance of being a distinct new religion. It was a very remarkable achievement.

IVAN THE TERRIBLE

Born 1530, died 1584.
First Tsar of Russia, brutal dictator.

ACHIEVEMENTS:
Reduced the power of the Russian nobility, using dictatorial
*   powers.*
Re-organized the administration of Russia.
Created an expanded and more powerful state of Russia.
Destroyed the city of Novgorod and its 60,000 inhabitants.
Founded the black riders, a kind of secret police force, to carry
*   out political assassinations.*
Became a role-model for later dictators.

IVAN IV WAS born in 1530, the son of Vasily, Grand Duke of Moscow. He was orphaned at an early age; his father died when he was only three and his mother, acting as regent, was poisoned by political enemies when he was eight. After that, Ivan claimed he had 'no human care from any quarter'. A power vacuum followed his father's death, and a struggle for power developed among the leading Muscovite families. Ivan himself was a pawn in this struggle. One of his uncles was seized and murdered by a Moscow mob during a rising.

In this brutal environment Ivan had to learn quickly by example how to survive. It was not long before he organized his own first political murder. He was 13 when he threw his victim's body, a troublesome prince, to his dogs. In 1547, Ivan proclaimed himself Tsar and at a specially arranged beauty contest he selected himself a bride, a 15-year-old girl called

159

Anastasia. She gave birth to six children, though four had died by the time she herself died in 1560. It is possible that the loss of the children followed by the loss of his wife, who had been a steadying influence on him, caused him to topple over into bloodthirsty megalomania after that date.

In his grief, he accused his chaplain, Father Silvestr, and another close adviser, Alexei Adashev, of plotting to kill Anastasia, and banished them both. Then he went into retreat, leaving Moscow in order to go into seclusion in the provinces. He was begged by every level of Moscow society to return, for fear of another power vacuum in his absence, something they must later have regretted. Ivan agreed, but on one terrible condition – that he would be free to govern without hindrance. He was assuming dictatorial powers, and he used them. He re-organized the country into huge administrative units; he would be absolute ruler in one, while the others were governed on his behalf by teams of bureaucrats.

This is when the terror began. He created a force of oprichniki, black-cloaked assassins riding black horses. In their saddles they each carried their emblems of office, a broom and a dog's head. The black riders descended like Furies on anyone who was suspected of opposing Ivan and slaughtered them. Ivan used them, among other things, to settle scores dating back to his childhood. Anyone he could remember thwarting him during his early years was marked for a visit by the black riders. More than 4,000 aristocrats were murdered in this way, including the entire Staritsky family; they were relatives of Ivan's, but this made them potential rivals. When the leader of the Orthodox Church, metropolitan Philip, condemned the oprichniki attacks and withheld his blessing from the Tsar, with ruthless inevitability the black riders came for him and executed him.

Throughout history, dictators have behaved in this way, getting underlings to commit their murders for them. Ivan was unusual in wanting to take part himself. He joined in orgies of rape, torture and killing.

The peak of Ivan the Terrible's terrible reign came when he was informed that the city leaders of Novgorod, at that time the second city of Russia, were planning to rebel. Ivan's rage knew no bounds. He did not bother to check whether his informant was telling him the truth, which he probably was not, but summoned the black riders and rode to Novgorod with them. First they pillaged the monasteries and homes of the aristocracy of the area, laying waste to the lands within 50 miles of the city. Then he built a wooden wall round Novgorod to prevent anyone from escaping. For the five weeks that followed, he and his men systematically slaughtered everyone inside the wall. Nor was the killing quick and merciful. Sometimes families were forced to watch while fathers, husbands or wives were tortured. Women were roasted alive on spits. Ivan joined in with relish. He mounted a horse, took a spear and rode about, running people through as if it was a sport.

Russian historians have been keen to keep alive the memory of a great king, and have put the death toll at Novgorod at 2,000, but historians in the West put it nearer to 60,000. Ivan's savagery at Novgorod, and his similar treatment of Pskov on a similar pretext, had the effect of suppressing opposition. Many who knew they had become suspects killed themselves rather than risk the unimaginably horrible death that Ivan would inflict on them. When Ivan invaded the adjacent state of Livonia, one doomed garrison that was under siege blew itself up rather than risk falling into Ivan's hands.

In 1572, Ivan suddenly disbanded the black riders, and forbade any future mention of their existence. Unpredictability and capriciousness are hallmarks of the dictator. Ivan was probably a manic depressive, with bouts of frenzied sadism alternating with periods of static religious depression. During these religious phases, he would wear sackcloth and publicly confess his sins. Perhaps it was real, deep-seated shame that brought the six-year reign of terror to an end. Perhaps there was no need to go on because all Ivan's enemies were dead, but that had not stopped him killing thousands of imaginary enemies. Perhaps there was a more political reason. Perhaps it was an attack from outside Russia that caused him to call off the debilitating internal revenge attacks; the Turks were advancing from the south.

It is hard to see how any state can survive such destructive leadership. Ivan survived partly because he had the Orthodox Church's support. While Western Europe was going through the challenge of Protestantism, and the trauma of the Reformation was in full swing, Ivan was allowing no protest of any kind in Russia, and would maintain the status quo. Ivan took a predictably tough line on religious dissent, with the depressingly familiar burnings for heresy, and in this way he bought the support of the Church. In return, the Church acted as a propaganda machine for the Tsar. When peasant revolts were crushed with brutal cruelty, it was never the Tsar who was behind it. The atrocities were always blamed on the excessive zeal of underlings.

In 1581, Ivan murdered his son and heir with a spear during a quarrel. His licentious sex life had left him riddled with disease. Ivan was about to play a game of chess when he collapsed and died. But even Ivan's legacy was terrible. He had recently killed his heir, the young Ivan, and left his imbecile son Theodore on the throne. Russia was plunged again into decades of chaos, with invasions by both Poles and Swedes.

Ivan created an expanded and more powerful state of Russia, and in so doing changed the face of western Asia. He reduced the power of the Russian nobility, using dictatorial powers. He re-organized the administration of Russia. He destroyed the city of Novgorod and its 60,000 inhabitants, partly out of bloodthirsty revenge, partly to show that he was not to be crossed. He founded the black riders, a kind of secret police force, to carry out political assassinations. In his various actions, some of them entirely unpredictable and therefore engendering even greater fear, Ivan the Terrible became a role-model for later dictators. His was a destructive and egocentric career that would be repeated several times over, as late as the twentieth century; it is possible to see Ivan reincarnated in Stalin.

RICHARD TARLETON

Born about 1530, died 1588.
Great comic actor and jester.

ACHIEVEMENTS:
The last of the great English court jesters.
The first of the great stand-up comedians.

RICHARD TARLETON WAS born at Condover in Shropshire. He evidently started off as an inn-keeper and developed his skills as an entertainer, bantering with customers across the counter. Then he became a professional comic actor and comedian. Not a great deal is known about him except that he occupied a very special place in the Elizabethan theatre. He was the greatest comic actor of his day, and universally regarded as the funniest man alive. Richard Tarleton had a funny-looking face and he had only to show it round the curtain to bring the house down. Every time he went on stage there was uproar.

For a thousand years at least there had been court jesters, often called 'fools'. These characters more or less disappeared in the sixteenth century. Charles I was the last English monarch to have a fool, which has a certain irony about it; Charles I need not have employed a fool as he was one already.

Today we do not have jesters or fools. We have stand-up comedians, the best of which achieve national and occasionally international celebrity, like Bob Hope. Richard Tarleton was at the divide between these two traditions. He was the last of the great court jesters: he was the first of the great comedians.

Tarleton was introduced to Queen Elizabeth I through the Earl of Leicester and became one of the Queen's Players. He is known to have been a member of that company in 1583 and remained with them until the time of his death. By the 1580s he was a very experienced actor indeed and Queen Elizabeth's favourite clown.

Richard Tarleton had a particular talent for making up impromptu doggerel on subjects suggested to him by the audience. He became so well-known for this trick that doggerel became known as 'Tarleton'.

Richard Tarleton wrote *The Seven Deadly Sins* for the Queen's Players to perform. He may well have written many other pieces, but they have not survived. After his death a three-part series called *Tarleton's Jests* was published, from 1592 onwards. It is not certain whether he wrote these works. Probably they represent a compilation of material recalled and reconstructed from live performances by other members of the Queen's Players, who must have heard his routines many times and known them well enough to write them down with fair accuracy, just as many people today can remember and recite whole scenes from *Fawlty Towers* or *Monty Python*. *Tarleton's Jests* includes some material that pre-dates Tarleton, but he may still have used it on stage. Many comedians make us laugh by telling us jokes we have heard many times before – that becomes part of the joke.

William Shakespeare would have been very familiar with Tarleton's style and personality. He probably had Tarleton in mind when he affectionately described the dead clown, Yorick, in a meditation on death in the gravedigger scene in *Hamlet*.

A fellow of infinite jest, of most excellent fancy; he hath borne me on his back a thousand times . . . Where be your gibes now? Your gambols? Your songs? Your flashes of merriment, that were wont to set the table on a roar?

The grave-digger says of the skull as he holds it up for Hamlet to see, 'Here's a skull now: this skull hath lain in the earth three-and-twenty years.' The number of years is interesting, because Shakespeare wrote

Hamlet in 1601, 1602 or 1603, by which time Tarleton had been dead for 23, 24 or 25 years. Shakespeare still remembered him fondly, and probably some in the audience would have remembered him too. We always remember with fondness and gratitude the people who make us laugh. The 'three-and-twenty years' was a nudge to the audience to think back to what must have been a very sad day in 1588 – the day Richard Tarleton died.

HIDEYOSHI TOYOTOMI

Born 1536, died 1598.
Japanese soldier, unifier of Japan.

ACHIEVEMENTS:
Unified Japan, creating the modern state of Japan.
Unsuccessfully attempted to conquer Korea.

NOBUNAGA WAS A military genius, but without any administrative ability. His most important achievement was to bring to the Japanese people the idea that under an emperor supreme authority was vested in one man. It was Hideyoshi Toyotomi – the remarkable man who succeeded Nobunaga – who was to exploit this important idea to the full.

Hideyoshi became the second of the three great historical unifiers of Japan, the others being Nobunaga and Ieyasu Tokugawa. Hideyoshi's career was extremely unusual, in that he started as a mere peasant who became a groom to Nobunaga, and then rose to become Nobunaga's leading general. Hideyoshi became Nobunaga's trusted lieutenant and clearly had the ability to succeed him – but he did not have the rank or title.

When Nobunaga died, Hideyoshi supported the claim of the child of Nobunaga's deceased eldest son and became the child's guardian. Nobunaga's surviving sons challenged Hideyoshi. One of them, Nobuo, raised an army and had the support of Ieyasu, who had previously worked with Hideyoshi. Now they found themselves in opposition, they saw that the issue was not great enough to justify the conflict. In the end, none of Nobunaga's descendants played a major role.

Hideyoshi emerged from this melee as emperor. His first move was to wage a campaign against Echizen. The result of this was that four provinces on the Sea of Japan submitted to him. The island of Shikoku had drifted into virtual independence, and Hideyoshi attacked, conquered and reclaimed it for Japan.

Alongside these conquests, which in effect enlarged Japan, Hideyoshi began to set up an efficient central government supervised by five ministers. He also reformed the coinage and the administration of justice.

By 1585, Hideyoshi was master of all of Japan except Kyushu and the Kwanto with the provinces that lay to the north. Hideyoshi then turned his attention to these areas, starting with Kyushu. Some of these expeditions brought Hideyoshi into contact with Christianity as a political power. Up until this time, Hideyoshi had shown no prejudice against Christians, but now he made restrictive laws to reduce the influence of Christianity in Japan. What Hideyoshi saw and heard in Kyushu convinced him that the Jesuits there were not confining their activities to religious matters. He saw the Jesuits as trying to establish a kingdom within his kingdom. He cleverly put five leading questions to a Jesuit official, including 'On what authority do the Jesuits constrain Japanese subjects to become Christians?' Hideyoshi considered the answers unsatisfactory and, in 1587, he published an edict ordering all Jesuits to leave Japan within 20 days, or risk being put to death.

The situation was aggravated by a Spanish shipwreck. The pilot was anxious to impress the Japanese and boasted of the expansion of the Spanish empire. When asked how these conquests had been made, the pilot foolishly said that 'the catholic king first sent ministers of the Gospel to convert the natives, who then uniting with the captains of his majesty made their work of conquest easier.' This report made Hideyoshi very angry and confirmed his suspicion about the insidious nature of the Christian mission. He had 26 missionaries executed and many churches destroyed.

Now only the east and the north remained to be conquered. By 1591 he had achieved this. Hideyoshi became known as the Napoleon of Japan, and he began to show more and more of the classic signs of megalomania.

His moves to conquer and assimilate the various provinces of Japan into a unified whole were reasonable, understandable and achievable. But reaching out to conquer Korea and China was foolishly over-ambitious. His armies invaded Korea in 1592, and the Jesuits claimed that Hideyoshi was just looking for somewhere to dump all the Christians. It was certainly true that he sent 20,000 Christian troops to Korea, and may have thought that it would be no bad thing if they didn't come back. The scheme to conquer Korea and then China seems to have been in Hideyoshi's mind for a long time, and may even have been an ambition of Nobunaga's.

The Koreans had had long experience in fighting off pirates. They had evolved special 'turtle-shell' ships, which were covered and gave them a great advantage. The Japanese invading fleet was virtually destroyed. The Chinese realised that their country was threatened and sent an expeditionary force of 5,000 men. They were routed by the Japanese. The seriousness of the situation was then brought home to the Chinese and a much larger army was dispatched. The Japanese fell back on Korea.

In 1596, the Chinese tried diplomacy, sending an embassy to Hideyoshi at Osaka. The embassies handed Hideyoshi a document. It was a patronizing letter from the Ming emperor recognizing Hideyoshi as king of Japan. Hideyoshi was furious and sent them packing. Another huge force was sent off to Korea in 1597, and in 1598 the Japanese gained a substantial victory over the Koreans. A gruesome monument raised by the Japanese boasted that 38,000 of the enemy had been killed.

Hideyoshi himself died in September 1598. It is said that before he died he asked Ieyasu to make arrangements for the invasion of Korea to cease. The Japanese armies withdrew from Korea as soon as he was dead.

Hideyoshi was responsible for a huge and unnecessary amount of suffering in his invasion of Korea, which achieved nothing whatever. The attack on the mainland of Asia was simply an expression of power-madness. Hideyoshi's earlier career, in building the modern state of Japan, was far more constructive. His treatment of the Christian missionaries has been condemned – but perhaps he was right. The British were after all, a few hundred years later, to use Christianization as a pretext for empire-building.

AKBAR

Born at Umarkot 1542, died 1605.
Great Mogul Emperor.

ACHIEVEMENTS:
Won back the empire taken from his father.
Extended and consolidated the Mogul empire in North India.
Abolished slavery and suttee in the Mogul empire.
Introduced a policy of genuine religious toleration.
Became the greatest of the Mogul emperors.

AKBAR WAS BORN at Umarkot in Sind, when his father Humayun was escaping to Persia after being driven from the throne of Delhi by a usurper. Thirteen years passed before Humayun felt able to attempt the reconquest of Hindustan, and he had achieved little by the time of his death in 1556. Then Akbar succeeded his father. Akbar was only 13, and not ready to rule. For four years the government was competently run by his tutor Nairam Khan, whom became regent. In 1560, Akbar dismissed his regent and assumed power for himself.

The early years of Akbar's reign were troubled by civil war and rebellion. Eventually Akbar was able to overcome these internal problems and triumph over his enemies. After that, he was able to turn his attention to neighbouring states. He rapidly extended his empire by conquering Malwa in 1561, Rajputana in 1569, Gujarat in 1573 and Bengal in 1576. Akbar was not content with this, and went on to conquer Kashmir in 1586, Sind in 1592, Kandahar in 1595 and Ahmadnagar in 1600. These great military successes made Akbar the undisputed master of the whole of northern India.

Akbar made major reforms to the tax system, abolishing the hated poll-tax inflicted on non-Muslims and the tax on Hindu pilgrims. He encouraged the advancement of science and promoted trade. In 1582 he abolished slavery. He also put a stop to enforced suttee, the barbaric practice of burning widows on their dead husbands' funeral pyres, and legalized the remarriage of widows. Akbar was himself a Muslim, but his beliefs were wide-ranging, and he tolerated other religions among his subjects; in this he practised a formal tolerance policy rather like that of his great contemporary, Elizabeth I of England. Akbar may have been a Muslim, but he did not want his many Hindu subjects to feel excluded or resentful. It was rather similar to Elizabeth I's attitude to her Catholic subjects.

Akbar was himself illiterate, but he was very interested in promoting thought. In 1575 he created the Ibadat Khana (House of Worship), a meeting-place for scholars and theologians of all kinds. Akbar became disillusioned at the intolerant and narrow-minded wrangling that became the hallmarks of the meetings there, and closed the institution in 1582. To replace it he created a new institution, an inter-denominational order called the Din Alahi. Its motto was 'God and the King'. His tolerance extended to inviting three separate Jesuit missions to his court, to see what they had to say in favour of Christianity. Through the 1580s, he had to put up with a rude and bigoted campaign by these Portuguese missionaries to convert him to Christianity, treating them with a patience and respect they did not deserve. The missionaries found him ready to listen and to accept some of their ideas, but entirely unwilling to give up the pleasures of his harem; he also refused to accept the idea that Jesus was God made man and rejected the concept of the Trinity.

When Akbar the Great died in 1605, he was an invincible political, cultural and spiritual force, the ruler of 15 provinces, in command of an empire that stretched from the Hindu Kush to the Godavari, from Gujarat to Bengal. But perhaps his greatest achievement was his policy of universal religious toleration. He was an uncompromising autocrat, but that was probably the only way he could have achieved what he did. His successors presided over a gradual decline in the Mogul empire, largely because they did not pursue Akbar's policy of religious tolerance.

SIR JOHN HARINGTON

Born at Kelston 1561, died at Kelston 1612.
Courtier, soldier, writer, inventor of the flushing water closet.

ACHIEVEMENTS:
Invented the first flushing lavatory.
Introduced an era of greater domestic hygiene, promoting health
    and longer life.

JOHN HARINGTON WAS born at Kelston near Bath in 1561. His father, also called John Harington, became rich by marrying Etheldreda, an illegitimate daughter of Henry VIII. After his wife's death, Harington's father entered the service of Princess Elizabeth, and married Isabella Markham, one of Elizabeth's ladies in waiting. When Mary Tudor came to the throne, Harington's father and mother were imprisoned in the Tower along with Elizabeth. When the young John Harington was born he became Princess Elizabeth's godson.

Harington was educated at Eton and Christ's College, Cambridge. His tutor at Cambridge was John Still, later Bishop of Bath and Wells. He went to London with a view to becoming a lawyer, but he was clearly more suited to court life than the bar. At court he was popular and noted for his wit. Harington nevertheless shocked the queen by translating the story of Giocondo from Ariosto and passing his indecent translation across to her ladies. He was ordered to withdraw to his seat at Kelston to complete the translation of the entire work. The verse translation of Orlando Furioso was published in 1591.

In 1592, Harington became high sheriff of Somerset. He produced a three-part work, *The Metamorphosis of Ajax, An Anatomie of the Metamorphosed Ajax* and *Ulysses upon Ajax* in 1596. These were lightweight, absurd, facetious pieces showing a coarse sense of humour. An incautious reference to the Earl of Leicester in these bawdy writings turned out to be unwise, and Harington found himself in disgrace for a while.

In 1598 he received a commission to serve in the ill-fated campaign in Ireland under the Earl of Essex. Harington was one of those knighted in the field by the Earl of Essex. This was a well-established medieval custom, but it annoyed the autocratic Queen Elizabeth, who decided she was the only person entitled to award knighthoods. His association with Essex and in particular his acceptance of the knighthood from him put Harington into difficulties. Essex returned to England against orders, and was soon in total disgrace, facing the block for treason. Harington managed to distance himself from the earl's disgrace by writing an account of the Irish campaign which directed Elizabeth's anger against the earl.

Ever the courtier, Harington wrote a *Tract on the Succession to the Crown* in 1603, a manuscript that was clearly intended to win favour with the new king. In 1605, once the new king James I was installed, he cheekily asked for the posts of Chancellor and Archbishop of Ireland, supporting his double request with an essay that is conspicuously modern in tone, entitled *A Short View of the State of Ireland.*

Sir John Harington died at his home at Kelston in November 1612. He would probably not be remembered as anything more than one of a bevy of self-advancing popinjays that constantly fluttered and postured wittily round Queen Elizabeth I – but for one thing. When the queen visited him at Kelston in 1592, he showed her his invention. It was a flushing lavatory, nicknamed 'Ajax', which Harington had designed and built in 1589. The queen insisted on trying it out for herself, was greatly impressed, and ordered an Ajax for herself. The Spanish Armada was defeated, England was safe from foreign invasion, peace was assured and the age of the flushing lavatory had arrived; modern civilization had begun in earnest.

GALILEO GALILEI

Born in Pisa 1564, died at Arcetri 1642.
Italian astronomer and experimental philosopher.

ACHIEVEMENTS:
Established rigorous observation as a scientific method.
Discovered observational evidence that Copernicus was right.
Proved that the Sun is at the centre of the solar system.
Anticipated modern discoveries, such as measuring distances to
    planets and stars using parallax.
Realised that moonlight is reflected sunlight.
Observed the mountainous landscape of the moon.
1583 – Discovered the properties of pendulums.
1591 – Discovered the properties of falling bodies.
1609 – Perfected the modern refracting telescope.
1610 – Discovered four of Jupiter's satellites.
1610 – Discovered sunspots.
1611 – Used sunspots to deduce that the sun rotates.
1613 – Letters on the Solar Spots.
1630 – Dialogo dei duo massimi sistemi del mondo.
1636 – Dialogo delle nuove scienze.

GALILEO GALILEI WAS born in Pisa in 1564. He came of an impoverished noble Florentine family. His father was Vicenzo Galilei, a competent mathematician and musician. Galileo was educated at the monastery of Vallombrosa near Florence. There he studied Latin and Greek, but found the science he was taught distasteful. He came to disagree with and despise the Aristotelian philosophy that prevailed in his day. He showed a practical aptitude for mechanical invention.

His father sent him to Pisa University in 1581 to study medicine. Just two years later Galileo inferred, first from casual and then from systematic observations of a swinging lamp in Pisa Cathedral, the properties of a pendulum; whatever the range of the oscillations, the time scale is the same (isochronism). He then applied the same principle to the human pulse. Until this time he was kept completely ignorant of mathematics by his father, who uncannily sensed that Galileo would become preoccupied with it and that it would lead him to neglect medicine. Galileo by chance overheard a lesson in geometry, which caught his interest. He pleaded with his father to be allowed to study mathematics and his father reluctantly agreed.

In 1585, Galileo was withdrawn from university before taking a degree, because his father could no longer afford to keep him there. Galileo returned to Florence, where he lectured to the Florentine Academy.

His mathematical studies led to the invention of a hydrostatic balance and a work on specific gravity. His paper on the hydrostatic balance made his name as a scholar throughout Italy. Now supported by a patron, he put forward the first principle of dynamics. After he was appointed lecturer in Mathematics at Pisa, he carried out his famous series of experiments (1589–91) which dramatically proved to all the professors and students of the university that all falling bodies fall at equal velocities, whether they are large or small. His work aroused strong opinions. Unfortunately Galileo dealt abrasively and sarcastically with contradiction and consequently became unpopular. He had to resign his lectureship and move to Florence in 1591.

In 1592 he became Professor of Mathematics at Padua, where his lectures attracted students from all over Europe. The refracting telescope was invented by the Dutch in 1608; rumours of its invention reached northern Italy in June 1609. Galileo investigated the principle of the instrument, started work on it at once and made significant improvements on it shortly afterwards, for example raising the magnification to x32. Galileo's telescopes – and that is what people were calling the new instrument – were much in demand, and he made hundreds of them with his own hands.

Using this wonderful new invention, Galileo launched on a series of observations, which convinced him that the Copernican theory of the universe, with the sun at the centre, was correct. It seems that Galileo knew from early on in his researches that Copernicus was right. He held back from publicly supporting Copernicus for a long time – not because he feared persecution, but because he feared ridicule. This is clear from a letter he wrote to Kepler.

He concluded that the Moon's brightness was due to the reflection of sunlight from the Moon's surface, and he could see for himself that its surface was covered with mountains and valleys. He saw the Milky Way as a track of innumerable stars. In January 1610 he discovered that Jupiter has four satellites. He saw spots on the Sun, and used their movement across the Sun to infer that the Sun rotates.

These amazing discoveries led in September 1610 to a summons to Florence, where he was warmly received by the Grand Duke of Tuscany; he was awarded a professorship for life, on a high salary. He was also appointed as philosopher and mathematician extraordinary to the Grand Duke. In 1611 he was received with similar honour in Rome, where he exhibited his telescopic discoveries to the highest dignitaries at the Pope's court. He was a compelling lecturer because of his enthusiasm and also because of his ability to argue logically. Unfortunately his presentations were so clear that some began to see that what he was arguing ran counter to certain passages in the scriptures.

Things began to go wrong for Galileo in 1613, when he published his dissertation on sun spots; in it he boldly declared his support for the Copernican system. This brought down on him the displeasure of the church authorities. Galileo was not looking for a fight with the Church authorities, but once the discrepancies were pointed out to him he did not hold back.

In 1615 he was given a semi-official warning to keep off issues that were fundamentally theological. In 1616 the theologians of the Holy Office declared that the propositions that the sun is immovable at the centre of the universe and that the earth rotates on its axis once a day were heretical – though we now know that they were true. Shortly afterwards, Pope Paul admonished Galileo, and required him to promise never to advocate the forbidden doctrine of Copernicus again. Galileo tried in vain to get the ban lifted.

In 1632 he published a *Dialogue* on the solar system, in which he again supported Copernicus. This work was hailed as a work of genius all over Europe. It was lively, elegantly expressed, and full of lucid scientific argument. Pope Urban VIII was led to believe that Galileo was satirizing him as a timid and blind traditionalist, and Galileo was summoned to appear before the Inquisition. After a trial and a period of imprisonment, Galileo was forced to relinquish his belief in the sun-centred system. He was sentenced to indefinite imprisonment by the Inquisition. At the request of the Duke of Tuscany, the pope commuted this sentence to house arrest for life. Galileo first went to live at the house of the Archbishop of Siena, a trusted friend, Ascanio Piccolomini, then to Arcetri near Florence where he spent the remaining eight years of his life.

While under house arrest, Galileo continued to carry on his researches, even though he was losing both his sight and his hearing. He discovered many important physical properties of the universe. One was the law of uniformly accelerated motion towards the earth, the parabolic path of projectiles. Just before Galileo became completely blind in 1637, he discovered the Moon's monthly and annual librations. He developed a fever, of which he died on 8 January 1642.

Galileo contributed little to the theory of science. He can also be criticized for failing to incorporate into his work the discoveries made by his great contemporary, Kepler. He was a great observer, especially with the telescope which he perfected. Not only did he discover Jupiter's satellites: within two years of discovering them he had constructed fairly accurate tables of their periods of revolution. His observations of sunspots are similarly scrupulous and scientific; they were not only accurate in themselves, but he used them to make accurate inferences about the rotation of both sun and earth. He seems to have had an idea of a universal force of gravitation hovering at the edge of his mind, though it was not an idea he explored – he would leave that to Newton.

He anticipated modern discoveries, in that he established the idea of parallax, which involves measuring distances to heavenly bodies by observing their apparent position from two different points on the earth's orbit. Galileo predicted that it would one day be possible to measure distances to bodies beyond Saturn in this way – as indeed it now is. In all his work, he combined careful measurement and calculation to reach his results.

WILLIAM SHAKESPEARE

> *Born at Stratford-upon-Avon 1564, died at Stratford-upon-*
> *Avon 1616.*
> *Playwright, poet, actor-manager.*
>
> ACHIEVEMENTS:
> *Wrote 37 plays that dominate world literature.*
> *The outstanding playwright of the Renaissance.*
> *The greatest playwright of all time.*
> *Showed great insight into a wide range of human*
> *predicaments.*
> *Typified the questioning humanism of the Renaissance.*
> *Set new standards for all subsequent writers.*
> *Defined the full potential of the English language.*

WILLIAM SHAKESPEARE WAS born in Stratford-upon-Avon on 23 April 1564. He was the eldest son of John Shakespeare, a well-to-do glover and wool dealer.

Shakespeare's life fell into three distinct periods. The first was his boyhood in Stratford, where his parents lived, where he was educated, where he was married and where his three children were born. There can be no doubt that he attended Stratford Grammar School, to which John Shakespeare's civic status entitled him to send his son free of charge. This outstanding school evidently gave the young William a very thorough classical education; his plays are full of references to the Latin and Greek poets, and he learnt a lot by studying drama, philosophy and history while at school.

In 1582, when he was 18, Shakespeare married Anne Hathaway. She was a farmer's daughter who lived just outside Stratford. She was 26 and pregnant by Shakespeare. It cannot have been a happy situation – the shotgun wedding followed by moving in with the elder Shakespeares because William had no means of supporting his wife on his own. The child, Susanna, was born six months after they were married. In 1585, Anne gave birth to twins, their only son, Hamnet, and another daughter, Judith.

The second period of his life began when, still a very young man, he left Stratford to make his fortune in London. The domestic situation in Stratford and his lack of income probably forced this sudden decision upon him. He settled on the London theatre as his career. As a youth Shakespeare probably saw many plays performed in Stratford by touring companies and may simply have joined one of these companies as they passed through – the equivalent of running away to join the circus. However it happened, Shakespeare became an actor in a company of actors in London in the 1580s. He quickly became a permanent and leading member of the company.

Very soon after the beginning of his acting career, Shakespeare started writing plays of his own. He seems to have had immediate success. There is no trace of any 'apprentice work' that is sub-standard or unworthy of performance. He wrote historical plays that were from the start immensely popular and commercially successful, the three parts of *Henry VI* (1592). The theatre impresario Philip Henslowe wrote in his diary that 'Harey the vj' played to packed houses at the Rose Theatre between March and June 1592. The young Shakespeare's triumphant debut on the London stage was not universally applauded. There must have been many who were jealous. In September 1592, a frustrated writer called Robert Greene wrote a pamphlet called *Greene's Groatsworth of Wit, Bought with a Million of Repentance*. This included a ranting, envy-fuelled attack on 'an upstart crow', a 'Shake-scene'. It must have been very galling indeed for Greene to see Shakespeare make an immediate hit with his very first play.

His first seven years in the theatre included several other successes too.

He completed two more history plays, *King John* and *Richard III*, a revenge tragedy, *Titus Andronicus*, and three comedies, *The Comedy of Errors*, *The Taming of the Shrew* and *The Two Gentlemen of Verona*. So, by 1592, William Shakespeare had attempted and succeeded to write in each of the three most popular forms of drama of his day. Not only that, he had extended their range, and made his own highly original contribution to each genre. The play-goers in London must have been very aware that a dazzling new talent was at work, eclipsing even Christopher Marlowe, then generally thought to be the best playwright in England.

For two years, starting in 1592, the London theatres were shut because of plague. While the theatres were shut, Shakespeare turned his hand to narrative poetry, writing the long narrative poems *Venus and Adonis* and *The Rape of Lucrece*. These poems, dedicated to the Earl of Southampton, were highly praised for their eloquent treatment of classical subjects. He wrote many sonnets too at this time when plays were banned, and these were in private circulation by 1598.

In 1594, when the theatres re-opened, Shakespeare joined the prestigious acting troupe called The Lord Chamberlain's Men, and soon became its joint manager. He was responsible for day-to-day business management and also for the artistic direction of the company, receiving a share of the profits. He also became part-owner of one of the two theatres where the company operated. The Lord Chamberlain's Men was an excellent choice of company. It was stocked with highly talented men. Richard Burbage was highly thought of as a tragic and heroic actor, as good as the great Edward Alleyn, who acted for the Admiral's Men. There was also Will Kempe, who was a very popular comic. The Lord Chamberlain's Men were also making a very clever choice in inviting Shakespeare in as a 'sharer'. Up to this point he had been freelance, and any company could perform his plays; now the Lord Chamberlain's Men had his exclusive services. Shakespeare had security; the company had his plays.

There followed a torrent of great plays: a tragedy (*Romeo and Juliet*), three more histories and five more comedies.

In addition to managing and writing, Shakespeare was a performer.

He regularly acted in his own plays, as well as those of other playwrights whose plays were in the company's repertory. While working in London, Shakespeare had lodgings in London and used most of his increasing income to secure the status and comfort of his family back in Stratford.

Shakespeare was sufficiently well-off in 1596 to meet his father's heavy expenses when John Shakespeare received his grant of arms. From this point on the elder Shakespeare was entitled to style himself 'Gentleman', a modest honour that would be inherited by his son in due course. The style and the arms that went with it meant a great deal in an age when fine social divisions made a great deal of difference, not just socially but in business. As if to reinforce this, Shakespeare bought New Place, an imposing mansion in Stratford. He spent a considerable amount of money having it improved before moving his family into it.

When James I came to the throne in 1603, Shakespeare's company became The King's Men, and this change in status brought great benefits to the company. His later plays included tragedies such as *Hamlet* and *Macbeth*, plays that rank among the darkest plays ever written. Shakespeare crafted his later plays so that they could be performed with equal success on very different stages. His plays were still performed in open-air theatres like The Globe, but now also indoors in the great halls of great houses, where artificial lighting and more elaborate stage effects were possible. Shakespeare was always an intensely practical man, well able to adjust to changing technical conditions – and changing fashion. Tragi-comedy was a form of drama now much in fashion, so Shakespeare supplied it. These 'last plays', as they are known, included *Pericles, Cymbeline, The Winter's Tale* and *The Tempest*.

Shakespeare was very prolific, writing 37 plays that have survived and several more that have not. *The Tempest* shows a thinly disguised Shakespeare taking his leave of the stage. He formally handed over the role of The King's Men's chief dramatist to John Fletcher and retired in 1612 to Stratford, where he died four years later.

The third period of his life, the return to Stratford, is difficult to explain. He evidently planned his withdrawal from the London theatre in a careful and business-like way. He was not giving up because his career was failing; quite the reverse, it was extremely successful. He was not giving up because he was old; he was still in his forties. Shakespeare's approach to his career was very business-like, and it may be that he simply wanted to enjoy the fruits of his labour. He had lived for years in lodgings in London and may well have wanted to reap the benefit of the improved lifestyle he had created for his family back in Stratford. Old John Shakespeare was now dead, and Shakespeare may have wanted to assume his position in Stratford as head of the family, and not only that but as a 'Gentleman'. Given that he did not live very many years after his return to Stratford, it may alternatively be that he was ill. Whatever the reason, he left London in 1612 to live full-time in Stratford again. He left a formal document stating that he was withdrawing from management of the company in the safe hands of his fellows, styling himself 'William Shakespeare of Stratford-on-Avon in the County of Warwick, gentleman of the age of 48 years.'

Shakespeare did a little writing in retirement. In 1613 he wrote *Henry VIII* in collaboration with John Fletcher. Shakespeare died on 23 April, 1616. In 1623, two of his friends in the King's Men, John Hemminge and Henry Condell, assembled all of Shakespeare's plays and published them in what is called the *First Folio*. It was not just a tribute to the greatest playwright of the age; it saved the plays from extinction. Without that publication, many of the surviving plays would have been lost.

Shakespeare was the outstanding playwright of the Renaissance, outshining all of his contemporaries and setting new standards for all subsequent dramatists. His plays range widely in subject and tone – challenging histories loaded with political agenda, atmospheric and romantic comedies and the darkest of tragedies. His work is astonishing for the richness and beauty of its language, showing the full potential of the English language for the expression of thought and feeling. It also shows great insight into a wide range of human predicaments. Shakespeare typifies the questioning humanism of the Renaissance, and he stands as an unmatchable role model for all later writers.

III

THE
ENLIGHTENED
WORLD

CARDINAL RICHELIEU

Born 1585, died 1642.
French statesman, virtual dictator.

ACHIEVEMENTS:
Developed an aggressive foreign policy for France.
Created a climate of fear and distrust throughout France.
Built the French army into one of the best in Europe.
Raised the status of France in Europe.
1628 – Organized the suppression of the Huguenots.
1631 – Bribed Sweden, Denmark and the Netherlands to fight the Hapsburgs.
1635 – Initiated a war between France and Spain.

ARMAND JEAN DU Plessis, duc de Richelieu was born in Paris in September 1585, into an ancient family of the lesser nobility of Poitou. Armand's father Francois, Seigneur de Richelieu, fought through the wars of religion, first as a favourite of Henry III and then under Henry IV. Armand's mother Susanne came from a family of a lawyers. Armand was the third son and, as was often the fate of younger sons, he was destined for the Church. At the age of only 21 he was nominated Bishop of Lucon by Henry IV. As he was so young, he went to Rome to receive a special dispensation and was consecrated bishop there in April 1607. Armand returned to his poor bishopric and devoted himself conscientiously to his episcopal duties there for six years. In 1614, he was elected by the clergy of Poitou to the last States-general to meet before the Revolution. It was there that he attracted the attention of Marie de' Medici, the Queen

Mother, and was chosen at its close to present a plenary statement on behalf of the clergy, embodying its petitions and resolutions.

After the assassination of Henry IV of France in 1610, there was a power vacuum. The dead king was succeeded by his nine-year-old son, Louis XIII. The young king's mother, Marie de' Medici, acted as regent. Four years later, Armand became the queen's adviser, during her exile at Blois. One of the duties involved in this complex role was to spy on the Queen Mother and report back to the young King on his mother's activities. The situation was made more complicated still, it was said at the time, by the Queen Mother's unrequited love for the young man. Armand's own patron, Concini, had been assassinated, so he was very vulnerable, and he did his best to ingratiate himself with the King. Two years later in 1616 he was promoted to secretary at war and for foreign affairs. It is hard to understand his meteoric rise, though he certainly had tremendous ability and cunning as a diplomat.

But Richelieu's tight-rope walk between the King and his mother brought no instant gratitude. He was of course a priest as well as a politician and he was able to retreat to his diocese (Lucon) for a while. He was even so exiled to Avignon with his brother and brother-in-law in 1618. But his august personality saved him. Even the King quailed before his stern, severe, ascetic face. He was thin-faced, sickly, wasted by disease, but still an awe-inspiring presence – and even more so after 1622, when he was created a cardinal, and could wear the red robes. He also tried his hand at writing drama.

When Louis XIII came of age in 1624 he appointed Richelieu as his minister of state. Richelieu was now a great churchman, at least in title and appearance, with his scarlet robes, but his true ambition was to make France greater than she was. He used his new position at the young king's right hand to set about destroying his rivals in France. He was a harsh ruler as far as his fellow countrymen were concerned. He also pursued a very aggressive foreign policy.

It was in 1628 that Cardinal Richelieu personally supervised the suppression of the Huguenots, the French Protestants who had for a long time been a thorn in the King's side, resisting his overlordship. Richelieu organized a military strike. He destroyed the Huguenot stronghold at La Rochelle after starving the occupants out in a siege that lasted a year. Richelieu went on to destroy the last Huguenot refuge at Montauban. After that, the Protestants in France were too weak to cause Richelieu any further trouble.

Richelieu appointed intendants, officers who toured France, supervising taxation, policing and law courts. The intendants were in effect spying for Richelieu, reporting back to him any subversive activity. Anybody who plotted against Richelieu was taking a terrible risk; ahead lay prison and possibly death.

In 1630, the two Queens, Louis XIII's wife Anne of Austria and his mother Marie de' Medici, made friends at last and made a pact that they would get rid of Richelieu. Together they might do it. They persuaded the King to promise to get rid of him. He agreed to do so when the war with Spain was over. When news of the truce of Regensburg came through, the King went to his mother's apartments at the Luxembourg to discuss the situation, ordering that nobody was to disturb them. Richelieu entered by way of the unguarded chapel door. Marie was flabbergasted at Richelieu's audacity in entering her chamber uninvited, then rebuked him in the strongest terms, declaring that the King must choose between them. Richelieu withdrew, certain that all was lost. Later though, the King sent for Richelieu and assured him of his support. The King hated Richelieu personally, hated him deeply, but knew also that he needed his abilities to run France. He could not throw him over, even though he detested him just as much as everyone else in France did.

When the Austrians had overrun Germany and threatened the whole of Europe in 1631, Richelieu paid Sweden, Denmark and the Netherlands to fight the Habsburgs. In 1635, Richelieu initiated a war with Spain, a war that dragged on after his death, which came in 1642. By that stage the French army had proved itself to be one of the best fighting forces in Europe. Richelieu certainly succeeded in setting France up as a great European power, but it was at a very great cost. By the end, when he was both a cardinal and a duke, Armand Jean Du Plessis, duc de Richelieu was deeply hated by the French, and by all levels in French society, for his harsh and tyrannical style of government. He was hated for being over-bearing, for being a dictator, for creating a universally oppressive climate of fear and distrust. The bad plays could just be ignored, and he did at least offer patronage to some better writers, such as Corneille. He was the most arrogant of courtiers, claiming precedence even over princes of the blood. He was proud, ambitious and behaved as if he were the king. Richelieu nevertheless did raise the status of France in Europe by pursuing an assertive foreign policy; he gave France self-respect. He also turned the French army into one of the best in Europe.

OLIVER CROMWELL

Born in Huntingdon 1599, died 1658.
Leader of the Parliamentarians in the English Civil War, Lord
* Protector.*

ACHIEVEMENTS:
Groomed the New Model Army.
Developed military tactics that won the English Civil War.
1644 – Won the Battle of Marston Moor for the
* Parliamentarians.*
1645 – Won the Battle of Naseby for the Parliamentarians.
1647 – Ordered the arrest of Charles I.
1648 – Took the leading role in bringing Charles I to trial.
1649 – Became a regicide, one of those responsible for Charles I's
* execution.*
1649 – Invaded and conquered Ireland.
1649 – Ordered the massacre at Drogheda.
1649 – Invaded and conquered Scotland.
1649 – Worked to make an English republic.
1653 – Became military dictator.
1657 – Refused the crown when offered it.
1657 – Became Lord Protector, a substitute king.

OLIVER CROMWELL WAS born in Huntingdon on 25 April 1599, the son of Robert Cromwell and Elizabeth Stewart. He was a gentleman farmer, but had to sell up to repay debts. He was a devout member of the Puritan sect and became a Member of Parliament for Huntingdon in 1628, using his position to defend Fenland people from wealthy landowners who wanted to drive them off.

When the Civil War broke out, Cromwell joined the Army. He was 43 and had no previous military experience whatever, yet he recruited a cavalry unit and acquired fighting experience in a series of East Anglian battles. Rising to become General in charge of cavalry in the New Model Army, he trained his men to regroup rapidly after an attack, a tactic he used to great effect at the Battle of Naseby. Following this great military success came political power, and he quickly became the leading British politician of his time.

The so-called Second Civil War broke out when Charles I escaped from prison in 1648. This behaviour of Charles convinced Cromwell that no negotiated peace, no compromise with the King would be possible. Cromwell became convinced that the King must die. Many still hold Cromwell responsible for the King's execution, and Cromwell was a regicide, but it must be remembered that there were 58 other signatures on Charles I's death warrant besides Cromwell's. Had the King been ready to accept the military defeat and simply abdicated, he might have been spared, but the King's persistent attempts to escape and arrange secret treaties with the Scots showed that he could not be trusted.

Cromwell's actions in Scotland and Ireland were far more questionable. Scotland and Ireland were nominally independent nations. What Cromwell did was, in effect, to invade and conquer them. One episode in particular is a blot on Cromwell's record. He suppressed the Royalists in Ireland in 1649 with undue force and undue violence. When he captured Drogheda, he massacred nearly 3,500 people, including 2,700 Royalist soldiers and all the men in the town who carried arms, including civilians, prisoners and Catholic priests. Cromwell justified the atrocity on the grounds that the city's defenders should have surrendered the moment the walls were breached; the defenders instead went on fighting after the battle was formally lost. It was a pointless atrocity that tarnished Cromwell's – and England's – name ever after. The Drogheda massacre is one of the bitter historical memories that has fuelled strife between Ireland and

England, and Catholics and Protestants, ever since. What Cromwell committed there was a war crime.

The Republic that Cromwell presided over from 1649 was a period of uneasy peace. Many of Cromwell's actions following the end of the war seem unwise or hypocritical. There were mutinies within his own army, which he put down with great savagery. He showed little sympathy for the Levellers, an egalitarian movement that had contributed significantly to the Parliamentary cause during the Civil War. He moreover dismissed the Rump Parliament in 1653 and took dictatorial powers to himself. He became in effect a military dictator.

In 1657 a reconvened Parliament offered Cromwell the crown. This gave him a terrible dilemma. He had abolished the monarchy himself. He had even had the previous monarch beheaded. Would he now become 'King Oliver'? He took six weeks to think about it. He was evidently tempted, not least because the republican structures that had been tried were unsatisfactory. In the end he turned it down because senior officers in his army made it known that they would resign if he accepted. Instead he went for near-monarchy, accepting the title Lord Protector, having himself installed as such in Westminster Abbey (of all places), and sitting on the King's throne. He was as good as king, and there was even a succession, with his son Richard Cromwell, 'Tumbledown Dick', to follow.

Cromwell died on 3 September 1658, possibly of malaria, possibly of poison. Within two years the British establishment saw to it that the monarchy was restored, and Charles I's son Charles II was on the throne. In 1661, Cromwell's body was exhumed for a very odd ceremony indeed, a posthumous execution. On 31 January 1661, Cromwell's body was hanged, drawn and quartered. The body was then thrown into a pit and the head displayed on a pike outside Westminster Abbey until 1685. The head changed hands, in a box, a number of times until it was finally buried in the grounds of Sidney Sussex College, Cambridge in 1690.

Cromwell did much good, in stoutly opposing a very bad king, but when he achieved power himself he abused it. Opinions about Cromwell are naturally divided. Some thought him a madman, a fanatic. He had 'a temper exceeding fiery,' and was 'a brave bad man'. But even hostile royalists could see 'a great spirit, an admirable circumspection and sagacity, and a most magnanimous resolution'. He was a man of incredible ability. He was nowhere at the age of 43, a man with no military experience whatever; within two years he was second in command of an army. His command of men on the battlefield was outstanding, and there is no doubt that he was the most important individual behind the Parliamentarian victory in the Civil War. He was also the driving force behind the arrest, trial and execution of the king.

BLAISE PASCAL

Born at Clermont-Ferrand 1623, died 1662.
Child prodigy, religious philosopher, mathematician.

ACHIEVEMENTS:
Worked out for himself 23 propositions of Euclid, by the age of
 11.
Produced original work on geometry.
Discovered that atmospheric pressure decreases with altitude.
Discovered the principles that led to the barometer and the
 syringe.
Developed the concept of probability.
Invented a calculating machine.
1640 – Essai pour les coniques.
1657 – Lettres provinciales.
1662 – Pensees.

BLAISE PASCAL WAS born at Clermont-Ferrand in the Auvergne in 1623.
He was the son of Etienne Pascal, a local official (president of the Court
of Aids at Clermont). Pascal's mother, Antoinette, died when he was only
four years old, and the family moved to Paris in 1630, where the father
undertook the education of Blaise and his two sisters himself. Etienne
Pascal was a considerable mathematician, but had a very cautious approach,
refusing to broach a subject unless he was sure Blaise was ready to master
it. The boy responded to this unfashionably laid-back approach to
education in a remarkable way. Young Blaise had a very active mind and
was left to work out a lot on his own; his father had a great surprise when,
at the age of 11, the child prodigy revealed that he had worked out for

himself the first 23 propositions of Euclid. He referred to straight lines as 'bars' and circles as 'rounds', discovering their properties yet without knowing their proper names. It was a total vindication of Etienne Pascal's enlightened and liberal approach to education, which anticipated the ideas of Rousseau by many decades.

Etienne Pascal incurred the displeasure of Richelieu when he protested about the reduction in the interest rate on some bonds, and had to go into hiding to avoid being thrown into the Bastille. It is said that he was restored to favour by a performance before the cardinal given by one of his daughters. Etienne Pascal was in any case later appointed to an important post at Rouen, which he held for nine years.

At the age of 16, Pascal published an essay on conics, which so advanced that Descartes refused to believe had been written by a boy of only 16.

Pascal and his father collaborated in experiments to prove Toricelli's theory that nature does not abhor a vacuum. The experiments involved carrying two glass tubes containing mercury inverted in a vessel of mercury – carried up a mountain; the Pascals noted the fall in the mercury columns as altitude increased and atmospheric pressure decreased. This discovery led to the invention of the barometer, the hydraulic press and the syringe. The idea of mathematical probability evolved out of a correspondence between Blaise Pascal and Pierre de Fermat about the division of stakes in games of chance.

The year 1646 was a turning-point in Pascal's life. His father had an accident and was confined to the house. The family was also suddenly fired by Jansenism. The Pascal family had not been unduly religious, but the arrival of visitors who were convinced Jansenists amounted to a conversion experience for them. Blaise continued with his mathematics for the time being though.

In 1647, Pascal patented a calculating machine, which he had built to help his father with his accounts. In 1651, Pascal's father died and his sister entered a convent. From then on, Pascal divided his time between mathematics and his roistering social life in Paris, especially in the company of his friend the Duc de Roannez. Pascal's correspondence with Fermat in 1654 laid the foundations of probability theory.

Then an event occurred that changed the direction of his life. In the night of 22–23 November 1654, at the age of 32, Pascal had the first of two religious revelations. It was in effect a full religious conversion. He joined his sister in her retreat, gave up both mathematics and his social life and took up the Jansenist cause, in particular trying to save Antoine Arnauld, who had been denounced as a heretic. In a series of 18 anonymous pamphlets (*Lettres Provinciales*), Pascal attacked the Jesuits for their moral slackness, false arguments and meaningless jargon. The masterly style of Pascal's pamphlets did not save Arnauld, but they greatly influenced Voltaire. The composition was a landmark in French literature, a substantial and serious piece of work, diverse in its scope, and beautifully written.

Pascal's last years were dominated by his austere Christian beliefs and practices. He became an extreme ascetic, hating to see children 'spoilt' by patting or fondling, hating to hear the beauty of any woman being praised. At the time of Pascal's death in 1662, which seems to have been the result of a brain tumour, he was preparing a book of Christian truths, its style deriving from Montaigne. These were published after his death as Pensees.

Pascal was a notable child prodigy, who went on to make major breakthroughs in mathematics. His work led the way towards differential calculus. The idea of mathematical probability came from his corres-pondence with Fermat; probability led on to a range of modern actuarial concepts such as life expectancy and assessment of risks. Pascal also made original contributions to natural philosophy. His work on the equilibrium of fluids ranks with that of Galileo on hydrodynamics. He was a great original genius, creating new ideas, as well as seizing on and pursuing a range of existing ideas into fresh and unfamiliar areas. His work can also now be seen as a major stepping stone to future developments.

SIR ISAAC NEWTON

Born at Woolsthorpe in 1642, died 1727.
Scientist and mathematician.

ACHIEVEMENTS:
The greatest scientist of all time.
Invented a steam engine.
Discovered gravitation.
Discovered the mechanics of the solar system.
1665 – Invented calculus.
1666 – Measured the moon's orbit.
1668 – Invented the reflecting telescope.
1672 – Discovered that white light is made up of all the colours of the rainbow.
1684 – On the Motion of Bodies.
1687 – Principia Mathematica.

ISAAC NEWTON WAS born at Woolsthorpe, in Lincolnshire, in December 1642. His father had died two months earlier. His mother, Hannah Ayscough, remarried, but the stepfather, Revd Barnabas Smith, also died and she then returned to her parents' home, taking Isaac with her. He was educated at Grantham Grammar School, where he made little progress until he won a fight with another boy and it occurred to him that he could 'beat' other boys academically as well as physically. After that he became head boy. At the age of 14 he was removed from school to help his mother on her farm, but this was a failure as he was preoccupied with mathematical problems. Isaac's uncle was a member of Trinity College, Cambridge, and at his advice Isaac was sent back to school to prepare him for Cambridge. He went up to Cambridge in 1661.

Isaac Newton was an experimenter as well as a mathematician. He built a small steam engine on wheels – just to prove a law of motion.

In 1665 he wrote up his first discovery concerning what he called 'fluxions', which was a form of calculus. In 1666, when he withdrew to Lincolnshire on account of the plague outbreak in London, he made his first steps in understanding gravitation when, in his garden, he watched an apple fall from a tree. Newton 'began to think of gravity extending to the orb of the moon,' though he did not publish anything about it for 18 years.

He turned to the study of light and the construction of telescopes. After a range of experiments on sunlight refracted through a prism, he concluded that rays of light of different colour are refracted by different amounts. This discovery suggested to him that the indistinct, fuzzy, coloured-edged images seen through Galilean telescopes might be due to the different coloured rays of light having different focal lengths. This led on to the abandonment of the refracting telescope of Galileo and the invention of a new type of reflecting telescope. This was used to great effect by William Herschel and the Earl of Rosse. Newton's account of his work on light (not all of which was correct) was sent to the Royal Society in 1672. Robert Hooke had carried out similar experiments but come to no particular conclusion. Hooke refused to accept Newton's conclusions, and so began what was to become a long-standing scholarly rivalry between the two men.

Newton became a Fellow of Trinity College, Cambridge in 1667, and two years later he became Lucasian Professor of Mathematics at Cambridge, when Barrow generously resigned so that he could have the post.

In discussions at the Royal Society, Robert Hooke boasted to Edmond Halley and Christopher Wren that he had discovered all the laws of celestial motion. Halley admitted that he had not and Wren, in his own words 'to encourage enquiry', said he would give a prize of a book to the value of 40 shillings (£2) to the one who found the solution. Wren was unconvinced by Hooke's boast, but hoped that he might flush him out with the prospect of a prize, and make him publish it so that others better equipped than himself could evaluate it. Halley afterwards visited Newton at Cambridge and discussed the matter with him. Newton generously gave him a mathematical formula to explain the movements of heavenly bodies, and Halley knew, as he wrote in a letter to Newton later, that he 'had brought the demonstration to perfection.' Halley excitedly reported back to fellow members of the Royal Society that Newton had shown him the draft of an important paper entitled *De Motu Corporum (On the Motion of Bodies)*. It was in 1684, in *De Motu Corporum,* that he gave his first account of his theory of gravitation, and he expounded it more fully in his great work, *Philosophiae Naturalis Principia Mathematica,* in 1687.

This masterpiece was financed by Edmond Halley, which was a truly heroic gesture. In *De Motu Corporum,* he had treated the planets and the sun as points in his equations, but by 1685 he had realised that it was inappropriate to treat the sun, which is huge, in the same way as the planets, which are small. He then came up with the crucial idea that the gravitational pull of a heavenly body must be proportional to its mass. This was immediately refined to allow for distance, because objects a long way away cannot have the same gravitational pull as those close by. He then arrived at one of the most momentous discoveries – that bodies attract one another with a force that is proportional to the product of the masses of the two and inversely proportional to the square of the distance between them. Like many great ideas, Newton's law of gravitation seems very obvious, even self-evident, once it is said. However, until Newton no-one had even thought it, let alone said it. This was one of those moments which utterly change the world; after the first expression of Newton's law of gravitation, science and our general everyday perception of the universe were different.

In 1703, his ideas on light were published as Opticks.

Jean Bernoulli set two problems for the mathematicians of Europe in 1696, allowing six months for their solution; Newton received copies of the problems from France on 29 January 1697, and sent the solution back the next day. When Bernoulli received the solution, which had no name on it, he knew at once that it could only be from Newton! In 1716 Newton performed a similar feat in answer to a challenge from Gottfried Leibniz.

Newton supervised the publication of Flamsteed's *Greenwich Obser-vations*, which he needed in order to build his own lunar theory. This was only done after a major dispute with Flamsteed, who was not ready to publish, but Newton virtually hi-jacked the process. There was a major altercation between Newton and Leibniz over which of them discovered differential calculus; it seems it was probably a case of almost simultaneous independent discovery, which happens more often than one would expect – a case of 'improbability'. Mathematicians agree that Leibniz was the better mathematician in this instance, giving a more complete method, though he did invent the calculus after Newton. The conflict with Hooke, Flamsteed and Leibniz is typical of Newton's career as an academic. He was an extremely difficult, aggressive, confrontational man, a man at constant high tension, a man determined to beat his colleagues. In some ways Newton was a symbol of the Age of Reason, yet because he was prepared to challenge and investigate everything from scratch he repeatedly pushed his own mind to the limit – and sometimes beyond. At one stage he suffered a serious mental breakdown. He was the madman at the centre of the Age of Reason.

Even so, the difficult and reclusive man was an international celebrity, the great mind of his age. He was man with many admirers and few friends. When William III, another unpopular man, became king of England in 1689, his first request was to lunch with Isaac Newton the next day.

In 1703 he became President of the Royal Society. Newton died in 1727.

Alongside his great scientific work, Newton was also spending a considerable amount of time in esoteric studies that now seem futile – investigating the prophecies contained in the Book of Daniel and the pursuit of alchemy. In his epic work, the *Principia Mathematica, he* explained how the universe worked – an amazing achievement. Newton laid down a comprehensive scheme for the mechanics of the solar system that would be used for two hundred years and more, though it was to be added to in the twentieth century by Einstein. Newton's model for the solar system, with the principle of gravitation at its heart, was to be of great benefit to all subsequent astronomers and physicists – and to astronauts too.

GOTTFRIED LEIBNIZ

Born in Leipzig 1646, died in Hanover 1716.
German philosopher and mathematician.

ACHIEVEMENTS:
His philosophy was the bedrock of 18th century rationalism.
Developed a theory of substance based on monads (sub-atomic
   particles?)
The original for Voltaire's Dr Pangloss.
1671 – Invented an advanced calculating machine.
1674 – Discovered differential and integral calculus.
1686 – Theological System.
1710 – Essays on the Goodness of God.

GOTTFRIED WILHELM LEIBNIZ was born on 1 July, 1646 in Leipzig. His father was the Professor of Moral Philosophy at Leipzig University. The young Gottfried was sent to the Nicolai School in Leipzig, but after his father died in 1652, when the boy was only 6, Gottfried seems to have organized his own education. He proved to be something of a prodigy, as his learning was far beyond his years – and his schooling. He got hold of two books in Latin and taught himself Latin at the age of eight. He was overjoyed when he was finally given access to his father's library. By the age of 12, he was starting to learn Greek, write Latin verse, and turn to the study of logic.

When he was 15 he entered the University of Leipzig as a law student. For his first two years he was taught philosophy by Jakob Thomasius, a Neo-Aristotelian philosopher who founded the rigorous study of the history of philosophy in Germany. It was probably at this time that Leibniz first encountered the ideas of contemporary thinkers, philosophers and scientists such as Bacon, Cardan, Galileo and Kepler.

Leibniz devoted himself to legal studies at Leipzig and in 1666 he submitted for the degree of Doctor of Law. He was turned down on the grounds that he was too young. His response was to leave Leipzig for ever. The doctorate he was refused at Leipzig was immediately forthcoming at Altdorf, the university town of Nuremberg, where he was also offered a professorship on the strength of his brilliant dissertation. It was an extraordinary offer made under extraordinary circumstances. Even more extraordinarily, the 20-year-old Leibniz declined the flattering offer. He said he had 'very different things in view'.

In 1667, he gained a position at the court of the Elector of Mainz on the strength of an essay on legal education. At the Elector's court he codified laws, drafted schemes for the unification of the Catholic and Protestant churches, and his position required him to be a courtier and international lawyer as well as a civil servant. The post was an important one, as the Elector's job was to maintain the security of the German empire, which was under threat from France, Russia and Turkey. While performing all these tasks, Leibniz absorbed the philosophy, mathematics and science of his time, reading the work of Pascal, Descartes and Robert Boyle.

In 1672, Leibniz was sent to Paris on a diplomatic mission, at the request of the French Secretary of State, Simon Arnauld de Pomponne. Leibniz had sent a memorandum to King Louis suggesting that Holland might best be attacked indirectly via Egypt, which was a vital link in the Dutch trading operation; it would also have been very easy for France to take Egypt. While in Paris, Leibniz was able to meet Huygens and Malebranche, but he was refused an interview with the French king. It seems Pomponne was nervous about launching what might well look like a medieval crusade in the east. Undeterred, Leibniz wrote a full account of his plan for the king, but it seems the letter was intercepted and never reached him. The idea of an expedition was shelved – until Napoleon revived it. The plan for invading Egypt was stored in French archives, though uncredited. It was not until 1803, when Napoleon took Hanover, and the Consilium Aegyptiacum written by Leibniz was discovered, that Napoleon realised that his plan for a French annexation of Egypt had actually come from Leibniz.

But Leibniz had other reasons for visiting Paris anyway. The city was a great centre of science and literature, and in the midst of his political activity he never lost sight of his philosophical and scientific interests.

Four years later he travelled on to London, where he had discussions with members of Newton's circle of mathematician friends. This led later to a rather juvenile squabble about whether it was Leibniz or Newton who had invented infinitesimal calculus. Leibniz published his work in 1684, Newton in 1687, though Newton could relate his findings to earlier work. In 1711, the Royal Society formally decided that Newton had been first, but the controversy continued. It was during his second visit to Paris in 1673 that Leibniz devoted himself seriously to geometry under Huygens; these studies led him almost at once to his discovery of the differential and integral calculus.

In 1676 Leibniz visited the Hague, where he met and had many discussions with Spinoza. Spinoza gave him his unpublished Ethics to read, and Leibniz copied various passages from it. He was on his way to take up his last post in Hanover, as librarian to Duke John Frederick of Brunswick, with whom he had been corresponding for some time. In Hanover, where he remained for the next 40 years, working under three successive princes, Leibniz continued elaborating his philosophical and mathematical theories without publishing, but kept up a huge correspondence with scholars all over Europe. In 1687–90, he travelled extensively in Germany, Austria and Italy, researching a book the Elector had commissioned him to write on the history of the House of Brunswick.

In 1700 he went to Frederick I of Prussia to persuade him to set up a Prussian Academy of Sciences in Berlin. This Frederick did, and Leibniz became its first president.

Leibniz was not popular with George of Hanover and, when the Elector moved his court to London to become the King of England as George I,

Leibniz was simply left behind like an old hat. His final years were profoundly unsatisfactory. He was ill, harassed by controversy, embittered at the way he had been treated. He felt the snubs and the pointed neglect very keenly, and knew that the world had turned its back on him. He nevertheless went on working with the same incredible energy and persistence that characterized his entire life. Leibniz died in Hanover two years later, on 14 November 1716. No notice was taken of his death in Berlin, where he had founded the Academy; no notice was taken in London, where his prince had gone to be king. He was, in end, a kind of pariah. At his funeral in Hanover, his secretary Eckhart was his only mourner. An Englishman who witnessed the funeral, John Ker, commented, 'he was buried more like a robber than what he really was, the ornament of his country.' It was only in the French Academy that some appreciation was offered, and an appropriate eulogy made.

The philosophy of Leibniz centres on his original theory of substance. His position is closest to that of Descartes, and Leibniz was fond of saying that Descartes was the anteroom of truth, but only the ante-room. Everything is made of monads, simple, self-active beings or centres of force that are the constituent elements of all things. They are held together in harmony by the omnipotence of God. It is not clear why he emphasized that monads are individual and self-active, when it would be more consistent with his theological position to say that they are manifestations of a single universal force. Leibniz was aware from his observations that individuality is fundamental to the nature of things. He saw the monads as metaphysical points or spiritual beings whose very nature is to act. In each monad, the past determines its present state, but is unchanged by neighbouring monads. They are all, nevertheless, in a perfect pre-established harmony, in the best of all possible worlds. The monads have existences and histories independent of one another, it follows that energy can be neither created nor destroyed.

Space and time are mere relatives. Space is an order of co-existences. Time is an order of successions. The rather strange universe envisaged by Leibniz in some ways looks forward to the world that physics entered in the second half of the twentieth century: he seems to have seen beyond atoms to particle physics.

His major difficulties arose from the theological side. If this is the best of all possible worlds, how does evil exist within it? He distinguished between metaphysical evil, willed by God as essential to all created beings, physical evil, like pain, willed by God as punishment to certain beings and moral evil, which he cannot explain. Leibniz fell back on the suggestion that maybe God saw a world with evil as better than a world without it. The great central problem was thus unsolved.

Leibniz had a strange career. He had remarkable, encyclopaedic knowledge, was a great philosopher and mathematician, and has been described as a universal genius. But his knowledge and his achievement were unquestionably the result of intense and sustained hard work; he had incredible intellectual stamina and tenacity, and worked continuously. He made original contributions in a great many different branches of science; optics, statistics, mechanics, logic, probability theory. In 1671, he invented a more advanced calculating machine than Pascal's, one that was able to multiply, divide and calculate square roots, as well as adding and subtracting; it was built and displayed at the Academy of Paris and the Royal Society in London. He had the idea of devising a universal language. He wrote on history, law and political theory.

His philosophy was the bedrock of 18th-century rationalism. He had a great effect on other scholars, because he made a point of meeting many of them, discussing issues with them, corresponding with them; he was an intellectual dynamo, energizing a whole generation of European thinkers. They in their turn respected his work and honoured him for it. He was made a Fellow of the Royal Society in 1673 and a foreign member of the French Academy in 1700. His popular work on theology, *Essays on the Goodness of God* (1710), expressed optimism and a faith in enlightenment and reason, which Voltaire satirized brilliantly in Candide: 'all is for the best in this best of all possible worlds.' Leibniz thus finds his way into literature as Doctor Pangloss. His work on mathematics and logic looked forward to that of Bertrand Russell. He has not been recognized for what he was mainly because he wrote so little down; he was Socrates without Plato. In fact, Essays on the Goodness of God is the only extended published piece of work he produced, the only complete philosophical work. The rest is contained in a mass of letters, notes and memoranda, which stand as a solemn warning to other scholars who fail to get round to publishing.

THOMAS SAVERY

Born about 1650, died 1715.
Inventor and military engineer.

ACHIEVEMENTS:
Invented the paddle-wheel.
Invented the steam pump.
Made deep coal-mining possible.
Initiated the Industrial Revolution in England.

THE TWO DRIVING forces behind the Industrial Revolution were steam power and the depletion of the English forests. The woodlands had been over-exploited for timber (for building houses and ships) and fuel (both domestic and industrial). The expansion of England's mercantile ambitions, and the creation of a British Empire meant an increased demand for ships, and ever-greater demands on the forests that supplied the timber to build them. Iron needed to be smelted and charcoal (roasted wood) was needed for smelting. Increasing use was made of coal, which was at first thought to be an inferior fuel. In the early days coal was dug out at the surface, but as demand intensified, the miners had to dig deeper. Then a problem was encountered – the water table. Not far below the surface, mines started to fill up with water, a problem that had been encountered for hundreds of years. The water table, in effect, forced the miners to stop mining at a certain depth.

What was needed was an effective pump to keep the mines dry. This was where Thomas Savery, who was born in about 1650, came in.

In 1696 he patented his invention for rowing vessels by means of paddle-wheels. In 1698 he patented the first practical high-pressure steam engine for pumping water out of mines. Though it was superseded in 1712 by an improved version which Savery designed in collaboration with Thomas Newcomen, it was Savery's 1698 steam pump that marked the very beginning of the Industrial Revolution.

With effective water pumps, coal mines could be driven deeper underground, opening up vast reserves of coal and other minerals. Once the steel-making process was revolutionized so that it depended on coke (roasted coal), not charcoal, the demand for coal increased, year after year, not only in Britain but in other European countries too. British coal production went on increasing, using ever-deeper mines, until it peaked just before the First World War. It was Thomas Savery's steam pump that made this phenomenal industrial growth possible.

PETER THE GREAT

Born 1672, died 1725.
Tsar and modernizer of Russia.

ACHIEVEMENTS:
Took a Grand Tour of Europe in 1697 (= commercial
  espionage).
Forced Russia into line with developments in western Europe.
Achieved a cultural revolution in Russia.
Turned Russia into a major European power for the first time.

PETER THE GREAT, Tsar of Russia from 1682, was the fourth son of Tsar Alexei I Mikhailovitch, by his second wife, Natalia Naruishkina. He was born on 30 May 1672. He was made co-tsar jointly with his half-brother Ivan V, when their elder brother Fedor III died; the boys ruled under the regency of their sister, the Grand Duchess Sophia. His election as tsar seems to have been a signal for general rebellion. He saw one of his uncles dragged from the palace and butchered by a savage mob. He saw Artamon Matvyeev, his mother's mentor and his own best friend, pulled away and cut to pieces. These awful childhood experiences made Peter a twitchy and anxious boy, and it is thought that the convulsions he experienced in later years had their roots in these early traumas.

During the regency of his sister, Peter was free to indulge himself. His new friend, a Swiss adventurer called Francois Lefort, introduced Peter to all the delights of a dissolute lifestyle in a special house, which was built at Peter's own expense. Peter's mother was understandably alarmed at her son's antics, and hastily arranged his marriage to the beautiful but stupid

Eudoxia Lopukhina, the pious daughter of a nobleman, when he 'came of age' in 1689. The marriage was a disaster, and Peter virtually abandoned Eudoxia only a year later. He also had his sister, the Grand Duchess, arrested and immured in a convent, where she died in 1704, so that he could rule on his own with his feeble-minded brother as a figurehead. In 1690, Eudoxia had a son, the Tsarevich Alexis.

Peter's strength and failing lay in his boundless energy and curiosity. This gave him a great capacity for work, but also an appetite for roistering. He had a coarse contempt for religious ceremony and political formality, and therefore made an unusual king.

In 1695, after six years of preparation, Peter moved his army against the Turks. Peter characteristically served in this army as a humble bombardier. The following year, he captured the crucial Black Sea port of Azov.

In 1697, Peter the Great set off incognito on a Grand Tour. The official purpose of this 'Grand Embassy' of Europe was to win allies for Russia against the Turks. Peter spent a year and a half touring Holland, Germany, England and Austria, even working as a shipwright in shipyards in Holland and at Deptford on the Thames. Peter's private mission, his personal agenda, was to gather a comprehensive knowledge of western technology so that he could modernize Russia. He hired thousands of specialist craftsmen and military personnel to return to Russia with him to instruct the Russian people in western methods. The 'Grand Embassy' was thinly disguised commercial espionage.

Peter had to return to Russia in a hurry in 1698 to deal with a rebellion of the musketeer regiments (streltsy). This he suppressed with great savagery with the help of a Scottish general, Patrick Gordon. The Tsarina Eudoxia was accused of conspiracy, divorced and sent to a convent. He then started introducing many western customs, by force, and caused a great deal of unnecessary offence by doing so. He ordered all beards to be shaved off at court. He insisted that 'German' dress must be worn. Houses were to be built in western style. Peter's son Alexis was put in the charge of a German tutor.

In 1700, he launched the Great Northern War against Sweden, but Karl XII of Sweden marched his troops on a pre-emptive strike, routing the Russian army at Narva in Estonia. Peter ordered the church bells of Moscow to be melted down to make extra cannons. He refused to allow a new patriarch to be elected, enabling him to take all ecclesiastical revenues for the war effort. In 1703, Peter founded the new city and port of St Petersburg, which became the new capital of the empire.

Possibly appalled at his father's example, the Tsarevich Alexis decided that he never wanted to become Tsar. Peter was dangerously angry with his son and heir. In 1718, when the Tsarevich renounced the succession, Peter had him imprisoned and tortured to death. Alexis himself had a son, the Grand Duke Peter, but the Tsar did not want him to succeed. Peter's next step was to denounce primogeniture in the male line as the normal title to succession to the throne. With the 1722 ordinance (an Act of Succession) Peter assumed the right to choose his own successor, and the following year he took the precaution of issuing a second manifesto in November 1723 to explain at length why he was nominating his new wife Catherine as his heir. It was extremely unpopular, a scandalous innovation, and doubly so because of his new wife Catherine's low birth, but on Peter's death she succeeded him without any opposition. She was crowned empress in May 1724.

Peter the Great had more convulsions and died in agony on 28 January 1725.

Peter the Great achieved an extraordinary modernizing and westernizing cultural revolution in Russia, forcing it, with undue harshness, into line with developments in western Europe and making it a major European power. The war with Sweden was unnecessary, except in that dictators seem frequently to need foreign adventures to rally support at home.

ABRAHAM DARBY

Born about 1678, died 1717.

ACHIEVEMENTS:
A key figure in the Industrial Revolution.
1708 – Founded the Bristol Iron Company.
1709 – Became the first man to use coke to smelt iron.

ABRAHAM DARBY WAS born near Dudley in Worcestershire. In 1708 he founded the Bristol Iron Company. In 1709 he became the first man to use coke successfully in the smelting of iron.

With the depletion of English forests, charcoal had become scarcer and scarcer. A new fuel was needed. Coal was tried but almost always had too many impurities such as sulphur in it to be used for smelting. A decontaminated version of coal was what was needed. Roasting coal without actually igniting it drove off many of the impurities; coke quickly caught on as the principal fuel for iron smelting.

Abraham Darby's new iron-smelting process marked an important step in the Industrial Revolution, freeing industrial production from the depleted forests, and enabling industry to enlarge in scale. The Darby factory at Coalbrookdale manufactured large numbers of cast-iron cylinders for Newcomen's steam engines, and also, later on, the first high-pressure steam boiler for Richard Trevithick. Darby knew a good commercial secret when he saw one, and kept his process to himself and his workforce, but it inevitably got out. By the 1780s, Henry Cort was producing coke-smelted iron on a modern industrial scale, based on Darby's process.

Abraham Darby, contribution to the Industrial Revolution was not recognized in his lifetime. Indeed, when he died in 1717 he was buried like a labourer, in an unmarked grave.

VOLTAIRE

Born 1694, died 1778.
French author.

ACHIEVEMENTS:
Saw the Lisbon earthquake as evidence that there was no
  presiding God looking after human welfare.
Embodied the 18th century Enlightenment.
Satirized aristocrats, kings and philosophers.
Rebelled against religious intolerance and injustice.
Championed and gave refuge to persecuted Protestants.
1718 – Oedipus.
1723 – The League or Henry the Great.
1738 – Elements of the Philosophy of Newton.
1751 – The Age of Louis XIV.
1759 – Candide.

FRANCOIS MARIE AROUET was born in Paris, the son of a civil servant, Francois Arouet. Voltaire was educated at the principal Jesuit college in France, which he left at the age of 17. He was intended to enter a career as a lawyer, but the idea repelled him. His father became concerned at the dissipated life he was leading, and let him enter the service of the French ambassador to Holland. Unfortunately the young man misbehaved there too, conducting an undiplomatic affair with a French Protestant in The Hague, so he was sent back home again.

His return to the lawyer's office was short-lived. He wrote a notorious satire on a rival who won the poetry competition for an Academy prize. In 1716 he was suspected of satirizing the regent, the Duc d'Orleans, and he was banished from Paris for several months. The next year he wrote a savage attack on the regent accusing him of a range of crimes, and this resulted in his imprisonment in the Bastille for a year.

In the Bastille, he rewrote his tragedy *Oedipus* and assumed the pen name 'Voltaire'. The play was performed in 1718 and it was a triumph. Voltaire's next dramas were less successful. He devoted himself to a poem about Henri IV. Because it championed Protestantism and religious toleration, the authorities refused to allow its publication. Voltaire was not that easily defeated though; he had the poem printed in Rouen and smuggled into Paris.

By now Voltaire was a well-known and popular figure at court. He was denounced by the Chevalier de Rohan-Chabot as an upstart. Voltaire inevitably responded by circulating scathing epigrams about the Chevalier, who had Voltaire beaten up. Voltaire challenged the Chevalier and was again imprisoned. He was freed only if he agreed to leave France. He left for England in 1726.

In England, Voltaire met a lot of interesting people including Alexander Pope, the Duchess of Marlborough and John Gay. He also soaked up a lot of English literature: Shakespeare, Milton, Dryden, and the Restoration dramatists. He became interested in the philosophy of Locke and the science of Newton.

Allowed back into France in 1729, Voltaire behaved with more circum-spection, trying not to offend courtiers and wisely investing in the government lottery, which led to his increasing wealth. The patronage of Madame de Pompadour procured him the post of official royal historian. A piece of ill-placed flattery by Pompadour made the queen jealous and Voltaire once again had to leave France. This time he travelled to the court of Frederick the Great. By 1750, he was in Berlin as the king's chamberlain on a huge salary. However, once again Voltaire caused offence by writing satirical criticisms and was ejected. He was stopped at Frankfurt by a representative of Frederick the Great, who demanded the return of a book. Voltaire characteristically retaliated by writing a malicious character sketch of Frederick, which was not published until Voltaire's death.

In 1756–59, his pessimistic poem about the Lisbon earthquake appeared, *Customs and the Spirit of Nations*. The Lisbon earthquake was a great natural disaster in which earthquake, fire and tsunami followed one another in remorseless succession. It was a demonstration that there was no presiding God looking after human welfare; the human race was after all alone in the universe. It was in a sense the dawn of humanism, and certainly a landmark in the Enlightenment. He then wrote his masterpiece, *Candide*, a satirical short story ridiculing the philosophy of Leibniz.

Then, naturally, the first of Voltaire's anti-religious writings appeared. In 1762 the Protestant Jean Calas was falsely accused of killing his son to stop him from converting to Catholicism. The judicial murder of Jean Calas roused Voltaire to establish the man's innocence, and he made great efforts to rescue the surviving members of the Calas family from further persecution. This and similar efforts made on behalf of victims of French religious fanaticism won widespread admiration. He even set up a refuge for persecuted Protestants.

Voltaire was a friend of Rousseau – until Rousseau decided to throw his support behind the Swiss government. In 1778, when he was 83, Voltaire was given a 'royal' welcome in Paris when he arrived to mount a production of his last tragedy, *Irene*. The excitement of this reception was too much for him, and he fell ill and died. After the Revolution, Voltaire's body was buried in the Pantheon, recognized as one the great figures of European culture.

MIKHAIL LOMONOSOV

Born at Denisovka 1711, died 1765.
Influential Russian scientist and man of letters.

ACHIEVEMENTS:
Reformed and rationalized the Russian language.
Wrote great poetry.
Set up the first chemistry laboratory in Russia.
Founded the University of Moscow.

MIKHAIL VASILIEVICH LOMONOSOV was born in the village of Denisovka, on an island near Arkhangel. Denisovka later changed its name in honour of the poet, which is a rare tribute, giving an idea of Lomonosov's unusually central importance in the development of Russian culture. He was the son of a fisherman and he was forced to follow his father into the trade when he was 10. The boy had a passion for learning, though, and when he was 17 he ran away from Denisovka to Moscow in search of education. Later he studied at St Petersburg, where he was chosen as one of an elite group of young Russians who were sent to complete their education abroad. Lomonosov was sent to Marburg in Germany, where he studied metallurgy and was taught by the philosopher Christian de Wolff. He was also writing poetry on the side, mainly in imitation of German authors.

Lomonosov turned towards science, eventually, in 1745, becoming Professor of Chemistry at St Petersburg Academy of Sciences. He set up the first chemistry laboratory in Russia at the academy. Just ten years later, he founded Moscow University. He became rector of St Petersburg Academy, and secretary of state in 1764. He died in 1765.

Mikhail Lomonosov wrote many works on scientific issues and was toweringly influential in Russian science. At the same time, he had a wide-ranging intellect, writing poetry, works on rhetoric, grammar and Russian history. Probably his greatest single contribution to Russian culture was the system he imposed on Russian grammar and spelling, which was a great stimulus to Russian literature as well as science. He in effect reformed the Russian language, helping to make it a more effective literary medium. While pursuing his reforms, he followed a middle path between the vernacular Russian spoken by ordinary people and the complicated Slavonic language that was used for Church services. Lomonosov rationalized and fixed the Russian language. He also wrote magnificent poetry, which had a lasting effect on later Russian poets. Lomonov's influence outside Russia was minimal, and many outside Russia have not even heard of him, but he is a giant in Russian cultural history.

JEAN JACQUES ROUSSEAU

Born in Geneva 1712, died in Ermenonville 1778.
French philosopher, educationist and writer.

ACHIEVEMENTS:
Proposed a new social order in which individuals surrender
 their rights to the collective 'general will'.
Provided the philosophical basis for the French Revolution.
Attacked the private ownership of property.
Wrote, 'Man is born free; and everywhere he is in chains.'
Coined the revolutionary slogan, 'Liberty, Equality,
 Fraternity'.
Inspired the leaders of the French Revolution.
Proposed a new, more liberal, child-centred style of education.
1745 – Les Muses Galantes *operetta performed.*
1750 – Discours sur les arts et sciences *published.*
1752 – Le Devin du village *operetta performed.*
1758 – Lettre a d'Alembert sur les spectacles *published.*
1762 – Du Contrat Social *and* Emile *published.*
1770-78 – Confessions *written.*
1770-78 – Rousseau, juge de Jean Jacques *written.*

JEAN JACQUES ROUSSEAU was born in Geneva in 1712. His mother died when he was born, and he had little early family life. He was also unusual in having no formal education, which may be significant in view of his later, highly individual, views on education. In 1728, he ran away to Italy and Savoy, where he lived with Baronne Louise de Warens and was baptized a Catholic. He eventually became the Baroness's lover and general factotum. In 1741, the baroness took a new lover and Rousseau had to move out. He went to Paris, where he made his living from secretarial work and music copying.

In Paris he developed a life-long relationship with Therese le Vasseur, an illiterate servant at the inn where he lodged. Rousseau had five children by Therese, all of whom he discarded by dumping them in orphanages. His irresponsibility, callousness and cruelty with regard to his own children make his later writings about the idyll of childhood look extremely hypocritical.

In 1745, he wrote an operetta called *Les Muses Galantes*, which led on to a correspondence with Voltaire and meetings with Diderot. Through his new acquaintance with Diderot he came to contribute articles on political economy and music to Diderot's *Encyclopedia*.

In 1750, he made his name with a prize essay entitled *Discours sur les arts et sciences*. In this essay, Rousseau argued that civilization had corrupted people's natural goodness and restricted their freedom of action. In 1752, he wrote a second operetta, *Le Devin du village*, which was a great success. Rousseau had by this stage become a celebrity, and he went on to write another anti-civilization work, *Discours sur l'origine et les fondements de l'inegalite permi les hommes*. In this he attacked private ownership of property and argued that the (originally perfect) nature of man was corrupted by society.

Rousseau was a restless man, itinerant by nature, and he travelled first to Geneva, where he was greatly and perhaps rather surprisingly influenced by Calvinism, then to Paris, and then on to Luxembourg. The Calvinist influence bore fruit in his 1758 *Lettre a d'Alembert sur les spectacles*, in which he inveighed puritanically against the establishment of a theatre in Geneva. The inconsistency of the composer of two operettas campaigning against theatres is nothing short of breath-taking.

In 1762, Rousseau published his most influential book, his masterpiece, *Du Contrat Social (On the Social Contract)*, which explains his presence in this book. Because of this one work, Rousseau stands out as possibly the most important single figure in the 18th century. Eloquently written, powerfully argued, the *Du Contrat Social* seemed to sum up the new spirit of the age, questioning the moral foundation of the existing social order, and preparing the way for both the French Revolution and the American Revolution. The book opens with the ringing statement, 'Man is born free; and everywhere he is in chains.' Rousseau proposed a new social order in which each individual surrenders his rights to the collective 'general will', which is the only source of legitimate sovereignty and defines the common good. Rousseau's anti-monarchy text, complete with its slogan, 'Liberty, Equality, Fraternity,' became the blueprint and the Bible for the French Revolution twenty years later, and of other radical social movements. *Du Contrat Social* was written out of frustration with the injustices of the *ancien regime* in France, so it was understandably extreme in its recommendations. It was even so profoundly unfortunate that he advocated a totalitarian substitute for absolute monarchy. The 'general will' found its expression in such abominations as the Committee of Public Safety, and the rights of individuals were trampled underfoot. Rousseau must take his share of the blame, alongside Robespierre, for the appalling excesses of the Reign of Terror.

The publication of Rousseau's landmark book *Du Contrat Social* was accompanied by the publication of another book, also extremely influential, but in a very different area – *Emile*. *Emile* was a treatise on education, written as a kind of narrative fantasy describing the ideal education of a child. Rousseau's *Emile* is brought up apart from other children in an experimental way. The child is not forced; he learns at his own speed from the situations around him. It was a major landmark in educational thinking, a pioneer work which paved the way for a number of different liberal experiments. Rousseau's *Emile* was a major influence on great educationists like Pestalozzi and Froebel. It also paved the way for a long-continuing discussion about the desirability of a return to 'nature' and a debate about what exactly we mean by the word 'natural'. This can be seen continuing in the present environmental movement.

Rousseau's ideas were quickly adopted into the Romantic literature, with the English poet William Wordsworth advocating the moral power of landscape. Wordsworth attempted in *The Prelude* (1805) to persuade readers that he had been reared by the mountains and streams of the English Lake District.

Rousseau's *Emile* so affronted the political and religious establishment that he had to leave Switzerland. In 1766, at the invitation of the philosopher David Hume he moved to England; Rousseau went to live briefly at Wootton Hall near Ashbourne in Derbyshire. It was there that he started to write his *Confessions*, a full, frank and self-admiring autobiography. Rousseau became unstable at this time, and seems to have suffered a serious mental breakdown. He quarrelled with his English friends, including Hume, and in 1767 he returned to France suffering from persecution mania. He went on to write a further autobiography, *Rousseau, juge de Jean Jacques*, and went back to music copying to make a living. His mental decline continued and he died insane in Ermenonville in 1778.

He became a posthumous hero during the French Revolution, and in 1794 his remains were buried in the Pantheon – beside Voltaire's. His writings, to a great extent, defined the spirit of the age. In his writings he was the ultimate spokesman for Romanticism in Europe generally, and his socio-political writings were blueprints for the revolutions that swept Europe and North America for the next few decades.

JAMES HUTTON

Born 1726, died 1797.
Pioneer, Scottish geologist and physical geographer.

ACHIEVEMENTS:
Identified igneous and metamorphic rocks.
Put forward the uniformitarian theory of geology.
Introduced prediction as an element in science.
Founded the modern sciences of geology and geomorphology.
Contributed useful ideas on meteorology.
Established a much longer history for the earth than hitherto
    acknowledged.
1785 – A Theory of the Earth published.

JAMES HUTTON WAS born in Edinburgh in June 1726. Hutton studied medicine in Edinburgh, Paris and Leiden, but in spite of this thorough training medicine was not to be his career. In 1754, based in Berwickshire in southern Scotland, he devoted himself to chemistry and agriculture, where he made many pioneering improvements. Even so, neither of these pursuits would be the field of endeavour where he made his mark, but they led him stepwise into mineralogy and geology. It was in geology, and in some of the greatest and most fundamental concepts in geology, that James Hutton was to make his mark.

In 1768, at the age of 42, James Hutton retired from agriculture and moved to Edinburgh, which became his base for pursuing his academic studies. It was a remarkable undertaking, in that geology as a science did not yet exist. His interest in minerals and rocks extended far beyond the concerns of the mineralogists of his time; he wanted to know how and when the rocks had been formed, and in this way he hoped to arrive at an understanding of the history of the Earth. It was an incredibly ambitious programme of work, to pursue issues of this magnitude as a second career, almost as a retirement hobby.

On the way to his greatest contribution to knowledge, Hutton published a paper entitled *A Theory of Rain*, in 1784. In this, he proposed that the amount of water vapour that air can contain increases with temperature. This very useful idea explained why when air is chilled the water vapour it contains tends to condense – a concept that has become one of the fundamentals of meteorology. It does indeed explain why it rains.

He made several major geological discoveries. One was that some rocks are igneous, originating from volcanic activity. Another was that many rocks are made of the disintegrated remains of still older rocks. Another was the fact that some rocks originated as sedimentary rocks but have been transformed by heat generated within the earth to make metamorphic rocks. He also saw that old sedimentary and metamorphic rocks have been penetrated by veins of younger molten rock; he thus discovered igneous intrusions as a geological feature.

Hutton also proposed that rocks, once formed, are later disrupted and heaved up above sea level, and that once above sea level they are subject to erosion. Hutton therefore introduced the idea of cycles of erosion in the landscape, and provided one of the key ideas of physical geography.

Perhaps Hutton's biggest idea was the principle of uniformitarianism – that on the whole rocks have been created by processes that are observable in the world today. The present is the key to the past. The past is the key to the present. This was a major break from the theory of catastrophism, which proposed that the past was to be explained by great upheavals that are no longer experienced. The uniformitarian theory – or Huttonian theory as it is sometimes called – was expounded before the Royal Society of Edinburgh in the spring of 1785 in his paper, *A Theory of the Earth, or an Investigation of the Laws Observable in the Composition, Dissolution and*

Restoration of Land upon the Globe. Hutton modified and expanded this major work in a second edition, which was published 10 years later.

He predicted that sediments now resting on the seabed will one day become sedimentary rocks. The processes of the past continue into the present – and will continue into the future. Prediction was an entirely new element in science.

Several major steps forward were made in this great work. Hutton avoided cosmogony – big theories about the nature of the universe – and confined himself to the inferences he had made from studies of visible exposures of rocks. In fact, he made a point of stating that geology must operate in this way; it must confine itself to the study of the materials in the earth. Hutton wrote other essays as well; *Dissertations on different Subjects in Natural Philosophy* and *An Investigation of the Principles of Knowledge.*

Hutton died two years after publishing the second edition of *A Theory of the Earth*, on 26 March 1797. His ideas were taken up immediately. Five years after James Hutton died, in 1802, John Playfair published *Illustrations of the Huttonian Theory of the Earth*, which contained an excellent summary of Hutton's theory and added fresh arguments and illustrations of his own to support the theory.

Hutton's *Theory of the Earth* was the basis for most subsequent developments in the science of geology, and marks the beginning of geology as a modern science. The individual observations were in themselves original and ground-breaking; put together, they made a theory that hung consistently together. In the Age of Reason, as the eighteenth century has sometimes been called, the biblical version of the ancient past was challenged. The account of Noah's flood in the book of Genesis seemed to support the catastrophists. The uniformitarian approach instead implied that a flood of global proportions was unlikely, and brought geology close to a collision with the Church. The Bible-based scholars had been using the genealogies given in the Old Testament to calculate the date of the Creation, and by that method Bishop Ussher had famously come up with 4004 BC.

James Hutton looked at the layers of sedimentary rocks, their great thicknesses suggesting thousands of years of accumulating sediment. He looked at the discontinuities, which seemed to imply intervals of thousands of years' worth of erosion. The passage of time involved must have been immense, far too great even to calculate. Hutton commented on the history of the planet as he saw it with awe; he could find 'no vestige of a beginning, no prospect of an end'. James Hutton was undoubtedly one of the greatest figures of 18th and 19th century science, laying the foundations for not one but three sciences – geology, geomorphology and meteorology.

JAMES COOK

Born at Marton 1728, died in Hawaii 1779.
English navigator and explorer.

ACHIEVEMENTS:
Surveyed the Gulf of St Lawrence and Newfoundland.
Circumnavigated New Zealand.
Discovered and surveyed the east coast of Australia.
Discovered the Great Barrier Reef.
Discovered Cape York (northern tip of Australia).
Surveyed the west coast of Canada and Alaska.
*Proved that no large landmass lay undiscovered in the Pacific
   Ocean.*
*Excited Europe with the exotic South Sea world that he
   discovered.*
Kept crews healthy at sea for long periods.

JAMES COOK WAS born at Marton in Cleveland, Yorkshire. His father was a farm labourer and later a farm bailiff. From the age of 12 Cook worked in a haberdasher's shop in Staithes but was then apprenticed to Walker's, who were ship-owners at Whitby. He spent several years working for Walker's in the coastal and Baltic trade.

In 1755, after rising to the rank of mate, Cook joined the royal navy and after only four years' service in 1759 became a master, on the recommendation of his commander, Sir Hugh Palliser. He was master of the sloop *Grampus*, then the *Garland*. Then for eight years he was engaged in a detailed survey, including soundings, of the Gulf of St Lawrence and the coast of Newfoundland on the *Solebay*. In 1766–68, Cook brought out volumes of sailing directions for the region, showing remarkably high ability. He also began to make a reputation for himself as a mathematician and astronomer as a result of his write-up of observations of the solar eclipse of 5 August 1766.

In 1768–71, Cook was appointed to undertake a major voyage – his first major voyage of exploration – as captain of the *Endeavour*. He was to take to a team of observers to the Pacific to observe the transit of Venus. During the return journey, Cook explored the Society Islands, sailed round New Zealand and surveyed its coastline; he sailed along the east coast of 'New Holland' (Australia), claiming it for Britain and surveying it in minute and accurate detail as he went. The voyage culminated in a rounding of the northern tip of Australia, Cape York, and proving by sailing through the Torres Strait that New Guinea was not attached to Australia.

The first voyage was such a resounding success that Cook was given command of a second voyage, taking the *Resolution* and *Adventure* to discover the gigantic but unseen southern continent that was for some reason thought to occupy the South Pacific. Between 1772 and 1775, Cook took his ships in a zig-zag course through the South Pacific, reaching 71 degrees South and seeing ice but no continent. By sailing so far south, Cook put his ships seriously at risk from floating ice.

Cook headed for Easter Island, whose position he accurately established for the first time. Cook also visited the Marquesas and Tonga, again fixing their positions more accurately. He discovered several previously unknown islands, including New Caledonia. On the way home, he crossed the South Atlantic at a high latitude, showing that there was no large landmass there either. It was an incredible voyage of discovery, truly epic in scale; in the one voyage, Cook's ships travelled the equivalent of three times round the world.

Cook was a careful expedition leader and lost only one man during the three-year cruise. He had successfully conquered scurvy.

The goal of the third and final voyage of discovery (1776–79) was to find a sea passage round the north of North America from the Pacific side.

On his way, Cook surveyed the west coast of North America from 45 degrees North as far as the Bering Strait. There, at Icy Cape, he was forced to turn back, reaching Hawaii in January 1779. The natives of Hawaii were friendly at first but suddenly turned hostile. When Cook landed with a party to recover a stolen boat, he was unexpectedly attacked and killed on the beach.

If Cook had returned home, he would undoubtedly have received a hero's welcome; King George was preparing to make him a baronet. As it was, a pension was awarded to his widow. Cook's achievements were certainly under-acknowledged and under-rewarded during his lifetime.

Captain Cook's voyages produced an astonishing amount of information about the geography of the Pacific and Southern Oceans. He returned with detailed descriptions and accurately surveyed charts. He gave Britain New Zealand and Australia as colonies. His exploits were the talk of Europe, and everyone was intensely excited about the exotic new world that was suddenly opened up. Cook's discoveries showed conclusively that there was no large landmass in the Pacific Ocean, that the Pacific was virtually empty of land, apart from the hundreds of small islands. Any large 'Unknown Land' must lie in very high latitudes, beyond 71 degrees South. He prepared the way for the eventual discovery of a smaller Antarctica.

GEORGE WASHINGTON

Born at Bridges Creek 1732, died at Mount Vernon 1799.
General, statesman, first president of the USA, commander-in-
  chief of the American army in the American War of
  Independence.

ACHIEVEMENTS:
Led the American army to victory in the American War of
  Independence.
Secured the American colonies' independence from England.
Presided over the creation of the American constitution.
Presided over the inauguration of the federal United States of
  America.
Became the first president of the United States of America.
Gave his name to the capital of the USA.

GEORGE WASHINGTON WAS born at Bridges Creek, Virginia, in 1732, the son of Augustine Washington. He came of English stock, the family originally coming from the village of Sulgrave in Northamptonshire; John Washington, George's great-grandfather, had emigrated to America in 1657. Washington's father had gone to school in England. George Washington's early years were spent with his five siblings in a humble four-room farmhouse on the Rappahannock. Little is known of George Washington's childhood, but the story about his chopping down the cherry tree is almost certainly untrue, made up to fill a gap. He was educated. His copy-book, in which at the age of 14 he transcribed *Rules of Civility,* was carefully preserved, presumably as something he was proud of. Later he taught himself a good deal of mathematics. However, most of his education was on a practical level. His father owned 6 plantations and George learnt the practical art of surveying; by the age of 14 he was able to measure and map the fields of his family and neighbours.

George's father died when he was 11, leaving him under the guardianship of his eldest half-brother Lawrence. In 1747, George went to Mount Vernon, Lawrence's residence. Lawrence had had the good fortune to inherit most of the Washington family estate. Here, George's life opened up considerably. He now had access to books and also came to know the Fairfaxes, his brother's wife's family. In 1748, Lord Fairfax gave George the job of surveying his property. For a while survey work, which was becoming his trade, alternated with hunting. George learned about weapons and the art of war.

In 1751, he accompanied his half-brother, who was dying of consumption, to Barbados for his health, but it was to no avail. The next year Lawrence Washington died at Mount Vernon and George was left guardian to his daughter and he was also left as residuary heir to the Mount Vernon estate if she should die without issue.

The French were at this time connecting their settlements on the Great Lakes with colonies on the Mississippi with a chain of outposts on the Ohio River, which was inside the English sphere of influence. Governor Dinwiddie of Virginia decided to warn off the intruders and organized an expedition to the Ohio. In 1753, Washington was put in command, but he was driven back, trapped in a fort and forced to surrender. It was not an auspicious start to a military career.

Next, Washington served on General Braddock's personal staff, and was instrumental in saving the remnant of Braddock's army in 1755. After that he was put in command of the Virginia forces. In 1759, he married Martha Custis, a rich young widow. His niece had died without issue, and Washington inherited the Mount Vernon estate; with that and Martha's estate as well, he had suddenly become one of the richest men in America. He entertained lavishly, danced, led the fox-hunting and was a successful farmer. He even flirted, but was very awkward and clumsy at it.

In the run-up to the War of Independence, Washington at first favoured a peaceful solution to the mounting friction with England. Gradually he became convinced that only force would guarantee the rights of the American colonists. He represented Virginia in the first and second Continental Congresses (1774 and 1775). He was no great speech writer and no orator either, but he was a good manager and exuded common sense.

By this stage he was the one American soldier with a nation-wide reputation and was the inevitable choice as a commander-in-chief. He was a gifted strategist and tactician, and he was also good at leading men; he was a dignified, aristocratic figure with natural authority. He had experience at managing his plantation, with strict common sense. He was physically commanding, six feet tall and heavily built, with unusually big hands and shoulders. It was, even so, almost incredible that he was able to lead a mixed bag of untrained, poorly disciplined and poorly armed men from all manner of backgrounds, turn them into an army, and win. In 1776 he was able to organize this army, which fought with itself as much as with the enemy, to the point where they were able to bottle up a well-trained British army in Boston and force an evacuation. The slaughter at Bunker Hill was less to do with Washington's brilliance than with the incompetence of the English command. Cornwallis was an able commander, but he was hampered by the stupidity of his superior.

Washington suffered setbacks round New York; he inflicted defeats on the English at Trenton and Princeton, but was himself defeated at Brandywine and Germantown. After forming an alliance with France in 1778, Washington's reinforced army was able to force the defeat and surrender of Cornwallis at Yorktown in 1781, bringing the War of Independence to an end.

On 23 December 1783, in a solemn ceremony at Annapolis, Washington resigned his commission and received the formal thanks of the nation. He left Annapolis at sunrise on 24 December and was back home at Mount Vernon by nightfall. He could not get home fast enough. He would have preferred at this stage to spend the rest of his days as a gentleman-farmer.

At Mount Vernon, Washington set about enlarging his house, re-arranging the grounds, installing ha-has, experimenting with new crops. It looked as if he really meant to retire. He was nevertheless alarmed by the increasing chaos in America in the wake of independence, alarmed enough to make him re-enter public life. It was a decision that made him America's first president. He declared in May 1786 that 'something must be done, or the fabric will fall, for it is certainly tottering.' He set about creating a strong government by way of a constitution. In 1787 he presided over a convention at Philadelphia which formulated the American constitution. He completely lost confidence in the existing American institutions after an outbreak of virulent personal abuse, warning the quarrellers that they must consider 'whether the Revolution must ultimately be considered a blessing or a curse.' He went over heart and soul to the federalist party, warning that an indissoluble union was the only answer.

Washington's style as president was cool, dignified and aristocratic. At presidential receptions, he came dressed in a black velvet suit with gold buckles, yellow gloves and powdered hair, a cocked hat with an ostrich plume in one hand and a sword in a white leather scabbard in the other. He arrived in a coach and six. Guests at his receptions commented that he served good wines and the menus were elaborate, but the atmosphere was grave and solemn. Some Americans, especially the more radical ones, thought he was conducting himself much too much like a king, which was not what they wanted at all. They had after all just got rid of a king. It is nevertheless likely that Washington's cool, reserved manner had more to do with his innate shyness than to an inflated sense of dignity.

He retired from the presidency after eight years in 1797. Two terms in office were enough, he was getting tired and he winced at some of the opposition's verbal abuse. He died at Mount Vernon on the Potomac in December 1799. His death plunged America into mourning. In the House of Representatives a tribute included the remark that George Washington was 'first in war, first in peace, and first in the hearts of our countrymen.' When the news reached Europe, in the throes of the Napoleonic Wars, both the British Channel fleet and the armies of Napoleon paid tribute to him. The federal capital of the United States was, appropriately, named after the man who had done more than any other man to create the USA not only as a sovereign state but as a federal state.

JAMES WATT

Born at Greenock 1736, died 1819.
Engineer, civil engineer, inventor.

ACHIEVEMENTS:
Invented the modern condensing steam engine, improving on
   the inefficient Newcomen engine.
Invented the governor and micrometer.

JAMES WATT WAS born at Greenock on the Clyde in 1736, the son of a
merchant and town councillor who lost his money in unsuccessful specu-
lation. At the age of 19, James Watt became an apprentice mathematical
instrument maker with John Morgan in 1755 in London. The work was
very hard and he was living too frugally; he was so exhausted after a year
of this apprenticeship that he had to return to Glasgow to rest and
recuperate. In 1756 Watt tried to set himself up in business as an
instrument maker in Glasgow but he encountered serious difficulties. The
Hammermen's Guild were obstructive because he had not served his full
term of apprenticeship with Morgan, and he was unable to open his shop.
But his position was secure once Glasgow University formally employed
him as its mathematical instrument maker in 1757.

Watt made some useful friends at the university. He became close
friends with Joseph Black, a chemistry lecturer who discovered latent heat.
In 1759, Watt began to think of steam power as a force that might be
harnessed, way beyond its current restricted use to drive mine pumps. In
1763, in the course of his routine work, he was sent a working model of the
Newcomen steam engine to repair. He put the model engine back in order,
and while doing so saw the design defects in the machine. It was extremely

inefficient, consuming enormous quantities of steam (and therefore coal) to do relatively little work. He also saw fitting a separate condenser as a way of improving it. Later he found other ways of improving the engine's performance, including an air pump to remove the spent steam, a steam jacket for the cylinder to make sure the cylinder was as hot as the steam entering it and a double-action for the engine.

Watt's design improvements were relatively easily made in Watt's mind, but testing them cost him a lot of money and he put himself in debt in order to demonstrate the merits of his engine. He allowed Dr Roebuck, the founder of the Carron Ironworks, two-thirds of the profit from his invention in return for bearing the costs. An engine was then built at Kinneil near Linlithgow; in the course of constructing it, Watt saw further ways of improving the machine.

Watt was meanwhile gaining a reputation as a civil engineer of considerable ability. He was employed to undertake survey work on the Forth and Clyde Canal in 1767, and then the Caledonian Canal. He was also engaged to improve harbours at Ayr, Port Glasgow and Greenock and dredge rivers to improve navigation.

In 1768, Watt met Matthew Boulton, who owned the Soho Engineering Works. Boulton agreed to buy Roebuck's share of Watt's steam engine so that they could work together. In 1774, Watt set up in partnership with Boulton, and the improved steam engine went into production at the Soho Engineering Works, protected by a patent Watt had prudently taken out in 1769. The partnership was a very happy one; Watt saw to the engineering side and Boulton looked after the business. Between 1781 and 1785 he took out no fewer than 6 patents for further devices, including the centrifugal governor, a self-regulating device that ensured an even running speed in a rotating steam engine.

Watt's steam engine soon superseded Newcomen's as the engine of choice for mine and other pumps. For one thing, it used only a quarter of the fuel. But Watt's imagination ran on ahead. Why should this extremely efficient machine be used just to drain mines? Why not use it to drive carriages along roads or ships across the sea? In 1784, Watt described a steam locomotive in one of his patents, yet for some reason discouraged William Murdoch, his assistant, from experimenting with steam locomotion. What they had in mind was a steam carriage that would travel along ordinary roads. Watt had not thought of using rails, and when that was proposed by others in the last years of his life he would not consider it at all.

The watt, a unit of power, is named after him. Horsepower, another power unit, was invented by him. Along the way, Watt discovered the composition of water, which is often overlooked, but was a major discovery.

James Watt retired in 1800 and died at his home, Heathfield Hall near Birmingham, in 1819. His last invention was a device for copying sculptures full-size, and another for making reduced copies. A pointer travelled over the surface of the original, while a rotating tool cut a corresponding surface on a second block. He experimented with these devices, presenting copies of busts of himself to his friends as the work 'of a young artist just entering on his eighty-third year.' This final episode shows what an engaged and engaging man he was. He was a man of warm friendships, full of anecdotes – and he was a great talker.

His son, also called James Watt (1769–1848), in 1817 fitted the steam engine to the first English steamship to leave port, the *Caledonia*. James Watt's outstanding contribution was the improved and more efficient steam engine, the engine that was to transform the 19th-century world. Watt envisaged using his improved engine for locomotion. It was largely due to Watt's inventions and the imagination behind them that the steamship era began – and in spite of himself the age of the railway.

TOM PAINE

Born at Thetford 1737, died at New Rochelle 1809.
English-born socio-political agitator, American revolutionary.

ACHIEVEMENTS:
Actively participated in the American Revolution.
Used journalism to promote the cause of American
* independence.*
Actively participated in the French Revolution.
Expressed in his writings the challenging, revolutionary spirit
* of the age.*
1776 – Common Sense.
1786 – Dissertations on Government.
1792 – The Rights of Man.
1796 – The Age of Reason.

TOM PAINE WAS born at Thetford in Norfolk. He was the son of a Quaker smallholder and corset-maker. Tom himself worked as a corset-maker from the age of 13. He went to sea for a time, and then tried his hand at teaching. In 1771 he became an exciseman but lost his job after agitating for an increase in pay for excisemen; he was seen by his employers as a trouble-maker. He soon turned out to be a trouble-maker on a grand scale, offering his helping hand in overturning governments in two continents.

In London he met Benjamin Franklin, and it was Franklin who in 1774 helped him to emigrate to America. There he settled in Philadelphia and worked as a radical journalist. When the American War of Independence broke out in 1775, he published a pamphlet entitled *Common Sense* (1776), outlining the events that had led to the outbreak of war, and urging a declaration of independence.

Paine served in the continental army, and issued a series of pamphlets called *The American Crisis*, which promoted the cause of the colonists. He became secretary to the congress committee on foreign affairs in 1777.

In 1781 Paine travelled to France to raise money for the American cause and in 1786 he published *Dissertations on Government*. He returned to England in 1787, where he published *The Rights of Man* (1792), which was a reply to Edmund Burke's *Reflections of the Revolution in France*. In it, Paine supported the French Revolution and daringly appealed for the overthrow of the British monarchy. He was in danger of being arrested for treason, but managed to escape to France. He immediately became a French citizen and with surprising speed became a member of the National Convention, representing the Pas-de-Calais.

Paine supported the Girondins, opposed the execution of Louis XVI and so became an enemy of Robespierre. Robespierre accordingly cancelled his French citizenship and had him arrested. This was in 1794. Tom Paine was very lucky to have escaped the guillotine. Once the Terror was over, he claimed that he was an American citizen, and was released in 1795. While he was in prison, he had never stopped writing, and *The Age of Reason* was published in 1796.

The Age of Reason lost Paine many of his old friends, including George Washington. After his release, Paine stayed on in Paris for a few years, perpetually writing and studying. In 1802 he returned to America, where he was now considered a dangerous extremist, far too radical. He was, after all, an atheist, a free-thinker, and that did not go down at all well in America; the Land of the Free was not the Land of the Free-Thinking. In 1809 Tom Paine died alone, ostracized and in poverty on his farm at New Rochelle – the farm that a once-grateful state of New York had given him for his services to the American Revolution.

THE MONTGOLFIER BROTHERS

Joseph Michel Montgolfier
Born 1740, died 1810.
Jacques Etienne Montgolfier
Born 1745, died 1799.
French aeronauts and inventors.

ACHIEVEMENTS:
Designed and built the first practical balloon.
Launched the first flights of hot-air balloons.
Made possible the first manned flight in 1783.

THE MONTGOLFIER BROTHERS were the sons of a paper manufacturer at Annonay in France, about 40 miles from Lyons. The brothers observed the way clouds were suspended in the air, and thought that if they could enclose vapour of the same nature as the cloud in a large and light bag it might rise, carrying the bag into the air.

In 1782 they constructed a small balloon which was lifted by igniting a cauldron full of paper underneath it. The smoke and warmed air inside the balloon decreased in density so that it became more buoyant than the surrounding air. They saw that their hypothesis was correct and decided to make a larger version of the balloon and demonstrate it in public. On 5 June, 1783, in front of a large crowd of spectators, a huge linen globe 30 metres in circumference was inflated over a fire fuelled with chopped straw.

When released, the balloon ascended rapidly to a great height, and then came down again 10 minutes later over a mile away. This event marked the invention of the balloon.

News of the experiment at Annonay quickly spread. In Paris, Barthelemy Faujas de Saint-Fond set up a fund to repeat the experiment. The second balloon was built by two brothers by the name of Robert, and the work was supervised by a physicist, J. Charles. Initially the idea had been to use hot air like the Montgolfier brothers, but Charles wanted to try hydrogen. This balloon too was given a public audition, and it obligingly rose rapidly to a height of about 1000 metres. Rain started to fall during the ascent, but the crowd stayed to see the spectacle, and many were drenched.

On 19 September, 1783, Joseph Montgolfier repeated the Annonay experiment in Paris, in the presence of Louis XVI, Marie Antoinette and an immense crowd. The inflation took only 11 minutes, after which the balloon rose to about 500 metres, floated along in the wind, and came down in a wood about two miles away. Suspended below the balloon was a cage containing a sheep, a cock and a duck, which became the first airborne travellers. The Montgolfier balloon was painted with ornaments in oil colours, and was very eye-catching, looking like a gigantic Christmas tree bauble.

The first person to ascend in a balloon was Jean Pilatre de Rozier. In October 1783 he made several ascents in a captive balloon; it was held to the ground with ropes. He demonstrated that the balloon could rise with people suspended beneath it, and also carry fuel so that a fire could be kindled under the balloon while in flight. On 21 November, 1783, Pilatre de Rozier and the Marquis d'Arlandes travelled in a free balloon about two miles from the Bois de Boulogne. They were in the air for about 25 minutes and this was the first manned flight in a balloon.

The Montgolfier brothers were unable to develop the balloon technology any further before the outbreak of the French Revolution. Etienne fell foul of the authorities, and Joseph went back to the family paper factory.

Joseph Montgolfier was eventually elected to the Academie des Sciences and created a chevalier of the Legion of Honour by Napoleon.

Whether the Montgolfiers would have developed their hot-air balloon technology any further if the Revolution had not intervened it is impossible to tell. They certainly succeeded in realising one of man's oldest dreams – flying through the air – and their success encouraged others to go several steps further. Within just a few months from the initial experiment, the newly invented hot-air balloon technology had led to a manned flight. The Montgolfiers opened up new possibilities that would lead on, not only to hot-air ballooning as a 'rich' sport but to passenger airships too.

PRINCE GEBHARD VON BLUCHER

Born at Rostock 1742, died at Krieblowitz 1819.
Prussian field marshal, victor of Waterloo.

ACHIEVEMENTS:
Defeated Napoleonic armies in a series of major battles.
Led the Prussian army to victory at the Battle of Waterloo.
With Wellington, joint victor at Waterloo.
Brought the Napoleonic Wars to an end.

GEBHARD LEBERECHT VON Blucher, Prince of Wahlstadt, was born at Rostock in Mecklenburg, Prussia, in 1742. Blucher's military career began when he was only 14, entering the Swedish service in 1756. In the Pomeranian campaign of 1760 he was taken prisoner by Prussian soldiers, after which he was persuaded by his captors to enter the service of Prussia. Blucher took part in the later battles of the Seven Years War as a hussar officer, distinguishing himself in the Prussian cavalry, from 1760 to 1770. His very promising career was halted at this point, when it ended because of his dissipation and insubordination. He was a very hot-blooded man, which made him a heroically courageous fighter, but in peacetime he was often in trouble, giving himself over to wild living. He was passed over for promotions he thought he deserved and in 1773 sent in a letter of resignation. Frederick the Great's response was, 'Captain Blucher can take himself to the devil.'

For 15 years, Blucher attended to the farming on his own estates. But his military career was far from over. In 1787, following the death of Frederick the Great, he rejoined the army with the rank of major, taking part in the expedition to Holland. The following year he was promoted to lieutenant-colonel. At last he was getting the promotion he thought he deserved. In 1789 he was awarded the high honour, *pour le merite.*

In 1793 he fought against the French on the Rhine as full colonel of hussars. In 1806 he fought against them again at Auerstadt. He fought well at Lubeck and Stralsund, though the battles were lost and the campaign was a disaster.

In 1809, Blucher was made general of cavalry. When the Prussian rose against the French in 1813, it was Blucher who took command in Silesia. He fought with conspicuous courage at a sequence of battles at Lutzen, Bautzen and Haynau. At the Battle of Katzbach he succeeded in clearing Silesia of Napoleon's troops. In January 1814, Blucher led his troops across France. When Paris was taken in 1814, Blucher wanted revenge; he wanted to inflict on Paris what Napoleon had inflicted on other cities all over Europe, the severest retaliation, and in particular he wanted to wreak revenge on Paris for what Prussia had suffered at French hands. In this he was restrained by Wellington. In June 1814, Blucher was made prince of Walstadt, which is on the Katzbach battlefield. After the peace, Blucher retired to Silesia, but the return of Napoleon quickly brought him out of retirement again.

He was put in command of the Army of the Lower Rhine with General Gneisenau as his chief of staff. At the outset of this new campaign the Prussians received a very severe defeat at the Battle of Ligny. In the course of this battle the old field marshal was ridden over in a cavalry charge and only rescued from being trampled to death by the bravery of his aide-de-camp, Count Nostitz. Blucher showed remarkable resilience, in that after a few hours he was able to resume command. In the meantime, Gneisenau took over.

Relations between the English and Prussian headquarters were complicated, and it is not clear how events unfolded. It seems that it was

Blucher's own decision, and a very daring decision, to march to the aid of Wellington. Blucher subjected his army to a very demanding and severe march to reach Wellington in time to save him.

His role at the Battle of Waterloo, Napoleon's final defeat, was crucial. The battle between the French under Napoleon and the English under Wellington was fairly evenly matched, but the result could have been a victory for Napoleon. Blucher and his Prussian army arrived on the battlefield at Waterloo in time to turn the battle decisively against Napoleon. The Prussians relentlessly chased the French as they fled from the battlefield all through the night; it was a killing spree that made it absolutely certain that the French army could not fight again.

The allies re-entered Paris, where Blucher remained for some months. Age and infirmity compelled him to retire to his estate in Silesia, where he died in September 1819. He retained to the very end of his life the wild character and tendency to excess that had caused his dismissal from the army when he was young. But in war, that wildness expressed itself as a fierce patriotism, bloodlust, reckless courage and the determination to win – precisely the qualities needed to beat Napoleon. He was the man for the moment.

Blucher must be given joint credit with Wellington for bringing the Napoleonic Wars to a final, decisive conclusion. As a result of Blucher's intervention at the Battle of Waterloo, Napoleon was finished.

JOHANN PESTALOZZI

Born in Zurich 1746, died at Brugg, 1827.
Swiss educational reformer.

ACHIEVEMENTS:
Introduced a more liberal form of education.
1774 – Founded an experimental farm school.
1780 – Evening Hours of a Hermit.
1781 – Leonard and Gertrude.
1801 – How Gertrude Educates her Children.

JOHANN HEINRICH PESTALOZZI was born in Zurich in 1746. His father died when he was young and he was brought up by his mother. When he was a youth in Zurich he was associated with Lavater and the reforming party. From early on he was involved in schemes for improving the conditions of the poor. When his friend Bluntschli died, Pestalozzi switched his attention from politics to education, but still with liberalizing reform as the keynote.

Pestalozzi devoted his adult life to the liberal education of very poor children. Pestalozzi shared Rousseau's ideal of the rural idyll, of the inherent virtue of the rural way of life. He set up a residential farm school at his farmhouse at Neuhof in Aargau in 1774, and collected waifs and strays to stay there and learn rural occupations and values. Unfortunately the financial management of the school was flawed and it was therefore doomed. He bought a piece of adjacent waste land and tried to cultivate madder on it, but this business venture failed too. After five difficult years, in 1780, Pestalozzi had to abandon both the school and the madder cultivation. For a time Pestalozzi withdrew to think over his views on education and wrote *Evening Hours of a Hermit,* a collection of reflections and aphorisms.

He then wrote *Leonard and Gertrude,* which some people consider to be his masterpiece. It describes the gradual reformation of a household, then of a whole village, through the efforts of a good and devoted woman.

The French invasion of Switzerland in 1798 brought the ideas of Pestalozzi into high relief. Many children were left on the shores of Lake Lucerne without parents, homes or food. Pestalozzi's response to the emergency was to open an orphan school in a deserted convent at Stanz. He gathered some of the orphans together and gave them shelter and education, but his school folded after only eight months when the French claimed the premises for use as a hospital. The orphans were once again homeless.

Pestalozzi was appointed to the people's school at Berthoud (Burgdorf) in 1799, but was forced out by the envious senior master. Then under the patronage of the Swiss government and with help from others, Pestalozzi opened his own school at Berthoud. While he was working there he published *How Gertrude Educates her Children,* a landmark book in which Pestalozzi expounded his educational ideas in full. The method is to begin with observation, to proceed from observation to consciousness and from consciousness to speech. Then come measuring, drawing, writing, number and mathematics.

In 1805 he moved his school to Yverdon on Lake Neuchatel, where he applied his method in a large secondary school. Pestalozzi's liberal approach to education, which was in large measure an attempt to apply in practice the principles of Rousseau, was of great interest to his contemporaries, and many distinguished people were actively interested: Mme de Stael, von Humboldt and Talleyrand, for instance. Pestalozzi had enormous influence on the later evolution of education through his pupils. Among them were Carl Ritter, Zeller and Froebel. Unfortunately, Pestalozzi was not a practical man and his impracticality led to the school's decline. There was an outbreak of dissent among his teaching staff in 1815 and the school closed ten years after that. Johann Pestalozzi's life was a difficult one, with many setbacks, and his closing years were sad and weary. He characteristically addressed a final farewell prayer to mankind, *The Song of the Swan,* and retired to Brugg, where he died in 1827.

Johann Pestalozzi's main importance lies in his attempt to put into practice, in schools, the educational theories of Jean Jacques Rousseau. His pupils and disciples went on, through the 19th and 20th centuries, to develop a distinctive tradition of liberal education, a tradition that was more child-centred.

JOHANN WOLFGANG VON GOETHE

Born in Frankfurt-am-Main 1749, died in Weimar 1832.
German poet, dramatist, novelist, scientist.

ACHIEVEMENTS:
Germany's greatest lyric poet, dramatist, novelist and man of
  letters.
Embodied the German Romantic movement.
Established the Shakespearean form of drama on the German
  stage.
Wrote the great German national drama, Faust.
The modern universal man.
1771 – Gotz von Berlichingen.
1774 – Die Leiden des jungen Werthers.
1808 – Faust, Part 1.
1811 – Aus mein Leben.
1832 – Faust, Part 2.

JOHANN WOLFGANG VON Goethe was born in Frankfurt-am-Main in 1749, the eldest son of Johann Kaspar Goethe, a lawyer. The house where he grew up in Frankfurt was full of interesting curios that stimulated the boy's mind; a puppet theatre held a special fascination for him. Another early memory that impressed him was the picturesque coronation of Emperor Joseph II in Frankfurt town hall. In his boyhood he wrote a good deal, including a biblical prose epic about Joseph and a 'correspondence' novel in letters written in different languages. This highly imaginative and intelligent boy was educated privately, first by his father and later by tutors, and was unfortunately expected to follow his father into his law practice.

He consequently went off to study law at Leipzig with some reluctance in 1765, at the age of 16.

He fell in love with Kathchen Schonkopf, the inn-keeper's daughter at the tavern where he dined, and this experience inspired him to write two plays exploring the lighter and darker sides of love, *Die Laune des Verliebchen and Die Mitschuldigen,* while he was supposed to be studying law. In Leipzig, Goethe also found time for another of his abiding interests, art. As with everything else, Goethe pursued his studies conscientiously, taking drawing lessons from A. F. Oeser, the director of the Academy of Painting in the Pleissenburg.

Goethe had a sudden haemorrhage and was ill for a long while after this, and the period of convalescence was a time of deep introspection, a kind of incubation period. At his father's insistence, he then continued his law studies at Strasbourg from 1770, though now more seriously; in fact everything was undertaken more seriously now. At Strasbourg he fell under the influence of Herder, the pioneer of German Romanticism. Goethe's breadth of interests became more conspicuous; he was developing interests in anatomy, antiquity, alchemy and the occult. Another love affair generated another play, *Roslein auf der Heide,* and several fine lyric poems.

Goethe's best qualities seem to have been inherited from his mother. He had a lively, impulsive nature with great imaginative power; these were her attributes too, and she was perhaps the ideal mother for a poet. The stiffness of manner which he developed in later years was a characteristic of his father, but from him he also inherited an underlying stability that sustained him through all his passionate adventures.

In 1771, he at last qualified and went back to Frankfurt to begin the process of initiation into the legal profession, but he evidently intended to break free of it at the earliest opportunity. He became a newspaper critic. He wrote another play, this time capturing the thwarted spirit of German nationalism in a dramatic masterpiece, *Gotz von Berlichingen.* This play, showing a man of genius at odds with society, may have been in part Goethe dramatizing his own position in relation to the family law practice, but it was also very much in the fashionable new Sturm und Drang spirit of German Romanticism. Goethe was already looking well beyond the borders of Germany for inspiration, and seeing Shakespeare as the best model for dramatists; in Gotz, Goethe was applying Shakespearean principles to the German theatre.

Then Goethe began the work for which he is most remembered, *Faust*, and in 1774 wrote a self-revealing novel, *Die Leiden des jungen Werthers*, which was about his hopeless love for a friend's fiancee, Charlotte Buff. Werther, the hero, nobly resolves the dramatic problem by committing suicide. This popular novel had the unfortunate effect of making suicide fashionable for a time. Scores of young men killed themselves. Whereas Gotz exemplified the masculine Sturm und Drang side of German Romanticism, Werther exemplified the feminine sentimental side of it. Goethe encompassed it all.

The love lyrics he wrote in 1775 were inspired by another love, this time for Lili Schonemann.

In 1776, Goethe took the surprising step of accepting a court position, as privy-councillor to the young Duke of Weimar. He may have done this to ensure financial security while he continued his creative writing; he may have done it to pre-empt any further move by his single-minded father to involve him in the family law practice. He carried out his court duties conscientiously, interesting himself in a geological survey. Now emotionally steadied by his relationship with Charlotte von Stein, Goethe was himself able to exert a steadying influence on the young duke. But Goethe seemed to need difficult and turbulent relationships with women to stimulate his creative writing and the ten steady years he spent with Charlotte did little for his writing.

Goethe's scientific work included studies of bone structure and leaves. He even attempted to refute Newton's theory of light. He similarly supported Neptunism, the geological theory that the earth's crust had an aqueous origin, against Vulcanism, the rival theory that the crustal rocks were igneous in origin; he was wrong in this too. He wrote a novel about theatre life, called *Wilhelm Meisters Theatralische Sendung*, which did not come to light until 1910.

Goethe's revelatory visits to Italy in 1786 and 1790 brought an end to his emotional dependence on Charlotte von Stein. He had planned the first visit in great secrecy, presumably so that no-one, including Charlotte, could stop him. As a result of his Italian experience, Goethe became detached from the German Sturm und Drang movement, increasingly detached from the German Romantic movement generally, and more preoccupied with poetic form, with pagan classical aesthetics. He wrote classical verse dramas: *Egmont, Iphigenie* and *Tasso.* He fell in love with Christiane Vulpius, a girl who could offer no intellectual companionship, but could offer him home comforts. Christiane was never accepted in court society and she was ignored by Goethe's friends; but she seems not to have minded these snubs. Goethe lived with her for a long time and finally married her in 1806, when the invasion of Weimar by the French made life, property and human rights very uncertain.

In 1792, Goethe accompanied the Duke of Weimar on campaign in France, a campaign that ended in defeat for the Germans at the Battle of Valmy. Later, Goethe would write an account of this: *Campaign in France.*

Goethe's friendship with Schiller began in 1794; they corresponded about aesthetics and carried on a friendly contest in ballad-writing. This led to Schiller's *Die Glocke* and Goethe's *Hermann und Dorothea.* They both wrote articles deploring philistinism in a literary magazine. Their close friendship lasted until Schiller's death in 1805, at which Goethe was grief-stricken. It was an irreparable loss.

Goethe's final period of creativity saw him resuming his novel of the theatre, which he turned into a novel cycle. This resulted in the creation of two very popular novels about Wilhelm Meister, who became the idol of the German Romantics. Ironically, Goethe increasingly disapproved of the Romantics. He disliked their enthusiasm for the French Revolution, which he poked fun at in a number of works. He also deplored their disregard for style. Unquestionably, Goethe's masterpiece is his version of Christopher Marlowe's *Faust*, which he worked on for much of his adult life. It was started in 1775 and finished in 1832, the year of Goethe's death.

Goethe had no patriotic feelings; his sentiments were above such things. He had seen Germany prospering as a cluster of small absolute monarchies and had little confidence in the dreamers who saw unification as a way of reviving the glories of the past. He had no sympathy for the 'war of liberation' which so excited many young Germans. As nationalism soared, so Goethe retreated into his study. He kept back from the great political upheavals of his time – as far as he could. It was nevertheless difficult for a figure as celebrated as he was to remain completely in the background. Napoleon made a point of meeting Goethe at the Congress of Erfurt in 1803. Like Beethoven, Goethe initially admired Napoleon, identifying him as the saviour of European civilization, but later changed his mind and regretted his early praise.

Goethe was buried close to Schiller in the duke's vault at Weimar. He was a towering influence on German literature in particular, and a reverberating force in European culture generally. He read incredibly widely, absorbing not only German and Italian culture, but British culture too. Writers like Byron, Scott and Carlyle could all expect friendly and encouraging words from Goethe. Little escaped his attention, and it is said that he had one of the largest minds of all time. He succeeded in embodying Romanticism without surrendering classical forms of expression; he expressed Sturm und Drang but maintained balanced and civilized standards. The young Wordsworth welcomed the French Revolution: Goethe did not. It is possible find fault with Goethe's novels; not all of the poetry is marvellous; some of his science was completely wrong. However, the overall accomplishment was comprehensive and remarkable. The most outstanding thing about Goethe was his completeness as a human being, and perhaps his life was his greatest work. Napoleon came away from his famous meeting with Goethe profoundly impressed; he said, *'Voila un homme!'* – 'There is a man!'

WOLFGANG AMADEUS MOZART

Born in Salzburg 1756, died in Vienna 1791.
Pianist, composer, child prodigy, universal musical genius.

ACHIEVEMENTS:
The greatest composer who ever lived.
Wrote music that marks the culmination of the classical
    tradition and the beginning of the romantic.
Bridged 18th and 19th century musical traditions.
1773 – Symphonies 23–29.
1786 – The Marriage of Figaro, Prague Symphony.
1787 – Don Giovanni, Eine Kleine Nachtmusik.
1788 – Symphonies 39, 40, 41.
1790 – Cosi fan tutte.
1791 – The Magic Flute, Requiem.

MOZART, OR TO give him his full name Johann Chrysostom Wolfgang Amadeus Mozart, was born in Salzburg in 1756, the son of Leopold Mozart, a violinist and composer. Wolfgang was a child prodigy who became famous all over Europe, playing the keyboard confidently at the age of four, composing his first pieces for it at the age of five. He then learned to play the violin. Leopold Mozart could see the commercial potential of this extraordinary precocity, especially alongside the ability of his pianist daughter Nannerl, who was also a prodigy, and organized a series of recital tours.

In 1762 the two children played before the Elector of Bavaria in Munich and the Empress Maria Theresa in Vienna. In 1763 the Mozart family reached Paris, where they stayed for 5 months, and then went on to London for 15 months. In London, the young Mozart formed a friendship with J. C. Bach. During the next six months in the Netherlands both Wolfgang and Nannerl were taken seriously ill. In 1766 the journey home began, stopping once again to give concerts in Paris, Switzerland and Germany. The young Mozart was widely praised for his spirited playing and his clever improvizations.

In 1767, the Mozarts went to Vienna, where the 11-year-old composer wrote two operas, *La finta semplice* and *Bastien und Bastienne*. After this, there were extended visits to Italy. His experiences on these tours did much to help Mozart shape his style, especially in dramatic music. In his recitals, Mozart performed various tricks at the keyboard. One was to display his phenomenal musical memory. While in Italy, for example, he was able to write out *Allegri's Miserere* from memory.

By 1772, when he was still only 21 years old, Mozart had written around 25 symphonies, of which some have been lost, as well as some string quartets. It was in 1772 that Mozart first encountered Haydn's music.

Mozart was unhappy with the patronage of Archbishop Colloredo, the Archbishop of Salzburg, who was austere and unmusical, and friction between them led to Mozart's dismissal from his service. Unfortunately Mozart was unable to find an alternative employer elsewhere. There was no post for him at Mannheim and Leopold tried and failed to get him a court position at Vienna. Mozart travelled to Paris, but his father eventually persuaded him to return to Salzburg, where he became court organist. In 1781, Archbishop Colloredo summoned Mozart to Vienna for the coronation of Emperor Joseph II. After a blazing row with the archbishop Mozart again left his service – but remained in Vienna, which became his home for the rest of his life.

In Vienna, Mozart's reputation soared, as he wrote a sequence of incomparable operas that have remained the staple fare of the opera repertory ever since – *The Marriage of Figaro, Don Giovanni, Cosi fan tutte* and *The Magic Flute*. There were also a dozen piano concerti and a series of symphonies that are all played frequently in concert halls all round the world and are popular with audiences everywhere. An outstanding characteristic of Mozart's career is the fluency and facility with which he composed. Music seemed to flow unceasingly from him. In fact a great deal of mental preparation went on before he started writing; he worked out whole movements in his head before setting pen to paper, which entailed not only a strong musical imagination but a strong memory. Some of the writing down was very last-minute. The overture to *Don Giovanni* was written just two nights before the first performance. He was incredibly prolific. Among other pieces, he wrote 12 operas, 41 (surviving) symphonies, 21 piano concerti, 5 string quintets, 23 string quartets, 37 violin sonatas, 17 piano sonatas and 18 masses – and all of this was achieved before his early death at the age of 35.

In 1789, Mozart visited Leipzig, where he was able to discuss Bach's music with Bach's successor, Doles. Even at this late stage, Mozart was still hoping that he might find refuge with a more sympathetic patron. In 1790 he was disappointed that he was not made Kapellmeister by the new Emperor Leopold II. Financial worries closed in on him. In July 1791 he was visited by a mysterious stranger, who was the steward of a nobleman who needed a composition in order to pass himself off as a composer, and who commissioned Mozart to write a Requiem for this anonymous patron. Mozart accepted this strange commission, but died before he could complete it. The Requiem was completed by Mozart's pupil Sussmayr. Mozart was gripped by an unidentified fever and died on 5 December, 1791.

Mozart was a child prodigy and his experiences as a child both made and marred him. Over-praised and over-petted when young, dandled by Marie Antoinette, in some ways he remained a spoilt child to the end of his life. He did not organize the commercial side of his life responsibly, which caused him great problems in his last years. His music often conveys the exuberance of childhood delight, but always with incredible grace and polish; the music is never childish. The musical ideas are always very clearly expressed, but never banal and always cleverly avoid the predictable. He was not an intellectual. When not performing or composing, he enjoyed playing billiards; he seems to have had no interests outside music. The music perhaps absorbed most of his mental activity.

Mozart was the universal genius of music. His music always shows a total command of technique, and an infallible command of design and structure, qualities that make Mozart the ultimate flowering of the classical tradition. In *Don Giovanni,* he depicts a dynamic anti-hero at odds with the society he lives in, in other words the opera is the first Sturm und Drang piece. Mozart therefore marks not only the culmination of the classical tradition but the beginning of the German Romantic tradition. He is the bridge between the 18th and the 19th centuries.

Mozart's music reaches such a perfection and sublimity that it is still, over 200 years after his death, hard to believe that it was the creation of a human being. He was unquestionably the greatest composer who ever lived.

MARQUIS DE LA FAYETTE

Born at Chavagnac 1757, died in Paris 1834.

French soldier, reformer, revolutionary, fighter for American
   independence.

ACHIEVEMENTS:

Played key roles in both French and American Revolutions.

1777 – Fought on the American side in the American War of
   Independence.

1787 – Personally demanded that Louis XVI summon the
   States General, initiating the French Revolution.

1789 – Was appointed colonel-general of the French National
   Guard.

1789 – Presented a declaration of rights to the French National
   Assembly.

1789 – Devised the tricolour cockade and the flag of modern
   France.

1791 – Ordered the escaping Louis XVI to be arrested and
   returned to Paris, indirectly causing the death of the king.

1830 – Took command of the National Guard.

MARIE JOSEPH PAUL Yves Roch Gilbert du Motier, much better known as
the Marquis de La Fayette, was born in the Chateau de Chavagnac in the
Auvergne district of France. La Fayette's father was killed at the Battle of
Minden in 1759 and at the age of 13 he was left an orphan, though with a
considerable family fortune at his disposal. He married at 16 and entered

the army. He was a captain of dragoons when the American War of Independence broke out. He later wrote, 'At the first news of this quarrel, my heart was enrolled in it.' It was a political cause very close to his heart, and in a real sense the struggle was a dry run for the French Revolution; the French people were a colonized people, like the Americans, but colonized by their aristocracy instead of a foreign power.

In December 1776, an arrangement was made through Silas Deane, American agent in Paris, by which La Fayette was recruited into the service of America as major-general. At this moment news came of a major setback to the American cause, and La Fayette's friends urged him not to go to America. The American envoys gave him no encouragement, and Louis XVI forbade him to go. The British ambassador at Versailles insisted that La Fayette's ship should be seized at Bordeaux, where it was being fitted out, and La Fayette himself was arrested. But all was not lost. In 1777 the ship was moved to another port, on the north coast of Spain, out of the reach of the French authorities. La Fayette escaped in disguise and sailed to America to offer assistance to the American colonists in their struggle for independence from Britain.

La Fayette landed near Georgetown in South Carolina and hurried to Philadelphia, demanding to see the commander-in-chief. He showed Deane's authority and demanded to be given the most senior post after the commander-in-chief. He quickly realised that this was an unrealistic expectation, and asked instead to be taken on in some capacity as a volunteer. Congress passed a resolution recommending that he be given the rank of major-general, in recognition for his zeal and family connections – which still mattered in 'revolutionary' America. He was given the command of a division by Washington but never had many troops under his command. His prowess in battle was soon proved, and he greatly impressed the colonists with his military dash. Treaties of commerce and defensive alliance were signed by the insurgent colonists and France in February 1778, and these were promptly followed by England's declaration of war against France – for siding with the colonists. La Fayette's high-profile involvement itself implied France's connivance at the American

Revolution, and La Fayette can be held partly responsible for the momentous outbreak of war between England and France.

La Fayette asked leave to return home to France for a few months in 1779, to consult Louis XVI as to the further direction of his services. This was incredibly rash, as the French king had forbidden him to go to America in the first place, and La Fayette had escaped custody in disguise in order to flout the king's wishes. Even so, the Americans readily agreed to let him go, as there was the possibility that this 'golden boy' might be able to negotiate a peace.

In France, instead of being clapped in prison, La Fayette received startling advancement. He was made a major-general in the French army. It was in 1779 that his son was born; La Fayette named him Georges Washington Motier de La Fayette, and the boy would one day also to follow a military career in the Napoleonic Wars as aide-de-camp to General de Grouchy.

He then went back to America, where he was given the responsibility for defending Virginia. He fought at the Battle of Yorktown.

On his third visit to America, in 1784, Lafayette was welcomed enthusiastically. In France too he had acquired a reputation as a committed reformer and was called to the Assembly of Notables in 1787. It was La Fayette who made the demand – and courageously he alone signed the demand – that Louis XVI must summon the States General. La Fayette thus played a leading role in the French Revolution. He sat in the States General. He also sat in the National Assembly of 1789, where he laid on the Assembly's table a declaration of rights that was based on the American Declaration of Independence. On 5 July, 1789, the second day of the new regime, he was appointed by acclamation to lead the armed citizenry of France, the National Guard, as its colonel-general. It was La Fayette who proposed combining the colours of Paris, red and blue, with the royal white, to make the tricolor cockade and the tricolor flag of the modern state of France.

When Louis XVI made an attempt to escape, it was La Fayette who ordered his arrest at Varennes and return to Paris. He therefore indirectly brought about the death of Louis XVI and his family, bringing about the end of the dynasty.

Lafayette struggled ceaselessly for order and humanity, pleading for an end to arbitrary imprisonment, for the establishment of trial by jury, for the emancipation of slaves, and for the freedom of the press. The Jacobins, who were revolutionary extremists, came to hate his moderation, his liberalism. He nevertheless supported the abolition of all titles and all class privilege – though he himself was a marquis. In the end the hatred of the Jacobins became so intense that he thought it safer to get out of France before he went, like so many other moderates, to the guillotine. He rode across the north-east border to Liege, where he was captured and imprisoned first in Germany then in Austria as one of the prime movers of the Revolution. He was kept confined until long after the Terror ended. In fact Lafayette remained in detention until he was released on Napoleon's orders, contained in the Treaty of Campo Formio, in 1797.

Lafayette's political career was by no means over. In 1802 he voted against Napoleon being made life consul. In 1804 he voted against Napoleon being made emperor. He was still the moderate revolutionary. He sat in the Chamber of Deputies from 1818 until 1824, representing the extreme left.

In 1824, Lafayette visited America, at the invitation of congress. They voted him 200,000 dollars and a township. He was overwhelmed by the spontaneous applause and appreciation shown by the American people. They warmly remembered his inspirational role in America's struggle for independence.

From 1825 until 1830 he was again a leader of the opposition in France. In 1830, France went through another revolution, and once again Lafayette was in the thick of it, once again in command of the National Guard, in spite of being then 73 years of age. He sat in the Chamber of Deputies for Meaux until he died in 1834. His last speech, made in that final year, was on behalf of Polish political refugees.

La Fayette was a very unusual figure. He was unusual in fighting the causes of both the American and the French Revolutions, and surviving both. Few men with his profile in the French Revolution survived the bloodbath into which the Revolution descended. He went on from there to oppose the dictatorship of Napoleon – and survived that too. Incredibly, he was still there, very conspicuously there like a figure from a bygone age, in the Revolution of 1830, once again at the head of the French National Guard. He was impulsive, a man of spirited, courageous and even reckless action, yet he was also a fiercely moderate liberal. He believed in the freedom of the press, the freedom of the individual, the right to a fair trial – the very things that the French Revolution which he instigated swept away. He also strode the stage of major world events through sheer force of personality. His influence on the course of the American War of Independence was out of all proportion to his technical rank or specific military actions. In France, in much the same way he took power without rank. The audacity with which he, personally, commanded the King to convene the States General, was remarkable – and remarkable too in its effect. La Fayette was one of those rare individuals who manages to change the world by sheer force of personality.

MAXIMILIEN ROBESPIERRE

Born at Arras 1758, died in Paris 1794.
French Revolutionary leader, cruel dictator, regicide.

ACHIEVEMENTS:

1792 – Set up the Revolutionary Tribunal.

1793 – Responsible for the execution of Louis XVI, ending the French Bourbon dynasty.

1793 – Organized the Reign of Terror, ordered the murder of thousands of innocent people.

1794 – Introduced a short-lived new religion, the Reign of Virtue.

1794 – Became dictator of France for a few months.

MAXIMILIEN MARIE ISIDOR de Robespierre was born on 6 May 1758 in the French town of Arras. He was the eldest child of François de Robespierre, a lawyer, and Jacqueline Marguerite Carraut, the daughter of a brewer. Robespierre's childhood was unhappy, especially after the death of his mother in 1767, and he was left, along with three siblings, in the care of relatives when his father abandoned them. The father left Arras immediately after his wife's death, wandering disconsolately round Europe until he too died, in Munich, two years later.

Maximilien was sent to the college of Arras and the college of Louis-le-Grand in Paris. It was in Paris that he met and befriended Camille Desmoulins. As a boy and as a man Maximilien was nervous and hesitant when speaking, disliked crowds, and might have been thought timid and lacking in self-confidence. His reserve even so concealed a steely certainty and an underlying arrogance. Although hesitant in his ordinary speech, and tending to enjoy his own company, he turned out to have the gift of oratory, becoming the greatest public speaker of his time.

In 1780, Robespierre became a Bachelor of Law, receiving his licence the following year and opening a law practice in his home town of Arras. As a young man he had a reputation for honesty and compassion. He was not a good lawyer, losing many of his cases, though he began to think of ways in which society might be reformed through the law. He wanted to see the death penalty abolished and, when he became a criminal judge in the diocese of Arras in 1782, refused to give a death sentence when the law required it. He resigned his post rather than pronounce the death sentence.

He turned now to literature and society. He came to be admired as one of the best writers and most popular dandies of Arras. He was a member of a musical and literary society known as 'The Rosati'. It was the beauty of his speaking voice when he recited at meetings that won him great applause rather than the quality of his verses.

In 1788 Robespierre took part in the discussion on the way in which the States General should be elected. He argued lucidly that if the old mode of election was used, the next States General would not represent the people of France.

In this way the following year he found himself elected, at the age of 30, to the States General, to represent Artois. He gravitated to the extreme left wing and soon commanded attention because everything he said burned with fanatical fervour. His charisma ensured that his influence grew daily. Initially, he had no intention of overthrowing the monarchy or setting up a revolutionary government. Mirabeau referred to the left wing contemptuously as 'the thirty voices', because they were so few, but they were fanatically determined. Mirabeau's death brought Robespierre into higher profile. The radical Jacobin Club to which Robespierre belonged was soon advocating exile or death for the aristocracy.

In 1791, Robespierre proposed the motion that no member of the present Assembly should be eligible for the next, and revealed for the first time in public the streak of jealous suspicion that would come to the fore during the Terror to come. Robespierre's first great triumph as a demagogue came on 30 September, when the Constituent Assembly was dissolved and the people of Paris crowned Pétion and Robespierre as 'the two incorruptible patriots'.

In August 1792, Robespierre presented to the Legislative Assembly a petition for a Revolutionary Tribunal and a new Convention, where some bitter attacks launched against him by the Girondins threw him into a closer alliance with Georges Danton. Interestingly, and somewhat inconsistently, during that summer Robespierre took no part at all in the movement to end the Bourbon dynasty. At this stage, almost incredibly, it seems that Robespierre was still shocked at the idea of shedding blood. By December 1792 his position had changed to the extent that it looks as if his personality had changed. He said, 'I pronounce the fatal truth: Louis ought to perish rather than a hundred thousand virtuous citizens. Louis must die, that the country may live.'

The execution of the King without appeal to the people on 21 January 1793 represented a personal triumph for Robespierre and inaugurated the final life-and-death struggle between the Girondins and the Jacobins.

Robespierre's personality changed, or rather different traits emerged, after he gained power. There was now a strong streak of paranoia. He became extremely intolerant. He treated people who disagreed with him and criticized his ideas as 'enemies of the nation', and suspected conspiracy everywhere. In his position as leader of the Committee of Public Safety, he was easily able to send those enemies of the nation to the guillotine. People became terrified of him. Robespierre now developed a great love of power and acquired a reputation for self-righteousness and cruelty. He used his great skill as an orator to win the death sentence for both the King and the Queen.

It was largely due to Robespierre's efforts that Louis XVI went to the guillotine in January 1793 and Marie Antoinette followed ten months later. The first Committee of Public Safety was decreed in April 1793. It assumed the governance of France and now Robespierre, elected in July, formally became one of the rulers of France along with the rest of the Twelve. In his capacity as ruler, Robespierre supervised a three-year Reign of Terror. During this terrible episode, Robespierre and his associates committed the wholesale murder of entire families of aristocrats, and sent thousands of ordinary people to their death without proper trials.

Robespierre's paranoia led him to suspect everyone about him. His friends Danton and Desmoulins were sent to the guillotine. He placed his own men in all positions of influence in the Commune of Paris and assumed complete control of the Revolutionary Tribunal. Jacques-René Hébert, an atheist, closed the Catholic churches and started the pagan-style worship of a Goddess of Reason. Robespierre condemned this Cult of Reason and sent him and his friends to the guillotine in March 1794, and then in May recommended the Convention to acknowledge the existence of God. On 8 June he introduced his own alternative faith, the Reign of Virtue, at the inaugural Festival of the Supreme Being. It says a lot about Robespierre's vanity and megalomania that he thought he could make up a whole new religion and force France to adopt it. He gave an extraordinary speech 'On the Festival of the Supreme Being', the text of which has survived. It is full of ringing generalities and eloquence. One can sense what it must have been like to be there, listening to Citizen Robespierre persuasively rhapsodizing as the death sentence became more and more certain for some unlucky victim.

Robespierre's friend St Just demanded the creation of a dictatorship in the person of Robespierre. On 8 July, the dictator delivered another long and neurotic tirade, this time complaining that his enemies were out to get him. Many felt threatened and menaced by his tone.

Robespierre's grasp of France was mercifully short-lived and imperfect, so at least *his* Reign of Terror was quite brief. He succeeded in the course of a few months in executing many of his enemies, but the groups opposed to him recognized that they must act against him or they too would be executed. The only way to save themselves was to bring Robespierre down.

In 1794, the Committee of Public Safety impeached Robespierre. Most of his co-members of the Jacobin Club betrayed him during this trial. St Just was a rare exception. When Robespierre hesitated in his own defence, someone shouted, 'It's the blood of Danton that chokes him!' He had sent one too many of his comrades to the guillotine. He was rescued from prison and taken to the hôtel de ville, but Barras followed him there with the National Guards to re-arrest him. A young gendarme fired his pistol at him and hit him in the jaw. After a night of agony, Robespierre was taken before the tribunal where he was identified as an outlaw and taken away to be executed. On 28 July 1794, Robespierre was taken to the Place de la Concorde along with 19 of his comrades and executed with the same guillotine, on the same spot, as Louis XVI.

With that, the Reign of Terror came to an end. At the time, Robespierre was blamed for instigating many of the horrors, and probably rightly. Robespierre did not single-handedly invent the Terror, but he served it with his oratory. He persuaded his hearers of his honesty and virtue and made it seem that everything that happened was laudable and necessary, rather than monstrously evil. Robespierre liked to lay 'all the crimes and misfortunes of the world' at the door of the poor, dead, feckless King Louis, but the Reign of Terror was much more of Robespierre's making than the King's.

In himself, Robespierre was a respectable, hard-working, well-dressed, well-mannered, honest, truthful, charitable man. But for the Revolution, he would probably have made a comfortable and happy life for himself as a provincial judge and a writer – a traditional pillar of 18th-century bourgeois society. But reading Rousseau when young gave him disturbing, subversive, revolutionary ideas. Even those might not have led to trouble, but for his election to the States General, where he met a score of other fanatical young Rousseau addicts – and there among them the Revolution was kindled. It was a personal tragedy as well as a tragedy for France that the honest and incorruptible idealist who detested the idea of sentencing someone to death should have ended up successfully arguing for the death of his King and his Queen and thousands of other innocent people besides.

LORD HORATIO NELSON

Born at Burnham Thorpe 1758, died at Trafalgar 1805.
English naval commander, national hero.

ACHIEVEMENTS:
Gret naval tactician.
Inspirational commander.
Origin of the saying 'turning a blind eye'.
Won several major victories at sea against the French.
Prevented a French invasion of Britain.
Played a major role in defeating Napoleon.
The most famous of all seamen.
Britain's greatest combat hero.
1796 – Won the Battle of Cape St. Vincent.
1798 – Won the Battle of the Nile.
1801 – Won the Battle of Copenhagen.
1805 – Won the Battle of Trafalgar.

HORATIO NELSON WAS born at Burnham Thorpe parsonage in Norfolk. His family was middle class; his father, Edmund Nelson, was the rector and his mother, Catherine Suckling, was the grand-niece of Sir Robert Walpole. This connection might have been of some career advantage in what was an extremely class-conscious society, but it was not. In 1784, Horatio was to write to his brother, Revd William Nelson, that the Walpoles were 'the merest set of cyphers that ever existed – in public affairs I mean.' His uncle, Captain Maurice Suckling, later became comptroller of the navy, and this family connection was of great practical use to him. The young Horatio received a spasmodic and inadequate education at Norwich, Downham and North Walsham before going into the navy with his uncle.

He entered the Royal Navy as a midshipman in 1770, entering on the *Raisonnable*, Captain Suckling's ship, when there was a major naval alert. War with Spain seemed imminent, and Suckling and his distinguished nephew put to sea at once. When the emergency was over, Captain Suckling was transferred to the *Triumph*, the guardship at Chatham, and he took his nephew with him. Suckling realised that Nelson would get little in the way of useful experience on a ship stuck in an estuary all the time, so he sent him off on a voyage to the West Indies on a merchant vessel, and when he returned, Suckling gave Horatio plenty of work to do on boats on the Medway and Thames estuaries. With this experience, Nelson became a good pilot for small vessels from Chatham up to the Tower of London and down to the North Foreland, and became expert at navigating among shoals and sandbanks.

He served with Captain Lutwidge on the *Carcass* in the Arctic expedition of 1773, and then served in the East Indies on the *Seahorse*. It was on the *Seahorse* that he met his lifelong friend Thomas Troubridge. After two years in the Indies he was invalided home in September 1776. He was profoundly depressed during the return voyage, until:

> *After a long and gloomy reverie, in which I almost wished myself overboard, a sudden glow of patriotism was kindled within me, and presented my king and my country as my patron. My mind exulted in the idea. 'Well then,' I exclaimed, 'I will be a hero and, confiding in Providence, I will brave every danger.' He described to friends the radiant orb that from then on for ever hung before him, 'urging him onward to renown.*

After this near-religious conversion, Nelson passed his examination to lieutenant and was confirmed in rank the next day. As lieutenant in the frigate Lowestoft he went to Jamaica in 1777. In 1779 he was posted to the *Badger*, with an unusually rapid promotion to its command, and then to post captain of the frigate *Hinchingbrook*. He was by this time still only 20. In the main, Nelson owed his rapid rise in seniority to an extraordinary ability to win the affection of his comrades and superiors. Nelson was a very likeable man. One feature of his leadership was his thorough briefing; every officer knew before going into action exactly what their commander's battle plan was. The captains in any squadron were then able to bond with each other and their commander as a band of brothers. Another feature of his leadership was his common humanity, the bond he shared with the ordinary seamen; he knew all too well what it was like to be sea-sick and home-sick, and treated them with kindness. In return he was respected, even venerated by them.

In 1780, Nelson saw his first action, when he commanded the naval force attacking San Juan. He caught a fever, from which he almost died, and was invalided home again. In 1781, he joined the *Albemarle* and undertook some convoy service in the North Sea before joining the squadron under Lord Hood in America. In the West Indies he made the acquaintance of Admiral Lord Hood, who introduced him to the Duke of Clarence, later William IV, as an officer well qualified to instruct him in naval tactics, which was a telling compliment for a great tactician to pay such a young officer. William IV later described Nelson as:

> *The merest boy of a captain I ever beheld; and his dress was worthy of attention. He had on a full-laced uniform; his lank unpowdered hair was tied in a stiff Hessian tail of extraordinary length; the old-fashioned flaps of his waistcoat added to the general quaintness of his figure, and produced an appearance which particularly attracted my notice; for I had not seen anything like it before, nor could I imagine who he was or what he came about. My doubts were, however, removed when Lord Hood introduced me to him. There was something irresistibly pleasing in his address and conversation; and an enthusiasm, when speaking on professional subjects, that showed he was no common being.*

So the young Nelson made a deep impression, even on kings. The odd appearance, the ability to inspire affection, and the glowing fervour within were commented on by everyone who met him.

The Peace of Versailles that ended the American War gave Nelson a break in which he visited France, to study the language of the enemy and also to study the French literature on naval strategy. Then, when most naval officers were doomed to idleness, Nelson had the good luck to be appointed captain of the frigate Boreas for service in the West Indies. In Antigua another side of Nelson emerged – his high-handedness. First he refused to acknowledge the commissioner of the dockyard as his superior. Then he drew the Admiralty's attention to the corruption that prevailed in the dockyard, and introduced strong measures against interloping trade. The Admiralty found all this rather troublesome and thought Nelson's behaviour ostentatious. Nelson was vain, arrogant and egotistical – he was a show-off – and this was the negative side of his genius. While serving in the West Indies in 1784 he met and married Frances Nisbet, a widow, and retired from the navy for a time to live with his new wife at Burnham Thorpe.

When the war with Revolutionary France broke out in 1792, Nelson was given the command of the *Agamemnon*, which was his favourite ship. Nelson was in more or less continuous service for the next 7 years; he was active, busy and highly successful – though often controversial. In the *Agamemnon*, Nelson accompanied Hood to the Mediterranean. After Toulon was surrendered, Nelson was ordered to go to Naples. This was where he met Emma Hamilton, the wife of the British ambassador. His letters home to his wife mention Lady Hamilton, though only in terms of her kindness to his stepson, Josiah Nisbet, whom he had taken to sea with him. In 1794, he commanded the naval attack on Bastia and Calvi; it was in this action that he was wounded in his right eye. This did not necessitate surgery, and the wound healed without leaving him disfigured, but the sight gradually faded. Nelson never wore an eye-patch, contrary to popular belief. This fragment of the Nelson myth probably arose because there was talk of Nelson 'losing an eye' rather than losing his sight, and therefore assume there was an unsightly empty socket to cover. Not so; the eye was sightless, but appeared undamaged.

In 1796, together with Sir John Jervis, Nelson inflicted a major defeat on the Spanish fleet off Cape St Vincent. Nelson acted with promptness and initiative in the battle, proving again his worth as a naval commander.

After this he was promoted to Rear-admiral and sent with an inadequate squadron to capture a Spanish treasure-ship at Santa Cruz de Tenerife. In this action he lost his right arm. His elbow was shot through. The amputation was done hurriedly and badly, in the dark. He was forced to spend nine months at home in extreme pain, recovering not only from the injury but from the bad surgery.

In 1798 came one of Nelson's greatest victories, the Battle of the Nile, where, commanding *HMS Vanguard*, he inflicted a crushing defeat on the French fleet. It is often assumed that the British deliberately destroyed the French flagship, which blew up and sank during the battle, but it was accidental. The loss of the valuable flagship meant a huge loss in prize money to the British sailors; they were mortified. At the Nile, Nelson was wounded on the forehead; he went below for a while to recover, but was soon back on deck again. The victory of the Nile on 1 August 1798, was a landmark in his career, putting him in the front rank among the warriors of his time, and making him a national hero – his main ambition.

Nelson was now raised to the peerage, becoming Lord Nelson of the Nile and voted a pension £2,000 a year. The East India Company awarded him £10,000, and the King of Naples conferred on him the title Duke of Bronte. He characteristically wore all these honours at every opportunity. Nelson resigned his command after this triumph and returned to England with the Hamiltons; Emma was expecting a baby, undiplomatically named Horatia, and Nelson finally separated from his long-suffering wife.

In 1801, Nelson was promoted to Vice-admiral and appointed second in command on a new expedition to the Baltic, under Sir Hyde Parker. It is hard to see why someone with Nelson's proven ability should have been made subordinate to someone as ordinary as Hyde Parker. Parker himself seems to have been aware that he had a problem in giving orders to someone of Nelson's genius and, as is usual in such situations, became wary and suspicious of him. Nelson was good at handling people, though, and treated Parker with great tact. By the time they reached Copenhagen Nelson was able to make the decision to attack. But Parker was irresolute, and in the middle of the action stupidly tried to order Nelson to withdraw. Nelson took a massive risk, famously put his telescope to his blind eye, through which he genuinely could not see the signal flags that his officers were pointing out. He disobeyed orders, because doing so would have put his ships in increased danger, and continued to engage the enemy. He decisively won the Battle of Copenhagen.

During the short Peace of Amiens in 1802–3, Nelson stayed at the house and estate he had bought at Merton in Surrey. Sir William and Lady Hamilton were his guests. Nelson managed to secure a reconciliation with his father, who until then had found it hard to forgive him for his immoral association with Emma Hamilton, which had become a national scandal.

When the Napoleonic War resumed in 1803, Nelson was commander of the Mediterranean fleet, but in March 1805 the French fleet which he was trying to keep bottled up there escaped into the Atlantic. Nelson searched the Mediterranean in vain. He had a hunch that Villeneuve, the French admiral, had taken his fleet to the West Indies for safety and sailed there in pursuit. When Villeneuve heard that Nelson had arrived, he ran away again, taking his fleet hastily back across the Atlantic towards Europe, once more hotly pursued by Nelson. The French fleet was bottled up at Cadiz by Collingwood, while Nelson returned to Merton for a break. Then he offered 'to give Monsieur Villeneuve a drubbing', an offer which the Admiralty accepted with alacrity, and Nelson left Merton, and England, for the last time.

He eventually caught up with the French fleet off Cape Trafalgar, on the coast of Portugal, in October 1805. Nelson directed the action, which was planned brilliantly, from his flagship *HMS Victory* and the battle was a decisive British victory as well as a tactical masterpiece. Unfortunately, Nelson insisted on being seen on the quarter-deck of the Victory dressed as always in full uniform, decorated with all his honours like a bird of paradise, and was easily identified from a great distance. He was a sitting duck. He was picked off by a French sniper and mortally wounded. He languished in great pain for several hours in the cockpit, among the many other wounded and dying, receiving reports of the progress of the battle. He repeatedly muttered, 'Thank God I have done my duty', and died knowing that the battle was won. At the end he asked Hardy, one of the officers tending him, to kiss him.

An attempt was made to preserve Nelson's body in a barrel of brandy, and it was shipped back to London for burial in St Paul's Cathedral. Nelson was given a state funeral and his death was rightly regarded as a national disaster. An enormous crowd turned out to see Nelson's funeral; only 7,000 VIPs were allowed into St Paul's – but among them, extraordinarily, was Nelson's opponent Villeneuve. With Wellington in command of land forces and Nelson in command at sea, there was a good chance of defeating the dictator Napoleon. The damage done to the French fleet by Nelson's great victories – the 'drubbing' he had promised Monsieur Villeneuve – ensured that the French would not contemplate an invasion of Britain. Although the Napoleonic Wars dragged on for another ten years after the Battle of Trafalgar, Britain was at least safe from invasion.

WILLIAM WILBERFORCE

Born in Hull 1759, died in London 1833.
English philanthropist, reformer, freer of slaves.

ACHIEVEMENTS:
1788 – Started the campaign to end slave trade and slavery.
1797 – A Practical View of Christianity.
1807 – Ended the slave trade in Britain and British
   possessions.
1833 – The Emancipation Bill was passed by Parliament,
   ending slavery in the British Empire.
1834 – 750,000 slaves throughout the British Empire were
   freed.

WILLIAM WILBERFORCE WAS born in Hull, the only son of Robert Wilberforce, a rich merchant. At the age of nine his father died and he was sent to be looked after by his father's brother in Wimbledon. At the age of 12 he returned to Hull, where he was placed in the care of the master of the endowed school of Pocklington. William did not work very hard at school, but he was still accepted at St John's College, Cambridge, in 1776.

The deaths of his grandfather and his uncle left him with a large legacy, he had little incentive to work at Cambridge, and he neglected his studies. Wilberforce graduated successfully, but nevertheless later looked back on his student years with remorse at the opportunities he wasted when young. In 1780 he became MP for Hull, and he soon became caught up in the fast-moving political set in London. He became a close friend of William Pitt the Younger, although he remained independent in his views and above party affiliation. In 1783, he went on holiday with Pitt to France, and on their return, Wilberforce's eloquence was a great help to Pitt in his fight against the majority of the House of Commons. In 1784, Wilberforce was returned as MP for both Hull and Yorkshire, and took his seat for Yorkshire.

In 1784–85, Wilberforce went on a tour of the continent with Dr Isaac Milner, who had been one of his masters at Hull Grammar School and would later become President of Queen's College Cambridge and Dean of Carlisle. During this tour, Wilberforce became a convert to evangelical Christianity. This event had a major change on his behaviour. In 1787 he founded an association for the reform of manners.

In 1788, with the support of Thomas Clarkson and the Quakers, he began his historic 19-year struggle for the abolition of the slave trade. It had been just over 20 years since Jean Jacques Rousseau had drawn attention so dramatically and ironically to the state of mankind: 'Man is born free, but everywhere he is in chains.' Wilberforce wanted to remove those chains. Pitt encouraged Wilberforce to give himself to this monumental project as one that was ideally suited to his character and talents. Thomas Clarkson took the campaign round the country, while William Wilberforce took every opportunity to raise the matter in the House of Commons. This long, slow, arduous campaign resulted in success in 1807, when the slave trade became illegal in Britain and throughout the British Empire. Then Wilberforce worked towards getting the slave trade abolished globally and the total abolition of slavery itself. This was obviously far more difficult to achieve – and he failed.

In 1823, Clarkson and Wilberforce became vice-presidents of the Anti-Slavery Society, which continued to campaign for total abolition. In 1825 failing health forced him to retire from parliament and public life generally. He moved to Highwood Hill near Mill Hill. The Emancipation Bill, which was the culmination of Wilberforce's life work, was passed in August 1833, a few weeks after his death on 29 July. From 1834 onwards, slavery was abolished throughout the British Empire. On Emancipation Day, 1 August, 1834, 750,000 slaves were freed – largely thanks to the work of William Wilberforce.

In 1797, Wilberforce married Barbara Spooner and they set up home together in Clapham. There, for a long time, he was a leading figure in the Clapham sect of Evangelical Christians. Wilberforce's third son, Samuel Wilberforce, became Bishop of Oxford.

His major success in having the slave trade abolished in Britain ensured his place in history – he was buried in Westminster Abbey – but he promoted many other schemes for the welfare of the community too, such as the emancipation of Catholics and parliamentary reform. William Wilberforce was one of those movers and shakers who worked tirelessly to make life significantly better for other people.

WILLIAM SYMINGTON

Born at Leadhills 1763, died in London 1831.
Scottish engineer and inventor.

ACHIEVEMENTS:
Invented the paddle steamer, the first practical steamboat.

WILLIAM SYMINGTON WAS born in Leadhills and became a mechanic in the Wanlockhead mines.

In 1787 he took out a patent for a road locomotive. In that same year, over in America, James Rumsey drove a boat on the Potomac at 4 mph; it was powered, rather ineffectively and inefficiently, by a stream of water forced through the stern by a steam-powered pump. At the same time John Fitch was experimenting with an oar-driven steamboat on the River Delaware. The 24-year-old William Symington may have heard about these American experiments, because in the following year, 1788, he switched his interest from land to water transport, mounting his 'road locomotive' engine, a direct-action steam engine, onto a paddle boat. The steamboat Symington designed with Patrick Miller, another inventor and steamboat pioneer, was 25 feet long. It had twin hulls with paddle wheels mounted between them. The boat was essentially Miller's design, but Symington supplied the engine. Symington and Miller launched their unusual vessel on Dalswinton Loch at Miller's estate near Dumfries. Paddles turned out to be the most efficient device so far invented, yet the landmark invention attracted no commercial attention whatever.

In 1801–2 Symington built the *Charlotte Dundas* at Grangemouth on the Firth of Forth. The *Charlotte Dundas* was one of the earliest practical working steamboats ever to be built. Symington intended the ship to function as a tug, and she proved her capabilities by doing towing work on the Forth and Clyde Canal. Unfortunately vested interests prevented the ship from being taken into regular service; the argument used against it was that the steamboat would stir up too much wash, and erode the banks of the Forth and Clyde Canal.

Because he failed to capture any commercial interest in his invention, Symington died in poverty. Yet he was one of the great innovators of the Industrial Revolution. He made the first working steamboats, and prepared the way for the building of ever-larger steamships through the second half of the 19th century. Robert Fulton saw the *Charlotte Dundas* in action, was impressed by its effectiveness, and went back to the United States to build his own ship, the *Clermont*, on the Hudson River in 1807. Fulton used Boulton and Watt steam engines for his steamship, and it proved to be a very popular passenger ferryboat, running between New York and Albany. The first steamer to make a regular sea voyage was the *Phoenix*, built in 1809, which steamed from Hoboken, New Jersey to Philadelphia. The steamship developed very quickly, but certainly began decisively with the *Charlotte Dundas* built by William Symington.

THOMAS MALTHUS

Born near Guildford 1766, died at Haileybury 1834.
English economist and clergyman.

ACHIEVEMENTS:

Contributed many ideas to modern economic theory.

Invented the idea of population collapse.

Maintained that human population increases until it outgrows food supply.

Supplied Darwin with an explanation for evolution.

Supplied the 'population explosion' propagandists of the 1960s with a reason for promoting birth control.

1798 – Essay on the Principle of Population *first edition published.*

1807 – Essay on the Principle of Population *second edition published.*

1815 – An Inquiry into the Nature and Progress of Rent *published.*

1820 – Principles of Political Economy *published.*

THOMAS ROBERT MALTHUS was born at The Rookery near Guildford, a small estate owned by his father, Daniel Malthus, who was a friend and executor of Jean Jacques Rousseau. Thomas Malthus was educated privately before going to Cambridge. He was a very able student and was elected Fellow of Jesus College in 1793. In 1797 he became curate at Albury in Surrey.

In 1798 at the age of 32 he published, anonymously, his great work, *Essay on the Principle of Population*, following it with a greatly enlarged edition in 1807. Malthus was constantly adjusting and amending his ideas, and brought out six editions of his *Essay*, the last appearing in 1826.

In this landmark book, Malthus maintained that the optimistic views of Rousseau and William Godwin regarding population are baseless, and that population has a tendency to increase faster than the means of maintaining it. Food production increases at an arithmetic rate; population increases at a geometric rate. In other words, human population will go on increasing until there is no food left, or until there is some other check, such as pestilence or war, and then collapse through famine.

The book developed out of discussions with his father about the perfectibility of society. Daniel Malthus shared the optimistic views of Condorcet and Godwin, while his son Thomas took the pessimistic view that the achievement of a happy society will always be hindered by the problems caused by the tendency for population to grow faster than the means of supporting it. Daniel Malthus was very struck by his son's arguments and pressed him to put them into writing. When he read them, he pressed him to publish them. The first edition is really a long pamphlet, but a key feature is the high quality of Malthus's style of writing, which is both vivid and lucid.

Malthus was an amiable and benign man who has often been misrepresented and abused. Malthus drew from his own conclusion the unhappy thought that the poor-law system prevailing at that time, in his England, with its indiscriminate doles and bounties given to large families, was actually destructive rather than helpful. Saying so seemed, and to many still seems, heartless and illiberal but it was an honest inference, logically arrived at. It was not surprising that the first edition of his book provoked a storm of controversy. But in his second edition, Malthus fleshed the argument out with case studies to prove his points, and adopted a more sober and scholarly style. He also offered readers the hope that the birth rate might be reduced by 'moral restraint', by which he meant sexual abstinence and the use of birth control.

The problem of population growth had been handled by other thinkers, such as Franklin and Hume; what Malthus did was to express their views in a systematic form together with proofs from history. Nor was Malthus entirely pessimistic in his views. He argued that a population collapse could be averted by reducing the birth rate, but he was evidently not convinced that the human race as a whole would be prepared to regulate itself in this way.

In 1805 Malthus was married and also appointed Professor of Modern History and Political Economy at the East India College at Haileybury.

Malthusian ideas on population have been profoundly influential in economics, geography, demography, biology and ecology. Charles Darwin was strongly influenced by Malthus, whose *Essay* he happened to read by chance. According to his own account, he saw 'on reading Malthus *On Population* that natural selection was the inevitable result of the rapid increase of all organic beings.' Darwin inferred that a rapid increase in population necessarily leads to a struggle for existence. The phrase 'struggle for existence' actually occurs in Malthus's *Essay*. Darwin in effect used Malthus's theory to explain why evolution was necessary.

Writing at the end of the 18th century, Malthus was unaware of the effects that improved transport in the form of steamships and railways would have. He was unaware that colonization of new regions would open up new areas to food production. As a result, the population collapse he predicted was long delayed. He may not have been wrong in the long term, of course – only wrong for the 19th and 20th centuries.

Malthusian ideas also lay behind the scare-mongering that went on in the 1960s and 1970s, when many influential economists and ecologists argued that human population growth was running out of control – that starvation lay just round the corner. The simple Malthusian model may work well for organisms that have a narrow range of foods on which they depend, but the human race is more complicated than that. People have been able to develop new high-yield strains of wheat, rice and other key foods, so that the food supply is more elastic than once thought. The neo-Malthusian scare campaigns of the 1960s and 1970s nevertheless generated a great deal of interest in population control, and most countries now have more or less effective birth control programmes in place. Some countries have found that their attempts to reduce the birth rate were too effective and they now need immigrants in order to meet all their labour needs.

Malthus also had great influence on the development of economic theory. He was a close friend and correspondent of the economist David Ricardo, and he helped Ricardo to develop his ideas on the theory of value. Malthus was the first writer to formulate the law of diminishing returns as applied to agriculture, though he did not call it that. Malthus contributed other useful ideas too, such his views on rent.

For better or worse, the ideas of Malthus have continued to be extremely influential over the last 200 years.

LORD ELGIN

Born 1766, died in Paris 1841.
British diplomat, art connoisseur and collector.

ACHIEVEMENTS:
Rescued from the Parthenon sculptures (the Elgin Marbles) that
   would otherwise have been destroyed.
Created a cultural, political and ethical puzzle that has not
   been solved.

THOMAS BRUCE, 7TH Earl of Elgin, was born in 1766. He succeeded to
the title, succeeding his brother, in 1771. He was appointed ambassador to
Brussels in 1792, and to Berlin in 1795. From 1799 to 1802 he was envoy
extraordinary to the Porte.

It was while he was ambassador to the Ottoman sultan in Constantinople that he became interested in the decorative sculptures on the ruined
Parthenon at Athens. He could see that they were in significant danger
from wilful damage – possibly in danger of being completely destroyed –
and decided to rescue them.

Lord Elgin arranged for the sculptures to be transported to England for
safe-keeping. His action was criticized vehemently in some quarters at the
time as an act of vandalism and theft. A government committee looked
into the affair in detail and concluded that Lord Elgin acted in good faith.
In 1810 he published a pamphlet, *Memorandum on the Subject of the Earl of
Elgin's Pursuits in Greece*, in which he explained his actions and vindicated
himself. He did in fact contribute a major service to art history by making
sure that the great pediment sculptures and the frieze reliefs survived.

The Elgin Marbles were purchased for the nation in 1816 for what
sounds like a very generous sum, £36,000, but the Earl had spent over

£50,000 in acquiring and transporting the sculptures, so he made a serious financial loss from the enterprise. The Elgin Marbles have ever since been on public display in a special room at the British Museum, where they can be seen to best advantage.

Lord Elgin was a Scottish representative peer for 50 years. He died in Paris in November 1841.

The Elgin Marbles have re-emerged as an issue in the post-colonial period. The removal of the sculptures is seen by some as characteristic of the British approach to the world in the days of the British Empire. The Greeks see the ruins on the Acropolis as a symbol of their nationhood; they see the Elgin Marbles as an integral part of the monument, and accordingly want them returned. The counter-arguments offered on the British Museum's behalf include concerns for the sculptures' safety in the heavily polluted atmosphere of Athens, and the thorny problem of precedent. Many artworks and artefacts over many centuries have been acquired by fair means and foul; are they all to be returned as well? Museums and art galleries all round the world are stocked with material from other countries; should all of it be returned, simply because it is valued in its country of origin? If the answer to this is 'yes', then it follows logically that much of the material in showcases in national museums in the capital should be dispersed to local museums in the areas where the material originated. If Hampton Court Palace was stolen by Henry VIII from Cardinal Wolsey, should it now be returned by the Crown to Wolsey's heirs? A great deal of property was acquired in past centuries by unorthodox and unethical means. Can it all be returned to its rightful owners or their descendants? And what about objects bought with 'dirty money', for instance earned through the slave trade? Although Lord Elgin rescued the Elgin Marbles 200 years ago, they still represent a very live ethical issue. One thing is certain, though, and that is that the Elgin Marbles are in far better condition than they would have been if Lord Elgin had left them on the Acropolis.

IV

THE
NINETEENTH
CENTURY
WORLD

NAPOLEON BONAPARTE

Born in Ajaccio 1769, died on St Helena 1821.
Emperor of France, French national hero.

ACHIEVEMENTS:
Promoted to general at age of 26.
Improved the system of education in France.
Re-organized the government of France.
Gave France a new legal code.
Restored order to France after the chaos of the Revolution.
Modern France owes much to his reforming, centralizing
  changes.
Remembered in France as a great hero.
Attempted to conquer and unite Europe.
Fostered the ideal of a European union that would be revived
  in the 20th century.
Left a European legacy of death and destruction on the
  grandest scale.
1804 – Made himself Emperor of France.
1808 – Invaded Spain.
1812 – Invaded Russia.
1815 – Briefly returned to power before his defeat at Waterloo.

NAPOLEON BONAPARTE WAS born in Ajaccio on Corsica, the second son of Charles Bonaparte. Napoleon was granted free military education in France, first studying French at Autun before entering military schools at Brienne and Paris. He was commissioned second-lieutenant of artillery in the regiment of la Fere, which was garrisoned at Valence in the south of France. While he was at Auxonne he saw the beginnings of the French Revolution, but he was more concerned with Corsica than France and went home on leave to organize a revolution there. In 1792 he returned to his regiment late and was for a time struck off.

In 1793 he was put in command of the artillery at Toulon and promoted. When Robespierre fell in 1794, Napoleon was arrested on a conspiracy charge because he was a friend of the younger Robespierre, but no conspiracy could be proved and he was released. In 1795 he helped to defeat supporters of the counter-revolution in Paris, firing on a mob at the Tuileries. After that he was put in command of the French army in Italy in 1796. He was a soldier with very obvious ability, and he made very rapid progress through the ranks and was a general at the age of 26.

His success in capturing northern Italy for France in 1797 made him dangerously popular as far as the French government, the Directory, was concerned. It was suggested that he should take command of the army of England and invade England, possibly to make him fail, but Napoleon saw that that was futile while the British navy had command of the seas. He got himself out of this trap by cunningly proposing the invasion of Egypt instead, to sever Britain's trade route to India. This plan failed when Nelson destroyed the French fleet in 1798. Napoleon abruptly returned to France in 1799 and seized power in a characteristically bold way, marching into the government buildings with his bodyguards, dismissing the Council of 500 and appointing three consuls to run France, of which he would be one. Napoleon ruled France for 15 years, making himself emperor in 1804. Within France, Napoleon made many reforms including an improved system of education, a re-organized government, a new legal code, a restoration of order. Modern France owes much to his reforming, centralizing changes.

Napoleon's aggressive military policy against the rest of Europe nevertheless had a very destructive effect. With his huge army of over two million, he caused enormous loss of life and untold misery. The continuing war with Britain, the fighting in central Europe, the Continental System (a trade blockade against Britain), the invasion of Spain in 1808 and the disastrous invasion of Russia in 1812 all weakened France and contributed to Napoleon's eventual downfall.

The British victory masterminded by Nelson at the Battle of Trafalgar in 1805 saved Britain from a French invasion. In 1813, Napoleon was defeated at Leipzig. In 1815 he made a brief return to power before being defeated at Waterloo by a combined Prussian and British army under Blucher and Wellington. After that he abdicated and was exiled to St Helena in the South Atlantic where he died (perhaps by poisoning) in 1821.

In France, not least because of the 'martyrdom' on St Helena, Napoleon is remembered still as a great hero, and he knew that he would be remembered in this idealized way; he said, 'What a romance my life has been.' The romance was the unification of Europe, and in this Napoleon followed in a long procession of political idealists who have chased the will o' the wisp of European union. His effect on Europe as a whole was nevertheless a long way from this romantic vision. His legacy to Europe was death and destruction on the grandest scale.

DUKE OF WELLINGTON

Born in Dublin 1769, died at Walmer 1852.
Soldier and statesman, victor of Waterloo.

ACHIEVEMENTS:
A mainly reactionary, anti-reform force in British politics.
Helped consolidate British control of southern India.
Won the Peninsular War.
Inflicted final defeat on Napoleon.
1803 – Defeated the Mahrattas, captured Poona.
1808 – Defended the Portuguese against the French.
1809 – Won the Battle of Talavera.
1812 – Won the Battle of Salamanca, ending the
*   Peninsular War.*
1814 – Negotiated the formal ending of the Peninsular War
*   at Toulouse.*
1814 – Became Duke of Wellington.
1815 – Won the Battle of Waterloo.
1827 – Became Prime Minister of Britain.
1834 – Declined William IV's plea to become Prime Minister
*   for a second time; became Foreign Secretary under Peel.*

ARTHUR WELLESLEY, 1ST Duke of Wellington, was born in Dublin in
1769, the fourth son of Garrett Wellesley, 1st Earl of Mornington. The
family was related to the evangelical Wesley, and Wesley was the spelling
used until 1790, when they changed it to Wellesley. The young Arthur was
no great scholar, and studied very little at Chelsea, Eton or Brussels. Time
spent at a military school at Angers led in 1787 to a commission as ensign
in the 73rd Highlanders. He was something of a dilettante without any

particular loyalties, moving to the 76th Foot, then to the 41st, 12th Light Dragoons and 58th Foot. These moves nevertheless involved several promotions and by this point he had reached the rank of captain.

Thus far, Arthur Wellesley's military career did not as if it was destined for great heights of achievement. In the marriage stakes he looked equally mediocre. He wanted to marry Lady Katherine Pakenham. He was aide-de-camp to two Lords Lieutenant of Ireland (which involved little in the way of regimental duties) and member for Trim in the Irish Parliament, but he was not well off financially – and that prevented him from marrying Lady Katherine. His brother Richard at this point bought him the lieutenant-colonelcy and command of the 33rd Foot and he campaigned with it on the Ems in 1794. In 1797 his regiment was sent to India, with Arthur Wellesley now as full colonel, and his brother arrived there as Governor-general within a few months, and would be in a position to do him further career favours.

Napoleon was gaining ground in Europe, and winning victories in Egypt. Meanwhile, Arthur Wellesley was sent into southern India to deal with Tippoo Sahib at Mysore. He was a brigade commander under General George Harris and did sterling work throughout this expedition and subsequently as administrator of the newly conquered territory. He was appointed by his brother to supreme military and political command in Mysore. He conducted a military campaign against Doondiah, a robber-chief who was chased by Wellesley out of Mysore and into Mahratta territory; Wellesley followed him. His campaign against Scindia and Holkar led to the capture of the key town of Poona in 1803. The Mahratta war-lords were defeated at Ahmednagar, and Wellesley won a final victory at Argaum.

Wellesley's time in India marked a significant change in him. He wasted less time, took his career more seriously, gave up cards, stopped playing the violin. There was a new focus. He also showed a shrewd understanding of eastern ways of thinking. Wellesley's particular charisma appeared for the first time during the Mahratta campaign, when he gained a personal ascendancy over the Mahrattas, not just by military superiority but by knowing how to negotiate with them. The march on Poona and the capture of the town was a total success for him.

In 1805 Wellesley returned to Britain where he was now regarded as highly successful, and he was able to marry Lady Katherine Pakenham in

ABOVE: *Buddha, the founder of Buddhism.*

A unique Being, an extraordinary Man arises in this world for the benefit of the many, for the happiness of the many, out of compassion for the world, for the good, benefit, and happiness of gods and men. Who is this Unique Being? It is the Tathagata, the Exalted, Fully Enlightened One.

ANGUTTARA NIKAYA
PT. 1, XII

LEFT: *Homer, epic poet and writer of* The Iliad *and* The Odyssey, *two of the most enduring stories ever told.*

ΠΕΡΙΚΛΗΣ

ABOVE: *Genghis Khan was one of the world's greatest conquerors and creator of the Mongul Empire*

LEFT: *Leonardo Da Vinci the illegitimate son of a Florentine lawyer who produced many of the world's most accomplished and valuable paintings*

OPPOSITE PAGE: *Pericles, the great Athenian ruler who commissioned the construction of the Parthenon*

RIGHT: *Charles Darwin, the British naturalist who discovered the theory of evolution by natural selection*

BELOW: *Elizabeth Fry, the English campaigner and prison reformer who overcame a male dominated world in order to improve conditions for prisoners throughout Western Europe*

RIGHT: *Lord Horatio Nelson, the most famous seaman who ever lived. This inspirational leader is celebrated for having single-handedly rescued Britain from invasion by the French*

BELOW: *Ludwig Van Beethoven, German composer and child prodigy who became a romantic hero despite massive disadvantages*

LEFT: *Joseph Lister, the doctor who invented modern antiseptic surgery and pioneered cleanliness in hospitals*

RIGHT: *Thomas Edison, the school drop-out who went on to invent the electric light bulb the moving picture camera and talking pictures*

RIGHT: *W. G. Grace, the English cricketer who became the first modern sports personality*

BELOW: *Frank Lloyd Wright, the American architect behind the Guggenheim Museum of Art and some of the world's first skyscrapers*

RIGHT: *Marie Curie, the Polish-French scientist who coined the term 'radio-activity' and discovered the elements radium and polonium*

OPPOSITE PAGE: *Charlie Chaplin, the original irrepressible underdog and godfather of silent film comedy*

LEFT: *Marie Stopes, the straight-talking academic responsible for opening the first birth control clinic in Britain*

LEFT: *Edmund Hillary, the first man to climb Mount Everest*

RIGHT: *Peter Sellers, the Englishman who – alongside Spike Milligan – pioneered surreal comedy with the anarchic radio programme* The Goon Show

ABOVE: *Jesse Owens the record breaking black athelete who stunned Hitler by winning four gold medals at the 1936 Berlin Olympics*

ABOVE: *Marilyn Monroe, the definitive female sex symbol of the 20th century*

LEFT: *Che Guevara, Argentinian communist revolutionary leader and icon*

BELOW: *Fidel Castro, Cuban revolutionary and head of state*

OPPOSITE ABOVE: *Bill Haley, the pioneer of rock and roll music*

OPPOSITE BELOW: *Martin Luther King, the black civil rights campaigner responsible for the civil rights act of 1964*

RIGHT: *Elvis Presley, the first white performer to embrace a combination of country and western music and the traditionally black sounds of rythm and blues.*

BELOW: *Bob Geldof, the pop star who brought home the harsh reality of famine to millions of westerners*

LEFT: *Osama Bin Laden, Saudi Arabian leader of Al-Qaeda. The man who issued instructions for the World Trade Centre attack of September 11, 2001*

BELOW: *Bill Gates, the philanthropist founder of Microsoft who brought computing and computers into the everyday lives of millions of people throughout the developed world.*

1806. 'Kitty' Pakenham was to bear him three sons and three daughters.

Whether in genuine pursuit of a career in politics, or in pursuit of social status, the now-ambitious Wellesley took a seat at Westminster as MP for Rye in Sussex. He became Irish Secretary in 1807. That year he went with the Copenhagen expedition, defeating the Danes. In 1808 he was sent to assist the Portuguese against the French. He defeated Junot at Rolica and won a further battle at Vimeiro. He returned to England to resume his parliamentary duties, but was called back to the Iberian Peninsula in 1809 after Moore's retreat at Corunna. Wellesley assumed chief command in the Peninsula. At this crucial moment, Wellesley became one of the key warriors in the Napoleonic Wars.

He very nearly lost the Battle of Talavera in 1809 through a blunder, but retrieved the situation. For the victory at Talavera he was awarded a peerage. The Battle of Salamanca in 1812 was a more worthy victory. Gradually, Wellesley's determination succeeded in driving the French army out of Spain. He understood the physical geography of the Peninsula well enough to know that Napoleon could not sustain a large army there, in hostile country, indefinitely. Most of Spain was too poor to feed an army. If Wellesley held on for long enough, with the support of the Spanish, he could outlast a French army of any size. And he was right. A formal admission of withdrawal from the Iberian Peninsula was extracted from the French at Toulouse in 1814.

Wellesley's conduct of the Peninsular War was hailed as a major success in England, and he was rewarded by being appointed Duke of Wellington.

Napoleon was thought to be utterly defeated and out of the way, but his escape from Elba after a few months threw Europe back onto a war footing again. Wellington rushed from the Congress of Vienna to take command of a hastily mustered rag-tag army to deal with Napoleon. Wellington referred to it as 'an infamous army'. He had a pleasantly rough way with his men, chaffing them affectionately. They in turn loved him, often greeting his appearance at inspections with the unison chant, 'Nose! Nose! Nose!' The nickname arose because of Wellington's distinctively beaky Roman nose.

Napoleon had somehow mustered a huge French army, which defeated Blucher and his German army at the Battle of Ligny. It looked as if Napoleon might after all be the overall victor. Wellington chose to make his stand at Waterloo, a battlefield he reconnoitred beforehand and chose with considerable care. Wellington came close to losing the Battle of Waterloo, which took place on 18 June 1815, but Blucher arrived just in time, after a heroic march with his German army, and the allied forces together routed Napoleon's army. The outcome was decisive. It was Napoleon's final defeat and the start of a long period of peace.

Wellington was treated as a great national hero, given a country house (Strathfield-saye) and a place in government as master-general of ordnance. Then began Wellington's less successful second career, his post-Waterloo career. In 1829, he assisted Robert Peel in his reorganization of the Metropolitan Police force. Wellington's policy was to avoid foreign entanglements, as Britain did not possess an army large enough to impose its will. It was a lesson learnt at Waterloo, where he had needed Blucher's help to win. When Canning intervened to bind Britain, France and Russia to impose recognition of the autonomy of Greece on Turkey, he resigned.

In 1827, Canning died and the Ripon administration collapsed; the King called on the Duke, now called the Iron Duke, to form a government and he became Prime Minister. His policies alienated Huskisson and the Liberals. He did however support the cause of Catholic emancipation, and this led to a bloodless duel with the Earl of Winchelsea. He refused to intervene in the east after Navarino, and this lost him the support of a large section of his party. He was unlucky in being a staunch conservative at a time when many cried out for reform. He opposed the unqualified enlargement of the franchise; he did not believe in votes for everyone, and this made him extremely unpopular. On the anniversary of Waterloo, a mob broke the windows of his London home, Apsley House, to show what the people thought of their national hero now.

In the political crisis of 1834, the King again called on Wellington to form a government; this time it was an intensely personal plea, not a matter of form. Wellington was reluctant, but agreed on a compromise solution, proposing that Peel should head the new administration, and that he should serve under him as Foreign Secretary. While Peel was abroad Wellington temporarily acted for all the secretaries of state. When Peel was returned to power in the 1841 election, Wellington was made a minister without portfolio in his cabinet. Although not a popular politician, Wellington was a good man to have in high office because of his scrupulous honesty. From his earliest despatches on, everything Wellington said could be entirely trusted; no fact was misrepresented.

In 1846, approaching 80, Wellington retired from public life. Honours and positions were still showered on him. In 1848 he was made Lord High Constable of England, his task being to organize the military against the London demonstrations of the Chartists; in a way it was an emblematic role – the candid, direct and formal suppression of reform. As Warden of the Cinque Ports, the Duke of Wellington was given a third home, Walmer Castle. He loved Walmer, a fine clover-leaf fortress built by Henry VIII, probably because its simple functional austerity reminded him of his happier life as a soldier. He spent as much time at Walmer as he could.

The last years were calm and impressive. He was a very likeable old man. Many years ago I met an elderly Oxford academic who told me a delightful story, at only second hand, about the 'Iron Duke'. His father as a small boy had met the old Duke – and not only that but played with him. The Duke dined with his parents and apparently went to say goodnight to the boy and his younger sister, re-enacted the Battle of Waterloo with them in a spirited pillow fight and was so impressed by their tactics that he offered to promote them. 'I'll make you generals in one of my armies.' The boy was puffed up with pride, but his little sister demurred; 'I'm only a *dirl*, Mister Dook!' He died at Walmer in 1852, and was buried in St Paul's Cathedral after a colossal state funeral.

Wellington did much to consolidate the British occupation of India, assisting in the conquest of the southern Deccan. He also won the Peninsular War, driving the French army out of Spain. His main achievement was unquestionably the landmark victory at Waterloo, which brought Napoleon's domination of Europe to an end and opened a new phase of history. Wellington might have made a good 18th century British Prime Minister, but at a time when reform was needed he was the wrong kind of great man in the wrong place at the wrong moment. He resisted the Reform Bill as long as he could. The Iron Duke was a great figure in 19th century Britain – a national hero on a level with Nelson. But in terms of his reputation, perhaps it was his tragedy that he did not die at Waterloo.

LUDWIG VAN BEETHOVEN

Born in Bonn 1770, died in Vienna 1827.
German composer.

ACHIEVEMENTS:
First Romantic composer.
Bridged the traditions of 18th and 19th century music.
Became a symbol of the struggle of the Romantic hero against
  great odds.
1804 – Third Symphony.
1805 – Fidelio.
1824 – Ninth Symphony.

LUDWIG VAN BEETHOVEN was born on 16 December 1770 in Bonn, where both his father and grandfather were singers in the service of the Elector of Cologne. Beethoven was initially taught music by his ambitious, rough, unstable father, who tried to turn him into a second Mozart. Beethoven's first appearance as a keyboard prodigy was at the age of eight. Later he became assistant harpsichordist in the Elector's orchestra.

In 1787 he was in Vienna and probably had some lessons from Mozart. These were unfortunately cut short by news that his mother had died and he had to return to Bonn. By 1789, Beethoven was playing viola in the opera orchestra. He met Haydn in 1790 and two years later 'Papa' Haydn agreed to give him some lessons in Vienna. Then Beethoven moved permanently to Vienna, but the initially promising relationship with Haydn did not develop as expected. Beethoven was arrogant and ill-mannered, and he arrived at a bad moment. Haydn was in a state of profound shock at the unexpected early death of Mozart, who Haydn knew was the greatest musician ever. The two things coinciding – the loss of Mozart and the arrival of Beethoven – confirmed in Haydn's mind that the sun had set on music.

By 1802, the end of Beethoven's 'first' period as a composer, he had written three piano concertos and two symphonies. The 'middle' period produced the remarkable optimism and heroism of the *Third Symphony* in 1804, two more piano concertos and his only opera, *Fidelio* in 1805, while he battled with progressive deafness and a series of unhappy love affairs.

Beethoven's home life was a complete mess. He was untidy, dirty, quarrelsome, arrogant, and wasted a lot of time pointlessly fighting for the custody of his nephew, Karl. In spite of this chaos and the complete deafness, the 'last' period produced some remarkable music: the last six string quartets, the *Missa Solemnis* and the *Ninth Symphony*.

Beethoven died prematurely at the age of 56, of a lung infection and general self-neglect. The later Romantics revelled in the fact that he died in a thunderstorm. Many of his medical problems, including his deafness, resulted from lead poisoning.

Beethoven's music looks back to the classical tradition for structures, harmonies and models, but forward to High Romantic art for its spirit. The *Third Symphony* is the perfect synthesis of the 18th and 19th century traditions. Beethoven was the bridge from the old into the new. The Romantics embraced him, or rather his memory, as the great precursor. His music was heroic; the man himself was an icon of heroic struggle against adversity. Yet what he wrote about was not entirely internal; it also reflected what was happening in the wider world. He gave eloquent voice to the age of social transformation and political upheaval that was Napoleonic Europe.

RICHARD TREVITHICK

Born at Illogan 1771, died at Dartford 1833.
Engineer and inventor.

ACHIEVEMENTS:
Made the railway age possible, by inventing the railway
*   locomotive.*
1797 – Invented the plunger pole pump.
1800 – Invented the high-pressure non-condensing steam
*   engine.*
1801 – Invented the steam road carriage.
1804 – Invented the steam rail locomotive.
1812 – Invented the steam-powered threshing machine.

RICHARD TREVITHICK WAS born at Illogan, Redruth, Cornwall, the only son of Richard Trevithick, the manager of the Dolcoath mine and several other Cornish mines. The younger Richard started off as a mining engineer, devoting his life to the development and application of the steam engine. James Watt had preferred relatively low steam pressures for his engine. Trevithick preferred high steam pressures because they would give a greater power yield from smaller cylinders.

Trevithick's earliest invention of any importance came in 1797: his improved plunger pole pump, designed for use in keeping deep mines clear of water. The following year he applied the principle of the plunger pole pump to the design of a water-pressure engine. In 1800, he built a high-pressure non-condensing steam engine, which became a competitor to Watt's low-pressure steam-vacuum model.

Trevithick, like several other early pioneers of steam locomotion, saw the way forward as mounting a steam engine on a carriage and running it along roads. This was never to be developed. Once steam locomotives were invented and run along rail tracks, that was universally accepted as the way forward. But in 1800, the railway did not seem like an inevitable future. Watt himself did not think it was. From 1800 until 1815, Trevithick built several experimental steam road carriages.

He also built the first steam railway locomotives, as well as several stationary steam engines. Trevithick's steam locomotive was clearly the prototype for George Stephenson's commercially successful locomotives, and it is hard not to see Stephenson as a plagiarizing entrepreneur, who took Trevithick's invention, made money out of it – and took the credit.

It was on Christmas Eve 1801 that Trevithick's road locomotive carried the first load of passengers ever to be transported by steam locomotion. It was the first year of the 19th century, and the age of steam locomotion had begun. In March the following year he and Andrew Vivian applied for a patent for steam-propelled carriages. In 1803, another steam-powered carriage was driven through the streets of London, from Leather Lane along Oxford Street to Paddington, and returning from there by way of Islington.

In 1804, Trevithick worked on a tramroad locomotive for industrial use at Pen-y-darran; it proved capable of carrying 20 tons of iron. He built a similar machine for the Wylam colliery at Newcastle in 1805. In 1808 he built a circular railway track near Euston Square in London. To demonstrate the effectiveness of its technology, he took members of the public round the track on a steam locomotive at speeds up to 15 mph – and round some fairly tight curves.

He was very successful in applying his high-pressure steam engine to breaking and boring through rock, and also to dredging. In 1806, he was under contract from the board of Trinity House in London to dredge ballast from the bed of the River Thames at a rate of half a million tons a year. He was to be paid sixpence a ton. He even applied his steam engine to agriculture. In 1812, he built a high-pressure steam-powered threshing machine at Trewithen, That same year he wrote a letter to the Board of Agriculture stating his belief that every agricultural process might by aided by steam power, and that the use of steam power in food production would 'double the population of the kingdom and make our markets the cheapest in the world.' Presumably he meant that food production could be doubled and therefore support more people.

In 1814, Trevithick entered on a contractual agreement to build engines for mines in Peru. In 1816, he went to Peru to supervise the installation of the engines, and afterwards travelled to Costa Rica. He returned to England in 1827.

Trevithick was full of brilliant and highly practical ideas, and he knew how to publicize them effectively. He was one of the first people to recognize that iron was going to be the main construction material for ships in the future, and indeed iron was to dominate shipbuilding right through the 19th century. He was perhaps simply unlucky in not having enough wealth at his disposal, or finding a rich enough backer, to develop his inventions on a commercial scale.

Richard Trevithick's inventions, discoveries, successes and mistakes were to lead on to commercially successful steam locomotives shortly afterwards, but Trevithick was to gain nothing for himself out of it. In 1828 he was reduced to petitioning Parliament for a reward for his inventions, but had no success. Nothing he invented or developed was commercially successful and he died, penniless and in debt, at Dartford in 1833. Richard Trevithick was one of the great figures of the Industrial Revolution and, until recently, one of its unsung heroes. To him, rather than George Stephenson, should go the credit for inventing the railway locomotive.

ELIZABETH FRY

Born in Norwich 1780, died 1845.
English philanthropist and prison reformer.

ACHIEVEMENTS:
Improved conditions in prisons throughout Western Europe.
Established a concept of accountability to the public.
Initiated the first phase of social reform in 19th century
  Britain.

ELIZABETH GURNEY WAS born in May 1780, the daughter of John Gurney, a rich Quaker merchant and banker. As a girl she had a benevolent nature, as well as the strength of purpose and the independence of mind that would enable her to make her way in what was in the 18th century still seen as 'a man's world'. In 1800, when she was 20, she married Joseph Fry, a London merchant who belonged to another Quaker family of long-standing. In 1810, in the midst of increasing family worries, she became a preacher for the Society of Friends.

Early in 1813 Elizabeth Fry made several visits to Newgate Prison for women and was appalled by the conditions in which the 300 female prisoners were kept, along with their non-offending children. The visits changed her life. She devoted herself from that experience on to the reform of prisons and asylums, both in England and overseas. In 1817, she formed an association specifically to improve conditions for the women in Newgate. She sought to establish some very basic reforms, such as the supervision of women prisoners by women wardresses, the separation of different classes of offender, and appropriate provision for religious and secular education. She also wanted to ensure that prisoners were usefully employed.

The improvements at Newgate that resulted from Elizabeth Fry's strenuous efforts rapidly spread to other prisons.

In 1818, Elizabeth Fry travelled with her brother to visit the prisons in Scotland and northern England. The next year she published her notes on this inspection. The House of Commons committee on the prisons of London recognized the value of Mrs Fry's work and received her report with warmth and enthusiasm. This led on to an extensive correspondence with people in other countries who were interested in prison reform – in Denmark, Italy and even Russia. Her brother, Joseph John Gurney, was a Quaker banker and reformer; he campaigned for the emancipation of negroes in the West Indies and North America, as well as supporting Elizabeth's prison reforms.

Elizabeth Fry visited Ireland in 1827, where she looked at hospitals and asylums as well as prisons. Her observations led to a marked improvement in the British hospital system and in the way the insane were treated.

In 1838, she visited France, where she had discussions with many senior prison officials and visited many prisons in the north of the country. The following year, she was granted an official permit giving her access to all places of detention in France. She undertook a comprehensive tour of French prisons, wrote a thorough report and then submitted it to the Minister of the Interior and the Prefect of Police. In 1840–1, she was off again on the same mission in Belgium, Holland, Prussia and Denmark.

By 1842, Mrs Fry's health was failing and she had to stop travelling. The frustration at having to call off the crusade was offset by the news returning from the places she had visited. Everywhere, the authorities were listening and responding to her suggestions. Reform really was under way.

Elizabeth Fry was not only interested in prisons. She also founded hostels for the homeless and charity organizations. She carried on her good works in spite of her husband's professional problems; he became bankrupt in 1828.

Elizabeth Fry died in October 1845.

ROBERT OWEN

Born at Newtown 1771, died at Newtown 1858.
Welsh social and educational reformer.

ACHIEVEMENTS:
First English mill-manager to use American sea-island cotton.
First cotton-spinner in England.
Founded the first co-operative store.
Founded the co-operative movement in Britain.
Founded the first infant school in Britain (with James Buchanan).
Created the first school playground.
Pioneered trades unionism in Britain.
Attempted a socialist transformation of Britain.
The spearhead of social reform in 19th century Britain.
1813 – A New View of Society.
1815 – Started a one-man campaign for the reform of conditions in factories.
1817 – Proposed a British Socialist Co-operative movement.
1820 – Report to the County of Lanark.
1833 – Founded the Grand National Consolidated Trades Union.

ROBERT OWEN WAS born at Newtown in Montgomeryshire, the son of a saddler and ironmonger. His school education ended when he was ten years old and put to work in a draper's shop at Stamford. Then he moved to Manchester, a major industrial centre, and there he began to prosper. By the age of 19 he had risen to be the manager of a cotton mill employing 500 people. With his intelligence, energy and administrative ability, he made his mill the best of its kind in the country. In this factory, Owen used the first imports of American sea-island cotton ever to be used in Britain. He was the first cotton-spinner in England, and made big improvements to the quality of spun cotton. He became a partner in the Chorlton Twist Company in Manchester, and persuaded his partners to buy the New Lanark Mills and manufacturing village at New Lanark in Scotland.

In 1799, Robert Owen married Anne Caroline Dale, the daughter of David Dale, from whom his company had bought New Lanark. It was at New Lanark that Owen set about creating a model community for the 2,000 people who worked in the mills, with better housing, better working conditions and better education. Among the inhabitants were 500 children brought in as cheap labour from the various poorhouses and charities of Glasgow and Edinburgh. The children in particular had been well treated by Dale, but there was little provision for their education; the housing conditions were appalling; the sanitation was poor; and there was a high rate of crime and vice associated with very low morale amongst the employees generally.

Robert Owen set about improving every aspect of these people's lives, training them to higher standards of order and cleanliness and improving their houses. He built an Institute for the Formation of Character and a school which incorporated the world's first day-nursery and playground. The school offered evening classes for those at work during the day. He also built a village store which offered goods at little more than cost price; this was the birth-place of the co-operative movement.

Although his social reforms had been highly successful, they were expensive, and his partners complained about the effect they were having on profits. In 1813, Owen formed New Lanark into a new company with collaborators who included Jeremy Bentham and the Quaker William Allen. This time Owen forestalled criticism by guaranteeing his partners a 5% return for their capital; Owen was in return to have more freedom of action on the philanthropic side. In his book, *A New View of Society*, he expounded his ideas of educational philanthropy, arguing that character is formed by social environment. The great secret in the development of a person's character is to place him or her under the right influences from the earliest years; this was why he was prepared to invest so much care and attention in schooling and schools. From an early age he left all religious belief behind, becoming a thorough-going humanist and socialist and evolving his own creed. After New Lanark, Owen went on to create more co-operative 'Owenite' communities, including New Harmony in Indiana and Orbiston near Glasgow in 1825–28 and Ralahine in Ireland in 1831–33, but they were all failures.

In 1815, Owen launched a single-handed campaign to make factory-owners and managers adopt more humane practices. He drafted a bill directed at all textile factories, banning the employment of children under 10, banning night work for young people under 18, limiting working hours to 10 hours a day for all under 18, and providing for inspection. There were many who sympathized with Owen's bill. It was introduced in Parliament, but it was cut to the point where, when it was introduced in 1819, it had become so unrecognizable that Owen dissociated himself from it. He was a man a little before his time; he was very much at the spearhead of 19th century social reform in Britain – a very necessary man.

In 1817 he put forward a report to the House of Commons committee on the Poor Law, outlining his socialist co-operative scheme. His detailed and comprehensive plans for dealing with poverty in the wake of the Napoleonic Wars were initially given a warm reception in the press and by many influential people. Owen could count the Duke of Kent, Queen Victoria's father, among his many friends and supporters. But then, at a large public meeting in London, Owen declared his avowed hostility to all organized forms of religion. This lost him at a stroke the support of the establishment. He himself thought the radicals, to whom he might have looked for support, were wrong-headed. Owen threw away his chance of getting large-scale government support for his idea of comprehensive reform through whole communities. Instead, he had to work for reform piecemeal, finding supporters who would help set up small communities here and there.

In 1820, Owen declared in his *Report to the County of Lanark* that what was needed was not a reform but a transformation of the social order. This had a great appeal to the young and for the next ten years there was mounting pressure for Owen's doctrine to be accepted as the aspiration of the ordinary working class people of Britain. When Owen returned to

England from New Harmony in 1829 he found himself hailed as a leader.

In 1825, Robert Owen ceased to be a manager at New Lanark after long-term disagreements with his partners, including William Allen. In 1828 he sold all his shares in New Lanark, losing £40,000 – four-fifths of his fortune – on the project.

Robert Owen worked towards the empowerment of workers, emphasizing that labour is the source of all wealth. Various labouring groups formed craft-oriented unions, such as the National Operative Builders Union. Owen himself organized the Grand National Consolidated Trades Union in 1833, and huge numbers of workers joined. But the employers and other members of the British establishment became alarmed and adopted counter-measures to stop the trade union movement becoming any stronger. It was to be another two generations before socialism again directly influenced trade unionism.

Vigorous restoration work at New Lanark in recent decades has made it a living community once more; it was awarded a Europa Nostra Medal of Honour in 1988. Owen's ideas – fundamentally benevolent, practical and philanthropic – did not amount to a new philosophy, but their application to whole communities was entirely new. The New Lanark experiment was a model to those socialist activists who believe in social engineering. His work in the 1820s and 1830s to achieve social transformation through the trade union movement was heroic, though premature, and a model to later political activists. He prepared the way for the Rochdale Pioneers Co-operative Society founded in 1844, which in turn gave birth to the world-wide Consumers' Co-operative Movement. In a sense he prepared the way for socialist revolution.

To the end of his long life, Robert Owen attracted people with his great personal charm and his love of children. At 82, he took up his last great cause – spiritualism. He died on a visit to his birthplace, Newtown, in November 1858. His last act, the day before he died, was to draw up a plan for re-organizing education in the town where he had been born.

SIMON BOLIVAR

Born in Caracas, Venezuela, 1783, died near Santa Marta,
  Colombia, 1830.
South American revolutionary leader.

ACHIEVEMENTS:
Liberated five South American countries from Spanish rule.
Gave his name to Bolivia.
Gave his name to the unit of currency of Venezuela, the bolivar.
Hero of Latin America.

SIMON BOLIVAR WAS born in Caracas, Venezuela, of a noble and wealthy family. His father was Juan Vicente Bolivar y Ponte and his mother Maria de la Concepcion Palacios y Blanco. Simon's father died when he was very young, and his mother died when he was 15. His uncle, Carlos Palacios, sent him to study law in Madrid. There, in 1801, Bolivar married Maria Teresa Toro, niece of the Marquis of Toro, another Caracas resident, but she died less than a year after their return to Venezuela. After Maria's death, Bolivar went back to Europe, apparently to see friends. In Rome, he told one old friend, his tutor, that he was pledging his life to freeing Venezuela from Spain.

He travelled back to Venezuela by way of the USA, visiting many Americans in the eastern cities. He reached Caracas in 1806. The liberation movement in Venezuela was fuelled partly by the large-scale quarrel in Spain between Charles IV and his son Ferdinand VII, and the additional complication of Napoleon's imposition of one of his relations as king. Spaniards and colonists were divided into two camps. Bolivar and his friends were members of the Caracas junta, which after the crowning of

Joseph Bonaparte as King of Spain favoured the restoration of Ferdinand. In April 1810, this junta forced the Captain-general, Vicente Emparan, to abdicate; then the junta formed the very first locally-created government in Spanish America. Bolivar was sent to England as diplomatic representative of the new Venezuelan government.

On his return to Venezuela, Bolivar made a speech advocating a declaration of independence from Spain. Venezuela was accordingly declared independent in 1811, and the model of a federal republic, to be named Colombia, was decided on – though not by Bolivar. Bolivar travelled to New Granada (now Colombia) to raise an army. Fierce fighting followed in town after town, between the royalists and Bolivar's supporters. He was seriously outnumbered, but because he was mobile he was able to deal with the royalists group by group. In 1813, after fighting six pitched battles, he returned, entering Caracas as conqueror, and proclaimed himself dictator and Liberator of western Venezuela. The following year he was driven out, but made repeated attacks on Venezuela from the West Indies.

There were atrocities on both sides, and Bolivar has been severely criticized for the cold-blooded execution in 1814 of 886 Spanish prisoners at La Guaira as a reprisal. Battle followed bloody battle. At one point, in 1815, Bolivar was so disheartened by the lack of progress, and by delays and intrigues, that he resigned his command and set sail for Jamaica. From Jamaica, Bolivar wrote his famous 'Jamaica letter', in which he analyzed the causes of the failure of the enterprise and gave reasons for believing that it would eventually be successful.

In Jamaica, an attempt was made to assassinate the Liberator. A former negro slave of Bolivar's stabbed to death another man who happened to be sleeping in the hammock Bolivar usually slept in. Further intrigues followed, and the support of the President of Haiti was enlisted before Bolivar returned to Venezuela.

After a new series of pitched battles and skirmishes in Venezuela, Bolivar at last made visible headway against the Spanish. Then he took the struggle over the Andes into Colombia. In Bogota, he was given a rapturous welcome, and money and men were put at his disposal for the relief of Venezuela. In Bogota in January 1820, Bolivar proclaimed the union of Greater Colombia. Meanwhile the Spanish Government opened negotiations for peace. Bolivar refused to agree to any peace unless it was based on the independence of Venezuela and the other colonies. The offer of an armistice was nevertheless a great encouragement to the freedom fighters. They fought on.

In 1821, Bolivar was chosen as president of a new state of Colombia, which was to consist of Colombia, New Granada and Venezuela. In 1822, Bolivar added Ecuador to this 'republic' that increasingly looked like an empire.

In 1824, came the decisive victory which for ever ended the domination of Spain in South America. It came on 9 December 1824 at Ayacucho in Peru. This battle was won by Bolivar's lieutenant Sucre, as Bolivar had already set off for Lima to organize the new civil government of Peru. Simon Bolivar drove the Spaniards out of Peru, and made himself dictator there for a while. Upper Peru was turned into a separate state, and named Bolivia in his honour. He was to be 'perpetual protector' of Bolivia, but the state's constitution gave many cause for concern and the Colombian troops were thrown out.

After he returned to Colombia in 1828, he assumed dictatorial powers there, which made the republicans apprehensive. In 1829, Venezuela separated itself from Colombia. In 1830, Bolivar became ill, set aside his extravagant dictatorial claims, and relinquished his power altogether in April. In June he heard that Sucre had been murdered. It was crushing personal blow to him. Ill, exhausted, grief-stricken and disheartened, Simon Bolivar went into a steep decline. Ignoring calls for him to return as leader, he tried to find a place with a congenial climate, a place where he might recover.

He went out into the country, to San Pedro Alejandrino, three miles outside Santa Marta. There he died on 17 December 1830. He was only 47. Twelve years later, the body of Simon Bolivar was exhumed and reburied in the national pantheon in Caracas. Beside his tomb is an empty tomb, waiting still for the body of Sucre, which Ecuador has refused to hand over.

Simon Bolivar was a charismatic freedom-fighter who liberated five South American states from Spanish colonial rule. He was the hero of 200 bloody battles. His life was a colossal and tumultuous adventure in which failure and triumph alternated rapidly, and in which he covered enormous distances across wildernesses with armies, showing remarkable leadership skills. Bolivar wrote addresses, proclamations and letters, and these writings show that he was not only a very able general but a wise and prophetic observer of the conditions of the people and their political needs.

Bolivar spoilt an appealing anti-colonial movement by seeking grandiose dictatorial powers for himself – and by killing large numbers of people. He succeeded in getting the Spanish out of Venezuela, Colombia, Ecuador, Bolivia, Panama and Peru, but not in imposing his own dictatorship. The idea of a federation of Spanish-speaking South American states was a fruitful one, and was a major part of South American politics for some time to come. His style of government and his vision were far in advance of his time, and in some ways look forward to the great dictatorships of the 20th century. His was such a revolutionary way of governing that it is not surprising he had – and still has – vehement critics. He was nevertheless one of the most accomplished revolutionary leaders of all time.

ARTUR SCHOPENHAUER

Born in Danzig 1788, died in Frankfurt 1860.
German philosopher.

ACHIEVEMENTS:
Emphasized the importance of the Will as the driving force in
human nature.
Greatly influenced Wagner, Tolstoy, Proust, Mann, Freud.
1819 – The World as Will and Idea.

ARTUR SCHOPENHAUER WAS born in Danzig in 1788. His father was a banker and his mother wrote novels. After a move to Hamburg in 1793, Artur was prepared for a career in business, which was not to his taste. After his father died in 1805, Schopenhauer was free to pursue his own interests, which were academic. He studied medicine and natural science at Gotha, Weimar and Gottingen, before going on to Berlin and Jena, where he finished his thesis on philosophy in 1813.

Schopenhauer was a pessimist. He had an unhappy life and his temperament remained consistently gloomy; he distrusted others and hated women. Philosophically, he reacted forcefully against the idealist tradition of Hegel, and was inspired instead by the work of Plato, Kant and the ancient Indian Vedic philosophy. He also admired Goethe; indeed the two collaborated on Goethe's theory of colours.

He took a teaching post in Berlin in 1820 and characteristically timed his lectures to coincide with those of his rival Hegel. He failed to attract students by this extreme measure, and he retreated in great bitterness to live the life of a recluse in Frankfurt, with only his poodle for company. He carried on working, developing and defending his ideas in works such as *The Two Main Problems of Ethics* in 1841, and a second edition of his main book, *The World as Will and Idea*, in 1844. Schopenhauer did not attract a great deal of attention from his contemporaries, until he published a collection of essays and aphorisms, and his main influence was really on those who came after him – an extraordinary succession of writers, composers, philosophers and psychologists.

Schopenhauer's main work was *The World as Will and Idea*, which was first published in 1819. In this he emphasized the role of will as the principal creative force in human nature, an irrational and unconscious force. His ideas were to have a great influence on Wagner, Nietzsche, Tolstoy, Proust, Mann and Freud. He expressed puzzlement that philosophers had given so little attention to sex as a driving force, and that observation certainly foreshadowed the work of Freud.

In 1854, Wagner read *The World as Will and Idea*, and reacted to it as he had never reacted to any other book. He felt it as 'a gift from heaven'. He sent Schopenhauer a copy of his libretto for *The Ring*. In 1860, the last year of Schopenhauer's life, Wagner visited Frankfurt and talked of calling on him. He didn't in the end because he was afraid he might be inadequate to the meeting – Schopenhauer had the distinction of being the only living person to whom Wagner felt inferior. It is a pity the projected meeting did not take place, as Schopenhauer might have been genuinely cheered to think that a great opera, *Tristan and Isolde*, had been inspired by his ideas.

LOUIS DAGUERRE

Born at Cormeilles 1789, died at Petit–Brie–sur–Marne 1851.
French painter and photographic pioneer.

ACHIEVEMENTS:
1822 – Devised dioramas.
1838 – Invented the daguerrotype (early photograph).
1839 – Historique et description des procedes du
   daguerrotype et du diorama.

LOUIS JACQUES MANDE Daguerre was born at Cormeilles in the department of Seine-et-Oise. His first job was as an inland revenue officer. He then became a scene painter for the Paris Opera. In 1822, in collaboration with Bouton, Daguerre opened a Diorama in Paris. This was an exhibition of pictorial landscape views, painted on a large scale to deceive the eye into thinking that they were real three-dimensional landscapes. The way the dioramas were lit had a major effect on this *trompe l'oeil*. Daguerre went on to open a similar exhibition in Regent's Park, London. It was unfortunately destroyed by fire in March 1839.

This commercial setback for Daguerre was more than offset by the huge success that he had with his photographic process. From 1826 onwards he developed and perfected his 'daguerrotype' process, working with Joseph Niepce. Niepce had been trying since 1814 to make permanent pictures by the action of sunlight, and in 1826 he succeeded in making the first permanent photograph. In that year he heard that Daguerre was similarly preoccupied and proposed that they should start working together. The two inventors collaborated on what they called their heliographic pictures from 1829 until Niepce's death in 1833.

Daguerre went on experimenting alone, eventually discovering the photographic technique that bears his name – the daguerrotype.

Daguerre's process involved obtaining a photographic image on a copper plate coated with a layer of metallic silver that had been sensitized to light by iodine vapour. This revolutionary process produced some of the earliest, if not the earliest permanent photographs in 1838. On 9 January 1839, at a meeting of the Academy of Sciences, Arago emphasized the huge importance of Daguerre's discovery. In consequence, Daguerre was appointed an officer of the Legion of Honour. A law was passed that year awarding him an annuity of 6,000 francs, on condition that he would divulge the secret of the process to the Academy. Daguerre accordingly passed on to the Academy the details of his process, which was published by the government.

Daguerre died at Petit-Brie-sur-Marne near Paris in July 1851.

The invention of photography had far-reaching effects. By the end of the 19th century, photography was regularly used for recording the appearance of places and people, and this released painters from the need to produce 'likenesses'. Thanks to Daguerre, we can see exactly what the elderly Duke of Wellington looked like. The revolutionary art movements of the 20th century, such as expressionism, futurism and cubism, were made possible by photography. Daguerre made the career of Picasso possible. Photography also showed what people, places and events were really like, and this had a dramatic effect on the transmission of news stories. It would eventually be possible to capture on photographs historic events such as the assassination of John F. Kennedy and the attack on the World Trade Centre. The immediacy of these images has had the effect of making people more engaged with world events than they ever were before.

MICHAEL FARADAY

Born 1791, died 1867.
English chemist and physicist.

ACHIEVEMENTS:
Improved laboratory methods.
Pioneered modern physics.
Discovered two new chlorides of carbon.
Invented the terms electrolyte, electrode, anode, cathode, ion,
cation and anion.
1824 – Discovered the induction of electric currents.
1831 – Invented the dynamo.
1831 – Discovered electromagnetic induction.
1845 – Discovered the rotation of polarized light by
magnetism.
1862 – Instigated the use of electricity to power lighthouses.

MICHAEL FARADAY, THE son of a Yorkshire blacksmith, was born at Newington Butts in London in 1791. His parents belonged to a small Christian sect, the followers of Robert Sandeman, and Michael Faraday attended their meetings from childhood onwards. At the age of 14 he was apprenticed to a bookbinder, and it was through the bookbinder that he first gained access to books on science. It was these that sparked Faraday's first interest in science.

In 1813 he applied to Humphry Davy for a job, and was accepted as an assistant at the Royal Institution. In his role as assistant, Faraday attended Humphry Davy's lectures on chemistry, which were an inspiration to him.

He carefully wrote notes on all Davy's lectures, complete with illustrations, and then presented the volume of collected notes to Davy. He accompanied Davy on an 18-month tour of Europe in 1813–15 and during this tour Faraday had an opportunity to meet many of the leading scientists of the day. From his unique position at Humphry Davy's side, he also gained a broad and valuable scientific education.

In 1825, Faraday was appointed Director of the Royal Institution Laboratory and in 1833 he was made Fullerian Professor of Chemistry in the Institution for life. The understanding was that he need give no lectures; it was a research role. But Faraday gave lectures anyway, and very good lectures they were. His Christmas lectures to children were outstanding. In 1827 Faraday published his Chemical Manipulation. He went on to write papers on the condensation of gases and optical illusions. His great life work was the series of papers Experimental Researches on Electricity, which were published over a 40-year period.

At the end of a burst of intense and probably excessive mental activity in which he made many discoveries, Faraday had a severe mental breakdown. This period of insanity lasted from 1841 until 1845, when he made a recovery and a second great period of research and discovery began.

Faraday made many important discoveries, including electromagnetic induction, electrolysis and the rotation of polarized light by magnetism. For his work he was awarded a pension in 1835 and a house at Hampton Court in 1858. He was adviser to Trinity House and in 1862 he advocated the use of electricity to power lighthouses. Faraday died at Hampton Court in August 1867 and was buried in Highgate Cemetery.

Faraday had a poor memory and acquired the habit of writing down every experimental result and the development of every idea meticulously and immediately. His Diaries were eventually published in the 1930s. Faraday made major contributions to our understanding of electricity and its applications. He had a great influence on the way physics developed as a science. He was perhaps the greatest experimental physicist of all time. Rather surprisingly, Faraday had no pupils and only one long-suffering assistant.

WILLIAM HENRY FOX TALBOT

> *Born at Evershot 1800, died at Lacock Abbey 1877.*
> *English inventor of photography.*
>
> ACHIEVEMENTS:
> *1838 – Invented 'photogenic drawing' (early photograph).*
> *1839* – Illustrations of the Antiquity of the Book of
> Genesis.
> *1841 – Invented the calotype (first photographic negative).*
> *1844* – Pencil of Nature *(first book illustrated with
> photographs).*
> *1851 – Invented flash photography.*

WILLIAM HENRY FOX Talbot was born at Melbury House, Evershot, in 1800. He was educated at Harrow and Trinity College, Cambridge. From 1833 until his death, Fox Talbot lived at Lacock Abbey in Wiltshire. In 1839, Talbot announced that the previous year he had invented a photographic process, which he called 'photogenic drawing'.

Fox Talbot's technique involved making prints on silver chloride paper. In 1841 he patented another technique, the calotype or Talbotype. This was the first process involving the creation of a photographic negative from which prints could be made. He was awarded the Rumford Medal of the Royal Society in 1842.

He also invented a third photographic technique, in 1851, the creation of instant photographs using illumination by an electric spark; this was in effect the invention of flash photography.

Fox Talbot's book, *Pencil of Nature*, was published in 1844. This was the first book to be illustrated with photographs.

He was an inquisitive man and did not limit himself to photography by any means. He published works on mathematics, astronomy and Bible studies, and helped Rawlinson and Hincks in the decipherment of the cuneiform inscriptions found at Nineveh.

Fox Talbot's achievement is one of those recurring curiosities of history – a simultaneous invention. He devised his process for making photographs in the same year that Louis Daguerre invented his. Fox Talbot had produced his photographs in Wiltshire before Daguerre exhibited his pictures in Paris. As soon as Fox Talbot heard about Daguerre's work, he communicated his own work to the Royal Society.

ISAMBARD KINGDOM BRUNEL

Born in Portsmouth 1806, died at Westminster 1859.
English engineer and inventor.

ACHIEVEMENTS:

1831 – Designed the Clifton Suspension Bridge.

1841 – Designed the Hungerford Suspension Bridge.

1838 – Designed the Great Western, the first steamship to go
into regular service across the Atlantic.

1845 – Designed the Great Britain, the first large iron ship,
and the first ocean-going ship powered by propeller.

1853 – Designed the Royal Albert Bridge over the River
Tamar.

1858 – Designed the Great Eastern, the largest steamship for
the next 40 years.

ISAMBARD KINGDOM BRUNEL was born in Portsmouth in April 1806, the only son of Sir Marc Isambard Brunel, an engineer and inventor. In 1821, at the age of 14, Brunel was sent to the College Henri Quatre in Paris. Two years later he left to start work in his father's office as assistant engineer, at an exciting moment when his father's major project to design the Thames Tunnel between Wapping and Rotherhithe was taking shape. He first helped his father to plan the tunnel. Then, from 1825 until 1828, he was resident engineer in charge of the actual creation of the tunnel, until the fateful moment when the water broke in from the river bed and flooded it. That project was fated not to be completed until 1843.

In 1829 Brunel started working on his own plans for the Clifton

Suspension Bridge, which was only completed in 1864 using the chains from his own Hungerford Suspension Bridge, built in 1841–45 over the Thames at Charing Cross.

In 1833, at the age of 27, Brunel was appointed engineer to the Great Western Railway, and designed and built all the tunnels, bridges and viaducts along that line. The 'battle of the gauges' arose when Brunel introduced the broad gauge (7 feet) on the Great Western line, whereas other lines were using the standard gauge (4 feet 8 inches), which though offering less stability eventually held sway nationally. The last of Brunel's bridges, and the greatest, was the Royal Albert Bridge over the Tamar at Saltash, built between 1853 and 1859.

Brunel designed bridges, tunnels and viaducts, but also great and highly original ships too. As early as 1835 he was encouraging the directors of the Great Western Railway to 'make it longer, and have a steamboat to go from Bristol to New York, and call it the *Great Western*.' The directors took up his idea and commissioned him to design and supervise the building of the *Great Western* at Bristol in 1838. This was the first steamship to make regular voyages across the Atlantic. He then designed the *Great Britain*, which was the first large iron steamship, the largest ship afloat at that time, and the first large ship to be powered by a propeller. The *Great Britain* was the first ocean-going screw steamer; she made her maiden voyage across the Atlantic in 1845, and is now on display in Bristol.

Brunel was obsessed with the idea of a great ship, and this dream was eventually realised in the *Great Eastern*. This gigantic steamship was finally launched in 1858, a huge ship that was in many ways 40 years ahead of its time. It was a strange hybrid vessel, with screws, paddle wheels and sails. The *Great Eastern* was built in collaboration with John Scott Russell, who owned the yard at Millwall where the ship was built. Brunel also designed or improved docks at Bristol, Plymouth, Brentford, Monkwearmouth, Milford Haven and Cardiff.

Extreme anxiety, exhaustion and illness overwhelmed Brunel during the building of the *Great Eastern*. He was in the end too ill to see the great ship sail impressively off at the beginning of its maiden voyage on 7 September 1859, and he died 8 days later at his home in Westminster.

Brunel was one of the great engineers and innovators of the 19th century, full of drive, full of ideas, ambitiously and energetically pushing the technology of transport a long way forward. It is astonishing that he achieved so much, but in addition to his highly visible achievements he was also a vigorous promoter of the Great Exhibition of 1851, serving as a member of its building committee. He was also involved in the improvement of big guns, designing a floating gun carriage for the attack on Kronstadt in the Crimean War in 1854.

LOUIS AGASSIZ

Born at Motier-en-Vuly 1807, died at Cambridge, Mass.
  1873.
Swiss-American naturalist, geomorphologist and teacher.

ACHIEVEMENTS:
Discovered the Pleistocene Ice Age.
Disturbed pre-existing ideas of a stable climate.
Introduced the idea of periodic climate change.
Prepared the way for a variety of 20th century
  environmental scares.
1829 – Fishes of Brazil.
1840 – Etudes sur les glaciers.
1842 – History of the Freshwater Fishes of Central Europe
1847 – Systeme glaciaire.

JEAN LOUIS AGASSIZ was born at Motier-en-Vuly, on the shore of Lake Morat in Switzerland, in May 1807. He was the son of the Protestant pastor of Motier, the last of a long line of clergymen that began with a French cleric driven out of France by the revocation of the Edict of Nantes. Louis' mother, Rose Mayor, loved animals and plants, and the boy took his love of natural history from her. Louis spent four years at the gymnasium in Bienne, and later went to the academy at Lausanne. After that he attended three universities, Zurich, Heidelberg and Munich. When he had completed these academic courses, Agassiz took a doctor of philosophy degree at Erlangen and a doctor of medicine degree at Munich.

Although it looked as if he was heading towards a career in medicine, his main interest at that time was zoology. While he was still a 22-year-old student he published a Latin description of the *Fishes of Brazil,* a conscientious and accomplished classification of data collected by two other Munich men, Spix and Martius. It brought him to the attention of Cuvier. He built on the knowledge of fish that he had acquired by producing a *History of the Freshwater Fishes of Central Europe in 1839–42.* He moved to Paris in 1831 and in the following year he was appointed Professor of Natural History at Neuchatel.

When he arrived at Neuchatel, Louis Agassiz was the youngest and most eager teacher at the university. He was full of enthusiasm and activity. For a time in Neuchatel he even published his own material, and his home was always a hive of activity. Many students were co-opted to help him with his publications, on the understanding that they would share the proceeds from his publications and lectures. Agassiz was a dedicated and enthusiastic teacher, always treating his students as co-workers. In 1833–44 he published *Recherches sur les Poissons Fossiles.*

Then came Agassiz's breakthrough discovery. From 1836 onwards he started researching the Alpine glaciers. Several other writers had expressed the view that the glaciers had once been larger. The erratic boulders scattered across the Swiss Mittelland, right across to the Jura Mountains, must have been deposited by ice. He built a hut on the Aar glacier, where he and his co-workers could study the structure and movement of the ice. He observed the behaviour of glaciers in the Alps and their associated landforms, and noticed that the distinctive u-shaped troughs and the polished rock surfaces associated with glacial erosion could be found many miles down-valley from the places where the glaciers melt today. He deduced from this that the Alpine glaciers must once have extended much further down their valleys, and that they must have been deeper too than they are today; in fact in the recent past virtually the whole of Switzerland must have been engulfed in ice. 'Great sheets of ice, resembling those now existing in Greenland once covered all the countries in which unstratified gravel (boulder drift) is found.' These straightforward observations led him to the important conclusion that there must have been a time in the not-too-distant past when it was much colder than it is today. He discovered the great Ice Age.

Agassiz published his ideas in *Etudes sur les glaciers* in 1840 and *Systeme glaciaire* in 1847. In 1846 he went on a lecture tour of America, specifically to give series of lectures at Charleston and Boston, and was appointed Professor of Natural History at Harvard in 1847. From that time on he left his Swiss nationality behind and became more and more American – a new enthusiasm. In 1850 he married a Bostonian naturalist, Elizabeth Cabot Cary. Together they founded a girls' school at Cambridge, Massachusetts, and she later became president of Redcliffe College.

Agassiz himself founded a Museum of Comparative Zoology at Harvard in 1859. He published four out of a projected ten volumes of *Contributions to the Natural History of the United States* (1857–62) and went on several zoological expeditions, especially to Brazil. Agassiz died in December 1873 and was buried at Mount Auburn, Cambridge, Mass. By his grave, they placed a boulder from the Lauteraar; it was a glacial erratic – part of his evidence for the Ice Age.

Out of all of this scholarly activity, just one idea of Louis Agassiz's, one discovery, stands out as really momentous, really world-changing. It was the discovery that the world's climate is not stable or constant but has been subjected to major changes during the past few hundred thousand years. The Pleistocene Ice Age which has dominated the past two million years was Agassiz's great discovery, with all its consequent implications for the instability of present-day climate. Agassiz showed us that we live in a changing world, one where we cannot depend on the environment continuing just as it is. He radically and irreversibly changed our view of the world.

THOMAS COOK

Born at Melbourne 1808, died 1892.
Pioneer travel agent.

ACHIEVEMENTS:
Facilitated day excursions by rail in England.
Assisted British military operations in Egypt and the Sudan.
Encouraged the growth of foreign travel for the British middle classes.
Encouraged the growth of tourist resorts in Europe.
Created the first wave of mass tourism from Britain to Europe.

THOMAS COOK WAS born at Melbourne in Derbyshire in November 1808. He started work at the age of ten as a gardener's help. Then he became a wood-turner at Melbourne and printer at Loughborough. When he was 20 he became a Bible-reader and village missionary for the county of Rutland. He married in 1832, and from then on combined his missionary work with wood-turning.

He organized his first railway excursion on 5 July, 1841, persuading the Midland Counties Railway Company to run a special return trip from Leicester to Loughborough for one shilling a head for a temperance meeting. This was the first publicly advertized excursion by train ever run in England. By 1844, Cook had a permanent arrangement with the Midland Company to put trains at his disposal, for which he would supply the passengers.

At the Great Exhibition of 1851, Thomas Cook's profile was raised significantly when he helped 165,000 visitors to travel to and from London. Then in 1855, for the Paris exhibition, Cook ventured into the European market for the first time. He organized round trips from

Leicester to Calais for £1 10 s. In 1856, he organized his first circular grand tour of Europe.

At first, Cook's tours were personally conducted – guided, even – but in the early 1860s he started acting as an agent for the sale of travel tickets, and from then on the travellers travelled independently. Switzerland was the first country with which he made this ticket arrangement. Other countries followed and by 1865 it was possible to book tickets for almost every European country through Thomas Cook. In 1865, Thomas Cook initiated 'hotel coupons', offering accommodation at a fixed charge.

Thomas Cook's idea was to promote educational or recreational travel. There was one departure from this. In 1882, when Arabi Pasha's rebellion broke out, the British Army commissioned Cook to organize the transport of Sir Garnet Wolsey and his retinue to Egypt, and to transport the sick and wounded along the Nile. Thomas Cook & Son were employed in a similar way in 1884 to convey General Gordon to the Sudan, and the 18,000 men and stores later sent to relieve him. In 1889, the firm won the exclusive right to carry mail, soldiers and officials of the Egyptian government along the Nile.

In 1891, the firm of Thomas Cook & Son celebrated its jubilee. The following year Thomas Cook died. Thomas Cook did much to relieve 19th century travellers of the worry of buying tickets in unfamiliar currencies in unfamiliar languages. He also created the first wave of mass tourism. With Cook's help, large numbers of middle and upper class British people were encouraged to try taking their holidays abroad. Thanks to Thomas Cook, more visitors arrived at resorts in Italy and the Swiss Alps, which in turn encouraged the building of hotels and other tourist facilities. The modern tourist industry in Europe was under way. His chartered train arrangement was copied a hundred years later by travel companies using aircraft. It was Thomas Cook who opened the door on more adventurous holidays.

ABRAHAM LINCOLN

Born at Hodgenville 1809, died in Washington 1869.
President of the United States, victor in the American Civil
War.

ACHIEVEMENTS:
Coined the expression 'government of the people, by the people,
for the people.'
1863 – Declaration of emancipation of slaves as from January
1863.
1863 – Emancipation Proclamation.
1865 – Passed Thirteenth Amendment to US constitution,
abolishing slavery.
1865 – Presided over the Union victory in the American Civil
War.
1863 – Gettysburg Address.

ABRAHAM LINCOLN WAS born on a farm near Hodgenville, Kentucky in February 1809. The young Abe Lincoln grew up 'in the valley surrounded by high hills and deep gorges,' a rocky and infertile place where a big rain in the hills sometimes swept a crop 'clear off the field'. He was a good-humoured, imaginative but rather idle boy raised from the start to do farm work. His mother was Nancy Hanks and his father, Thomas Lincoln, was a restless pioneer, a rolling stone, a dreamer. After several moves, the Lincolns settled in Indiana in 1816. In 1818, when Lincoln was 9, his mother died and his father quickly remarried. The new stepmother encouraged Abraham's education, though there was little schooling to be had in the rural area where they lived.

In 1830, the family moved to Illinois and by now Abraham had grown into a very tall and lanky young man six feet three inches tall, and very strong. He was known for the strength with which he could wield an axe, and on arrival in Illinois earned his living splitting fence rails. His father had settled into a new farm, but Abe Lincoln had had enough of farming. He then worked as a clerk in a new general store at New Salem, a forlorn village, and the store soon closed for lack of custom. A local gang, the Clary Grove Boys, tried to bully Lincoln, but he was more than a match for these young roughs. He beat them, then charmed them, and became the nucleus of a more benign gang. Lincoln was not a good-looking man, yet he had an unusual ability to attract people with his geniality, strength and purity.

He was defeated as a candidate for the legislature, and he bought a small store in partnership with W. F. Berry. The project was a commercial failure and left Lincoln in debt for the next 15 years. He was then made village postmaster to earn a little money. He also borrowed a book on surveying, avidly learnt everything in it and managed to get himself taken on as deputy county surveyor. At around this time he enlisted, along with his Clary Grove friends (as they now were), as a volunteer in the Black Hawk War; they elected him captain of their company. Lincoln was already emerging as a natural leader, though a very easygoing one. He saw no action in this war, but he did arrive on the scene of a skirmish and was confronted with dead men who needed burial. He described the scene in mystical terms, revealing a semi-religious approach to events. He subscribed to no religion, belonged to no religion, but had a sense of the supernatural that seemed to come from the frontier landscape itself. Lincoln recognized in himself the seeds of insanity, and was terrified of it.

In 1834, he was elected to the legislature, serving until 1842; he became leader of the Whigs. He became engaged to Mary Todd in 1840, an engagement that was inexplicably broken off in January 1841. According to one story, it was on the wedding day itself that Lincoln went into a state of shock which prevented him from turning up for the wedding, and 'temporary insanity' is a possibility – given Lincoln's personality. But the bride's sisters told different stories about what happened. There is documentary evidence in the form of letters from Lincoln that he was in a state of extreme nervous excitability at the time.

A few months later, Lincoln was back to normal. One characteristic of these early years was his love of sarcasm, which he used openly in letters to the Sangamon Journal to make fun of a rival politician, James Shields. Lincoln pretended to be an illiterate countrywoman, signing himself Aunt Rebecca. Coincidentally, Mary Todd read this, thought it very funny and tried her hand at similar letter to Shields, who was not at all amused. He wanted to know who Aunt Rebecca was, and Lincoln gallantly owned up to writing both letters. Shields challenged Lincoln to a duel; Lincoln accepted; friends intervened to stop the duel; Mary and Lincoln were reconciled and married.

In 1842 Lincoln married Mary Todd. In 1846 he sat in Congress, but professional work was drawing him away from politics. Then in 1854 Stephen Douglas repealed the Missouri Compromise of 1820, and the question of slavery was reopened. There were strong feelings on both sides. Douglas defended his pro-slavery position in a speech at Springfield. Lincoln delivered a reply. It was this speech that showed for the first time Lincoln's power and eloquence as a debater.

When the Republican party was organized in 1856 to stop the spread of slavery, Lincoln was its most conspicuous leader in the state of Illinois. The delegates from Illinois proposed him for the vice-presidency. In 1858, Douglas canvassed in Illinois when he was trying for re-election to the Senate, and Lincoln stood against him. Douglas won that election, but it gave Lincoln a national profile for the first time.

In 1860, Abraham Lincoln was in one of those rising tides which from time to time carried him irresistibly forwards. In May that year, the Republican convention nominated him for president. The Democrats were divided between Douglas and Breckinridge. After an exciting campaign, in which Lincoln did extremely well, South Carolina withdrew from the Union and, in February 1861, together with the six Gulf states formed the Confederate States of America.

In his inaugural speech on 4 March 1861, Lincoln declared the Union perpetual and the secession futile, but in the circumstances – the imminent disintegration of the United States – it was scarcely an adequate speech. Lincoln's inner tide was on the ebb. He made a number of speeches after the inaugural that have been described as fatuous, and made a number of bad decisions that were to lead to the defeat at the Battle of Bull Run. He summoned generals before him to make reports, but failed to ask their advice. On 12 April, The Confederates opened the Civil War by attacking Fort Sumter at Charleston. Lincoln's response was to summon 75,000 militia and order the enlistment of 65,000 regulars. He also ordered a blockade of the southern ports. The first major battle, Bull Run, was a resounding defeat for Lincoln and the North.

Undaunted, Lincoln proclaimed that on and after 1 January 1863 all slaves in the states in rebellion should be free. Lincoln's great achievement was the enshrinement of this principle in the Thirteenth Amendment to the Constitution of the United States in 1865.

Lincoln was elected for a second term as president and in his second inaugural speech, in March 1865, Lincoln set out the profound moral issues involved in the Civil War. By now he was confident, master of the situation, in full command. His secretaries, who adored him, referred to him as 'The Tycoon'. One, John Hay, wrote:

The Tycoon is in fine whack. He is managing the war, the draft, foreign relations and planning a reconstruction of the Union all at once. I never knew with what tyrannous authority he rules the cabinet until now. The most important things he decides and there is no cavil. There is no man in the country so wise, so gentle and so firm.

On 3 April, 1865 General Grant captured Richmond, the capital of the South. Six days later, General Robert E. Lee surrendered to General Grant, bring the Civil War to an end. Lincoln's determination to free the slaves inflamed the passions of many racist extremists; many Southerners were bitter and frustrated at the Northern victory. One of them, John Wilkes Booth, shot Lincoln in the head on 14 April, 1865 at Ford's Theatre in Washington. Lincoln died the next morning.

Lincoln was a fair, direct and forthright man, highly principled and ethical, abstemious, charitable and sympathetic. How charitable and sympathetic he was can be seen from his generosity in victory. When the Civil War was over, he asked his cabinet to consider a proposal to award 400 million dollars to rebuild the South. It was a generous proposal, so generous that his cabinet forced him to set it aside. He was familiar with the precepts of the Bible, though not a member of any church; he was driven by a simple idea of what was right. He was a powerful and eloquent speaker, as can still be seen in the texts of his Emancipation Proclamation of 1863 and the Gettysburg Address of 1863. He ranks as one of the greatest of American presidents because he preserved the unity of America by winning the Civil War and preventing the Confederate states from breaking away – and because he abolished slavery in the USA.

CHARLES DARWIN

Born at Shrewsbury 1809, died 1882.
British naturalist.

ACHIEVEMENTS:
1842 – Discovered the theory of evolution by natural selection.
1858 – On the Tendency of Species to form Varieties; *and*
on the Perpetuation of Varieties and Species by Natural
Selection. *(Joint paper with Wallace)*
1859 – ON THE ORIGIN OF SPECIES BY MEANS OF
NATURAL SELECTION.
1868 – The Variation of Animals and Plants under
Domestication.
1871 – Descent of Man.

CHARLES DARWIN WAS born in Shrewsbury. His grandfathers were
Erasmus Darwin and Josiah Wedgwood. His mother, Wedgwood's
daughter, died when Charles was only eight. Charles had a brother, also
named Erasmus, who was interested in art and literature rather than
science. Charles later wrote that he agreed with Francis Galton 'in
believing that education and environment produce only a small effect on
the mind of anyone, and that most of our qualities are innate.' He was
educated as Shrewsbury Grammar School, and then studied medicine at
Edinburgh from 1825 until 1827, but it was apparent that he was
temperamentally unsuited to the medical profession. So then, with the idea
of going into the Church, he went to Christ's College, Cambridge in 1828.

Darwin was a serious student. Already at Edinburgh he had been a member
of the Plinian Society and read at one of its meetings his first scientific paper.

Darwin's first serious biological studies began at Cambridge, where John

Henslow encouraged his interest in zoology and geology. Henslow was a great guiding influence in Darwin's life; it was Henslow who was responsible for recommending Darwin as the naturalist for the Beagle voyage, which was about to begin. At Cambridge, Darwin also became friends with the geologist Adam Sedgwick.

Embarking on the Beagle voyage was to be the greatest and most momentous decision of his life. It was to be an epoch-making voyage, not only because of the huge volume of data which the young Charles Darwin collected, but because of the freshness and originality with which he interpreted what he saw. He said, 'I have steadily endeavoured to keep my mind free so as to give up any hypothesis, however much beloved, as soon as facts are shown to be opposed.' This approach was the key to his success. Darwin's mind and the 19th century's collective mind were opened wide by that five-year voyage round the world of *HMS Beagle*. The Magellan circumnavigation in the 16th century fixed the size of the world and the arrangement of its continents and oceans. The Darwin circumnavigation in the 19th century opened up a whole range of new geological and biological insights into the nature of that world, and transformed our understanding of it.

The intellectual journey of the years 1831–36 left Darwin with a colossal bank of data that would occupy him for the rest of his life, and some ideas that he would find hard to digest. But by the end of the voyage, when he was still only 27, he already knew what the principal minefield, the origin of species, was and where the key evidence lay. Already, in a pocket book of 1837, Darwin was writing:

In July opened first note-book on Transmutation of Species. *Had been greatly struck from about the month of previous March on character of South American fossils and species on Galapagos Archipelago. These facts (especially the latter) origin of all my views.*

By 1846 he had published papers on his findings that put him at the front rank of scientists.

Darwin is remembered for his theory of evolution, but he made important discoveries relating to geology and landforms too. He found seashells high in the Andes, showing that the rocks of which the mountains were made had been somehow lifted from the seabed, probably in a series of convulsions associated with earthquakes. He did a great deal of work on coral islands as well. His ideas on rocks and landforms naturally brought him into contact with Sir Charles Lyell, the great geologist. They corresponded, became close friends, and Lyell went on incorporating and interpreting Darwin's valuable data in successive editions of his authoritative key work, *Principles of Geology*, the standard 19th century work on the subject.

Lyell's brilliant book played a very important part in preparing people for Darwin's bombshell. It accustomed readers to the idea that enormous changes had taken place in the natural world as a result of powerful long-term processes. Lyell included a lucid and calm discussion of the views on evolution by Lamarck and other scientists; and this was valuable in acclimatizing readers and making them more receptive to Darwinian theory.

Darwin married his cousin, Emma Wedgwood, and in 1842 settled at Downe House in Kent, living the life of a reclusive country gentleman. At Downe, he devoted himself especially to the one great problem that preoccupied him, the origin of species. He had the idea that 'laws of change' governed species and led to their extinction, something like the laws that control the growth, maturation and death of individual organisms. He also had the idea that one species must somehow give birth to other species or die out, much as an individual organism either reproduces or becomes defunct. Darwin stumbled on Thomas Malthus's essay *On Population*, which struck him as profoundly truthful. He became convinced that favourable variations in a species would help it to survive in the Malthusian 'struggle for existence' and unfavourable variations would lead to its destruction.

He mulled over his evidence for five years, then wrote some notes in 1842, enlarged them in 1844 into a 231-page paper for his own reference. This was the theory of natural selection; evolution by the survival of the fittest, or what came to be known as the Darwinian theory. Darwin wrote to his friend Sir Joseph Hooker, 'At last gleams of light have come, and I am almost convinced (quite contrary to the opinion I started with) that species are not (it is like confessing a murder) immutable.' But Darwin was a cautious man, and probably understood the pain and furore that would follow publication. He knew that people would say his findings were blasphemous and contradicted what was plainly told in the Bible. He put off the evil day. He did not publish, though he did outline his ideas in letters. One letter, addressed to the American botanist Asa Gray, expressed his ideas with such eloquence that it later gained classic status, just as if it had been a publication.

After the Beagle voyage, Charles Darwin suffered for the rest of his life from a mysterious ailment. Some have suggested that it was a recurring tropical disease that left him drained and debilitated; some have suggested it was ME or a kind of agoraphobia; some have suggested it was a kind of nervous paralysis because he carried the burden of having made a dangerous discovery. He knew his theory of evolution would have to come out, and he dreaded the storm that would follow the revelation. It was almost as if he was harbouring a guilty secret.

Then, in June 1858, Alfred Russel Wallace sent him a paper on the Malay archipelago which, to Darwin's surprise, contained a summary of the same idea as his own on natural selection. Wallace wanted Darwin's opinion on his paper and also wanted Darwin to forward his opinion to Sir Charles Lyell. Darwin wrote to Lyell, 'Your words have come true with a vengeance – that I should be forestalled.' Discussing the tricky situation with his friends, Lyell and Hooker, Darwin was persuaded that he and Wallace should submit a joint paper based on Wallace's paper and his own 1844 sketch. It was read at the Linnaean Society on 1 July 1858 at the same meeting as Wallace's paper. Neither Wallace nor Darwin was present.

Now that the cat was out of the bag, Darwin set to work to argue the case for natural selection more fully, again urged on by his friends. This turned into his great book, *On the Origin of Species by Means of Natural Selection, or the Preservation of Favoured Races in the Struggle for Life*, which was published on 24 November 1859.

This explosive book made a bigger impact on the 19th century world than any other. It is hard now to imagine the furore that it caused. Many scientists were profoundly impressed by it. Some accepted its findings. Some violently rejected them. The Church was most hostile as the book seemed to fly in the face of the Biblical account of the creation of man and the animals. Darwin was ridiculed for suggesting by implication that people were descended from apes. The storm of controversy reached a climax in 1860, when at the British Association meeting in Oxford there was a noisy verbal duel between Thomas Huxley, who supported Darwin, and Bishop Samuel Wilberforce of Oxford ('Soapy Sam'), who opposed him.

Darwin went on to produce another important book on evolution in 1868, *The Variation of Animals and Plants under Domestication*. This was in effect a more complete version of the material that was included in condensed form in the *Origin of Species*. His third, long-postponed, work on evolution dealt with the thorny issue of human evolution, which he had until then tried to avoid, knowing the distress and fuss it would cause. This was *Descent of Man and Selection in Relation to Sex*, published in 1871.

Darwin was not the sole originator of the theory of evolution by natural selection – Wallace was thinking of it at the same time. Darwin was however the first thinker to argue the natural selection theory through in a way that was comprehensive enough for a large number of fellow-scientists to find it acceptable, perhaps because of the long mulling-over period he gave to it. Darwin took the crude evolutionism of Erasmus Darwin and Lamarck and grafted on his own idea of natural selection; this raised evolution from a hypothesis to a verifiable theory. Cultures and civilizations are by their nature conservative and resistant to large-scale change – that is how they defend themselves and preserve their identity. They are like fully-laden supertankers continuing under their own huge momentum. Darwin's great achievement lay in turning the great supertanker of western civilization through several degrees, away from religious fundamentalism and towards a new and frightening idea that the emergence of the human race might be a result of mere chance. He didn't say that – he was too cautious – but that was where his ideas would lead. Darwin changed the thought-world of the 19th century.

CYRUS McCORMICK

Born 1809, died 1884.
American inventor.

ACHIEVEMENT:
1831 – Invented the mechanical reaper (combine harvester).

CYRUS HALL McCORMICK was born in Rockbridge County, Virginia, in February 1809. He was the son of Robert McCormick, a farmer who invented and patented several labour-saving agricultural implements. Cyrus's father made several attempts to design a mechanical reaper, but in 1831 he abandoned the project.

In that year, at the age of 22, Cyrus took up the challenge to see whether he could succeed where his father had failed. He studied the technical problems carefully and came up with a successful working design before the end of the year. The machine was built and actually used to bring in the late harvest in 1831. Cyrus McCormick did not get round to seeking a patent for his reaper until 1834, by which time another reaper, designed by Obed Hussey, had been patented.

American agriculture had entered a phase of raid expansion and there was fierce rivalry between the two men, Hussey and McCormick, to manufacture harvesters. Other companies were involved in this lucrative struggle too. McCormick moved to Chicago in 1847, and manufactured his harvesters there. In the end the McCormick Harvesting Machine Company emerged as the leading manufacturer. The McCormick reaper, after a number of further improvements, had proved a complete success, not only technically but financially.

Cyrus McCormick died in Chicago in May 1884; his son carried on the business after his death. By 1902, the family firm had become the International Harvester Company. Cyrus Hall McCormick's son, Cyrus Hall McCormick Jun., was the first president and chairman of the board.

Between them, the McCormicks invented several labour-saving devices that helped on the farms of America. It was on the huge grain farms of the Prairies that the combine harvester was to make the biggest changes. With the new harvesters, huge fields of grain could be harvested at speed, making the best use of spells of good weather. The new technology allowed food production to be stepped up enormously. Thanks to harvesters, the Prairies regularly produced huge grain surpluses, which the USA could export, and which were to become of profound political significance in the Cold War. The Soviet Union frequently suffered from crop failures and needed the US grain surplus, which gave the US political supremacy. Mechanization also depended on the availability of cheap oil; as oil reserves run dry, it may be that the Prairies will one day need to return to man and horse power for farm production.

ELISHA OTIS

Born 1811, died 1861.
American inventor.

ACHIEVEMENTS:
1853 – Invented the passenger lift.
1861 – Invented the steam-powered passenger lift.
Made skyscrapers possible.

ELISHA GRAVES OTIS was born in Halifax, Vermont in 1811. He was a master mechanic for a bedstead manufacturer. He was put in charge of the construction of his firm's new factory at Yonkers. It was a factory that had several floors connected by a hoist. Elisha Otis knew of the mechanical dangers of runaway lifting platforms – existing models were dangerously unpredictable and could cause serious accidents. He designed a spring-operated safety device that would hold the platform in position if there was a failure in the tension of the rope. The device could position the lifting platform very precisely. This was invented and in use in 1853.

Otis patented his 'elevator' and exhibited it in New York in 1854. Once it had been seen there, orders came in thick and fast for Otis lifts – for passengers as well as goods.

In 1861, just before his death, he patented a new type of steam-powered lift. These high-powered lifts were installed in the multi-storey blocks that were built during the later 19th and 20th centuries. Many of the great multi-storey buildings in New York, dating back to the beginning of the last century, still have their Otis lifts and original Otis engine rooms, still in full working order. The Otis lift made it possible to conceive of buildings of almost any height, as stairs were no longer essential. Elisha Otis's invention, a safe lift that would stop reliably at each floor, and at exactly the right level to within a few millimetres, made the skyscraper possible. Elisha Otis, without intending it, instigated the skyline of Manhattan and other North American city centres.

CHARLES DICKENS

Born in Portsmouth 1812, died at Godshill 1870.
English novelist.

ACHIEVEMENTS:
Greatest English novelist.
1836 – Pickwick Papers.
1838 – Oliver Twist.
1839 – Nicholas Nickleby.
1843 – A Christmas Carol.
1844 – Martin Chuzzlewit.
1850 – David Copperfield.
1853 – Bleak House.
1857 – Little Dorrit.
1859 – A Tale of Two Cities.
1861 – Great Expectations.
1865 – Our Mutual Friend.

CHARLES JOHN HUFFAM Dickens was born at Landport, a suburb of Portsmouth, in 1812. His father, John Dickens, was a clerk in the navy pay office, attached to the dockyard. In 1814 John Dickens was transferred to London, and then two years later to Chatham. In 1821, the Dickens family was in serious trouble. John Dickens was an unsteady, insecure, unreliable character, always hoping that something would turn up; he was made redundant and the family had to leave Chatham for London. Dickens used his father as a model for *Mr Micawber*. Dickens referred to his nomadic and mercurial parent as 'the Prodigal Father'. They took a small house in Camden Town. John Dickens was arrested for debt and sent to the Marshalsea, the debtors' prison, with his family – apart from Charles, who was sent to work in a blacking factory at Old Hungerford Stairs, a stone's throw from where the poet William Blake was living – though young Charles would not have known that. There, with half a dozen rough boys, he spent his days labelling the blacking bottles. At night he was left to his own devices, and he had to walk four miles to his lonely bedroom in lodgings in Camden Town. On Sundays he was able to visit his family. He was extremely unhappy.

This bitter and profoundly unhappy early experience, with all the feelings of isolation, rejection, injustice, and the harshness and grotesqueness of society, was undoubtedly what made Dickens the powerful and committed writer he later became.

When John Dickens was released from the Marshalsea, Charles was sent back to school for three years, after which he worked as an office boy for a solicitor, Mr Blackmore of Gray's Inn. His father had got himself a job as a reporter for the *Morning Herald*, and Charles thought that he too might become a journalist. In 1828 he became a reporter of debates in the House of Commons for the *Morning Chronicle*, but writing was still a means to an end, and he secretly wanted to become an actor. Meanwhile his career as a journalist developed well. In fact the son soon outshone the father: but Charles Dickens had the drive and energy his father lacked. He had worked at his reading and shorthand, and after working for the *Morning Chronicle* for several years he started contributing articles and sketches for the *Evening Chronicle*, under the pen-name Boz. In 1836 the Sketches by Boz were collected and published; he was given £150 for the copyright. Later he bought the copyright back for 11 times that amount.

The year 1836 was a watershed year for Dickens. Not only did the *Sketches by Boz* appear, but the first part of the *Pickwick Papers* came out in March. Three days afterwards he married Catherine Hogarth, the daughter of the editor of the *Evening Chronicle*. She bore Dickens 10 children between 1837 and 1852; in 1858 they separated.

As well as writing, Dickens travelled widely, visiting America in 1842 and 1867, Genoa in 1844–45, Lausanne in 1846. He also spent several summers in Boulogne. Dickens made a great name for himself delivering public readings of his books; these were incredibly spirited one-man melodramas, in which the novelist gave full rein to his thwarted desire to be an actor. But they were also a means of promoting his books. He wore himself out with overwork. Dickens died suddenly at his home in Godshill near Rochester in 1870. It was a place he had coveted as a boy, and managed to buy for himself in 1856.

Dickens worked like a demon all his life. His output as a writer was prodigious. After *Pickwick Papers* came *Oliver Twist, Martin Chuzzlewit, Christmas Tales,* and so on until the final novel *The Mystery of Edwin Drood,* which was left unfinished at the time of his death. The drive and commitment with which Dickens worked were perhaps a reaction to the irresponsibility of his 'prodigal' father. He championed benevolence and geniality in his books and always stood up for the simple pleasures of the poor, but he also championed justice, industry, ambition and personal loyalty. He was in many ways a true Victorian, standing for upright citizenship and also revelling in the rich variety of 19th century society, from top to bottom. Dickens was a kind of conflagration in the heart of the Victorian era, and a conflagration all the more extraordinary for bursting from a man with no background, no culture, and little education – as extraordinary as the spontaneous combustion he used to destroy Krook in *Bleak House.*

Many of his novels incorporate a campaign against some social or legal injustice, and these were real campaigns, not just adopted to make a good story. He was a literary Robert Owen, catching his readers' hearts in the hope that they would want to change the world. He had no time for do-gooding charity workers who neglected their children while collecting money for missionaries in far-off lands; these he sent up in fine style in *Bleak House,* almost as an aside to his main target, the Court of Chancery.

Dickens and his friend Wilkie Collins made nocturnal expeditions to the East End of London together, 'slumming' in order to collect characters, locations and incidents for their fiction. When he was researching for *Nicholas Nickleby,* Dickens wanted to make the boarding school as life-like as possible – which now seems hard to believe. On a tip-off, he applied to a school in Yorkshire, and arranged an interview with the Headmaster, pretending to be a parent wanting to place his son with him. Dickens memorized the turns of phrase, the patter, the gestures, while Cruikshank, the illustrator he had taken along with him, surreptitiously sketched the Headmaster's features for the book. Wackford Squeers was not a caricature at all, but a very literal portrait of a real Headmaster of a real school. It was a very daring thing to do, but Dickens guessed that he would ultimately be safe. The real Headmaster in question initially threatened to sue Dickens for libel, but had just enough intelligence to realise that by doing this he would make himself a laughing stock. No-one in his right mind would claim in a courtroom to be the model for a Dickens villain!

What Dickens did was to show that a world of interest lies in every human being, however grand, however humble. There is a world of entertainment just in looking at people and listening to what they say. He did not always seek to understand or explain – goodness and evil simply exist in his characters – but above all he made us look harder at people, and see how compellingly full of interest they are.

Dickens changed the world in another, wholly unanticipated way. His novels set in the middle of the 19th century were taken in the old Soviet Union as a true picture of capitalist Britain a hundred years later. In this way, Dickens's picture of England was actually used as propaganda – against the West. Dickens would have loved the comic grotesqueness of that.

RICHARD WAGNER

Born in Leipzig 1813, died in Venice 1883.
German composer.

ACHIEVEMENTS:
High point of Romanticism in music.
Extended the length of musical movements.
Developed new musical structure based on 'leading themes'.
Influenced the Hollywood film score tradition.
Stimulated the atonal rebellion in the 20th century.
1843 – The Flying Dutchman.
1848 – Lohengrin.
1869 – The Rhinegold.
1882 – Parsifal.

WAGNER'S EARLY EFFORTS as a self-taught composer led to the public performance of an inept concert overture (which even the older Wagner laughed at). After that he had composition lessons from Weinlig. Wagner set out to be an opera composer from the start and with incredible ambition and self-confidence experimented in his first three operas with three different traditions, German, French and Italian. From this experience he concluded that the German model was the best way forward, and composed his next series of three operas with the development of the German operatic tradition in view. This produced *The Flying Dutchman, Tannhauser* and *Lohengrin*.

Wagner was then caught up in the revolutionary movement sweeping across Europe, and became one of the leaders in an abortive revolution in Dresden in 1848. His accomplices served long prison sentences, so Wagner was lucky; by escaping from Saxony and living in voluntary exile he escaped a long spell in prison.

Liszt gave him financial support that enabled him to travel to Paris and then Switzerland. It was Liszt who arranged the production of *Lohengrin* at Weimar in 1850, and tried generally to keep Wagner's name in the public eye. During his exile, Wagner made some money by writing essays, books and articles, while turning over in his mind the next stage of his opera-writing career. He decided on one of the most ambitious art works of all time, *The Ring of the Nibelung,* a string of four operas, consisting of 17 hours of music that would develop symphonically to make a single piece. It was an absurdly ambitious project for a penniless exile – but he did it, drafting the text in 1852. The music took much longer to complete, and Wagner underwent a philosophical and psychological transformation during the writing of it – a conversion to the ideas of Schopenhauer. In the hands of a lesser composer this could have de-railed the project, but the shift actually energized it, gave it an unexpected dynamic thrust.

Wagner even set out to write a 'Schopenhauer opera', which turned out to be *Tristan and Isolde,* one of the most depressing yet also most sublime pieces of music ever written.

Money was always a problem for Wagner; he could never get enough. Luckily he had a wealthy and powerful fan in the shape of King Ludwig II of Bavaria. Ludwig made productions of *The Ring* possible in the 1870s, and musicians and composers from all over Europe flocked to see and hear the new total artwork. This experience had far-reaching effects on composers for decades to come. The effects in popular art were to be powerful; the Hollywood film score tradition of the 20th century is firmly based on the principles of Wagner opera, based on the 'leading theme' idea.

Wagner died suddenly of heart disease in Venice at the age of 70. Liszt set Wagner up as the god of the Romantic movement. Wagner was a totally original artist. With his distinctive sumptuous style, rich orchestration, melody, harmony and key progression, he would have many imitators in the first half of the 20th century. But he also stimulated rebellion. The saturated lushness of Wagner's music led some composers to think music could develop no further in this direction. Stravisnky's spikiness and Schoenberg's music without keys were part of an anti-Wagner revolt. Yet the seeds of Schoenberg's atonal music were there already in the score of

Tristan. Wagner stands at the doorway between 19th and 20th century music, in much the same way that Beethoven stands at the doorway between 18th and 19th.

KARL MARX

Born in Trier 1818, died in London 1883.
German social, political and economic theorist, creator of
  communism.

ACHIEVEMENTS:
Became the prophet and inspiration for 20th century
  communism.
Founded 'Marxism', in effect a new world religion.
Taught that a new economic and political order would only
  come about through a class struggle.
Wrote 'The workers have nothing to lose but their chains.'
1848 – Communist Manifesto.
1867 – Das Kapital.

KARL HEINRICH MARX was born on 5 May 1818 in Trier in Germany. The Marx family was Jewish by origin, but Karl's pragmatic lawyer father converted to Christianity in 1824 to escape anti-Semitic prejudice. The young Karl was therefore baptized as a Protestant convert. He later went to the grammar school in Trier. Marx studied at Bonn University in 1835–36 and Berlin University from 1836–41, studying first law and then history and philosophy. There he met and mixed with radical followers of Hegel, the so-called 'Freien', including Bruno and Edgar Bauer, who were preoccupied particularly with a critique of religion. Marx's own doctoral thesis was about the philosophies of nature in *Democritus* and *Epicürus.*

Marx had the academic ability to pursue a career as a university lecturer and it was only his radicalism that made a university career impossible. He had to find some other way of making a living. From 1842, Marx was working as a journalist. He became editor of the *Rheinische Zeitung*, a Cologne newspaper which expressed the views of the most radical section of the middle classes. The paper regularly made virulent attacks on the government, which suppressed it in 1843. In the summer of that year, Marx married Jenny von Westphalen, the daughter of a high-ranking government official. Marx emigrated to Paris, where he became a communist. He believed that society must undergo revolutionary change, but now he stated his distinctive belief – that the proletariat (the working class) must itself be the agent of revolutionary change. Until that time revolutions had been instigated by the middle class. Danton and Robespierre had been members of the middle class, not the working class.

One article Marx wrote in Paris was a criticism of Bruno Bauer's treatment of the Jewish question. Marx argued that the Jews could only be emancipated along with the general emancipation of society from commercialism. Marx's approach was always root-and-branch like this; everything came back to the necessity for a socialist revolution.

Marx wrote a long critique of capitalism, *Economic and Philosophical Manuscripts of 1844*, which remained as manuscripts until they were published in 1932. This document contained the idea that people suffer alienation under capitalism; capitalism is bad for them. At the same time, Marx struck up a life-long friendship with Friedrich Engels. The two men collaborated on several tracts. Their first was a scathing attack on the high-sounding speculative radicalism of the Berlin 'Freien'. In Paris Marx also met and befriended the poet Heinrich Heine, who spoke very warmly and respectfully of Marx. Marx got involved in a radical magazine, *Vorwarts*, and the Prussian government applied leverage to the French government to have it stopped.

The French authorities sensed that Marx and his co-workers were trouble-makers, as indeed they were – professional trouble-makers. Virtually the entire staff of the offending magazine were given orders to leave France. Marx was forced to emigrate again, this time to Brussels, where he arrived in 1845. There, shortly afterwards joined by Engels, he wrote *The Misery of Philosophy*, an attack on Proudhon. With Engels he wrote *German Ideology*, which, like *Social and Philosophical Manuscripts* also remained in manuscript; this outlined their view of the materialist conception of history. Marx did not think that a revolution could begin in

Germany until it had happened in France; 'The day of German resurrection will be announced by the crowing of the Gallic cock.'

In Brussels, Marx and Engels came into closer contact with the socialist working-class movement. They set up a German workers' society, and then joined the League of the Just, which was an international secret society with branches in London, Paris, Brussels and towns in Switzerland. In 1848, he and Engels together wrote a handbook for the League of the Just, which now started calling itself the League of the Communists. The handbook was the famous *Communist Manifesto*, and this masterpiece of communist propaganda ended with the rousing words, 'The workers have nothing to lose but their chains. They have a world to win. Workers of the world, unite!' It was this major work, outlining the history and the future of the working-class movement in modern society which was the inspiration behind many communist movements in the 20th century and which transformed the socio-political geography of the 20th century world. Though dead well before the 20th century began, Karl Marx was a great unseen force in its history.

Entirely by chance, or perhaps because the incipient revolution was the whiff of cordite in the air that Marx and Engels breathed, revolution broke out in France and several other European states immediately after the *Communist Manifesto* was written. It was in February 1848, just a couple of months after the *Manifesto* was written, that revolution broke out in Paris. 'The crowing of the Gallic cock' proved to be the signal for revolution to spread through Germany, just exactly as Marx had prophesied.

Marx and Engels made a brief visit to France, and then went to Cologne in May 1848. There, with friends, they started a radical newspaper, of which Marx was to be the editor, the *Neue Rheinische Zeitung*. Marx and his collaborators advocated non-payment of taxes and the organization of armed resistance. A state of siege was declared in Cologne, the *Neue Rheinische Zeitung* was suspended and Karl Marx was put on trial for high treason. He had after all advocated the overthrow of the state. He was unanimously found not guilty by a middle-class jury, and acquitted. He was nevertheless persona non grata and obliged to leave Prussian territory. He first went to Paris, but it was made clear to him by the authorities there that he must either settle in a provincial French town or leave the country altogether. He opted to leave for England. He took refuge with his family in London, where he lived for the rest of his life.

At first Marx tried to reorganize and revive the Communist League, but dissent broke out. Some of its members were tried and condemned for treason in Germany. Marx tried to save those accused. When he failed, he dissolved the Communist League altogether. An attempt to revive the *Neue Rheinische Zeitung* in London was also a failure, though it did carry a remarkable series of articles describing the course of the French Revolution of 1848, which Engels later published in book form in 1895, under the title *The Class-conflict in France of 1848*, and Engels conscientiously credited the account to his friend – 'by Karl Marx'. Marx heartily supported the efforts of Ernest Jones to revive the Chartist movement, which was the British working-class movement, and contributed several articles to Chartist journals.

In London, Karl Marx and his family lived in poverty, in a small apartment in Dean Street, Soho, but he continued to develop his political thought, spending time in the British Museum Reading Room, where he began the research that led to his major works of political and economic theory. The most notable of these was *Das Kapital*, the first volume of which was published in 1867. Two further volumes were added in 1884 and 1894. *Das Kapital* became one of the most influential works of the 19th century. In it, Marx developed his doctrines of the theory of surplus value, class conflict, the exploitation of the working class; he also predicted that capitalism would be superseded by socialism and that the state would give way to a classless communist society. The new political and economic order would only be achieved through a class struggle, the working class fighting for its rightful supremacy. There was a strong element here of Darwin's theory of evolution through natural selection – the survival of the fittest. The timing of *Das Kapital* is interesting in this respect, its publication coming a few years after Charles Darwin's *Origin of Species*. The communist's role was to act as a midwife to this process, which was to be regarded as an inevitable historical evolution. Marx said, 'Philosophers have previously tried to explain the world; our task is to change it.' There is also in *Das Kapital* something akin to *The Ring*, written by Marx's almost exact contemporary Richard Wagner; in fact *The Ring* has been very successfully staged as a Marxist tract.

Throughout these difficult years, Marx was supported and encouraged by his friend Engels. He supported himself financially by acting as the New York *Daily Tribune*'s European correspondent, producing the 19th century equivalent of Alistair Cooke's *Letter from America*, but in reverse: *Karl Marx's Letter from Europe*.

After constructing his historic time-bomb, in the shape of *Das Kapital*, Marx was ready to become politically active again. He was a leading figure in the International Working Men's Association from 1864 until the anarchist followers of Bakunin, a friend of Wagner, split away in 1872. Marx was in fact, though not in name, the head of its general council. Marx here showed real leadership skills. He was wise, tolerant, and functioned more as a teacher than as an agitator.

The dissolution of the International at least allowed Marx time for his theoretical work. The final decade of Marx's life was a time of increasing ill-health and work on the second and third volumes of *Das Kapital* was repeatedly interrupted by illness. He died quietly in London on 14 May 1883 (the same year as Wagner) and was buried in Highgate Cemetery. He had been supported loyally through a very hard life by his wife Jenny, whom he outlived by only a year.

Many of the predictions Marx made turned out to be false prophecies, and the practice of 'Marxism' as a political system has turned out to be extremely unpleasant, far from classless, and far from just. The Marxist view of capitalist society is a generalized vision of a huge undifferentiated class of labourers dominated and exploited by a capitalist class. The reality of German, French or British society in the 19th century was far more complicated than that, as Marx must have known from first-hand knowledge. But in spite of these major – and all too obvious – defects, Marx's grandiose and almost novelistic ideas exerted a hypnotic grip on one society after another in the 20th century, and provided the dynamo for one revolutionary upheaval after another. And he was uncannily right about the 1848 revolution in France being necessary to trigger revolution in Germany. The secular adherents of Marxism outnumber the followers of most other religious or political creeds, and it has often been said that what Marx created was more than a political creed; it was nothing less than a new world religion.

LOUIS PASTEUR

Born at Dole 1822, died at St Cloud 1895.
French chemist, father of modern bacteriology.

ACHIEVEMENTS:
Became master of 'the world of the infinitely small'.
Discovered a method for making racemic acid.
Discovered that fermentation was the result of the activity of
  an organism.
Invented the technique of pasteurizing milk.
Made Lister's revolution in antiseptic surgery possible.
Invented a technique for vaccination against rabies and other
  illnesses.
Made immunization against TB, cholera and hepatitis possible.
Helped reduce the human death rate.

LOUIS PASTEUR WAS born at Dole in the Juras, the son of a tanner. The family, who were simple, devout Catholics, moved to Arbois, where Louis attended primary and secondary schools. In the autumn of 1838 he was sent to a school in Paris, but became homesick. He wrote home to his family, 'If only I could smell the tannery again I should feel well.' He was allowed to go back to Arbois, but soon went away again to the Royal College at Besancon. After qualifying, he became an assistant mathematics master, achieving his baccalaureat in sciences in 1842; in chemistry he was graded only 'mediocre'.

In spite of this unpromising beginning, Louis Pasteur was destined for success – because of his determination to succeed. He wrote to his sisters, 'Three things, will, work and success, between them fill human existence.' It was a revealing declaration, and his career was indeed to be dominated by hard work, dogged determination and success. Even on his deathbed, he asked his students, 'What are you doing? You must work.'

At the Sorbonne his research work was chemical, mainly on tartrates. He discovered that paratartrate contained two types of crystals. Then, after moving to Dijon as Professor of Physics, he discovered a method for producing racemic acid, for which he was awarded the Legion of Honour. Then, moving on to become Director of Scientific Studies at the Ecole Normale, he discovered that fermentation was the result of the activity of an organism. He showed that milk could be soured by injecting a number of organisms from beer, or kept unchanged if they were excluded. This major breakthrough led to the important process now known as pasteurization.

He discovered a living ferment, a micro-organism comparable to yeast, which in a solution of paratartrate selected for food one type of tartrate and left the other type alone. He went on to show that other fermentations – lactic, acetic and butyric – are also due to the activity of organisms. By this stage, Pasteur was acknowledged as the leading chemist of his time. Lord Lister saw the potential application to surgery. As a result of Pasteur's discovery of micro-organisms, and his discovery that they caused fermentation and putrefaction, Lister was able to revolutionize surgery by introducing, in 1865, the use of carbolic acid to exclude atmospheric germs and so prevent wounds from going septic. Pasteur's work thus led directly on to the invention of antiseptics and the improvement of survival rates after surgery.

In 1865, Pasteur was persuaded to visit the south of France, where silkworm disease was ruining the French silk industry. Three years later he was able to announce that he had discovered the micro-organisms responsible for two distinct diseases and had found a method of preventing the spread of these diseases. In 1868, Pasteur was struck by semi-paralysis, but was able to continue his experiments on fermentation in Paris.

The Franco-Prussian War of 1870, and the consequent disruption of trade, diverted Pasteur to perfecting the French brewing process. He succeeded in controlling harmful growths in beer. In 1874 he was awarded a life pension by the National Assembly.

He showed that it was possible to reduce the danger from micro-organisms by a range of different procedures. Exposure to air was one. Transmission though various animals was another. This apparently unexciting research led to a very significant result. In a landmark experiment, Louis Pasteur showed that sheep and cows that were 'vaccinated' with attenuated (weakened) bacilli of the dangerous disease anthrax were protected from the worst effects of the virulent form of the virus when they were injected with it later.

This was a major breakthrough in the treatment of diseases. It was later discovered that Pasteur's discovery had many applications. It was possible to inoculate not only sheep and cows but people too – and to inoculate them against a range of dangerous diseases. Because of Pasteur, it is now possible to inoculate people against diphtheria, tuberculosis, cholera, yellow fever, plague and hepatitis. Life expectancy itself has been transformed.

Pasteur himself applied the technique to another unpleasant disease, called rabies in dogs and hydrophobia in people. In July 1885, Pasteur took the ultimate risk, and inoculated a human being. It was a child who had been badly bitten by a dog infected with rabies, so there was a strong chance that the child would develop hydrophobia. The experiment was totally successful. In 1888, the Pasteur Institute was founded for the treatment of hydrophobia by inoculation. Since then, thousands suffering from hydrophobia have been treated at the institute, greatly reducing the mortality rate from the disease.

When opening his institute, Pasteur made a memorable speech ending with the following words:

> Two opposing laws seem to me now in contest. The one, a law of blood and death, opening out each day new modes of destruction, forces nations to be always ready for battle. The other, a law of peace, work and health, whose only aim is to deliver man from the calamities that beset him. The one seeks violent conquests, the other a relief of mankind. The one places a single life above all victories, the other sacrifices hundreds of thousands of lives to the ambition of a single individual . . . Which of these two laws will prevail, God only knows. But of this we may be sure, that science, in obeying the law of humanity, will always labour to enlarge the frontiers of life.'

It was a statement of faith, not a statement of science. As we shall see, scientists and their knowledge can be harnessed for killing as well as for healing. But Pasteur was an optimist, and he above all people had first-hand experience of the good that science could do. Pasteur was the father of modern bacteriology, the master of what he called 'the world of the infinitely small', devising vaccines for the prevention of a range of diseases. Tuberculosis was one of the great killer diseases of 19th-century Europe, carrying off huge numbers of people every year. Thanks to applications of Pasteur's methods, the disease was brought increasingly under control in the 20th century. A side effect of Pasteur's work has been a reduction in the death rate and a consequent increase in human population totals.

HEINRICH SCHLIEMANN

Born at Neubuckow 1822, died in Naples 1890.
German archaeologist.

ACHIEVEMENTS:
Excavated Troy, Mycenae and Tiryns.
Established that the Trojan War was a historical reality.
Generated worldwide popular enthusiasm for archaeology.
1868 – Ithaca, the Peloponnese and Troy.
1875 – Troy and its Remains.
1890 – Mycenae.
1881 – Ilios: the city and the country of the Trojans.
1884 – Troja.
1886 – Tiryns: the prehistoric palace of the kings of
  Tiryns.

HEINRICH SCHLIEMANN WAS born at Neubuckow in the grand duchy of Mecklenburg-Schwerin on 6 January 1822. His father, Ernst, had five children to feed. Ernst was singularly unpleasant man, egoistical, drunken, sexually promiscuous, and ill-suited to his profession; he was the village pastor. In 1829, he took in a young woman called Sophie Schwarz, ostensibly as personal maid for his wife, Louise, but actually as his mistress. When his much abused wife died, he published a long-winded and hypocritical eulogy in the local paper. This must have prompted pity for Louise and derision for Ernst in many households; everyone knew about the mistress. The young Heinrich must have had a miserable time in this household. When he wrote about it in his autobiography, everything was sweetness and light, and it may be that it was the early need to cover up the awful truth that turned Heinrich into an inveterate liar.

At first young Heinrich was apprenticed to a grocer in Furstenburg, then he decided to sail on the *Dorothea* bound for South America. He told his sisters he had a job in Colombia and the passage was free. He wrote in his 1851 'life' that he had to sell his belongings to buy his ticket. In *Ilios* he says he worked his passage as a cabin boy. There is no way of telling which if any of these versions was true. Characteristically, Schliemann tells us that he was shipwrecked on this voyage, off the island of Texel on the Dutch coast. He was rescued and taken to Amsterdam. He could never resist adding colourful and glamorous embellishments to his life story, or to his excavation reports. His imaginative leaps with the truth were, and still remain, a major problem.

Whatever happened, or did not happen, on the *Dorothea*, young Heinrich Schliemann returned to Europe, where in 1842 he became first an office attendant then a book-keeper in Rostock. He was dismissed from his job in Hamburg, for reasons that are unclear. The firm of B. H. Schroder sent him in 1846 to St Petersburg, where he worked until 1863. In St Petersburg he set up in business on his own, embarking on the indigo trade. He was extremely successful, amassing a great fortune at the time of the Crimean War, partly as a military contractor.

He happened to be in California in 1850 when the state became part of the Union, and decided to take American citizenship.

At the age of 46 he retired from commerce and started travelling. Later, when writing his autobiography, he claimed that after he had made his fortune he always intended to devote the rest of his life to realizing a childhood ambition – to find the places described in Homer. In reality, he spent quite a lot of time travelling the world, to Greece, Tunisia, India, China and Japan, writing an account of the last two countries, before homing in on Greece. It was only in 1868 that he started visiting Homeric sites, and it seems likely that his interest really dated from this time, not from childhood at all.

He was exploring the likeliest area for the location of the ancient city of Troy, in north-west Turkey, and had definitely settled on a site called Bunarbashi as his candidate for ancient Troy. He was lucky enough to meet

Frank Calvert, who had been living in the area and researching the question for some time and come to an informed conclusion based on finds at the site that Troy was at Hisarlik, further to the north. Calvert worked hard to persuade Schliemann that Hisarlik was the likelier of the two sites.

Then Schliemann produced a book, *Ithaca*, in which he proposed two theories that would later seem to have the authority of prophecies. One was that Troy was at Hisarlik, not Bunarbashi. The other was that the graves of Agamemnon and his dynasty were within the citadel wall at Mycenae.

Schliemann organized excavations at Troy from 1871 onwards, with the help of Wilhelm Dorpfeld. The mound at Hisarlik turned out to be a complicated layer-cake of ancient settlements one on top of the other – not one Troy but nine Troys. Without any real dating evidence, Schliemann decided that Troy II was the Troy described by Homer, *Priam's Troy*, ploughing the mound down to that level and destroying the later cities. In fact it was only at the end of his life that he realized that he had been wrong. Troy II instead of dating from 1100 BC dated from about 2400 BC. It was Troy VI that was *Priam's Troy* – and he had destroyed most of it.

Schliemann collected a haul of gold from Troy II, which he presented to the German nation in the hope of gaining several high honours. He got his friend Virchow to do the dirty work of negotiating the honours. In taking the treasure out of Turkey he had broken Turkish laws, and it was only after paying compensation to the Turkish government that the treasure was handed over to a museum in Berlin in 1882.

Meanwhile, because of his breach of Turkish law, Schliemann had difficulty in 1874 in renewing his licence to excavate at Troy. He filled in time by writing *Troy and its Remains* and in 1876 turned his attention to Mycenae. Troy II was paraded as the Troy of Homer, and many scholars accepted it – Gladstone included.

The famous Lion Gate at Mycenae had already been uncovered in 1841 and the walls of the citadel were fully visible, so there was never any doubt about the identity of this site. Schliemann's excavations spectacularly uncovered royal burials in an unexpected location within the walls of the citadel although, as at Troy, Schliemann got the period wrong. At both sites he focused on finds dating from centuries earlier than the Homeric period, which was around 1250 BC.

In predicting where the royal burials would be found, Schliemann followed a description in Pausanias, who put the tombs of Aigisthos and Clytemnestra 'a little further from the wall, as they were not judged fit to be buried where Agamemnon lay.' Most scholars in 1868 reasoned that the kings of Mycenae would not have put their wealth, whether in tombs or treasuries, outside the city wall, and they also reasoned that the beehive tombs, popularly known as 'treasuries', must have been defended by a city wall much further out. Schliemann, an amateur, was unaware of these considerations and just assumed Pausanias was referring to the citadel walls. It was Schliemann's ignorance that led him to discover the shaft graves with their rich royal burials and gold funeral masks. In fact it is likely that Agamemnon was actually buried in the beehive tomb known, rather confusingly, as the Tomb of Clytemnestra, and that was just outside the citadel wall.

Schliemann was a highly successful self-publicist and knew exactly how to grab headlines. On finding a gold funerary mask in one of the shaft graves, he cabled the King of Greece with the quite arbitrary claim, 'I have gazed upon the face of Agamemnon.' Schliemann was guessing the identity of the prince in this shaft grave, but it was almost certainly a prince who lived long before Agamemnon.

Schliemann was deceitful and unscrupulous in the extreme, and may have salted the shaft graves with finds from elsewhere during the last week in November 1876 in order to catch the interest of newspaper journalists round the world. He had done this three years earlier, when he gathered together the components of 'Priam's Treasure' at Troy. Both at Troy and at Mycenae, Schliemann himself made spectacular discoveries during the final fortnight of his excavation, finding practically all the gold and silver the sites were to yield at one spot. Then, to the consternation of his team of excavators, instead of digging furiously to find more he darted away to publish, lecture and trawl publicity.

As well as Mycenae, Schliemann excavated important Bronze Age sites at two other Greek sites, Tiryns and Orchomenos, uncovering the remains of spectacular citadels with distinctive and rich artwork. On Ithaca in 1878 he dug without any result, which was uncharacteristic for Schliemann. At Orchomenos in 1881 he excavated the great beehive tomb, uncovering the recently collapsed remains of its beautifully carved stone ceiling.

Schliemann provided archaeological evidence that there had been a Mycenaean civilization in Bronze Age Greece. Until his time, there had only been literary evidence of that civilization, which means that it could have been fictitious. On returning to Troy, he realized that it was the Troy VI layer that contained pieces of the distinctive Mycenaean pottery that he had been finding at the Greek sites; this meant that it must have been the inhabitants of Troy VI that had contact with the mainland Greeks, not the Trojans of Troy II.

Arthur Evans was in two minds about Schliemann, but he was certainly influenced by him. Just as Schliemann uncovered the scene of the Trojan War and the places where Agamemnon had been murdered and buried, Evans wanted to unearth the Palace of King Minos, at Knossos on Crete. Indeed, Schliemann almost certainly encouraged him to do so, and told him where to find it. Schliemann himself had tried to buy the Knossos site, but dropped out when the owner lied about the number of olive trees on the site; Schliemann remained at heart a hard-bitten businessman.

The final campaign of excavation at Troy was left to Dorpfeld to oversee. Schliemann himself was by then ill. In 1890 he had surgery to have growths cut out of his ears. Immediately after the operation, his ears became infected. His doctors wanted him to stay in the clinic until the infection was cleared up. On 12 December, Schliemann, impatient and strong-willed to the end, discharged himself from the clinic. Within days the infection in his left ear had formed an abscess on the brain. On 25 December 1890 he was found unconscious in the street in Naples and was taken back to his hotel, where he died the next day.

Sir Flinders Petrie described his appearance when he met him in Egypt as, 'short, round-headed, round-faced, round-hatted, great round-goggle-eyed, spectacled, cheeriest of beings; dogmatic, but always ready for facts.' Others found him unattractive, shifty, deceitful, arrogant. He was not only ready to take Calvert's identification of Hisarlik as Troy; he later ridiculed the idea that it was Calvert's idea. After visiting Crete, Schliemann wrote, 'I should like to complete my life's labours with a great work, the excavation of the age-old prehistoric palace of the kings of Knossos in Crete, which I believe I discovered three years ago.' Schliemann cannot have thought that he had discovered Knossos, when he knew that two other people had been there before him and identified the site. Too many lies.

Schliemann was an unpleasant man in many ways, inheriting or mimicking many of his father's personality traits. A continual problem is his dishonesty, his penchant for fraud. He gave a passage in Pausanias as his reason for digging in a certain spot to 'discover' the shaft graves at Mycenae. In fact it is more likely that he heard in the nearby town of Nauplion of an illicit dig that had produced gold. Someone else must have dug in the grave circle at Mycenae before him. How else could he have known exactly at what depth – an unexpectedly great depth – he was going to find the graves? As we have already seen, he had no childhood dream of excavating Troy, and he told at least three different versions of his voyage on the *Dorothea*.

Another problem was the current German idea of 'the great man', the giant among men, the infallible genius with a superhuman capacity for work. It was an ideal he tried too hard to live up to, and it led him into pig-headed mistakes that were in some cases very destructive. If he had more open-minded about what he was discovering at Troy, he might not have destroyed so much of Troy VI in order to get to the lower (older) layers. But Schliemann wanted to appear heroic, Promethean, and his achievement was certainly very great.

Heinrich Schliemann was a very unusual man. In his life and character there is much to deplore. He was egotistical and cynical, he was a liar and a philanderer. But some of these flaws become understandable in the light of his difficult childhood and the hopeless role model presented by his father. The most remarkable thing about him is that he achieved so much in spite of his huge defects.

Schliemann was an inspired amateur who consistently went his own way, independently of 'expert' opinion, and made some of the most startling archaeological discoveries of all time. He uncovered the site of Troy (though it had technically been discovered by Frank Calvert), discovered the Bronze Age Mycenaean civilization, which had not even been suspected, and offered evidence that Homer's Trojan War might after all be history rather than fiction. Schliemann opened the way for other archaeologists, like Evans, to explore other sites that might prove that the ancient epic poems contained history. Where Schliemann's influence was destructive was in pre-empting the results of a dig. Once he had decided that a particular archaeological layer represented the Homeric Troy, trinkets found in it had to represent 'Priam's Treasure'. The melodrama of this kind of archaeology was infectious – he was a 19th-century one-man *Time Team*. Arthur Evans was hooked on it; even before Evans started digging at Knossos he had already decided that he was going to find a Bronze Age royal palace. In fact, most of the archaeological evidence pointed to a temple – but the preconception ruled – and that was very much the Schliemann approach.

JOSEPH LISTER

Born at Upton 1827, died at Walmer 1912.
Surgeon, inventor of antiseptic surgery.

ACHIEVEMENTS:
1867 – On a New Method of Treating Compound
  Fracture, Abscess, etc.
Invented modern antiseptic surgery.
Invented modern antiseptic wound dressings.
*Pioneered cleanliness in hospitals as a means of preventing
  infections.*
Founded the British Institute of Preventive Medicine.

JOSEPH LISTER (LORD Lister) was born at Upton in Essex in April 1827. Lister's father was Joseph Jackson Lister, an eminent optical scientist who made improvements to the compound microscope. Joseph Lister went to London University to study medicine, training under two distinguished physiologists, Wharton Jones and William Sharpey, and qualifying in 1852.

Taking a letter of introduction with him from William Sharpey, Lister became a house surgeon to James Syme at the Edinburgh Royal Infirmary. He married Syme's daughter in 1856. Lister then launched into a very successful academic career, becoming Professor of Surgery at Glasgow University in 1859, Professor of Clinical Surgery at Edinburgh in 1869, and eventually President of the Royal Society from 1895.

Joseph Lister made important observations on the coagulation of blood and inflammation. When he started at Glasgow, he busied himself with articles on amputation and anaesthetics for a textbook on surgery. His ideas on inflammation took a new direction when his attention was drawn, in

360

1865, to the work of Louis Pasteur. What Pasteur was discovering, Lister could see, had enormous implications for medicine. Pasteur had shown that putrefaction, like other fermentations, was caused by airborne microbes. Lister saw straight away that if wounds were infected by microbes from the air there must be some way of cutting the seat of the wound off from the air and preventing the putrefaction from setting in.

He decided to experiment with chemical agents and his first experiment was to apply undiluted carbolic acid to a wound. The acid formed a crust, with the blood, and the result was a success. Lister wrote up his result in the medical journal *The Lancet* in 1867: *On a New Method of Treating Compound Fracture, Abscess, etc.*

Carbolic acid was unsuitable in many situations, and Lister worked to find a better alternative. He first settled on carbolic acid and shellac spread on calico, afterwards painted with a solution of gutta percha in benzene. Later he experimented more successfully with impregnated dressings of absorbent gauze.

After this, Lister worked on methods of stopping wounds bleeding. For a long time silk and flax had been used to tie up arteries; Lister replaced these with catgut. He refined his procedure for antiseptic surgery by ensuring that the air in the operating theatre was free of microbes, and this he achieved by ensuring that the room was kept scrupulously clean.

Lister's principal monument is the Lister Institute of preventive Medicine in London, created in 1891, and modelled on the Pasteur Institute in Paris. Lister's work was widely appreciated in his own lifetime all over western Europe and he himself was honoured several times over. He was made a baronet in 1883 and a peer in 1897. In 1902, he was one of the first people to be awarded the newly created Order of Merit. Lord Lister died at Walmer in Kent in February 1912.

The great innovation for which Lister will be for ever remembered is the introduction of the modern antiseptic approach to surgery in 1867. This ensured that from then on far more people survived surgery than before, and this in turn raised life expectancy.

LEO TOLSTOY

Born at Yasnaya Polyana 1828, died at Astapovo 1910.
Russian novelist, landowner, soldier and moral philosopher.

ACHIEVEMENTS:
One of the greatest novelists the world has known.
Taught the doctrine of non-resistance to evil.
Influenced Mahatma Gandhi's strategy of passive resistance.
1851 – The Story of Yesterday
1852 – Childhood
1869 – War and Peace
1876 – Anna Karenina
1884 – The Memoirs of a Madman

LEO NIKOLAYEVICH TOLSTOY was born on the family estate of Yasnaya Polyana in Tula province. The Tolstoys were country gentry (Petr Tolstoy had been made a count by Peter the Great), and Leo's father was Count Nicholas Ilyich Tolstoy; his mother was Princess Marie Volkonsky, who brought him a large fortune. Young Leo, who was one of five sons, was educated privately at first. Later he went to Kazan University, where he studied law and oriental languages.

Tolstoy did not graduate. Instead he led a dissolute life in town – the classic youthful excesses of the idle rich – and played the gentleman-farmer in the country. He was a member of the upper gentry, enjoying the last years of the old regime. He was to be a landowner and estate owner in the final days of serfdom in Russia, and he was brought up with a traditional 'peer-and-peasant' view of society. In his youth he cultivated the fashionable philistinism of his class. He was educated at Kazan, one of the great seats of learning, but refused to take academic work seriously, instead treating it with contempt. The city of Kazan was also a major centre of social life, and in old age he remembered those years as very happy ones. In 1847 he gave up the university and settled on the family estate with the intention of farming and looking after his serfs, but he was inadequately prepared for this and the attempt at acting the squire was a failure. The next few years were spent, or rather wasted, in Moscow, where he led a dissipated and idle existence, like many others of his class.

In 1851, he entered a new phase of his life. He went with his elder brother Nicolai to the Caucasus where he enlisted as a gentleman volunteer, joining an artillery regiment. Initially he led a quiet life in Cossack villages, spending his time hunting. He started writing at that time and started with a set of autobiographical stories. This consisted of *Childhood* in 1852, *Boyhood* in 1854 and *Youth* in 1856. *Childhood* was accepted enthusiastically by the editor of the leading Russian literary review, who published it immediately.

Tolstoy was commissioned at the start of the Crimean War in 1854, and he requested a posting with the army actively fighting against the Turks on the Danube. A few months later he was in command of a battery at the defence of Sebastopol, where he stayed until the siege ended. After the fall of Sebastopol he was sent to Moscow with military reports, and he stayed there, mixing in both social and literary circles. He still preferred the undemanding socialites, and disliked the literary types, whom he thought plebeian; he also found their ideals of European social and political 'progress' distasteful. It was at this time that Tolstoy had his notorious quarrel with Turgenev.

His experiences in the Crimean War sobered Tolstoy up a great deal. After seeing and being part of the horror of warfare, he could no longer be the dilettante he had been up to that time.

He tried to purge some of the horrific memories of the war in *Tales of Army Life* and *Sketches of Sebastopol*. He left the army in 1857 and was greeted in St Petersburg as a literary celebrity. Then he travelled abroad, visiting Britain, and returned to Russia with a profound disgust for the materialistic civilization of the West.

After that, Tolstoy tried to settle on his Volga estate, where he became a progressive landlord. He accepted a post as magistrate under the Emancipation Act of 1861; his job was to settle disputes between landowners and their former, newly-liberated, serfs. He also set up a school for peasant children based on new lines. He had great respect for the ideas of Rousseau, and his school was based on the idea that children's values and insights were superior to those of civilization. He published a journal, *Yasnaya Polyana*, which expounded his educational ideas.

But it was not long before Tolstoy had to give up both the magistracy and the school. He was on the brink of a psychological crisis, although the full devastating fruition of that crisis did not come for another 15 years. It was postponed by his marriage to Sophie Behrs, who was to bear him 13 children. When the crisis finally broke, it broke up the Tolstoy family and destroyed their marriage.

At the same time Tolstoy committed himself to writing. To a great extent the fiction was a working out of the processes of his inner life. His first literary effort, written in 1851, was *The Story of Yesterday*, an ambitious and exhaustive account of his feelings and reactions during the space of 24 hours. This was not published until 1926. *Childhood* is less analytical and more conventional in style, but expresses with great clarity the elusive wanderings of the conscious mind. He spent three years from 1863 writing *War and Peace*, perhaps the greatest novel ever written. It is a domestic story, a narrative of two families, and it throws a nostalgic backward look at the life of the Russian gentry, the life he himself had so enjoyed. The book is also a national epic of Russia's struggle against Napoleon. One of Tolstoy's themes is that 'great men' are merely people who happen to be in the right place at the right time – lucky people. Victory in battle is equally more to do with chance events than strategy or military superiority.

In 1874–76 Tolstoy went on to write another great novel, *Anna Karenina*, which contains hints Tolstoy's impending personal crisis, which in turn produced his *Confession* (1882), a work of great sincerity and power. He recorded his initial stage of utter despair in another piece, not published until 1884, *The Memoirs of a Madman*. It was in 1876 that his long-developing personal crisis finally erupted. Initially he turned desperately to the orthodox faith of the common people, hoping that the religion that gave them solace would save him. Unfortunately the rational side of his mind would not accept the necessity of rites, fasts or worship. Tolstoy renounced the Church, returned to reading the Gospels for himself and devised his own form of Christianity.

He wrote pamphlets outlining his version of Christianity, which was moralizing, ascetic and based on a doctrine of non-resistance to evil. He decided that the entire message of Jesus Christ was contained in the one instruction, 'that ye resist not evil'. All forms of violence were denounced as wicked. He denounced the worship of Jesus as blasphemous. His writings about Christianity were so unorthodox that he was excommunicated by the Church in 1901. His piece *What is Art?* took an equally ascetic line, arguing that only simple things like the biblical parables are really great art. Everything that is sophisticated and complex is worthless – including his own great novels.

He practised what he preached, handed over his money and his estate to his wife and lived the life of a poor peasant under her roof. It was a kind of one-man Russian Revolution. He took to dressing as a peasant, doing a lot of manual work, and learning how to make boots. He became a vegetarian. All this was too much for his wife and children to take; they were all hostile to his teaching, all except Alexandra, his youngest daughter. The Countess Tolstoy did not believe that her husband had the right to renounce his possessions; she took the view that he held them in trust for their children. Inevitably there was increasing tension and estrangement in the household. The poor Countess became more bitter, hysterical and tactless and Tolstoy family life became a continuous state of war between the Countess and Tolstoy's followers.

Tolstoy left Yasnaya on the night of 28 October, 1910, accompanied by one of his daughters and his doctor. It was a worldwide news event. He seems to have had no particular aim except that of getting away from his wife. He caught a cold. When he reached Astapovo railway station, he was too unwell to go any further. The stationmaster gave him shelter in his room and Tolstoy took to his bed. His wife found out where he was and hurried to the station to try to reason with him. Remarkably, the incident was recorded on film, which shows a crowd of onlookers and the Countess peering anxiously in at the windows of what looks like a waiting room on the station platform, but Tolstoy refuses to let her in. He died there, at Astapovo station, on 8 November, to the end refusing to see his wife.

Tolstoy's estate became a place of pilgrimage. Tolstoy had enormous influence, both direct and indirect. Gandhi corresponded with Tolstoy and adopted his policy of non-resistance as a major political weapon against the

British. This theme of non-violent demonstration was consciously continued, through Gandhi's example, by Martin Luther King and Bob Geldof. Here, once again, we stumble on a chain of influence. Tolstoy is also known as one of the greatest novelists the world has known, and the master of the psychological novel. The remarkable closing passage of *War and Peace* contains ideas that foreshadow those of Jung and Einstein.

GOTTLIEB DAIMLER

Born at Schondorf 1834, died at Cannstadt 1900.
German engineer and inventor.

ACHIEVEMENTS:
Invented the internal combustion engine.
1885 – Invented the motor bicycle.
1886 – Invented the motor car.
1887 – Invented the motor boat.

GOTTLIEB DAIMLER WAS born at Schondorf in Wurttemberg, Germany on 17 March, 1834. As a boy he attended the polytechnic school in Stuttgart. As a young man he worked in Britain and Germany before becoming, in 1872, the technical director for Gasmotorenfabrik in Cologne. There he worked with Otto and Eugen Langen on improvements to the gas engine.

In 1883, Daimler set up his own experimental workshop in Cannstadt in partnership with Wilhelm Maybach. Shortly after that he patented the first successful internal combustion engine. He was also among the first to use liquid hydrocarbons as fuel for such an engine.

In 1885, Daimler mounted his high-speed internal combustion engine on a bicycle, in effect making the first motorbike. The following year he mounted his engine on a four-wheeled vehicle, building one of the first roadworthy motor cars. In 1890, he founded the Daimler Motor Company at Cannstadt, with Maybach as its manager. The firm built cars, but specialized in the manufacture of engines for motorboats. Daimler died at Cannstadt on 6 March, 1900.

Daimler's inventions had an enormous impact. He in effect literally mobilized the 20th century, made possible the growth of cities and freed many people in the West from dependence on public transport. He also created the need for more road-building, and the creation of motorway networks across Europe and America. In designing a successful internal combustion engine that ran on petrol, he set the world on a course that led to dependency on oil, and therefore indirectly to the complex political and military history of the Middle East.

JOHN BOYD DUNLOP

Born at Dreghorn 1840, died in Dublin 1921.
Scottish vet and inventor.

ACHIEVEMENTS:
1887 – Pioneered the pneumatic bicycle tyre.
Made the idea of the pneumatic car tyre a practical reality.
Made long-distance travel by bicycle and car possible.

JOHN BOYD DUNLOP was born on a farm at Dreghorn in Ayrshire on 5 February 1840. He became a veterinary surgeon in Edinburgh. In 1867, he moved to Belfast, where he developed a large and successful practice.

In 1887, Dunlop fitted his little boy's tricycle with inflated rubber hoses instead of solid rubber tyres. Apparently unknown to Dunlop, the principle had already been patented in 1845 by Robert Thomson. Dunlop nevertheless took the idea and turned it into a practical reality. Dunlop himself took out a patent in December 1888. In 1889, Dunlop formed a business to manufacture inflatable tyres on a commercial scale. This business, which was called the Pneumatic Tyre and Booth Cycle Agency, was run in partnership with William Harvey Du Cros. Dunlop sold the pneumatic tyre patent to Du Cros for a moderate sum and took 1,500 shares in the company. Difficulties arose because it then emerged that the idea for the tyre had already been patented 40 years earlier, but the company managed to hold its position because it held patents on various accessory processes. He produced practical pneumatic tyres for bicycles, later producing them for cars as well.

Dunlop himself did not make a vast fortune out of pneumatic tyres, as he took no part in the great development that followed the sale of the company to E. T. Hooley in 1896. By then the business was worth £5 million. In October 1921, Dunlop died in Dublin, where he had a business interest in a drapery firm.

The effect of Dunlop's innovation was to make riding bicycles far more comfortable, and so to make long-distance cycling more practicable. Whether Dunlop can be credited with inventing the pneumatic tyre or not, he certainly made regular cycle journeys to work possible, as well as cycling for leisure. Dunlop tyres made cycling into the major recreational activity it has become today. Similarly, it is impossible to imagine the modern motor car without pneumatic tyres. Solid rubber tyres on a car would inevitably have meant short journeys at low speeds. Dunlop's invention – if that is what it was – made long-distance driving at speed possible. Dunlop made his contribution to 'the great car economies' of the West.

EMILE ZOLA

Born in Paris 1840, died in Paris 1902.
French novelist and journalist

ACHIEVEMENTS:
1864 – Contes à Ninon.
1867 – Thérèse Raquin.
1871 – La Fortune des Rougon.
1893 – Docteur Pascal.
1898 – J'accuse.
1902 – Justice.
Exposed the anti-Semitic conspiracy against Dreyfus.
Succeeded in clearing the name of Dreyfus.
Pioneered campaigning journalism.

EMILE EDOUARD CHARLES Zola was born in Paris on 2 April 1840. His mother was French. His father was an engineer who was part-Italian, part-Greek, an energetic and visionary man who died while Zola was still a young boy. Emile received his early education at Aix, which figures as the town of Plassans in many of Zola's novels. Then, in 1858, he went to Paris to find work. His first job was as a clerk in the publishing house of Hachette. Soon he became a writer and journalist in his own right. Tolstoy took the view that great men were just lucky; Zola was in many ways just an unlucky man. He was active in criticism, politics and drama, but much of this work turned out badly.

Zola's real talent was for short story writing. He produced *Contes à Ninon*, which was his first book, in 1864, *Nouveaux Contes à Ninon* in 1874 and *Attaque de Moulin* in 1880.

It was in 1866 he decided to abandon clerking and pursue literature for a living.

In the last days of the French Empire, Zola formed an informal society with other writers, including Daudet, Flaubert and Turgenev; out of this club grew the 'Naturalist school'. Zola's *Thérèse Raquin*, in 1867, was representative of their idea of naturalism, exploring remorse in a gruesome but powerful novel. But it was only later, after the Franco-Prussian War, that he started to find his way with a series of novels, a kind of family saga called *Les Rougon-Macquart*. In this he succeeded in creating a world of his own, like Balzac's *Comedie Humaine* or Galsworthy's *Forsyte Saga*. The two guiding themes of Zola's novel sequence were heredity and cerebral infirmity. He went to a great deal of trouble to research the settings and the occupations of his characters, and tried to incorporate a scientific study of heredity within the narrative of the novels. The first novel in the 20-novel series was *La Fortune des Rougon*, which came out in 1871. This was followed by *La Curée* in 1874, *Le Ventre de Paris* in 1874, *La Conquete de Plassons* in 1875, *La Faute de l'Abbé Mouret* in 1875 and *Son Excellence Eugene Rougon* in 1876. These were all books of high quality, but not popular with the public. The series continued until the final novel in the sequence, *Docteur Pascal*, in 1893.

Zola famously took up the cause of Captain Dreyfus, a soldier who was framed, unjustly convicted and unjustly imprisoned because of anti-Semitism. At an early stage in the public furore, Zola became convinced that Dreyfus was the innocent victim of a nasty anti-Jewish conspiracy. With characteristic courage, Zola decided to do something about it. On 13 January 1898, he published in the newspaper *Aurore* a stinging denunciation of those who had taken part in the hounding of Dreyfus. The article, presented in the form of a letter, was entitled *J'accuse*. Zola was deliberately trying to goad the authorities into prosecuting him for libel, so that there could be a judicial enquiry into the conspiracy against Dreyfus, and this took place in February. The authorities proved too powerful for him and he was condemned. Zola appealed and there was to be a second trial at Versailles. Before it opened, Zola was worked on by his lawyer and his friends, who could see that the French establishment was determined to destroy him, and they persuaded him to escape to England. He took their advice and remained in hiding in England until June 1899, when the news came that the Dreyfus verdict was to be overturned. It was safe for him to return to Paris.

Zola set a marvellous and heroic example of campaigning journalism, putting himself at significant risk in order to see justice done for Dreyfus. He had to leave France and lie low in England for a year, but he was welcomed back to France as a hero – and his campaign had succeeded. In this, at least, he was lucky. Dreyfus too was lucky to have such a champion; he was exonerated.

Emile Zola died suddenly in 1902 in his house in Paris. On the morning of 29 September, he was found dead of carbon monoxide poisoning by fumes leaking from a faulty flue. Zola was given a public funeral attended by Captain Dreyfus, who owed him everything; the eulogy was given by Anatole France. At the time of his death, Zola had been finishing his last novel, *Justice*, based on the Dreyfus case.

HENRY MORTON STANLEY

Born at Denbigh 1841, died in London 1904.
Welsh explorer of Africa.

ACHIEVEMENTS:
1872 – Found Livingstone at Ujiji.
1872 – How I Found Livingstone.
1877 – Discovered the course of the River Congo.
1878 – Through the Dark Continent.
1880 – The Congo and the Founding of its Free State.
1898 – Through South Africa.
1893 – My Dark Companions and Their Strange Stories.

THE BOY LATER known as Henry Morton Stanley was born at Denbigh in Wales in June 1841. His parents were unmarried, and he was at first known by the name John Rowlands. He seems to have been a totally unwanted child, brought up initially by his maternal grandfather, then, after the grandfather's death, boarded out. In 1847 John was taken to the St Asaph workhouse, where he was maltreated by the sadistic schoolmaster, James Francis. In May 1856, John was provoked into giving Francis a beating, and after that he ran away. Neither his mother's nor his father's family would help him, and he was reduced to becoming a teacher at Brynford. After a short time he was sent to Liverpool, where he lived in poverty with an uncle.

After this terrible neglected childhood, it is not surprising that young John Rowland decided to leave Britain for America. In 1859, he sailed to

New Orleans as a cabin boy, and he was there looked after by a merchant called Henry Morton Stanley, who found him a job and adopted him, but shortly afterwards died. John Rowlands adopted his benefactor's name and, when the American Civil War broke out in 1861, served in the Confederate army. Stanley was captured at the Battle of Shiloh and after spending two months in prison at Camp Douglas he accepted the way out his captors offered, which was to enlist in the Federal artillery. In 1862, after this unexpected ordeal in America, he returned, poor, shabby and ill, to Denbigh, to be turned away once more from his mother's door.

He returned to America, travelled, wrote as he travelled and became a good descriptive writer. He contributed pieces to several journals. In this way he started a series of adventures in search of newspaper copy.

In 1867 he joined the staff of the *New York Herald*, which sent him to accompany Lord Napier's expedition to Abyssinia as its special correspondent. As a result of Stanley's initiative, the *New York Herald* carried the first news of the fall of Magdala. Stanley next went to Spain. Then, in October 1869, he got the memorable instruction from his boss, Gordon Bennett, 'Find Livingstone.'

First he visited Egypt to witness and report on the opening of the Suez Canal, then he travelled through Palestine, Turkey, Persia and India. In March 1871, Stanley set off from Zanzibar for Tanganyika and on 10 November he found Livingstone at Ujiji. Livingstone was not really lost, but it was still a very good newspaper story. Together, Livingstone and Stanley explored the northern end of Lake Tanganyika, and found that it was not connected with the Nile; finding the source of the Nile was a 19th century obsession, and Stanley was to contribute enormously to improving the accuracy of maps of the drainage systems and watersheds of central Africa.

In 1872, Stanley returned to civilization to publish *How I Found Livingstone*. The finding of Livingstone was a big news story. There were many sceptics who thought Stanley had made the whole thing up, but Stanley had thought of that in advance and was streetwise enough to be able to produce Livingstone's journal as evidence that they had met. Queen Victoria gave Stanley a gold snuff-box and her thanks. Suddenly Henry Morton Stanley was an international celebrity. Stanley gave public lectures about his expedition, then accompanied Sir Garnet Wolseley's expedition to the Ashanti (now Ghana). During this expedition, in 1874, he heard that Livingstone was dead.

Exploration was now very big news, so an ambitious three-year expedition was financed jointly by the *New York Herald* and the *Daily Telegraph*, with the aim of completing Livingstone's work in central Africa. Stanley, heading the expedition, circumnavigated Lake Victoria, then proved the shape of Lake Tanganyika. Then he travelled down the Lualaba River and followed the Congo all the way to the sea. It was a very successful expedition indeed, adding more to the map of Africa than any other single expedition.

Then followed a dark and disreputable episode, Stanley's work for Leopold, King of the Belgians. Stanley's discovery of a great waterway penetrating to the heart of Africa could obviously be exploited, and Leopold quickly realised its commercial significance. Leopold sent agents to intercept Stanley at Marseilles with a proposal to go straight back to the Congo, but Stanley badly needed a rest and put the proposal aside for a time.

In 1879 the Belgian king succeeded in commissioning Stanley to lead an expedition to found the Congo Free State, which was to be a colossal private estate for the enrichment of the king, and under his personal sovereignty. This was set up with unbridled cruelty by Stanley and others, with no regard for the normal human rights of the Africans. Stanley gave his version of what happened in *The Congo and the Founding of its Free State*.

The only thing that was free about the Congo Free State was the behaviour of King Leopold. It was in 1876 that Leopold organized an international association as a front for his personal plan to 'develop' central Africa. Leopold commissioned Stanley to survey the area and sign treaties with tribes. In 1879, acting under Leopold's sponsorship, Stanley was aggressively competing with a French explorer to lay claim to the Congo region. For five years after that, Stanley worked frantically to open the lower Congo by building a road to connect with the navigable reach of the river; the idea was that this would open the lower Congo basin to commercial exploitation, which it did, on a nightmare scale. Stanley's behaviour was conspicuously ruthless, earning him the nickname 'rock-breaker' among the Africans. Leopold relied totally on Stanley, who must bear some of the responsibility for what followed.

At the Berlin Conference in 1884–85, Leopold gained formal international recognition as sovereign of most of the Congo Free State. In 1891 he hired William Stairs, a British soldier, to take control of the copper fields of Katanga.

So far, this is a fairly routine story of part of the *Scramble for Africa*, but it was the way in which Leopold exploited his vast new colony that makes it a story of almost incredible evil. At home, in Belgium, Leopold gave every appearance of being a rather brusque and strong-willed European monarch, ruling within the recognized constraints of a constitutional monarchy, but in the Congo he was the self-anointed sovereign. The Congo was his personal domain and only he made the rules there, and he ruled with a barbaric ferocity and a complete heedlessness for basic human rights.

The Congo was to be a source of rubber, which had historically never before been mass-produced. Leopold was determined to make the Congo produce masses of rubber, and determined to make money out of it. He let multinational concessionary companies set up the rubber production under his auspices, but that does not absolve him from responsibility for the inhuman treatment handed out to the rubber workers.

The native population was controlled by torture, mutilation and massacre, and Leopold must have known that this was how his estate was being run. The population of the Congo fell from 20 or 30 million at the start of Leopold's enterprise to around 9 million by 1911. Between 1880 and 1920 the population of the Congo halved. It was a 19th century African holocaust. The Africans were unaccustomed to the capitalist ethos of production, and they suffered in many ways, from culture-shock, from exhaustion through over-work, murder, starvation and disease. The punishment for a wide variety of offences, including failure to meet work quotas of sap from rubber trees, was amputation of a hand, or a foot, or an arm, or a leg – sometimes an ear or the nose. Over ten million people died as a result of Leopold II's greed, and Stanley helped Leopold to achieve this.

The atrocities did not become became public knowledge until 1908, by which time the Sir Henry Morton Stanley, loaded with honours, was safely beyond reproach in his grave.

In 1886 Stanley led an expedition for the relief of Emin Pasha, landing at the mouth of the Congo. Stanley and Emin met on the shores of Lake Albert. Stanley returned with Emin overland to the east coast, reaching

Bagamayo in December 1889. On the way, he discovered Lake Edward and Mount Ruwenzori.

In 1890, Stanley married Dorothy Tennant, the daughter of an English MP. Then he was off again on lecture tours of America, Australia and New Zealand. When he came back, in 1892 he was re-naturalized as a British citizen. In 1895 he became a Member of Parliament. In 1897 he paid a last visit to Africa, travelling to the Cape as a guest of the British South Africa Company. He gave a speech at the opening of the Cape to Bulawayo railway, visited the Victoria Falls and met President Kruger. Even this was copy to the seasoned journalist, and it saw print in 1898 as *Through South Africa.*

His last few years were spent in retirement at a small estate he bought at Pirbright. He died at his London home in Whitehall on 10 May, 1904.

Stanley was a pioneer modern journalist – the sort that doesn't just report news, but actually makes it. He had a great gift for dramatic narrative, which is why his story about finding Livingstone is so memorable. There was nothing much too it in reality, as Livingstone was not really lost – but Stanley made it into a classic ripping yarn. His exploratory work did clear up some of the missing pieces of central Africa's physical geography. In fact he discovered more about the physical geography of Africa than any other explorer of the 19th century. He was a racist, got into frequent conflicts with Arabs and negroes, yet had a remarkable ability to manage natives. He had tremendous drive, as people who have suffered tremendous adversity in childhood often do. Stanley's role in setting up the Congo Free State for the Belgian king was entirely reprehensible, but unfortunately typifies the way many Europeans and white North Americans were to behave in Africa and other parts of the Third World in decades to come.

KARL BENZ

Born in Karlsruhe 1844, died in Mannheim 1929.
German engineer and car manufacturer.

ACHIEVEMENTS:
1877–79 – Invented the two-stroke internal combustion
  engine.
1885 – Simultaneously invented the motor car.

KARL BENZ WAS born in Karlsruhe on 26 May 1844. He became an engineer and it was in the years 1877–79 that he built a two-stroke engine of his own design and set up a factory to manufacture it. He left the factory in 1883 when it emerged that his backers would only finance fixed engines; they refused to finance an engine that could be mounted in a vehicle. Since that was the application he had in mind, Benz then went on to found a second company, called Benz & Co. Rheinisch Gasmotorenfabrik, at Mannheim. Initially he built fixed engines, but later developed a relatively light high-speed four-stroke engine; this, he realised, was light enough yet powerful enough to power a road vehicle.

Benz built his first motor car powered by the new light four-stroke engine in 1885 and sold it to a French manufacturer called Roger. This was the first of many car sales. The first Benz car was capable of reaching speeds of 10–16 km per hour. Benz's 'invention' of the motor car, which he patented in 1886, is another example of a simultaneous or near-simultaneous invention. The Benz motor car was created just a few months before the first Daimler. The two men, Benz and Daimler, were working on closely parallel projects and both men recognized that much was to be gained by collaborating. In 1926

Benz merged his firm with the Daimler-Motoren-Gesellschaft to form Daimler-Benz. Karl Benz died in April 1929.

Daimler and Benz together share the responsibility for inventing the motor car, powered by a light internal combustion engine. Together they share the responsibility for transforming transport in the 20th century, creating the great car economies of the West, for putting unprecedented demands on road systems, and making necessary the expensive networks of motorways that cover Europe and North America.

THOMAS EDISON

Born in Milan, Ohio 1847, died 1931.

ACHIEVEMENTS:
1871 – Invented the ticker-tape machine.
1877 – Invented the phonograph (gramophone).
1879 – Invented the electric light bulb.
1883 – Invented the electric valve.
1891 – Invented the moving picture camera.
1912 – Invented talking pictures.

THOMAS ALVA EDISON was born in Milan, Ohio on 11 February 1847. He was of Scottish ancestry on his mother's side and Dutch ancestry on his father's. He was thought to be retarded at school, the public school at Port Huron in Michigan, from which he was expelled after only three months. At the age of only 12 he became a railroad newsboy on the Grand Trunk Railway, but soon he was printing and publishing his own newspaper on the train, which he called the *Grand Trunk Herald.*

During the Civil War, starting in 1861, he worked as a telegraph operator in various cities. In his spare time he worked hard to improve himself, studying and experimenting. It was in 1868 that he took out his first patent, after inventing an electric vote recording machine.

In 1871, he invented the paper ticker-tape automatic repeater for stock exchange prices. He then sold this invention in order to fund an industrial research laboratory at Newark in New Jersey. This was in effect an inventions factory, and Edison was quickly becoming the most prolific inventor of all time, which marks him out as a key figure in this gallery of world-changers. The Edison laboratory-workshop started in Newark, then moved in 1876 to Menlo Park, then finally to West Orange, all addresses in New Jersey.

In his laboratory, Edison was able to give full scope to his creative genius. He was bursting with ideas, but also had to work very hard to make them work. He once commented that genius was one percent inspiration, 99 percent perspiration. He invented automatic telegraph systems and an electric pen, which developed into the mimeograph. His 1877 invention of the carbon transmitter, in which compressed lampblack buttons were used to create variable resistance in a circuit, marked a huge advance in telephony and helped significantly in bringing the Bell telephone into practical use.

As an indication of Edison's prolific and astonishing inventiveness, he took out over 1,000 patents altogether. Conspicuous among them is the gramophone, which he invented in 1877, calling it a 'phonograph or speaking machine'. The first model, which cost 18 dollars, consisted of a cylinder covered with tinfoil and turned with a hand crank. Ten years later, Edison invented an improved model, a motor-driven machine using wax cylinders. Thanks to this invention, it is possible to hear the voices of people now long dead, which changes our perception of the past, bringing it slightly closer to us. Thanks to Edison's wax cylinders, we can hear the voices of Oscar Wilde, W. E. Gladstone, Lord Tennyson and Johannes Brahms – and hear Brahms playing the piano. Later still Edison developed a disc for recording music, the recognizable prototype of the bakelite and vinyl 'records' of the 20th century. Thanks to this invention, we can all hear music of any kind in our homes, which has not only enlarged the audience for music – and in effect democratized music – but changed the way music itself has developed. It became possible, for the first time, to listen to a piece repeatedly and so understand it better. Both composers and listeners were able to listen to a larger range of music, and as a result tastes became more sophisticated, more eclectic. The astonishing range of musical development in the 20th century can be put down to Edison's invention.

In October 1879, after a great struggle involving 40,000 dollars' worth of failed experiments, Edison invented the incandescent electric light bulb. This consisted of a loop of carbonized cotton thread glowing in a vacuum inside a glass bulb for over 40 hours. Edison spent much of the next 10 years of his life refining and improving the light bulb and devising a system of generating and distributing electric lighting. He experimented with a three-wire system, an underground mains system, dynamos and motors.

In 1891, Edison patented what was in effect a movie camera, which he called a 'kinetoscopic camera'. This took moving pictures on a band of film; these were then viewed on a peepshow, then later projected onto a screen. Edison thus pioneered cinema. Other inventions included the electric train, the megaphone, the electric valve and the storage battery. It was Thomas Edison who invented the first talking motion pictures, and therefore created the great new art form of the 20th century. The moving picture camera also made it possible to film historic events like the Battle of Jutland. For the first time it was possible for people to see them, rather than just reading about them in newspapers and this made warfare more immediate – and more repellent.

During the First World War, Edison switched his attention to solving naval problems for the US government. By 1928, Edison had been working incessantly and with terrific dedication on his inventions and taken out over a thousand patents. He died on 18 October 1931.

Edison transformed 20th century life through his various inventions – and especially the light bulb, the gramophone and the cinema.

ALEXANDER GRAHAM BELL

Born in Edinburgh 1847, died at Baddeck, Nova Scotia, 1922.
Scots-American educationist and inventor.

ACHIEVEMENTS:
1875 – Invented the telephone.
1881 – Invented the metal detector.

ALEXANDER GRAHAM BELL was born in Edinburgh in 1847. He was the son of the phonetics expert Alexander Melville Bell. He was educated at the Universities of Edinburgh and London, and then, starting in 1868, assisted his father in teaching elocution.

In 1870, because of health problems, Bell emigrated with his father to Canada, the following year moving on to the United States. In 1872 he opened a training school in Boston for teachers of the deaf and also gave lectures on the mechanics of speech. He became Professor of Vocal Physiology at Boston in 1873, devoting himself to the teaching of deaf mutes and promoting his father's system of 'visible speech'. In this system Bell's father devised an alphabet system of his own in which the alphabet 'letters' were graphic diagrams of the positions of the organs of speech needed to make the sounds. The elder Mr Bell was a respected authority on physiological phonetics.

Bell experimented with various acoustical devices, finally building a primitive telephone. He sent the first successful telephone transmission on 5 June 1875. He patented this major invention in March the following year. He had to defend his patent against Elisha Gray, and formed the Bell

Telephone Company in 1877. Bell's telephone consisted of two identical microphones and receivers, each made of a solenoid mounted next to a metal membrane. Vibration set up in the transmitting membrane induced a current in the solenoid that travelled down the wire, causing the membrane in the receiver to vibrate in the same way. It was on 10 March 1877 that Alexander Graham Bell gave his historic demonstration of the newly invented telephone. The first phone call was to his assistant; 'Mr Watson, come here. I want you.' Just a few weeks later, on 3 April, Bell made his first long-distance telephone call, from New York to Boston, again to his assistant, Thomas Watson.

In 1880, Bell set up the Volta Laboratory, invented the photophone, which was an instrument for transmitting sound by vibrations in a beam of light and then, in 1881, the metal detector. Bell was one of the large number of experts called to the bedside of the fatally wounded President Garfield; Bell used his metal detector to locate the bullets fired into the president by his assassin. He also invented the graphophone in 1887, an alternative form of phonograph.

In 1883, Bell and his father-in-law, G. G. Hubbard, founded the journal *Science*. Bell also founded the American Association to Promote the Teaching of Speech to the Deaf. For a time he was President of the National Geographic Society. He became a member of many learned societies. After 1897, Bell's main interest shifted to aeronautics. Here too he made some original contributions, inventing the tetrahedral kite. He died on 2 August 1922 at his summer home near Baddeck in Nova Scotia.

Bell's telephone was one of the inventions that transformed the 20th century. It made communications and decision-making quicker and easier, and was, along with the motor car, responsible for a major acceleration in the pace of life. The metal detector has also played its part, not least in the field of archaeology, where it is used to find metal objects from the past.

W. G. GRACE

Born at Downend 1848, died at Eltham 1915.
English cricketer.

ACHIEVEMENT:
Became the first modern sporting celebrity.

WILLIAM GILBERT GRACE was born at Downend near Bristol on 18 July, 1848. He started playing first-class cricket for Gloucestershire in 1864, and was immediately picked for the Gentlemen Players match. In 1871 he scored 2,739 runs in the one season's play. In 1876 he scored 344 runs in a single innings while playing for the MCC. He took his degree in medicine at the age of 31 in 1879 and set up in general practice in Bristol, but he still continued to devote most of his time to cricket. In later years he became secretary and manager to the London County Cricket Club. He received two national testimonials. One, in the form of a clock and a cheque for £1,500, was presented to him at Lord's in 1879. The second, amounting to the then-incredible sum of £10,000, was collected for him by the county of Gloucestershire, the MCC and the *Daily Telegraph* in 1896.

W. G. Grace toured Canada and the USA. Twice, in 1880 and 1882, he was captain of the English Test team against Australia. By 1895 he had scored 100 centuries in first-class cricket. In his long career in first-class cricket, which lasted from 1864 until 1900, Grace made 126 centuries and scored an astonishing 54,896 runs; he also took 2,864 wickets. He held nearly all of the records connected with cricket. As well as being a great batsman and bowler, he was one of the finest fielders in the game, a fine thrower, a fast runner and good at catching.

Grace had a tremendous physique, a lot of determination and he played with great care and self-restraint. He was 6ft 2in tall, powerfully built, yet very supple. He kept himself fit all the year round, shooting, hunting or running with the beagles as soon as the cricket season ended. He was a great runner. His finest performance was running 440 yards over hurdles. His general fitness and stamina were unusual; on 30 July 1860, he scored 224 runs not out in an England v. Surrey match, then two days later he won a race in the National and Olympian Association meeting at the Crystal Palace. W. G. Grace died at Eltham in Kent on 23 October 1915.

Cricket ran in the family. W. G. Grace's father, Henry Mills Grace, and his uncle, Alfred Pocock, were both keen players. His two elder brothers played with him in the Gloucestershire side and also played Test cricket for England. 'W. G.' also had a younger brother, George Frederick Grace, who was a cricketer. It was nevertheless W. G. Grace who was the big celebrity of British sport, and sometimes he took unfair advantage of the fact, intimidating those around him on the pitch. On one occasion he went in to bat and was declared out almost straight away. Grace pointed out that people had come to watch the match to see him play, not to see him bowled out. The umpire cravenly gave in to Grace and let him play on. This was an early example of a sportsman exploiting his celebrity and behaving badly.

W. G. Grace was, even so, the first genuinely great cricketer. He was also one of the earliest practitioners of gamesmanship. Grace became an English national hero early in his career and because he went on playing for a long time his name became more and more widely known. He had a very distinctive appearance – he was a big man with a powerful physique and a huge trademark dark bushy beard, making him instantly recognizable and easy to portray in cartoons. W. G. Grace was one of Britain's first big sporting celebrities.

FRIEDRICH ALFRED KRUPP

Born 1854, died 1902.
German arms manufacturer.

ACHIEVEMENTS:
Greatly expanded the Krupp steel and armaments empire.
Maintained the Krupp family's dominance of German heavy
  industry in the late 19th century.
Developed the programme of warship-building.
Partly responsible for the late 19th century arms race.
Partly responsible for the First World War.

FRIEDRICH ALFRED KRUPP was one of a powerful dynasty of arms manufacturers. He was the son of Alfred Krupp (1812–1887) and the grandson of Friedrich Krupp (1787–1826).

His grandfather, Friedrich Krupp, founded a small iron works at Essen in 1810 and started manufacturing arms there in 1837. At the Great Exhibition in London in 1851, his father, Alfred Krupp, exhibited a flawless solid ingot of cast steel weighing 4,000 kg; it was an impressive display of skill and power. He set up the first steel plant using the new Bessemer steel making process and became the leading arms supplier to Germany – and to the world in general. The first steel gun was cast at Essen in 1847. Alfred Krupp acquired coal mines and docks and became a dominating force in the development of the industrial resources of the Ruhr valley.

Friedrich Alfred Krupp inherited the Krupp family fortune and the family's dominant position in Germany heavy industry as well. He continued the tradition of arms manufacture, extended the business into shipbuilding and greatly expanded the Krupp industrial empire as a whole. Krupp acquired the Germania shipyards at Kiel in 1902. This put the Krupp family in a fine position to develop and build new warships, and they were soon investing in the development of armour-plate. In this way Krupp facilitated the expansion of the German navy.

Clearly, it was in the Krupps' interest to escalate international tension in order to generate demand for weapons of offence and defence. The arms race that developed between Germany and Britain from the 1890s through to the outbreak of the First World War was fuelled in part by the Krupps' business interests. Krupp was at the time of his death employing over 40,000 people, four times the number employed at the time of his father's death. This was entirely due to the war ramp. It was almost inevitable that Krupp himself would become a personal friend and political ally of the Prussian emperor; for their very different reasons they both wanted war.

When Friedrich Alfred Krupp died on 22 November 1902, the huge industrial empire he had built up was inherited by his daughter Bertha. In 1906 she married Gustav von Bohlen und Halbach, who was allowed to adopt the name Krupp and take on the running of the colossal business of manufacturing arms for Germany though two World Wars, first for the Kaiser, then for Hitler.

The enormous dynamism and power of the Krupp industrial empire was a driving force behind the Great War, and those heading the Krupp family must shoulder their share of responsibility for it.

OSCAR WILDE

Born in Dublin 1854, died in Paris 1900.
Irish playwright, poet and wit.

ACHIEVEMENTS:
1888 – The Happy Prince and Other Tales.
1890 – The Picture of Dorian Gray.
1891 – The Duchess of Padua.
1892 – Lady Windermere's Fan.
1892 – Collected Poems.
1893 – A Woman of No Importance.
1895 – The Importance of Being Earnest.
1898 – The Ballad of Reading Gaol.

OSCAR FINGALL O'FLAHERTIE Wills Wilde was born in Dublin on 15 October, 1854, the son of Sir William and Lady Jane Wilde. Sir William Wilde was a well-known Irish surgeon. Lady Jane was a well-known writer of verse and prose, writing under the pen-name Speranza. Between the ages of 9 and 16 the young Oscar attended the Portora Royal School in Enniskillen, which another but very different Irish playwright, Samuel Beckett, later attended. From school, Oscar went to Trinity College, Dublin and then, in 1874, to Magdalen College, Oxford.

He changed on arrival at Oxford from being a fairly ordinary though rather large schoolboy into a foppish dandy with strong sympathies for the 'aesthetic' movement that was fashionable at the time. He affected to scorn manly sports, wore his hair long and decorated his rooms with peacocks' feathers, lilies, sunflowers and blue china. The posing was not original at all, but merely copying the fashionable pursuit of 'art for art's sake', which the painter Whistler was bringing into prominence. In his aesthete's guise, Wilde looked remarkable. He was described as:

A big man with a large pasty face, red cheeks, an ironic eye, bad and protrusive teeth, a vicious childlike mouth with lips soft with milk. While he ate – and he ate little – he never stopped smoking opium-tainted Egyptian cigarettes. A terrible absinthe drinker, through which he got his visions and desires.

Oscar Wilde also emerged as a distinguished scholar, an achiever in spite of his decadent appearance. In 1878 he won the Newdigate Prize for his poem *Ravenna*. Oscar's biographer, Richard Ellmann, described Ravenna as 'a clever hodge-podge of personal reminiscence, topographical description, political and literary history.' Oscar Wilde had high intelligence and great literary skill, but it was already apparent that his judgement was suspect. To what ends would he put his high intelligence and his enormous skill with the English language?

In 1881, Wilde's first volume of poetry was published. Its title, *Patience*, was in that same year adopted by Gilbert and Sullivan for their operetta lampooning the aesthetes. Wilde's posturings lent themselves all too easily to lampoon, caricature and ridicule. He seems not to have minded this at all. As for a great many other exposers since his time, it was more important to be noticed than to be liked, and far more important to be talked about than respected. He was by this time the leading aesthete, and his witty paradoxes were quoted all round London.

In 1882, Wilde went on a lecture tour of the USA. When asked at customs control whether he had anything to declare, Wilde replied, 'Only my genius.' From the beginning, he seems to have been acting a part, dressing up for it like Little Lord Fauntleroy, and delivering well-practised camp jokes that he intended to be passed around as quotations. He set out to be an enfant terrible. Perhaps surprisingly, Wilde went down very well in the wild west of America; working class Americans thought he was wonderful. Wilde can only have done it out of a hunger for self-advertisement. He returned to England claiming to have civilized America. While he was in America he wrote a play called *Vera*, which was performed in New York.

In 1884, Wilde married Constance Lloyd and they subsequently had two sons, for whom he wrote some children's stories, *The Happy Prince and Other Tales*, published in 1888. They include one of the most preposterous, mawkish, self-indulgent and badly constructed stories ever written, *The Selfish Giant.*

Two years later he published what looked like the creed of the aesthetes, *The Picture of Dorian Gray.* Then Wilde built his reputation as a playwright with a series of well-constructed plays, *Lady Windermere's Fan, A Woman of No Importance* and *The Importance of Being Earnest.* This last play was a huge success, and is generally regarded as Wilde's best work. It appeared in 1895, when some chickens were about to come home to roost. His success and popularity as a playwright had temporarily silenced some of the gossip about his private life, but that could not last. Many of his friends assumed the moral looseness he had affected since his days at Oxford was just that, an affectation, and it was a great shock to them when evidence emerged in a court hearing that Wilde had been slumming with male prostitutes.

Early in his marriage, Wilde was experimenting with homosexual affairs, but to begin with they were discreet. His affair with the young Lord Alfred Douglas was far from discreet, and his homosexuality was an open secret in some circles of London society. Lord Alfred's father, the Marquess of Queensberry, was aggressively homophobic and did everything he could to separate Wilde and his son. He left a card for Wilde at his club, addressed, 'To Oscar Wilde posing as a somdomite.' Queensberry's spelling was poor, but his point was very clear. The secret, if Wilde thought it was a secret, was out – with a vengeance.

Wilde next did the worst thing he could have done. He sued Queensberry for libel. This inevitably meant a court case, and during the hearing Wilde was cross-questioned about his relationship with Lord Alfred. It was obvious from his answers that at the very least an extremely sentimental relationship existed between them. A poem by Lord Alfred was produced, in which the young man referred cloyingly to 'the love that dare not speak its name'. Now it was out. Wilde lost his libel case against Queensberry. It was only a matter of weeks or days before Wilde would be arrested and charged with homosexual acts, which was at that time an imprisonable offence. Wilde knew this prosecution must follow and he was urged by well-meaning friends to leave London at once, to take the boat train and take refuge, where many others of his kind had taken refuge before him, in France or Italy.

For some reason Wilde decided to stay and face the second trial, which took place in May 1895. He was found guilty and given a very harsh sentence – two years hard labour. The judge was evidently making an example of Wilde, who had after all flaunted his immoral aestheticism, his 'art for art's sake', and his man friends for years on end.

Wilde had a very bad time in prison. He developed medical problems and was a sick man when he was released in 1897. By then his wife Constance had divorced him and taken the boys away; he would never see them again. Trusted friends like Walter Sickert and Aubrey Beardsley refused to have anything further to do with him; to be fair to them, it would probably not have been safe for them to befriend him. Now Wilde did go to France to live, first at Berneval, then in Paris. It would have been better if he had gone before the trial. He adopted the pseudonym Sebastian Melmoth. Some friends visited him in exile, including Ernest Dowson. Wilde was evidently attracted to Dowson, but Dowson persuaded him to try sex with women again. Wilde tried, with a Dieppe prostitute, and commented afterwards to Dowson, 'The first these ten years, and it shall be the last. It was like chewing cold mutton. But tell it in England, where it will restore my reputation.'

There were two more pieces of writing to come from him – *The Ballad of Reading Gaol* in 1898 and *De Profundis*. This last piece was his bitter reproach to Lord Alfred Douglas, who had turned out to be a broken reed; it was not published until after Wilde's death, which was not a long time coming.

Wilde was already ill with syphilis when he started his exile in France. He declined gradually and died of meningitis on 30 November 1900, at the age of only 46. It is easy now to forget what a short career Wilde had as a writer. From *The Selfish Giant* to *The Ballad of Reading Gaol* it lasted only 10 years, 1888 to 1898, and he spent two of those years in prison. The quality of writing achieved in *The Importance of Being Earnest* makes us wonder what Wilde might have achieved if he had not allowed himself to be so fatally distracted.

But Wilde was a flawed genius. Time and again he followed his ear, and went for the facile witticism ('more dined against than dining'), the obvious shallow play on words. He was facetious, endearing and entertaining. He was once reported to be 'overjoyed' when he saw a photograph of Kruger in a fur coat. But when he tried to be profound, he often misfired. Wilde was a likeable, entertaining but fundamentally silly man with a strong self-destructive streak. He was capable of great kindness, as when in 1891 he went to the Westminster Police Court to offer guarantees for the good behaviour of a mad friend, John Barlas, who had threatened to blow up the Houses of Parliament. Wilde discovered that Barlas thought he was a biblical prophet and said, 'My dear fellow, when I think of the harm the Bible has done I am quite ashamed of it.' But posturing in the streets of London in absurd velvet and satin suits, he was almost crying out to be ridiculed, rejected and vilified. From the very beginning in Oxford he ran the gauntlet of ridicule, taking a ducking in the River Cherwell as well as getting his rooms wrecked. His performance in court at the libel trial was suicidal. Oscar Wilde needed psychoanalysis, and it is possible that if Freud had invented his psychoanalytical technique a decade or so earlier, Wilde might have been saved. As it was they were almost exact contemporaries; Freud devised his free association technique for exposing the unconscious in 1894. Earnest and the trial came in the following year.

Wilde has been hailed as a gay icon, as some kind of pioneer campaigner for gay rights, even a gay martyr. In a sense he was, but he also put the cause of gay liberation back several decades, associating homosexuality in the popular mind with all kinds of seedy decadence. For some time to come, to call someone an 'Oscar' was a damning slight, a term of abuse. Wilde could be pointed out to young men as a terrible warning, the sort of man into which they could not possibly want to turn.

V

THE MODERN WORLD

SIGMUND FREUD

Born in Freiburg 1856, died in London 1939.
Austrian neurologist and psychoanalyst.

ACHIEVEMENTS:
Founded psychoanalysis.
Founded modern psychology.
Invented 'free association'.
Discovered or invented the Oedipus conflict.
Discovered the existence of the unconscious mind.
Saw the unconscious mind as split between id, ego and superego.
Discovered conflicts among psychic forces within the mind.
Discovered 'repression'.
Defined the 20th century way of thinking about human behaviour.
Established the importance of sexuality in human behaviour.
1900 – The Interpretation of Dreams.
1905 – Three Essays on Sexuality.
1913 – Totem and Taboo.
1920 – Beyond the Pleasure Principle.
1927 – The Future of an Illusion.
1933 – Why War?
1939 – Moses and Monotheism.

SIGMUND FREUD WAS born at Freiburg in Moravia of Jewish parents. Strongly influenced by reading Goethe's essay *Nature*, Freud decided to study medicine. He had no inclination to be a doctor; he was far more interested in scientific research. This may explain some of the difficulties that arose later; he was more interested in his ideas than in the patients who were supplying him with his raw data. Sometimes, as with his Oedipus complex, he lost touch with the reality of human psychology. Anyway, motivated by reading Goethe, he decided to study medicine in Vienna. He worked in the physiological laboratory under von Brucke from 1876–82, later joining T. H. Meynert in the Institute for Anatomy. Money became a problem, and he had to put research to one side, taking on work as a clinical neurologist.

From 1884 Joseph Beuer, an Austrian neurologist, told Freud about an experience he had had, in which hysteria was cured by using hypnosis to help the patient recall painful past experiences. The recall had been a kind of catharsis. Freud was profoundly impressed by this and developed Beuer's cathartic technique until it became the foundation stone of modern psychoanalysis. Then in 1885 Freud moved to Paris to study under Jean Martin Charcot, who gave him the moral support he needed to make his determined world-changing switch from treating hysteria as a neurological problem to treating it from a psychological point of view.

As anticipated, Freud's medical colleagues disapproved of what he was doing. Returning to Vienna, he developed a new psychiatric technique – free association. He used this instead of hypnosis to find out what was under the surface of the patient's mind, and so gradually refined psycho-analysis as a method of treatment. In 1893 he persuaded Breuer that he ought to publish his breakthrough in the treatment of hysteria, and in 1895 Freud and Breuer in collaboration published a book called *Studies in Hysteria*. In 1897 their collaboration ended in disagreement over Freud's theory of infantile sexuality. Freud tried the patience of many friends and colleagues as he developed his revolutionary new ideas. Many of them thought he was too insistent on the role of sex in the mind, and especially on the role of repressed sexual urges. This obsession was very plain to see in his major work.

In 1900 he published his landmark work, The Interpretation of Dreams. *In this he argued that dreams are disguised manifestations of repressed sexual desires. His ideas excited enormous interest and controversy. In 1902 he was appointed Extraordinary Professor of Neuropathology at Vienna University. He also started weekly seminars at his home. These were meetings of men who were thinking along similar, though not necessarily the same lines, but all adventurously*

exploring the human psyche. Conspicuous among them were Alfred Adler,
Ernest Jones and Carl Gustav Jung.

Three Essays on Sexuality, in 1905, met intense and uncomprehending opposition.

In 1908, the informal weekly meetings at his home became formalized into the Vienna Psychoanalytical Society, which changed its name in 1910 to the International Psychoanalytical Association. Freud's ablest and most distinguished disciple Carl Gustav Jung was its first president. In 1908 the first International Congress of Psychoanalysis was held. Freud's ideas were rapidly spreading round the world. Freud's views were extremely doctrinaire and it was almost inevitable that several of his disciples would disagree with him so strongly that they had to part company. Adler left in 1910. Jung broke with Freud in 1913. The problem was that, having found his explanation for neuroses, Freud was not prepared to keep an open mind. He felt threatened by Jung and on two occasions when he thought Jung's remarks revealed a death-wish against him he fainted in front of him.

Freud was, even so, not put off by the departure of disciples or the loss of friends. He produced *Totem and Taboo* in 1913, *Beyond the Pleasure Principle* in 1920 and *Ego and Id* in 1923. Freud saw the human unconscious mind as divided into three behavioural compartments, the id, the ego and the super-ego. In 1927, he published a controversial view of religion, *The Future of an Illusion*.

As Nazism developed in the 1930s, Freud became preoccupied with the European situation. Together with Einstein, he wrote *Why War?* in 1933. Psychoanalysis was outlawed under Nazi rule, so it was difficult, professionally, for him to continue. Despite advancing age and infirmity, Freud continued to be as active as he could be, directing the *International Journal of Psychology*. When Austria was taken over by Hitler, in 1938, arrangements were made to rescue Freud, a conspicuous Jewish intellectual who was clearly in mortal danger from the Nazis. Interestingly, when Jung organized a go-between to deliver a substantial sum of money to Freud, literally on his doorstep, to enable him to escape, Freud refused to accept it; the money was tainted because it had come from Jung. A plan that did not involve Jung succeeded, and the Freud family was safely moved to London.

Freud made a new home for himself in Hampstead, and produced one more major work, *Moses and Monotheism*, in which he explored the psychology of anti-Semitism. Freud died of cancer not long after his arrival in England, on 23 September 1939.

Freud made several important discoveries. Possibly the single most important was the existence of the unconscious mind and its powerful and dynamic influence on the conscious mind. Closely connected with this idea is the concept of the mind as being split into layers because of conflicts going on among various psychic forces within the mind. He called one of these forces 'repression'. Another idea was the existence of infantile sexuality, still a controversial idea, and the complex of jealousies that children feel towards their parents which Freud called the *Oedipus* conflict. Freud's influence spread way beyond the 200 committed specialist practitioners of psycho-analysis. Medics, philosophers, artists, novelists and playwrights all over the world recognized that a whole new way of thinking about the human mind – and therefore thinking about the human race – had come into being. Freudian psychology, for better or for worse, came to dominate the 20th century. Because of Freud, we had D. H. Lawrence.

KAISER WILHELM II

Born in Berlin 1859, died at Doorn 1941.
Third Emperor of Germany, imperialist war-monger.

ACHIEVEMENTS:

Expanded the German navy to threaten British supremacy at sea.

Developed an overseas German Empire to challenge British supremacy in colonial Africa.

Developed an aggressive, jingoistic persona that made him a perfect war-time hate-figure.

Started the European arms race.

Directly responsible for World War I.

Indirectly responsible for World War II.

FRIEDRICH WILHELM VIKTOR Albrecht von Hohenzollern was the third and last German Kaiser (Emperor) and the ninth and last King of Prussia. He is invariably referred to as 'The Kaiser'; he was one of the most disastrous monarchs of all time. During the First World War he was universally reviled in Britain as the man who caused the war. He was born on 27 January 1859 in Berlin, the eldest child of Crown Prince Friedrich (later Kaiser Friedrich III) and Victoria, who was also Britain's Princess Royal, the daughter of Queen Victoria. The Kaiser was therefore Queen Victoria's grandson. The family trees of the European monarchs were closely intertwined, and there were occasional events, such as coronations and funerals, where they all met and were photographed together. The Kaiser's mother, for instance, was the aunt of the Russian Tsarina Alexandra and the sister of Britain's King Edward VII.

The baby Wilhelm was critically damaged at birth by a traumatic breech birth, which left him with a permanently withered left arm. He managed on public occasions and in photographs to conceal the fact that his left arm was much shorter and thinner than his right. He had various tricks for disguising his deformity. In some photographs, he holds the withered left hand inside the normal right hand, concealing it; in others he carries a pair of white gloves in the left hand to make the arm seem longer. Recent analyses of his birth records in the Imperial Archives suggest that he may have experienced some brain damage at birth as well. If so, there may be an explanation of his frequently aggressive, tactless, headstrong, bullying approach, both in public and personal life. By 1894, some were already referring to him as a megalomaniac. The personality defect, whether it originated in brain damage or in compensation for the physical deformity, was disastrous in a head of state. He conspicuously fell out with his first Chancellor, Bismarck, and also from much earlier days had a conspicuously poor relationship with his mother. This was not a man cut out for diplomacy.

Wilhelm was educated at Kassel Gymnasium and the University of Bonn. In 1881, he married Augusta Viktoria, Duchess of Schleswig-Holstein, by whom he had seven children. In 1888 Wilhelm's grandfather, Wilhelm I, died. His father, Crown Prince Friedrich, was crowned Emperor as Friedrich III, but he was already terminally ill with throat cancer, dying shortly afterwards. After only three months, in June 1888, Wilhelm II became Kaiser unexpectedly early, at the age of only 29.

Within two years he had forced the resignation of Chancellor Bismarck, who disapproved of the Kaiser's plan to make an appeal to the German working class for political support, and appointed von Bòlow. After Bismarck, Wilhelm wanted only civil servants as Chancellors, not politicians. Wilhelm's intention was that the Reichstag should accept whatever policies the Kaiser and the upper classes wanted. His entire mindset was in effect that of an 18th century princeling, and entirely inappropriate to the situation in Germany at the end of the 19th century. He had a profound belief in the divine right of the Hohenzollerns, his own family, to rule Germany; he was in effect making the same mistake as Charles I of England, but over 200 years later.

Bòlow's foreign policy included the German Naval Bills of 1897 and

1900, which were designed to challenge British naval domination. The British government was right to be worried by the implications of the massive enlargement of the German navy, and even more so by the Kaiser's tactless posturing, his constant emphasis on Germany's military power. He also wanted 'a place in the sun' for Germany, which was a euphemism for wanting a huge German empire; this too obviously involved treading on the toes of Britain. Bòlow was replaced by Theobald von Bethmann Hollweg, who was more conciliatory towards Britain and adopted a political outlook which was somewhat liberal for the time. This tactic foundered when the British refused to promise neutrality in the event of a Franco-German war unless there was a significant reduction in the German fleet; the only reason Germany would need a large fleet would be to take on the British fleet. The Kaiser promoted both the arms race and the scramble for Africa; he did everything he could to escalate the tension, though it is still not certain that he actually wanted the First World War.

A major problem was that the Kaiser was personally responsible for appointing top government officials, and he was commander-in-chief of the armed forces. He was therefore the only person who could ensure that diplomatic and military strategies were harmonized. During the First World War, the Kaiser was roundly accused by the British of causing the war. In fact, he could have done a great deal to reduce the friction between the two countries during the previous decade, some of which was inevitable because of Germany's rapid industrialization and consequent economic growth. The growth of the Krupp steel and armaments empire was a major factor.

The Kaiser could also have exploited his family ties with Britain to reassure the British that his intentions were friendly. Instead of this, he took every opportunity to escalate the tension, posing for swaggering photographs in a variety of military uniforms. Seeing these photographs made many people across Europe wonder whether they should be amused or alarmed. It was hard to tell whether he was a megalomaniac or just playing the fool. What was not generally known was that the Kaiser had had a mental breakdown in 1908, and made fewer decisions after that.

After the assassination of Archduke Franz Ferdinand in 1914, the Kaiser encouraged the Austrians to adopt an uncompromising line. When it came to his own country, he lost his nerve and was unable to stop his generals from mobilizing. On paper the Kaiser was commander-in-chief, but the reality of the war must have disappointed him in more ways than one – the defeat at the end must have been the biggest disappointment of all – he found himself excluded from decision-making. As the war progressed his impotence became more and more obvious; he was reduced to pinning medals on soldiers who were lucky enough to return from the front. As the losses at the front mounted and civilian living conditions in Germany declined, his popularity evaporated.

When the war ended, he was forced to abdicate and he was exiled to the Netherlands. There was talk of bringing him to trial as a war criminal, but he evaded this by threatening suicide. Queen Wilhelmina refused to extradite him as a war criminal; the ex-Kaiser continued to live under her protection in the Netherlands for the rest of his life. He cunningly stopped wearing military uniforms now, and instead acted the role of an English country gentleman, trying to appear just a harmless old buffer. During the 1930s, he nursed the futile hope that the Nazis would revive the monarchy. It seems he was deluded enough to think that he might make a come-back.

Kaiser Wilhelm II died at Doorn on 5 June, 1941, while the German occupying troops stood guard at his gates. One consequence of his disastrous reign and the unsatisfactory circumstances surrounding his abdication was that there was no possibility of any sort of monarchy in the 1920s. He had an heir, Crown Prince Wilhelm (1882–1951) but there was no chance, after the Wilhelm II fiasco, that the German people would have wanted him. A vacuum was left which someone like Adolf Hitler could fill.

The Kaiser directly created the arms race with Britain, expanding the German navy so that it could beat the British navy. He was also directly responsible for promoting German imperialism and intensifying the Scramble for Africa. He made it clear that he sided with the Boers against the British in the Boer War. He made aggressive, militaristic speeches. He deliberately stirred and heated Europe towards boiling point. His actions led directly to the First World War. The outcome of the war was that the German people were left with war reparations they could not pay and resented paying, and this in turn led to the rise of Hitler and the Second World War.

FRANK LLOYD WRIGHT

Born 1867, died 1959.
Innovative American architect.

ACHIEVEMENTS:
Applied civil engineering principles to architecture.
Pioneered modern technology in architecture.
Pioneered open-plan interiors.
Designed some of the first skyscrapers.
Applied cubist art style to architectural design.
Father of modern architecture.
1910 – Robie House.
1911 – Taliesin.
1920 – Imperial Hotel, Tokyo.
1931 – Modern Architecture.
1939 – Falling Water.
1959 – Guggenheim Museum of Art.

FRANK LLOYD WRIGHT was born at Richland Center in Wisconsin on 8 June 1869. He studied civil engineering at Wisconsin University until 1888. His life was changed by a singular event – the collapse of a newly-built wing of the Wisconsin State Capitol. This spectacular event instantly turned his interest to architecture. The building must have fallen down because of an engineering failure, and he resolved to apply good engineering principles to architectural designs, to prevent such things happening in the future. He was already a man with a mission, and one that he carried through very successfully.

Wright set up in practice in offices in Chicago in 1894, and soon became known for his distinctive designs for residences. He specialized in low-rise prairie-style bungalows like Robie House in Oak Park, Illinois, built in 1910. At that time, most domestic architecture was still stoutly Victorian, with high-pitched roofs, vertical lines and ornate detailing. Wright's designs marked a break with that tradition. His houses were simple and clean-looking, with low-pitched roofs and horizontal thrusts – a look that we now see as characteristically 20th century in style. Then he launched into more adventurous and experimental designs using modern technology and materials – and cubist spatial concepts borrowed from Picasso. By going in this direction, he became one of the finest and most influential architects of the 20th century.

In 1911, Frank Lloyd Wright designed his own house, called Taliesin, at Spring Green in Wisconsin. He built another house and school, Taliesin West, near Phoenix, Arizona in 1938.

Wright became more famous still for his large-scale public buildings. He designed the earthquake-proof Imperial Hotel in Tokyo, completed in 1920, the Johnson Wax offices in Racine, Wisconsin, in 1936 and the Guggenheim Museum of Art in 1959. The Imperial Hotel design was widely criticized for its use of the floating cantilever, which was regarded as an unsafe feature. But Wright was totally vindicated when a major earthquake struck Tokyo in 1923; his hotel was one of the few buildings in the city to remain undamaged.

Falling Water, a house he designed at Bear Run, Pennsylvania in 1939, is regarded as his masterpiece. It is cantilevered out over the rock ledges of a waterfall and stream. The vertical accents in the house design had their origins in the natural lines of the tall straight trees surrounding the site. Wright was always conscious of the setting of his buildings and designed them so that they fitted naturally into that setting.

In his later years, Frank Lloyd Wright spent more time teaching and writing. A select group of apprentice architects was trained at Wright's workshop-homes. As a writer, Wright began as early as 1909 to present his theories of architecture in a series of essays called *In the Cause of Architecture*. *Modern Architecture*, published in 1931, is a collection of lectures Wright gave at Princeton the previous year.

Frank Lloyd Wright pioneered the high-rise style that gave 20th century urban architecture its distinctive look. With reliable passenger lift technology supplied by Elisha Otis, reinforced concrete and steel frames, it became possible to build skyscrapers of almost any height. Wright did much to change the look of central business districts in cities all round the world. In terms of interiors, Wright made major innovations too. He pioneered open-plan designs for homes and offices. He also designed furniture and textiles.

ORVILLE WRIGHT

Born at Dayton 1871, died at Dayton 1948.
American inventor and aviator.

ACHIEVEMENTS:
Co-invented the aileron principle.
Co-invented the aeroplane.
Piloted the first aeroplane.

ORVILLE WRIGHT WAS born at Dayton, Ohio on 19 August, 1871, the younger son of Milton and Susan Wright. Milton Wright was elected a bishop of the Church of the United Brethren in Christ. With his brother Wilbur, he early on worked in the cycle repair business, and they both became interested in the problems of flying when they read of the experiments of Otto Lilienthal in Germany. Lilienthal's experiments were suddenly ended when his glider crashed in 1896 and he was killed; he had lost control of the balance of the glider and the Wright brothers believed that his attempt to maintain equilibrium just by shifting his body weight about was inadequate.

They developed the theory that the air pressure exerted on different parts of the machine could be altered by making the wings adjustable, and that this would maintain equilibrium. This system, now known as aileron control, is used on all modern aircraft. The Wright brothers took out a patent on it. They carried out workshop experiments, using a wind tunnel, to test the aileron principle.

Starting in 1902, Orville and his brother developed a full-sized power-driven heavier-than-air machine. The machine weighed only 750 pounds and was powered by a four-cylinder petrol engine of 12 horsepower. It was piloted by Orville Wright on its first successful flight on 17 December, 1903 at Kitty Hawk in North Carolina; on that day the machine made four sustained free flights, the longest lasting 59 seconds and at a speed of 30 mph. The epoch-making machine was a major exhibit at the Science Museum in South Kensington for 20 years. On 17 December, 1948, the 45th anniversary of the Kitty Hawk flight, the pioneer plane was installed as an exhibit at the Smithsonian Institute in Washington D. C.

The experiments continued. In 1905, they learned how to prevent the tail-spin that had made short turns a problem. After that the flights became longer and in September that year Wilbur piloted the plane in a circle over a distance of 24 miles.

The brothers worked on an improved aeroplane which in 1908 stayed in the air for 1 hour 15 minutes. Further tests in 1909 satisfied the US government and led to the machine's general acceptance. In 1908 and 1909, Orville Wright and his brother flew their plane at numerous demonstrations in Europe. Flights at Le Mans, Pau and Rome attracted huge crowds to see them – crowds that included the kings of England, Spain and Italy.

Orville Wright spent most of the rest of his life engaged in research. He died on 30 January, 1948.

WILBUR WRIGHT

Born Indiana 1867, died Dayton 1912.
American inventor and aviator.

ACHIEVEMENTS:
Co-invented the aileron principle.
Co-invented the aeroplane.
Piloted the first aeroplane.

WILBUR WRIGHT WAS Orville Wright's elder brother, born in Indiana on 16 April 1867. At the time when he might have expected to go to college, Wilbur was involved in an accident while playing ice hockey, which put him out of active work for eight years. He spent these fallow years looking after his invalid mother and helping his father with legal matters relating the church.

Wilbur and Orville became simultaneously interested in solving the problem of powered flight, and their joint efforts succeeded in creating what is generally agreed to be the first successful aeroplane.

For the last three years of his life, Wilbur was president of the Wright Company, which had taken over the aeronautical patent rights for America. He spent much of this time defending and upholding their patents in law courts in America and Europe. Wilbur Wright caught typhoid fever and died at Dayton, Ohio on 30 May, 1912.

MARIE CURIE

Born in Warsaw 1867, died in Savoy 1934.
Polish-French scientist.

ACHIEVEMENTS:
Coined the term 'radioactivity'.
Discovered the elements radium and polonium.
Laid the foundations for later work on radioactivity and atomic
  energy.

MARIE CURIE WAS born as Manya Sklodowska in Warsaw in 1867. She received her early scientific training from her father. After she became involved with the students' revolutionary organization it became clear that it would be better if she left Warsaw. She studied first at Cracow, which was at that time under Austrian rule, and then at the Sorbonne in Paris. After graduating in science, in 1895 she married Pierre Curie, a chemist.

Marie Curie worked side by side with her husband on magnetism and radioactivity. She invented the word 'radioactivity' in 1898, though it was Henri Becquerel who had actually discovered the phenomenon two years before. The Curies also isolated two new elements from the mineral pitchblende, radium and polonium, which she named after her native Poland. They went on to explore the properties of radium and its transformation products. The work that Marie Curie and her husband did on radium laid the foundations for much of the later research on nuclear physics and chemistry.

In 1903, Marie and Pierre Curie were jointly awarded the Nobel Prize for physics, together with Henri Becquerel. The prize was for the discovery of radioactivity. In the same year, Marie submitted the results of her work in a doctorate thesis. It was a remarkable achievement, to have been awarded the Nobel Prize before being awarded her doctorate.

In 1905, Pierre Curie was elected to the Academy of Sciences. The following year, on 19 April, he was killed instantly when he was run over by a cart in a Paris street. After her husband's unexpected death, she succeeded him as Professor of Physics at the Sorbonne. In 1910 she isolated pure radium and was awarded the Nobel Prize for chemistry in 1911, this time for discovering radium and clarifying its properties.

After the First World War, Marie Curie was director of the research department of the Radium Institute in Paris, and she continued in this post until 1934. She set up another laboratory in Warsaw and in 1929, President Hoover gave her 50,000 dollars donated by American friends of science, so that she could buy radium to use at her Warsaw laboratory. Her elder daughter Irene became a nuclear physicist who shared a Nobel Prize for artificially producing radioactive elements, and after the Second World War joined the French Atomic Energy Commission. Marie Curie's younger daughter, Eve, became a well-known musician and writer, as well as working for the French resistance in the Second World War. Marie Curie died in the south of France on 17 March, 1934, having laid the foundations for research that would lead to the development of nuclear bombs and nuclear power stations.

TSAR NICHOLAS II

Born in St Petersburg 1868, died at Ekaterinburg 1918.
The last Tsar of Russia.

ACHIEVEMENTS:
Precipitated the First World War: ordered the mobilization of
the Russian army.
Precipitated the Russian Revolution.

NICHOLAI ALEKSANDROVICH ROMANOV was born on 6 May, 1868, the son of Tsar Alexander III and the Empress Marie. He became tsar in 1894. At his coronation in Moscow, several thousand people were trampled to death trying to get presents from the new Emperor. Nicholas was told about the disaster later in the day, but refused to cancel the ball he had arranged for that evening. This was the first of many bad decisions, showing him as tactless and lacking in imagination. At his coronation ceremony, the imperial chain broke and fell from his neck. He was deeply and fatalistically impressed by the two bad omens of his coronation day; the air of mystic resignation made him a supremely unsuitable head of state for the time.

Nicholas had not been well prepared to rule any country, let alone one that was in social and political turmoil. His father had died relatively young, which meant that he had little training to be head of state. His English tutor, Charles Heath, taught him fluent English and a love of physical exercise, and General Danilovich gave him military training, but he had no education in geography, history, economics or politics. He relied too heavily on his wife, Alix, who fully embraced the old Russian traditions of autocratic rule and religious mysticism. He also relied too heavily on the advice of his wife's unstable cousin, Kaiser Wilhelm; most of this advice was in Cousin Willy's interests and Cousin Willy was more interested in preventing Britain and Russia from getting too close to each other politically or diplomatically than he was in helping Nicholas.

Nicholas had only a poor understanding of Russia's problems. His grandfather, Alexander II, had done much to improve the situation, but revolutionaries had assassinated him anyway, because they wanted a different regime altogether. Nicholas could have won the support of liberals, but he instead alienated them by refusing to reduce the weight of autocracy by giving some constitutional guarantees. In the later years of his reign, he allowed Alix to step in to prevent him from making any concessions – concessions that just might have averted revolution. As a result, he ended up with both the liberals and the revolutionary extremists against him.

Nicholas was preoccupied with family problems. The first was the succession; he and Alix had four daughters before their son Alexei was born in 1904. Then Alexei proved to have haemophilia. Because of the fragility of the monarchy, Nicholas decided to keep this secret; no-one outside the royal household was to know about Alexei's illness. This in turn led on to another problem. Alix looked for help from a monk and mystic, Grigori Rasputin, who seemed to be able to relieve the boy's pain when he suffered from internal bleeding. Alix's increasing dependence on Rasputin gave Nicholas's many enemies a strong propaganda weapon against him.

Russia was seriously unprepared for war with Germany when the First World War broke out in 1914. There were huge losses on the Russian side. Nicholas then made a huge mistake, which was to assume responsibility for leading the army himself. He assumed the role of commander-in-chief in September 1915. This decision was a mistake twice over. First, it meant that he was in neither St Petersburg nor Moscow and he had to leave his wife in his place as an unofficial Regent. He had no awareness that Alix was deeply unpopular, because she was believed to be dependent on Rasputin, and because she was German and therefore, it was wrongly believed, on the side of Russia's enemies. Second, it meant that he was taking on himself the responsibility for the outcome of the war. Since the war was going against Russia, it was particularly stupid to associate himself (and the monarchy) with the responsibility for losing it. He was setting himself up for what amounted to a court-martial.

After the so-called February Revolution of March 1917, Nicholas was forced to abdicate in both his own name and that of his son in favour of his brother Michael. Michael too abdicated a few hours later. The provisional government confined Nicholas and his family and moved them to Tobolsk to prevent their escape or rescue. To prevent a restoration of the monarchy, the Bolsheviks shot them all at the Ipatiev House in Ekaterinburg in the night of 16-17 July 1918. There were rumours that one or more of the Romanovs had escaped, and a number of people in the 1920s and 1930s claimed to be survivors of the shootings, probably with the idea of inheriting the Romanov fortune. In the 1990s the bodies of the Romanovs were found, exhumed and identified using DNA. Two were missing, Alexei and one of the girls. The remains were reburied in the Romanov family crypt in 1998, on the 80th anniversary of the murders. It was at a time when the Soviet Union had imploded and there was an economic crisis, and the Romanov funeral generated a (short-lived and misplaced) nostalgia for the Russian monarchy.

If the Russian monarchy could have survived the first two decades of the 20th century, Nicholas II was certainly not the man to see that it did. Much has been made of his goodness and kindness as a family man – as with Charles I – but that did not in any way qualify him as a national leader. It should not be forgotten, either, that it was Nicholas II who gave the order for the Russian army to mobilize, so he played a part in precipitating the First World War. And it was in the mayhem of the First World War that the Russian Revolution was hatched. Without Nicholas there would have been no Lenin and no Russian Revolution. Without the Russian Revolution, there would have been no Stalin. Nicholas II has much to answer for.

MOHANDAS GANDHI

> *Born at Porbandar 1869, died in Delhi 1948.*
> *Indian nationalist leader, visionary moral teacher.*
>
> ACHIEVEMENTS:
> *Advocated non-violence as a positive principle.*
> *Advocated passive resistance as a political weapon.*
> *Gained the independence of India, Pakistan and Bangladesh.*
> *Brought about the collapse of the British Empire.*
> *Undermined the caste system in India.*
> *Encouraged individual self-help as the path to economic*
>   *development.*

MOHANDAS GANDHI, KNOWN as Mahatma Gandhi, was born at Porbandar in western India on 1 October, 1869. He was born into a Hindu family with a tradition of public service; his father was chief minister of one of the Gujarat states. When Mohandas was 18 he was sent by his family to study law in London, where he was called to the bar in 1891. There was already evidence of the asceticism and extremism that would come to the fore in later life. On the voyage to England he almost starved, after promising his mother he would not eat meat. Once in London he became an active member of the Vegetarian Society. This marked the beginning of a lifelong concern with diet, personal hygiene and moral scruple.

After qualifying as a lawyer, Gandhi set up in legal practice in Bombay, but had too little confidence in what he was doing to be successful. In 1893, he gave up this practice, which was worth £5,000 a year, in order to live on one pound a week in South Africa. There he neglected his legal practice and devoted 21 years to opposing legislation that discriminated against Indians. At one stage, Gandhi and his friends set up a self-supporting commune, which they called Tolstoy Farm, with a view to freeing themselves from dependence on the rest of the community. In the development of his ideas about social reform, Gandhi was profoundly influenced by the writings of Leo Tolstoy (with whom he corresponded) and John Ruskin, though the deepest influences were the *New Testament* and the *Bhagavadgita*.

Gandhi was profoundly committed to his social and political goals, but he was not by any means dour. With all of his friends and visitors he was courteous, patient, tolerant, sometimes playful and always ready to be amused. But behind the geniality, there was an unconquerable driving force, his ambition to change the face of India.

In his struggle against the South African authorities, Gandhi was arrested, imprisoned and assaulted. During the Zulu rebellion of 1906, he assisted in the ambulance corps, seeing it always as his duty to help others, and that obligation cut across political affiliation. At this time he was a supporter of the British Empire, seeing the British influence as mainly benign.

The climax of the South African struggle came in 1913, when a series of repressive measures culminated in a demand that every Indian seeking to live in the Transvaal must register. Gandhi organized a typical protest event, in which 2,000 Indians rallied behind Gandhi, and he led them repeatedly backwards and forwards across the Transvaal frontier. It was what later in the century would be called a publicity stunt – but it worked. Public opinion swung in favour of the well-behaved Indians, and the measures were repealed. Gandhi also won the respect of General Jan Smuts, who at first had done his best to crush the movement.

In 1914, feeling that he was no longer needed by the Indians in South Africa, Gandhi returned to India. He supported Britain through the First World War, but took an increasing interest in the Congress movement for home rule for India. He quickly came to dominate this movement. His civil disobedience campaign of 1920 created serious and violent disorder, and in consequence he was imprisoned from 1922 to 1924 for conspiracy. While he was in prison, relations between Hindus and Muslims deteriorated conspicuously.

In 1925, he disagreed with the Congress leaders' acceptance of proposals that they should join the new legislatures. In protest Gandhi announced that he was retiring from politics for a year. In fact he dropped out for several years, during which he toured villages, teaching people the principle of self-help, urging them to take up spinning as a way of escaping absolute poverty. He also urged them to give up the caste system. At every village meeting he addressed, he found that the organizers had divided audiences into two, caste people and untouchables. To counteract this, he always went and sat with the untouchables to speak. He also fought hard against alcohol and drug-taking, urged people to take proper care of their cattle, urged them to develop goodwill between the religious communities. It all added up to what he called 'the constructive programme', a crusade that was a preparation of India for the freedom struggle to come.

In April 1930, Gandhi led a 300 mile march from his ashram (settlement) near Ahmedabad to the coast at Dandi to make salt from the sea. The salt march was a grand symbolic gesture in defiance of the government monopoly on salt, and it had an electrifying effect on the whole country, leading to further scenes of disorder. This too led to his arrest. On his release from prison in 1931, Gandhi negotiated a truce between Congress (the home rule movement) and the government. When he returned to India, Gandhi relaunched his civil disobedience campaign in protest against the various compromise measures that were being introduced. Inevitably, he was rearrested. Another political device he used at this time was fasting. He threatened to 'fast unto death' when one of the new measures in effect condoned the different treatment of untouchables. Gandhi started calling the untouchables by a new name he invented – Harijans, children of God. He published a weekly paper using this name as its title.

When the Second World War broke out, Gandhi wanted to support Britain in the struggle against Nazi Germany, but gave in to Congress pressure, insisting that India could only co-operate if it was promised full independence. No such promise was forthcoming from the British. He started to press for complete independence more and more vehemently. By 1942, Stafford Cripps for the British government assured India of independence on certain conditions once the war was over, but Gandhi dismissed this as 'a postdated cheque'.

In 1944, after his release from another spell in prison, Gandhi tried to establish an understanding with Jinnah, the Muslim leader, who was demanding an independent Muslim state. But Gandhi and Jinnah were unable to agree. Gandhi's ideal was one India, an undivided India – but it was unachievable. In the summer of 1946 there were terrible massacres and atrocities. By the spring of 1947, the Partition of India was agreed by the Congress leaders, in spite of Gandhi's disapproval.

In May 1947, he praised Britain's decision to give India independence as 'the noblest act of the British nation'. Independence was sullied by outbreaks of violence between Hindu and Muslim communities. Once again he went on hunger strike to influence the situation, and a semblance of order was restored. The strife among the communities could only be resolved by segregating them, and creating a separate Muslim state of Pakistan (East and West) on either side of a predominantly Hindu India. Gandhi's promotion of home rule for India resulted not only in the independence of the Indian sub-continent, but the disintegration of the British Empire. India was, inevitably, just the first of the British possessions to wrest itself free.

On 30 January 1948 Gandhi was walking to his daily prayer meeting in the garden of Birla House in Delhi, when he was shot dead by a Hindu fanatic – only ten days after the previous assassination attempt. Hindu extremists saw that as long as Gandhi lived India could never be Hindu-dominated, so they were determined that he should die.

Mahatma ('great soul') Gandhi was venerated by many as a great moral teacher who wanted to free India from materialism as well as caste prejudice, and as a great patriot who wanted to free India from British rule. He was a kind of socialist, but it was a socialism that had nothing to do with Marx or Marxism. Gandhi's socialism was based on the principle of non-stealing. Anyone who took more than he needed was stealing from the poor. He did not object to employers or capitalists, but urged them to abandon their wealth. His view of social reform was based on personal reform, on changing people rather than systems. In many ways his mission was nearer to that of Jesus.

His critics saw him as self-deluded, blind to the violence that his 'non-violent' campaigns would lead to. Overall, he is seen as a great force for peace, progress and justice, with a message not just for India but for the rest of the world. His 'grass roots' self-help approach to social and economic development now looks very far-sighted indeed. What the Third World needs is not aid in the materialist form of hydro-electric dams or nuclear power stations, still less in the form of money or food, but the means to make a subsistence living – and this was Gandhi's big idea, a way forward for the 21st century.

VLADIMIR ILICH LENIN

Born at Simbirsk 1870, died at Gorki 1924.
Russian revolutionary leader and regicide.

ACHIEVEMENTS:

Carries the major responsibility for the bloodshed and the crimes
  against humanity committed during the Russian Revolution.
Adapted Marxism into a practical instrument for socialist
  revolution in Asia.
Advocated violence as the essential means for political change.
1899 – The Development of Capitalism in Russia.
1903 – Became leader of the Bolsheviks.
1917 – Encouraged the lawless seizure of the land by the
  peasantry.
1917 – Engineered and led the 'October' Russian Revolution.
1918 – Transformed the Bolsheviks into the Russian
  Communist Party.
1918 – Became Russian dictator.
1918 – Responsible for the execution of the Russian royal
  family.

Vladimir Ilich Ulyanov was born at Simbirsk on 22 April 1870, the son of a Russian civil servant called Ilya Nikolaevich Ulyanov. He had a Jewish ancestry through his mother's father, who later converted to Christianity, though he himself was baptized into the Russian Orthodox Church. At school he was particularly good at Latin and Greek. In May 1887 his eldest brother, Alexander, a student, was hanged for taking part in a plot to assassinate the Tsar, Alexander III. This traumatic event had the effect of electrifying Lenin, making him become extremely radical; it was his brother's execution that turned Vladimir Ilich into a revolutionary. Later in that same year he was arrested and expelled from Kazan University, and from Kazan itself, for taking part in student protests.

This did not stop him from continuing his studies at various places on the Volga and by 1892 he had a licence to practise law. But the earlier events took over now, and he decided to devote more of his time to politics. He involved himself in revolutionary propaganda efforts. He also studied Marxism, mainly in St Petersburg, and became an authority on it. On 7 December 1895 he was arrested as a subversive and held for a year, after which he was sent to Siberia. While there, in 1898 he married Nadezhda Krupskaya, a socialist activist. In April 1899 he published a book, *The Development of Capitalism in Russia*. The next year his exile came to an end and he settled for a time in Pskov, not far from St Petersburg, from which he was still banned. He used his freedom to travel in Europe, leaving Russia on 29 July, 1900 for more than five years. He travelled to Switzerland, Germany, London, Paris, then back to Switzerland, at the same time publishing tracts about the revolutionary movement. He also founded a newspaper, which he called *Iskra* (the Spark), which was published abroad but circulated in Russia.

At the end of 1901, Vladimir Ilich Ulyanov assumed the pseudonym, or nom de guerre, of Lenin. As he became more of a public figure, he evidently felt he needed a short name, possibly because it looked and sounded monolithic, possibly because it could be chanted or shouted more effectively. Stalin would later do the same.

Lenin was a small man with a sharp Slavonic face. His huge forehead gave his face strength and he had piercing eyes. He worked tirelessly. He was an intellectual, with a love of the arts and sciences, but led a simple frugal personal life. His life towards the end, when he was the dictator of Russia, was not very different from the life he led in exile.

Lenin became active in the Russian Social Democratic Labour Party (RSDLP) and from 1903 he became the leader of the Bolshevik faction after a split with the Mensheviks that was in part precipitated by his pamphlet *What is to be Done?* The prevailing Populist/Economist view was that the revolution would happen as a result of the workers' agitation for rights and that then socialism would 'come naturally'. Lenin's paper argued that this was not the case, that workers are not natural socialists at all; left to themselves they rise to the level of trades unionism, but no further. Socialism would only come out of the philosophical, historical, economic theories that were propagated by the educated middle classes. Only a disciplined party of professional middle-class revolutionaries under the command of a central committee could bring socialism to Russia. With such a party, Lenin joked, the whole of Russia might be turned upside down. Lenin's ideas were indeed revolutionary.

The revolution of 1905 fell short of Lenin's expectations. He arrived in St Petersburg in November and stayed for a while, but lived for the next two years in Finland, visiting Stockholm and London. In 1906 he was elected to the Presidium of the RSDLP. As his profile increased, so also did the danger of arrest, so in 1907 he moved to Finland again for safety, but he continued to travel and to participate in socialist meetings. He was unhappy during these years, partly because he was an unwilling migrant, partly because of ongoing faction-fighting between Mensheviks and Bolsheviks and within the Bolshevik camp itself.

When the March 1917 Revolution broke out, Lenin was in Switzerland, unable to get back to Russia without crossing enemy territory. The Germans provided the facility of a sealed train, in which he and other Russian socialists might travel across Germany. On 16 April, Lenin arrived in St Petersburg, now Petrograd (and one day to be named Leningrad in his honour), to take a leading role in the Bolshevik movement. The Tsar, Nicholas II, had been deposed. A Bolshevik rising in July failed, and Lenin had to withdraw to Finland once more. In October he returned to Russia to lead an armed coup, this time successfully, against the Provisional Government led by Kerensky.

Lenin was elected Chairman of the Council of People's Commissars by the Russian Soviet Congress in November 1917. There was a threat of German invasion, and Lenin advised that Russia should sign the proposed peace treaty because, though harsh, it would at least ensure the integrity of the Russian territories. The Russian delegation failed to take Lenin's advice, and the eventual Treaty of Brest-Litovsk in March 1918 did indeed entail the loss of much of the western territory. Sometimes Lenin displayed the wisdom of a great statesman, showing real insight. But sometimes he displayed the instinct of a raw anarchist. In 1906, for instance, he calmly wrote that what he really wished to see was not the confiscation of the landlords in the interests of the peasantry as a result of legislation to that effect, but the seizure of the land by the peasantry. Only a literally lawless rush for land by the peasantry in its scores of millions could shake the fabric of the state of Russia profoundly enough for him to be able to seize power with a hope of retaining it. What he overlooked was that anarchy is a Pandora's box. Once you have empowered people in that way, it is difficult to get them to accept restraints and laws. In 1917 the peasantry did indeed rush lawlessly for the land. Lenin came up with a soviet constitution, better than any constitution so far known, he said, a constitution based on seizures by any and every mob rather than on any central authority. Lenin called this principle 'the dictatorship of the proletariat'. His associates were understandably amazed and alarmed, not least because this new 'Leninism' was very different from the control by central committee that he had been advocating in the past.

On 30 August 1918, Fanny Kaplan tried to assassinate him, but he survived. The Bolsheviks prevailed and became the Russian Communist Party. In 1921 a New Economic Policy was adopted, allowing a limited amount of private enterprise, in an effort to modernize industry and agriculture.

In May 1922 Lenin had a stroke which left him partially paralyzed on his right side and his role in government contracted. After a second stroke in December and a third in March 1923, Lenin was bedridden and unable to speak. The fourth stroke, in January 1924, killed him. Petrograd was renamed Leningrad in his honour. After his first stroke, Lenin wrote a number of papers. The most famous of these is the *Last Testament*, which criticized Joseph Stalin, the Communist Party's General Secretary since April 1922. Lenin thought he had 'unlimited authority concentrated in his hands' and asked that 'comrades think about a way of removing Stalin from that post'. Naturally, Stalin and his supporters suppressed these papers for decades. Lenin's criticism of Stalin was rich, given that he himself had virtually dictatorial powers; Stalin was simply about to assume them for himself.

Lenin's speeches and writings were highly regarded by his successors. His major contribution to Marxism were his analysis of imperialism (stressing the importance of colonies as breeding grounds for revolution) and his concept of a highly disciplined revolutionary party.

Because of his leading role in instigating the Russian Revolution, Lenin must carry the major responsibility for the bloodshed and the crimes against humanity committed during that revolution. He was by far the greatest single driving force: the man who made it happen. Not only that, he advocated violence as the means to achieve change; he was the very opposite of Gandhi. He was responsible for the execution of the Tsar and his family; he may not have explicitly ordered it, but he created a climate within which it was bound to happen. He was responsible for unleashing the peasantry in the chaotic grabbing of property; he gave millions of people the freedom to rob thousands of others, with all the misery, unfairness and social and economic dislocation that that was bound to entail. Russia was no better off after the Revolution than it had been before, and thousands died in the process. It was Lenin who adapted Marxism as a practical instrument for socialist revolution in Asia, and therefore he was responsible for all the ills that followed – including the long, cruel, destructive reign of Stalin. It is interesting that, like Robespierre, Lenin was to a remarkable degree changed by power. He became besotted with the idea and the actuality of dictatorship, the very thing the revolution was supposed to remove.

BERTRAND RUSSELL

Born at Trelleck 1872, died 1970.
Welsh philosopher, mathematician and peace campaigner.

ACHIEVEMENTS:
Advanced the disciplines of mathematics and philosophy.
Popularized many new ideas to ordinary people.
1896 – German Social Democracy.
1903 – The Principles of Mathematics.
1912 – The Problems of Philosophy.
1913 – Principia Mathematica.
1919 – Theory and Practice of Bolshevism.
1925 – The ABC of Relativity
1945 – History of Western Philosophy.
1957 – Why I am not a Christian.

BERTRAND ARTHUR WILLIAM Russell, 3rd Earl Russell, was born at Trelleck in Gwent. His parents died when he was only three and he was brought up by his grandmother, the widow of Lord John Russell, the Liberal Prime Minister. His grandmother lived in Richmond Park. As a boy, Bertrand was educated by governesses and tutors. He then went to Trinity College, Cambridge, where he had to adjust to education in company, and initially he was very shy. He graduated in mathematics and philosophy in 1894.

Russell was briefly a British Embassy official in Paris, but became a Fellow of Trinity College in 1895, shortly after marrying Alys Smith. He visited Berlin and on the strength of that visit wrote his first book, *German Social Democracy*. This marked the start of a long and wide-ranging intellectual career. After his return from Germany, Bertrand and Alys lived in Haslemere, where he devoted himself to philosophy.

His most original contributions to mathematics, logic and philosophy were made in the period before 1914. His outstanding works in the field of mathematics were *The Principles of Mathematics*, in which he argued that all mathematics could be derived from logic, and *Principia Mathematica*, where (with Alfred Whitehead's collaboration) he developed the idea fully. *Principia* stands as a landmark in the development of both disciplines.

The young Wittgenstein came to Cambridge to be Russell's student in 1912–13. Ten years later, Russell was to write the introduction to Wittgenstein's *Tractatus*.

Russell was not just a great academic; he was also a great popularizer of his subject. His first populist book was *The Problems of Philosophy*, which came out in 1912. The First World War broke across his intellectual career in 1914 and he became immersed in political issues. He was a militant pacifist, which caused Trinity College to deprive him of his Fellowship in 1916 and the authorities to imprison him in 1918. Now Russell was forced to make his living by lecturing and journalism, and he went out of his way to become a well-known controversialist; now he needed to be noticed. He knew and quarrelled with the novelist D. H. Lawrence.

He briefly visited the Soviet Union immediately after the Revolution, and met Lenin. Russell asked Lenin how people with different views would be accommodated in the new system and was startled by Lenin's instant savage reply: 'We will shoot them!' Of course, Russell should have known that that would be the case, but he was still struck by Lenin's gangsterish barbarism. He also met Trotsky and Gorky. The Russian experience sobered Russell considerably; from that point on he was less enthusiastic about communism. He wrote *Theory and Practice of Bolshevism*. Even more remarkably, in the same year Russell visited China, where he lectured on philosophy at Peiping University. By now he was already divorced from Alys, and in 1921 he married Dora Black.

The need to earn money was ever-present and he wrote more populist works, such as *The ABC of Atoms* and *The ABC of Relativity*.

Russell went on being controversial between the two World Wars. His impending second divorce (1935) led him to reflect on *Marriage and Morals* in 1932. In 1940 his lectureship at City College, New York was terminated on the grounds that he was 'an enemy of religion and morality'. He did however eventually win damages for wrongful dismissal. The rise of fascism in Europe led him to renounce his pacifism in 1939. His Fellowship at Trinity was accordingly restored in 1944. He returned to England after the war ended to be awarded the Order of Merit. He also produced the best-selling book *History of Western Philosophy*. He was awarded the Nobel Prize for Literature in 1950.

His journalistic side drove him to publish a stream of provocative pieces, such as *Why I am not a Christian* (1957). The Cold War and the development of huge armouries of atomic weapons alarmed him greatly, and he immediately took a leading role in the British Campaign for Nuclear Disarmament (CND). In connection with this, Russell, who was by now an international celebrity, launched into correspondence with all the major political leaders of the world, as well as participating in CND demonstrations and rallies. In 1961 he found himself in prison again for his part in a sit-down demonstration in Whitehall.

Lord Russell's final years were spent in quiet retirement in Wales. To the end – and he lived to be almost 100 – he retained his resolute independence of mind, his lucidity of argument and his chirpy sense of humour.

Bertrand Russell was strongly influenced by the German philosopher and mathematician Gottfried Leibniz; Russell as a mathematician and a logician owed much to the pioneer work of Leibniz. Russell's importance lies in his role as a lucid and logical commentator on a wide range of 20th century intellectual and moral issues, and on his application of logical analysis to ethical and metaphysical matters. He showed that it is possible to construct a morality without falling back on a religious faith. His academic work on mathematics and philosophy carried both disciplines forward, and his popular works brought many new ideas to ordinary people.

GUGLIELMO MARCONI

Born in Bologna 1874, died in Rome 1937.
Italian physicist and inventor.

ACHIEVEMENTS:
Invented wireless telegraphy.
Launched the age of radio and mass entertainment.

MARCHESE GUGLIELMO MARCONI was born on 25 April 1874 in Bologna. His parents were an Italian country gentleman and his Irish wife, who was originally from County Wexford. He was educated first in Bologna and then in Florence. He later attended the Technical Institute of Livorno, where he studied physics under Vincenzo Rosa.

He became fascinated with the electromagnetic waves discovered by Heinrich Hertz, experimenting from 1894 onwards with a way of converting them into electricity. He carried out these experiments on his father's estate at Pintecchio, just outside Bologna. He used fairly crude apparatus: an induction coil with a spark discharger and a simple filings coherer at the receiver. He also started transmitting over short distances, then tried ways of extending the range of transmission. He found that using a vertical aerial increased the distance of transmission to over one mile; with reflectors fitted round the aerial to concentrate the signal into a beam, he could increase the distance still further.

Marconi was convinced that he had stumbled on something of great importance, but received little encouragement in Italy. He was advised by his mother's relatives to take his invention to England, where its value would be appreciated, and this proved to be the case. In February 1896 Marconi arrived in London, where he met William Preece, engineer-in-chief to the

Post Office, and Preece gave him every encouragement and all the help he could. Marconi filed his first patent for wireless telegraphy in London in 1896. Marconi gave several demonstrations of his wireless telegraph system, trying out kites and balloons to give his aerials greater height in order to increase the transmission distance. He succeeded in this way in sending radio signals four miles on Salisbury Plain and twice that distance across the Bristol Channel. The demonstrations and Preece's lectures on the technology attracted a lot of public interest, both in England and abroad.

Now even the Italians were interested. Marconi was able to erect a wireless station at La Spezia, and a communication link was established with warships up to 12 miles away. A further major step was taken when in 1898 he set up a land station on the South Foreland in Kent, to communicate with Wimereux in France, 30 miles away; he used this to transmit radio signals right across the English Channel. With finance from his cousin, Jameson Davis, Marconi was able to set up the Marconi Wireless Telegraph Company in 1900. The great advance of Marconi's invention was that it allowed practical communication between places without using any connecting wires – hence the name 'wireless'.

Marconi's greatest breakthrough was yet to come. Many physicists thought that the curvature of the earth would put a natural limit on the distance radio waves could be transmitted. Probably 100 miles would be the limit. In December 1901 Marconi proved the experts wrong; he managed to send signals in Morse code right across the Atlantic. The signal was transmitted from Poldhu in Cornwall and received at St Johns in Newfoundland. This achievement was sensational news. Many improvements and refinements remained to be made during the next 50 years, but the principle of international and even intercontinental radio transmission was established.

On a voyage of the US liner *Philadelphia* in 1902, Marconi received radio messages from distances up to 700 miles by day, and three times as far by night. Marconi had discovered that conditions for reflecting radio waves on the upper layers of the atmosphere were more favourable at night. By 1918, Marconi was able to send radio signals from England to Australia.

For this epoch-making invention, Marconi was awarded the Nobel Prize for physics, with Karl Braun. Later, in 1924, Marconi was commissioned to developed a short-wave radio network for the British government, so that London could communicate instantly with any country in the British Empire. Marconi's wireless made world-wide communication possible; it was first used merely for messages, but later it was used for entertainment, and eventually it spawned television. Marconi inadvertently launched the age of mass entertainment.

The instant communication it allowed was invaluable for police work too – and almost straight away. In 1910 Dr Crippen was famously arrested while trying to escape across the Atlantic after murdering his wife – thanks to a wireless message sent by the captain of the *SS Montrose*, when he suspected he had the murderer aboard his ship. Chief Inspector Walter Dew pursued the Montrose across the Atlantic on the *Laurentic*, ambushing the Montrose in the Gulf of St Lawrence. The outside world followed the sensational chase in successive newspaper editions. The arrest of Crippen was a world news story, and this in turn was very good news for Marconi's business. From then on, most large ships were equipped with wireless. Thanks to Crippen, the *Titanic* was fitted with wireless and at least those who took to the boats in 1912 were rescued by the *Carpathia*, which was summoned by the Titanic's wireless operator. After the Titanic disaster, there was some criticism of the way Marconi sought to exploit the sinking in order to advertize his company; he had an acute commercial sense, which on this occasion he overplayed.

From 1921 Marconi lived aboard his yacht, named the Elettra. In the 1930s, he became a staunch supporter of Mussolini. Honours were showered on him for his world-changing invention. He died in Rome on 20 July, 1937 and was given a state funeral by the Italian government.

ARNOLD SCHOENBERG

Born 1874, died 1951.
Austrian composer.

ACHIEVEMENTS:
Reacted against the German late Romantic style of Wagner.
Invented twelve-note music.
Taught Webern and Berg.
Left a legacy of two generations of classical music in the West to
  which very few people wanted to listen.
Created a gap between serious composers and the general public.
Created a gap between classical and popular music.
1899 – Verklarte Nacht.
1901 – Gurrelieder.
1923 – Piano Suite.
1934 – Suite for Strings.

ARNOLD SCHOENBERG WAS born in Vienna in 1874. As a child he taught himself to play the violin. In his 20s, he made a living by orchestrating operettas. From 1901 to 1903 he conducted a cabaret orchestra in Berlin.

From this unpromising beginning, it is hard to see how Schoenberg could have become one of the most influential composers of the first half of the 20th century. At first he wrote music that was strongly influenced by Wagner, such as the sextet *Verklarte Nacht* (Transfigured Night), the symphonic poem *Pelleas und Melisande* and the large-scale choral and orchestral piece *Gurrelieder*. It was appropriate that he should be writing about transfiguration in the final months of the 19th century; he himself was about to transfigure Western music of the 20th century.

As his composing style changed he was able to influence others. Throughout his career he was a teacher, and his two most famous pupils, Webern and Berg, joined him in Vienna in 1904. A reaction to the German late Romantic style of Wagner was setting in. His *Second String Quartet* caused an uproar at its first performance in 1908. *Pierrot Lunaire* (1912) used an extremely chromatic harmony that had its roots in Wagner's *Tristan*.

In the midst of his artistic crisis which, like the psychological crisis of Carl Jung, coincided with the First World War, Schoenberg looked to the visual arts for an escape route, and his own paintings were exhibited with those of Kandinsky's group. The revolution that Picasso's Cubism created was something he was to mirror in music. By 1920 Schoenberg had formulated his twelve-note method, producing what is sometimes called serial music, in which a melody is built out of the 12 semitones of a scale, each used only once. Because the new music rejected keys it was called 'atonal'. This extraordinarily rigid and doctrinaire method of composing was so arid and limiting that Schoenberg himself gave it up eventually, returning to music based on keys. But in the meantime, his pupils and other composers took it up and created a new fashion in music that ran parallel to abstract art in painting and sculpture.

Schoenberg lived on until 1951, by which time he could see the destructive effects of his revolution in music. He left a legacy of two generations of classical music in the West that very few people wanted to listen to; young composers in the 1960s still felt honour-bound to compose in Schoenberg's style, and they mocked those who composed music with melody. Schoenberg was responsible for creating a virtually unbridgeable gap between serious composers and the general public. As a result of serial music, many people stopped bothering with serious music written in the 20th century altogether, switching to popular music instead.

WINSTON CHURCHILL

Born at Blenheim Palace 1874, died 1965.
British Prime Minister and inspiring war leader.

ACHIEVEMENTS:
Ordered the disastrous Gallipoli landings.
Introduced Labour Exchanges (Job Centres).
Prepared the British navy for the First World War.
*Promoted the production of tanks, helping to win the First
  World War.*
Resisted the movement towards independence for India.
Won the Second World War.
Connived at Communist control over Eastern Europe.
Warned of the approaching Cold War.
Coined the phrase 'Iron Curtain'.
*Nominated the disastrous Eden to succeed him as Prime
  Minister.*
1898 – The Story of the Malakand Field Force.
1899 – The River War.
1900 – London to Ladysmith via Pretoria.
1929 – The World Crisis.
1938 – Marlborough.
1954 – The Second World War *(6 volumes).*
1958 – History of the English-Speaking Peoples *(4
  volumes).*

WINSTON LEONARD SPENCER Churchill was born at Blenheim Palace, Woodstock, on 30 November 1874, the eldest son of Lord Randolph Churchill and Jennie Jerome. As a child he was neglected by his mother, whom he adored, and he developed a compensating close relationship with his nanny. He had little attention from his father, who was busy with his political career. He was a lonely, attention-starved little boy, and this may have played a part in making him the avid attention-seeker he became in adult life. Lord Randolph died of a brain tumour, not of syphilis, as shown in Richard Attenborough's film *Young Winston*.

He was educated at Harrow, where he was a mediocre scholar, and then at Sandhurst; he was gazetted to the 4th Hussars in 1895. With the army he saw service with the Malakand field force in 1897 and with the Nile expeditionary force in 1898. During this expedition he was involved in hand to hand fighting with Dervishes at the Battle of Omdurman. At Omdurman he took part in the very last cavalry charge in British history.

He recognized that to have any chance of following his father into a political career he needed to be noticed. He was a gong-hunter. One way of getting noticed was to write up his experiences, such as they were. He wrote *The Story of the Malakand Field Force* and *The River War*. These were brilliantly written and won him the attention he craved.

In the Boer War, he acted as a newspaper correspondent for the *Morning Post*. He was captured by the Boers in an ambush, taken to a prison camp, but managed to escape. This adventure too was turned into a book, *London to Ladysmith via Pretoria*. In 1900 he became Conservative MP for Oldham, but at first he was up against the House of Commons' excessive expectations; could he be as good as his father, Lord Randolph? He was good at writing a set speech from classical models, but far less good at impromptu speech. Lord Balfour described him as carrying 'heavy but not very mobile guns'. It was only much later that he learned how to parry comments from opponents. His views diverged from those of his party, particularly when protectionist measures were introduced, and he joined the Liberals in 1906. He became President of the Board of Trade from 1908 to 1910, and in this role introduced Labour Exchanges, the forerunners of the modern Job Centres.

In 1910, Winston Churchill became Home Secretary and in this capacity became involved in the Siege of Sidney Street controversy in 1911. He turned out to be rather unsuccessful at dealing with industrial and other domestic disputes; he was by instinct a warrior rather than a diplomat. He then became First Lord of the Admiralty, within which he developed a 'war staff' and organized an embryonic air force. He was explicitly ordered by Asquith to put the navy into a state of instant readiness in case of an attack from Germany. He made organizational changes in readiness for the war with Germany which both he and Asquith saw as inevitable. When war came in 1914, the British navy was indeed ready, thanks to Churchill's efforts. Churchill was a great advocate of declaring war on Germany, and once it broke out he favoured all-out attacks by land and sea.

In 1915, Churchill was rightly blamed for the Dardanelles disaster. He went ahead with the Gallipoli landings against the advice of the First Sea Lord, Sir John Fisher. After the huge loss of Allied lives at Gallipoli, Churchill had to leave the Admiralty; he was moved to the Duchy of Lancaster, and Sir John Fisher resigned.

When the Liberal government collapsed in the political crisis following Gallipoli, Churchill abandoned politics. He went on active service, joining the army in France, where he commanded the 6th Royal Scots Fusiliers.

In 1917, when David Lloyd George was returned to power, Churchill was recalled to London, where he became Lloyd George's Minister for Munitions. He concentrated on the production of thousands of tanks, which were very much his own project; these bullet-proof vehicles were able to overrun barbed wire and trenches, and Churchill rightly saw them as the key to winning land battles.

When the First World War was over, he became Secretary of State for War and Air. From 1924 to 1929 he was Chancellor of the Exchequer. To this point, Winston Churchill's political career was a brilliant success story, with the exception of the Gallipoli landings. With the fall of the Conservatives in 1929, a breach opened between Baldwin and Churchill, mainly over the independence of India, which Churchill opposed. Then, in the 1930s, he found himself in the political wilderness. He became increasingly angry and frustrated at the supine National Government's passivity in the face of the growth of fascism in Europe. The dictators on the European mainland were arming ready for conquest, while the British government futilely hoped to dissuade them through diplomacy.

When the Second World War broke out, Churchill's call to arms was vindicated, and he was seen as someone the government needed. Neville Chamberlain responded to a wide popular demand by appointing

Churchill to his old, pre-Gallipoli, post back at the Admiralty. In May 1940, Chamberlain resigned as Prime Minister, and Churchill formed a Coalition government and began what he called his 'walk with destiny'. He saw all his earlier life as leading to this moment, when he was to face down Adolf Hitler in the greatest war the world had ever seen.

Churchill encouraged and inspired the British people to fight in a series of brilliantly composed war speeches, which were broadcast on the radio, his words spoken by an actor. In one of these stirring speeches, he offered the British nation nothing but 'blood, toil, tears and sweat.' He had a rock-like faith that Britain and America together could win the war, and conveyed this conviction to the British people – and to the troops – which was a significant factor in the eventual victory. He managed to make the withdrawal from Dunkirk – a crushing defeat – into something that seemed like a glorious step towards victory; 'We shall go on to the end, whatever the cost may be.'

He worked unceasingly through the war years, making all the key decisions himself, from shaping the Atlantic Charter in 1941 to working on the strategy for the Battle of El Alamein in 1942. Churchill advocated invading Europe from the Mediterranean in 1944, to coincide with the Normandy landings, but in this he was overruled by the American generals. In the end, Churchill thought an agreed strategy was better than having his own way. He cultivated a close personal relationship with the American President F. D. Roosevelt, which greatly helped to harmonize the American and British war efforts. He also worked hard to maintain a working relationship with the Russian leader, Stalin, whose support he needed to keep Germany fighting the war on two fronts.

After the stunning success of the Allied victory over fascism in 1945, Churchill fought and lost the July election in Britain. He was seen as the perfect war leader, but he was not what the people of Britain needed in peace time. Britain needed a range of social and economic reforms, and it was obvious from the speeches he made that Churchill was not really interested in them. He made a disastrous speech in which he addressed the British electorate as 'you in your cottages', which showed how completely out of touch he was; three-quarters of the British population lived in cities. There is film of him addressing a crowd in the street, stumbling through an ill-considered address and unable to deal with a heckler. Churchill suddenly looked like a figure left over from the 19th century, a beached whale.

Churchill's voice was still heard, still to be reckoned with, and he drew attention to the 'iron curtain' (his own phrase) that was falling across eastern Europe. At the same time, he and Roosevelt had agreed that Stalin would 'caretake' eastern Europe – Stalin's price – which they must have known meant consigning them to decades of repressive Communist rule. He also ordered the return of Russian refugees, at Stalin's request, knowing that they would all be shot. Churchill encouraged a stronger bond between Britain and America, and in these ways became both a prophet and a promoter of the Cold War. In 1951, he did become Prime Minister again, at the age of 77, retiring in 1955 at the age of 81. He handed over power to his own ill-chosen nominee, Anthony Eden, who turned out to be a disaster. After that he took his place on the back benches, where he was regarded with awe and veneration. He died in London in 1965. His body lay in state in Westminster Hall before a state funeral, which produced an outpouring of national mourning not seen since the death of Queen Victoria.

When relaxing, Churchill developed his garden at Chartwell in rural Kent, and was a keen amateur landscape painter. His paintings are bold, confident and alive with sun-drenched colour harmonies. He was also a card-carrying bricklayer.

Winston Churchill achieved a world-wide reputation as a far-sighted war strategist and an inspiring war leader of great courage and imagination, ready to seize on new inventions if they could be used to outwit the enemy. He once described his opponent, the Labour leader Clement Attlee, as 'a modest little man, with plenty to be modest about.' Churchill was not a modest man, but he was occasionally capable of modesty. In 1954 he said in a speech given to both Houses of Parliament on the occasion of his eightieth birthday, 'I have never accepted what many people have kindly said – that I inspired the nation. It was the nation and the race living round the globe that had the lion heart. I had the luck to be called upon to give the roar.'

He was a master politician, with a shrewd, incisive and impish sense of humour. In his last years as a back-bencher, two admiring MPs were talking about him, as they thought safely out of earshot, commenting kindly and sympathetically on his age and infirmity. He swung round and said, 'Yes, and they tell me he's very deaf too.' He had great powers of oratory, with a supreme mastery of the English language, which he used very explicitly and deliberately to make people proud to be English. In some ways he represented the epitome of English nationalism, actually looking rather like the 19th century cartoon image of John Bull, or the pugnacious British bulldog. He hated the Graham Sutherland portrait which showed this pugnacity all too well. He was greatly aided, both as an orator and as a war leader, by his profound sense of the great sweep of history. It was no accident that he used his politically fallow period in the 1930s to write a biography of his ancestor, the 18th century war leader, John Churchill, Duke of Marlborough. Like Alexander, Churchill saw his place in that great sweep of history and had the same sense of walking with destiny as he took control of events.

CARL GUSTAV JUNG

Born in Basle 1875, died in Zurich 1961.
Swiss psychologist and psychiatrist.

ACHIEVEMENTS:
Co-founder (with Freud) of modern psychology.
Coined the terms complex, introvert, extravert, collective
unconscious.
Discovered the collective unconscious.
Identified psychic archetypes.
Identified the phenomenon of synchronicity.
1907 – The Psychology of Dementia Praecox.
1934 – Archetypes of the Collective Unonscious.
1937 – Psychology and Religion.
1944 – Psychology and Alchemy.
1945 – After the Catastrophe.
1952 – Symbols of Transformation.
1957 – The Undiscovered Self.
1958 – Flying Saucers: a Modern Myth.
1962 – Memories, Dreams, Reflections.

CARL GUSTAV JUNG was born in Basle on 26 July 1875, the son of a clergyman. His outwardly ordinary childhood was shaping him into the profoundly thoughtful adult he would become. His father was often stern and tyrannical and his parents quarrelled a good deal; this cold and arid environment drove him deeper and deeper into himself. He invented solitary games. The tension within the family intensified when his parents started sleeping apart. Mental disturbances generated vivid dreams that he would recall and analyze later in life.

He studied medicine in Basle and then continued his psychology studies in Paris under Pierre Janet. He worked as a physician under Eugen Bleuler at the Bergholtzli mental clinic in Zurich from 1900 until 1909, and lectured in psychology at the University of Zurich from 1905 to 1913. Jung was an incredibly prolific writer, and one of his early publications was *Studies in Word Association*, in which he coined the term 'complex'. He also wrote *The Psychology of Dementia Praecox* (now called schizophrenia). These publications led directly to a meeting with Freud in Vienna in 1907. Along the way he acquired a wealthy wife, a marriage which made his life much easier and more comfortable. He also met and became friends with Einstein.

Carl Jung became Sigmund Freud's leading disciple and collaborator and in 1910 he was elected president of the newly created International Pschoanalytical Association. But Jung was an independent researcher with a mind of his own, and he was soon moving off into new realms of thought. The moment Jung set out his new ideas on the libido and the unconscious, in 1912, there was tension between the two men as Freud felt his authority challenged. Jung became increasingly critical of Freud's insistence on the psychosexual origins of neuroses; to Jung this insistence on the sexual was too narrow and too doctrinaire. Jung substituted his own term, libido, for a general non-specific underlying life force; Freud remained fixed on the sexual drive per se as the root of most psychological problems. They regularly exchanged dreams and analyzed them. When, one day, Freud refused to tell Jung one of his dreams 'because it would undermine his authority', Jung knew that it was time for him to go his own way and in 1913 he parted company with Freud. Jung felt that Freud lacked a philosophical background; Jung himself was steeped in philosophy. He also saw that Freud made a mistake in restricting analysis to the personal. We are all steeped in history and zeitgeist; the way our parents treat us and the way we are educated are historical, not personal.

There was an exchange of over-heated letters. Freud made the mistake of analyzing some of the things Jung had said: 'Are you objective enough to consider the following slip [a slip that Jung had made in his earlier letter] without anger. "Even Adler's cronies do not regard me as one of *yours*." ' Jung had obviously meant to write "one of *theirs*".' What Freud was pointing out was that Jung had made a significantly revealing mistake, a slip that has come to be known as a 'Freudian slip'. Freud knew this shallow analysis would annoy Jung, which is probably why he wrote it. Jung replied at length, including the comment, 'Your technique of treating your pupils like patients is a *blunder*. In that way you produce either slavish sons or impudent puppies.' Freud was humiliated at being addressed like this, composed a reply, but did not send it. It included the remark, 'I'm sorry my reference to your slip annoyed you so; your reaction seems out of all proportion to the occasion.' The two great psychologists were actually struggling to understand their own minds and emotions, and unable to understand the strength of their effect upon one other. It was like a tiff between teenage lovers.

A Freudian bystander might have judged that Freud was playing the father, and Jung was reacting badly to this as he had not enjoyed his relationship with his father, so he was playing the ultra-rebellious son. One tyrant-father was quite enough. Probably this is what their colleague Ernest Jones thought, as he watched this personal and professional tragedy unfold. But the two great founders of modern psychology had said unforgivable things to each other. They went their separate ways. Possibly as a result of this loss, Jung had a serious mental breakdown which lasted – significantly – for the duration of the First World War. Jung even made the extraordinary suggestion that the external struggle was a projection of his own breakdown, but that was part of his insanity. He went on seeing patients during this period; one wonders whether he can have helped them in any significant way. He diagnosed one patient as being in the final stages of syphilis and gave him only weeks to live. The patient wisely sought a second opinion; he turned out to be manic-depressive and lived for another 50 years.

In later life he admitted that he had nearly lost his reason between 1913 and 1918. He fell back on repeating to himself, 'I have a diploma from a Swiss university, I have a wife and five children, I live at 228 Seestrasse, Kusnacht.' Nietzsche had gone through a similar ordeal and drowned in his inner world. Jung managed to use his knowledge of the unconscious mind to swim through it and turn the episode into a rebirth. He and Freud had exchanged dreams and psychoanalyzed one another. He knew a lot about the workings of Freud's mind, but even in his final year he was not prepared to divulge what he knew. He smiled and said, 'There's such a thing as a professional secret.'

From 1920, his composure recovered and some travels abroad behind him, Jung decided he needed a special retreat. He tried first to buy the island of Schmerikon at the end of Lake Zurich, intending to build a kind of stone temple on it. Then he chose a peaceful lakeshore site at Bollingen, a large plot sealed off from the outside world by a railway line. Here he built his own tower-refuge. It was to be a representation in stone of his psyche. The Tower, which he built with his own hands and decorated with his own symbolic stone carvings, was gradually developed. A second tower was added. Gradually it turned into a beautiful miniature medieval castle, built round a courtyard. The architecture consisted of a trinity of principal buildings together with a loggia along the waterfront; he had unconsciously worked his way towards a quaternity, representing the four parts of his mind. Personal mystification of this kind was very important to Jung. It was essential – for everybody – to connect with the mythic world, and confront the archetypes. Bollingen became, and still is, a very beautiful place. It was an ideal place to retreat to – whether to think, or to entertain a mistress, as he often did.

Jung's Tower at Bollingen recalls the well-known tower of W. B. Yeats, a poet who was in many ways a similar type of person to Jung – down to the right-wing politics and the interest in the occult. The difference was that Yeats made his tower a retreat for his family, and Jung made his tower a retreat from his family. Bollingen was very cut off. It was a long walk from the nearest railway station, and the only other way to reach it (Jung did not have a car until 1929) was by water. Jung's preferred, and highly romantic, way of reaching The Tower was by sailing boat; he used to sail from his family home at Kusnacht to Bollingen. Bollingen was beautiful, but also eerie. Jung experienced 'hauntings' of various kinds there. One night he dreamt that several hundred darkly-dressed peasant boys were laughing and dancing round The Tower. Typically, Jung read intensively to illuminate the experience. He eventually came upon a reminiscence by Rennard Cysat, who had climbed Mount Pilatus in the seventeenth century and been disturbed at night by a noisy crowd, singing and playing music as they passed the mountain hut. The next day a herdsman explained to Cysat that the crowd was Wotan's army of departed souls. Jung was delighted to think that he too had witnessed a supernatural event.

Jung founded his own school of analytical psychology with Maeder in Zurich. Jung held professorships at Zurich in the 1930s and Basle from the 1940s onwards. What Jung shared with Freud – and he never deviated from it – was the profound belief in the fundamental importance and truthfulness of dreams. Dreams were a window onto the unconscious mind. Where the two men differed was in the interpretation of dreams. Freud delved into a patient's dream until he found the sexual metaphor, which might be a tree or a tunnel, and was then satisfied that he had reached the interpretation; once he had reached a sexual stratum he had interpreted the dream and looked no further. For Jung, the sexual content of a dream might be no more than metaphorical language, and still deeper layers might lie beneath; where Freud stopped, Jung went on digging.

After the Second World War, Jung was invited to give a lecture 'explaining' the war. He developed the idea that the German people have a tendency to be dominated by a particular archetype, which he called Wotan, the great Teutonic god of war. Hitler, he argued, was a kind of shaman or witch-doctor who had worked the German people up to a pitch where the Wotan archetype had taken over the entire nation. It was a characteristically daring view of the world – one that no-one before Jung could possibly have considered. After Jung, we see the world differently.

Jung read incredibly widely, as is evident from his writings. He also travelled widely. He was in London on one occasion and went to the British Museum Reading Room, where the librarian asked him his name. 'Jung,' he said. 'As in Freud, Jung and Adler?' the librarian asked lightly, not dreaming that it could be the great man himself standing there. 'No,' he said irritably. 'As in Jung.' In old age, Jung cultivated the image of the wise old man – it was a powerful archetype, after all. But he was more complex than that. He was quite a vain old man, and cared what the world thought of him. But it was professionalism and courtesy more than vanity that made him answer all his correspondence personally. Some correspondents were clearly mad, others were eccentric, others relentlessly persistent. Some correspondents were sending fan mail, some were crying for help. He answered them all.

In his 85th year he deteriorated noticeably, and he sat dressed in a Japanese ceremonial gown staring across Lake Zurich, and looking like a medieval magician (or indeed the dying George V). Towards the end he became fretful and was occasionally overwhelmed by despair. Then he went into a coma, which ended in his death on 6 June 1961.

Jung introduced the terms 'introvert' and 'extravert' for two personality types. He judged that in every person one or more of four primary functions dominate the mind: the quaternity of thinking, feeling, sensation and intuition. Jung's book on *Psychological Types* was characteristically dismissed by Freud as 'a new production by Jung of enormous size, 700 pages thick, the work of a snob and a mystic, no new idea in it.' Jung identified Zwingli, Schiller and Kant as introverts, Luther, Goethe and Stanley as extraverts.

Instead of searching for the psychosexual origin of a patient's mental health problems, Jung looked more at the specific immediate conflicts the person was undergoing. He emphasized the possibility of resolving the behaviour of a dysfunctioning conscious mind by making the conscious mind and unconscious mind work in harmony. Many psychological problems result from an artificial separation between the two parts of the mind. Jung made the very interesting observation that the people who 'see' flying saucers (which he treated as a projection from the unconscious mind) are very often policemen or pilots or others who are trained to deal only with the rational; in other words they do not give their unconscious minds the freedom they need, so there are occasional eruptions which take the form of involuntary visions.

He also developed a highly controversial theory of the collective unconscious, which held that people are born with a set of archetypes (basic images and situations) which they then recognize in the outside world and respond to accordingly. This extraordinary idea implies that some kind of memory transcends death and that certain images and situations in our minds are ancestral. Another controversial idea is synchronicity; the idea that thematically related events can sometimes happen close together without any causal relationship.

Jung's approach to the human mind is immeasurably richer and more exhilarating than Freud's, which often seems squalid, mundane and over-simplified by comparison. Jung was able to use his analytical method to explain the dreams of disturbed patients, the content of great literature like Goethe or Shakespeare, or the content of myths and religions; Jung offered a more universal gateway to the mind of man. If Freud opened the door on the 20th century way of looking at things, Jung opened the door on the 21st.

MUHAMMED
ALI JINNAH

Born in Karachi 1876, died in Karachi 1948.
Pakistani statesman.

ACHIEVEMENTS:
1916 – Became President of the Indian Muslim League.
1947 – Directly responsible for the Partition of India.
1947 – Created the Muslim state of Pakistan (East and West
Pakistan, now Pakistan and Bangladesh)

MUHAMMED ALI JINNAH was born in Karachi on 25 December 1876, the son of a Karachi merchant. He studied in Bombay and from 1892 in Lincoln's Inn, London. He was called to the bar in 1897 and then set up a very successful legal practice in Bombay.

In 1910, Jinnah, known to his people as Quaid E Azam (Great Leader), was elected to the Viceroy of India's legislative council. He was already a member of the Indian National Congress, the movement that steered India towards independence. In 1913 he also joined the Indian Muslim League when it extended its goals to include self-government for India. In 1916 he became its president; it was in this role that he was to make his lasting mark on the sub-continent.

Jinnah brought about a peaceful co-existence between the Indian Muslim League and he Congress by way of the Lucknow Pact of 1916. For many years he consistently advocated Hindu-Muslim unity in the cause of Indian nationalism. He supported the efforts of Congress to boycott the Simon Commission in 1928, but strongly disapproved of Gandhi's civil disobedience policy. He came to see the Congress party as exclusively fostering Hindu interests, and because of this and Gandhi's strategy he resigned from Congress. At the London Round Table Conference of 1931, Jinnah continued to advocate '14 points' to safeguard the interests of Muslims. After this conference, Jinnah withdrew from politics for a time, but in 1934 he was back again as leader of the Muslim League. Relations between Hindus and Muslims continued to deteriorate.

By 1940, because of the attitude of Congress, he became so convinced that the independence movement was going to result in Hindu supremacy in India that he fiercely advocated separate statehood for Muslims. He was not going to accept second-class citizenship for Muslims in a Hindu-dominated India; the Muslims must have their separate state. The British government (the Stafford Cripps mission in particular) and Gandhi both tried to save the united India, but Jinnah resisted. He would not compromise. In the end it was Congress who had to compromise.

On 14 August 1947, Jinnah's goal of Partition became a reality. The Dominion of Pakistan came into being. Jinnah became Pakistan's 'Great Leader', its first governor-general. This success was nevertheless accompanied by some terrible consequences. There were mass migrations of refugees in both directions across the new frontiers, many fights and skirmishes, riots in Punjab and Kashmir, many lives lost – and the responsibility was his.

The experience was traumatic – for India, and for Jinnah. Jinnah's health suffered terribly from the enormous strain of the independence process and he died at Karachi on 11 September 1948, only a year after his Muslim state had been created.

JOSEPH STALIN

Born at Gori 1879, died in the Kremlin 1953.
Soviet dictator.

ACHIEVEMENTS:
Subjected a large area of Europe and Asia to a 25-year reign of
terror.
Ordered genocides and deportations that still drive separatist
movements in the Russian Federation.
Responsible for the deaths of 20 million people.
1922 – Became General Secretary of the Communist Party.
1928 – Became supreme leader of the Soviet Union.
Initiated the Five-Year Plans to develop the Soviet economy.
Introduced collectivization (disastrous agricultural
reorganization)
1932–33 – Caused 5 million people to die in famines.
1937 – Ordered the Trial of the Red Army Generals.
1939–45 – Deported over 1.5 million people to Siberia and
central Asia.
1940 – Ordered the assassination of Trotsky.
1945 – Created a Communist zone (empire) in eastern Europe,
generating the Cold War.

JOSEPH DZHUGASHVILI WAS born at Gori in Georgia on 21 December 1879. His parents were illiterate peasants: in fact, they were serfs at the time of Stalin's birth. He was severely beaten by his father, who was an alcoholic, and this bad treatment in childhood may explain his harshness and the vengeful feelings he had towards anyone who might wield authority over him. The young Joseph was forced to work with his violent father as a cobbler until he was eleven, when his father was killed in a fight. His mother enrolled him in a religious seminary with a view to his becoming a priest!

Joseph Dzhugashvili's time at the seminary brought him into contact with socialists and led to his involvement with the socialist movement. In 1899 he failed to turn up for school examinations and was expelled. For ten years after that, he worked as a political activist in Georgia. From 1902 onwards he was repeatedly arrested and sent to Siberia. He admired Lenin's idea of a strong centralist party of professional revolutionaries, and he would be one of them. His practical experience in Georgia made him useful to the Bolsheviks, and he gained a place on the Bolshevik Central Committee in 1912. Some historians think that at this time Stalin was not a genuine revolutionary at all but a spy working for the Tsar, infiltrating the Bolshevik movement. Certainly Stalin was capable of playing a double game like that; he was not interested in personal or group loyalty.

In 1913 he adopted the name Stalin. Koba was his revolutionary nickname. Koba was a Georgian Robin Hood-like folk hero. Stalin used a dozen other secret names to ensure his own anonymity before the Russian Revolution. The nickname 'Stalin', combining 'stal' (steel) with Lenin, was one of his noms de guerre from revolutionary days, and that was the one that stuck.

In the Russian Revolution of 1917, Stalin was at first opposed to the idea of overthrowing Kerensky's provisional government, and he was only won over to Lenin's position after Lenin returned from exile in April 1917. He played only a minor role in the Bolshevik seizure of power in November. His stand-off at this crucial moment is very peculiar, and would fit in with the idea of a lack of genuine commitment; it would also fit in with the proposition that Stalin was an observing agent rather than a real revolutionary. If so, it would account for the thoroughness of his later purges; he must have wanted anybody who knew what his role was during the First World War eliminated. Stalin was a personal and political opportunist, not an idealist; like many others, he was able to exploit a chaotic political situation for his own personal advancement.

Stalin spent the first years after the Revolution in a sequence of senior posts in the government and party. He became General Secretary of the

Communist Party in 1922, and built up the post into the most powerful position in the state.

When Lenin died in January 1924, a triumvirate consisting of Stalin, Kamenev and Zinoviev ran the party, putting themselves ideologically between Bukharin (on the right) and Trotsky (on the left). Stalin advanced a policy of building 'Socialism in One Country', in stark opposition to Trotsky's policy of 'Permanent Revolution', which would involve working towards triggering revolution in other countries. Stalin and Bukharin joined forces against Trotsky, Kamenev and Zinoviev. By 1928, Stalin had emerged as supreme leader and the following year Trotsky was exiled. After that, Stalin exercised dictatorial power until his death in 1953.

Russia was at the time of the Revolution the poorest and economically the most backward country in Europe. To modernize its economy, Stalin introduced a system of centrally-organized Five-Year Plans. These involved ambitious programmes of rapid industrialization and collecti-vization of agriculture. The first two plans were successful in achieving rapid industrialization. This was financed by restraining consumption by ordinary Soviet citizens and the ruthless extraction of wealth from the peasants. It was odd. Stalin came from the peasant class, yet these were the people he treated worst.

The collectivization scheme was a disaster. In theory the large new mechanized farms would produce more food more efficiently than the small-scale and inefficient peasant farms. But collectivization meant destroying a way of life that had gone on for centuries, taking control over the land and food production away from the peasants, and their consequent loss of motivation. It also meant a drastic fall in living standards for many peasants. Many of them violently resisted the collective movement. Between 1929 and 1933 Stalin introduced shock brigades to go in and force peasants to join the collectives. Many peasants slaughtered their livestock rather than give in, leading to a major drop if food production. Stalin blamed this on the kulaks, rich peasants who were 'capitalist parasites' and therefore enemies of the people. Kulaks who resisted collectivization were to be shot, transported to Gulag labour camps or deported to remote areas.

These measures were the background to thousands of infringements of human rights, thousands of deaths and untold misery throughout the

Soviet Union. The disruption caused by collectivization led to major famines and up to five million deaths in 1932–33, especially in the Ukraine and lower Volga valley. Ironically, at this time Stalin was exporting millions of tonnes of grain.

On the good side, Stalin invested heavily in the provision of basic medical services, increasing the number of doctors and launching campaigns against diseases such as typhus, cholera and malaria. Infant mortality rates steadily dropped. Education was another major growth area.

Stalin feared assassination. He robbed, disinherited and killed many and there were many who would have liked to get revenge. On a day-to-day basis, he disliked attending functions where he had to cross rooms full of people; these were places where he might be assassinated.

He organized a Great Purge designed to get rid of all actual and suspected political and ideological opponents. Some were imprisoned in the labour camps, some were executed after show trials, some were assassinated. Trotsky and Kirov, the Leningrad party chief, were both assassinated. Stalin is said to have personally signed 40,000 death warrants, but many more than this died. During this reign of terror, there were mass arrests, torture and executions without trial. Anyone suspected by the secret police of opposing the regime was rounded up and killed. The word 'troika' acquired a horrible new meaning – a quick trial by a committee of three – it was a euphemism for summary execution. The scale of the atrocities ordered by Stalin is hard to imagine. There were three major purges, in 1935–38, 1942 and 1945–50. During those purges about a million people were shot and millions more were deported to labour camps.

The big show trials in Moscow were intended as examples for local courts to follow across the rest of the Soviet Union. The big show trials included the Trial of the Sixteen in 1936, the Trial of the Seventeen in 1937, the Trial of the Red Army Generals in 1937 and the Trial of the Twenty-One, which included Stalin's old colleague Bukharin, in 1938. Stalin was never to be known for personal loyalty. He ordered the assassination of Trotsky in 1940, eliminating the last of his opponents from the old Party leadership. Only two men now survived out of Lenin's Politburo, Stalin and Molotov, and Molotov must have felt very lucky to be alive, though not very safe.

In addition to the judicial murders, Stalin uprooted and deported hundreds of thousands of people. During the Second World War, he organized deportations an a massive scale. Over 1.5 million people were sent to Siberia and central Asia. The reasons given were separatist movements, resistance to Soviet rule, and collaboration with the Germans. Underneath this whole programme there seems to have been an unspoken desire for ethnic cleansing. Various ethnic minorities were removed from the Black Sea region: Tatars, Kalmyks, Chechens, Ingush, Karachai, Greeks and Armenians. The conditions under which these deportations took place were appalling. It is estimated that 60% of the 200,000 people deported from the Baltic states died. Half of the Crimean Tatars died of hunger within a year of being deported.

In 1956, three years after Stalin died, Khrushchev condemned Stalin's deportations as contrary to Lenin's principles. He said the Ukrainians escaped deportation by Stalin only because there were too many of them. Not only were the deportations a savage and totally unjustified act, they left a legacy of hatred which lives on. The memory of the deportations still plays a major role in shaping and driving the separatist movements in various parts of the former Soviet Union long after Stalin's death. The Baltic States were among the first to demand independence from a collapsing Soviet Union; Chechnya still hopes for separation.

Famines, deportations, prisons, labour camps, torture and political purges accounted for around 20 million deaths, maybe more. Stalin himself was responsible for these, in many cases directly responsible by issuing direct orders, in other cases indirectly responsible by creating situations in which he knew people would die. It is said that he had to have a medical team in constant attendance at his reception desk, because people who were summoned to an interview were literally in fear of their lives and often had to be sedated either before or after seeing him. It is also said that he had a button under his desk. If Stalin was not getting the answers he wanted, or he had found out enough to be sure of the interviewee's guilt, he just pressed the button and two or three men came and dragged the interviewee away to be shot. The harshness and cruelty of the man are hard to understand, yet the simplest explanation may be the right one – that he was getting his own back for the unjustified violence he himself experienced in childhood.

Stalin got a nasty surprise in June 1941, when Hitler broke the Molotov-Ribbentrop Pact, which divided Eastern Europe into agreed German and Russian spheres of influence. Hitler surprised Stalin by invading the Soviet Union, with the intention of reaching, and helping himself to, the Baku oilfields on the shores of the Caspian Sea. Stalin had not expected this invasion and was not prepared for it. In fact, he was too stunned to react appropriately to the invasion for several days. The Germans advanced quickly, capturing or killing hundreds of thousands of Soviet soldiers. Stalin had very unwisely executed many of his most experienced Red Army generals. Now he needed them. Stalin addressed the Soviet Union for only the second time in his 30-year reign. On this memorable occasion he told the Russian people two very big lies – that the Germans had lost 4.5 million troops and that Soviet victory was near. Neither of these facts was true. Russian losses were staggeringly high and Russia was losing the war. Stalin had executed his generals. Now he started executing his soldiers. Order 227 (27 July, 1942) dictated that any soldier who retreated or left his position without orders would be summarily shot. He also ordered a scorched earth policy. Infrastructure and food supplies were to be destroyed before German troops could make use of them; this inevitably meant that even greater suffering was inflicted on the civilian population. In the end about 25 million Soviet citizens died in the war between Germany and Russia.

This episode was a traumatic experience for Stalin, and shaped his post-war strategy in Europe. Communist-led governments were installed in the East European countries occupied by Soviet troops, forming a Communist Bloc. This was to be a buffer zone, protecting Russia from Germany. It was strengthened in 1955 in the Warsaw Pact. So, the freezing of eastern Europe into a Communist zone was the joint posthumous legacy of two evil dictators, Hitler and Stalin.

The knock-on effects were to be global. Many in the West believed that the Soviet Union's encroachment in Eastern Europe was a sign that the Soviet Union intended to spread Communism round the world. But that was Trotsky's aim – it was never Stalin's. Stalin only ever wanted control over the Soviet Union. The misunderstanding nevertheless led to a Cold War, a long period of distrust and tension.

In the post-war period, Stalin promoted himself as the great war-time leader who had defeated the Germans. He also cultivated the image of the wise and genial elder statesman, and the thousands of gigantic posters showed him as affable, kindly 'Uncle Joe'. Many in the West fell for this image; it was not until after his death that the full horror of the purges and the labour camps became known. In the aftermath of Stalin's death, his successors, Malenkov, Bulganin and Khrushchev, launched a programme of destalinization in an attempt to put the record straight about Stalin's period in office. Meanwhile, behind the genial smiling posters, the repression and the executions continued. In 1953, Stalin was apparently preparing a new purge – this time of Jews – but he died before he could put this scheme into action.

On 1 March, 1953, Stalin had a long dinner in the Kremlin with Beria, Malenkov, Bulganin and Khrushchev: too long a dinner – he collapsed at the end of it. He was apparently having a stroke, though the cause of death is still uncertain. Molotov later claimed that Beria boasted to him that he had poisoned Stalin. Either way, because of the centralization of power in the person of Stalin himself, none of the others felt they could take any action. That at any rate is the story they later told, but it may instead be that they deliberately did nothing for several hours in order to ensure that he died. They were safer with Stalin dead. Everybody was safer with Stalin dead. He died four days later on 5 March, aged 73.

Stalin's body was embalmed and displayed, for a time, alongside Lenin's; Lenin had disliked Stalin intensely and warned his successors to get rid of him. If only they had taken his advice, Eurasia would have been spared one of the worst democides the world has ever seen. Stalin helped to bring down Hitler, but he had a devastatingly damaging effect on Eastern Europe and northern Asia, destroying millions of people and leaving a legacy of social, economic and political damage that will take a century or more to repair. Stalin was one of the key world-changers of the 20th century, and probably its greatest destructive force.

ALBERT EINSTEIN

> *Born in Ulm 1879, died at Princeton, New Jersey 1955.*
> *German–Swiss–American mathematician.*
>
> ACHIEVEMENTS:
> *1905 – Proposed the theory of relativity.*
> *1921 – Awarded Nobel Prize for physics.*
> *1939 – Proposed constructing the atomic bomb.*
> *1945 – Made possible the annihilation of Hiroshima and*
> *Nagasaki.*

ALBERT EINSTEIN WAS born in Ulm in Germany on 14 March, 1879. His father was a German-Jewish industrialist. As a boy, Albert attended school at Aarau in Switzerland and then the Polytechnic School in Zurich. He went on to Zurich University where he studied mathematics and took his PhD. Einstein considered taking up geography, but decided the subject was too difficult; it is interesting to speculate what might have happened, in both geography and physics, if Einstein had followed this alternative path.

While studying for his doctorate, Einstein worked in the Swiss patent office. It was while working in the patent office, in 1905, that Einstein published his first, restricted, theory of relativity.

This was prompted by the difficulties encountered by Michelson and Morley when they tried to measure the absolute value of the Earth's movement through space. Their negative result, which they put down to a property of light, prompted Einstein to put forward the idea that if the speed of light was to be taken as a constant, as measured by all observers, anywhere and moving in any direction, then that would require a modification of Newtonian mechanics. Einstein also proved mathematically that nothing could move faster than the speed of light, that objects must become shorter and shorter as they approach that speed, and that clocks would slow down and stop as they approached the speed of light.

Some of these propositions had been put forward before, but as absurdities. Einstein was putting them forward as actual properties of the universe. At the time, there were no means of testing his theory, and only a few German mathematicians accepted what he was saying.

Ten years later, Einstein put forward his epoch-making general theory of relativity. In this, Einstein added the idea that gravitation might affect measurements through space and time. He also suggested that observations already made might be used to prove this, such as the observed irregularity in the orbit of Mercury, and the slight shift in positions of stars when they were observed close to the sun. The differences in position were very slight, but enough to suggest that gravitation might bend light. Measurements of high-speed electrons were showing changes in mass that agreed with Einstein's formulae.

Because of the real-world evidence Einstein was able to offer, his theory was given much more serious attention from scientists everywhere. One important implication was that the two forms of universal energy readily available for measurement, mass and the energy locked up in matter, were in a sense equivalent. The energy locked up in matter, E, was equal to its mass, m, multiplied by the square of the velocity of radiation, c . This formula, $E = mc^2$, is now one of the most famous equations of all time.

Marie and Pierre Curie had already realized that vast amounts of energy were locked up in matter, but it did not occur to them that that energy was accessible. Einstein was a key reaction in a long intellectual chain reaction that resulted in the releasing and harnessing of nuclear energy. It remained for Rutherford to verify Einstein's formula experimentally; for James Chadwick to discover the neutron; for Enrico Fermi to transmute half the elements in the atomic table; for Otto Hahn and others to recognize that a certain uranium isotope might be split; and for Fermi to design the first nuclear reactor.

From 1916 onwards, Einstein spent much of his own energy on trying to find a 'Theory of Everything'. He searched for an all-inclusive explanation of the energy in all phenomena in one all-embracing unified theory. He finally published this in 1953, but it did not meet with general acceptance. Einstein himself expressed dissatisfaction with it in that he had been unable to find any way of testing it experimentally.

But Einstein was not just the creator or discoverer of relativity. He extended Max Planck's quantum theory and made major contributions in other areas of mathematics and physics. His discovery of the law of photoelectric effect became one of the bases of modern electronics, and for this – not for relativity – he was awarded the Nobel Prize for physics in 1921.

As a young man, Einstein had become a Swiss citizen, but in 1913 he returned to Germany to become Director of the Kaiser Wilhelm Physical Institute. In 1932 he was offered a post at the Institute for Advanced Study at Princeton, New Jersey. He did accept this job offer straight away, but later that year, when it became clear to him that Hitler was about to come to power, Einstein set sail for America. He became an American citizen in 1940, when it was obvious that he would be unable to return to Europe.

On 2 August 1939, Einstein wrote a letter to President Roosevelt about the possibility of constructing a new and extremely powerful weapon, the atomic bomb. Roosevelt was very interested and promptly set up the Manhattan Project to investigate the possibility of developing the atom bomb. Ironically, Einstein was a confirmed pacifist, and had opposed Germany's invasion of Belgium at the beginning of the First World War. He was a great exponent of Zionism, socialism, world government and total disarmament. And yet he knowingly set in motion the research project that culminated in the nuclear bombs that destroyed Hiroshima and Nagasaki, and the entire arsenals of nuclear weapons that gave the Cold War its icy bite.

Einstein died at his home in Princeton on 18 April 1955, a decade into the Cold War.

MARIE STOPES

Born near Dorking 1880, died 1958.
British palaeobotanist, early advocate of birth control.

ACHIEVEMENTS:
Pioneered birth control in Britain.
Pioneered public discussion of sexual matters.
Opened the first birth control clinic in Britain.
1916 – Married Love.
1918 – Wise Parenthood.
1926 – Sex and the Young.

MARIE STOPES WAS born near Dorking in Surrey in 1880. She first studied at University College, London, then took a PhD at Munich. In 1904 she became the first female science lecturer at Manchester University, specializing in fossil plant remains and the palaeobotany of coal seams. From 1907 she lectured in Tokyo and with Professor Sakurai wrote a book on Japanese No plays, which was published in 1913.

In 1916 her first marriage was annulled, and this unhappy experience turned her attention to the general question of marital unhappiness caused by ignorance of sex. Information and education, including sex education, were the answer. Marie Stopes blazed a trail in a difficult area. Traditionally, even in economically and socially advanced countries like Britain, sex was a taboo subject, something that people never talked about. All too often, men and women went into marriage knowing too little to make their partners happy, and too little to control the sizes of their families. The typical Victorian family was huge, and the typical Victorian/Edwardian marriage was unhappy.

Marie Stopes started a crusade to spread information about contraception. Her 1916 book, *Married Love,* caused a sensation and brought her widespread disapproval. The book was banned in the USA.

In 1918, she married the aircraft manufacturer Humphrey Roe, with whose help she opened the very first birth control clinic in Britain, in North London. In all, Marie Stopes wrote 70 books on themes related to birth control, parenting and sexual matters generally.

Marie Stopes's crusade paved the way for more birth control clinics, which are now a routine facility in every town and city. She also established a healthier climate in which sexual issues could be discussed openly and freely, and sexual problems could be resolved.

PABLO PICASSO

Born in Malaga 1881, died 1973.
Spanish painter.

ACHIEVEMENTS:
Dominated early 20th century art.
Invented Cubism.
Broke away from conventional realism.
Freed the visual arts from dependence on perspective.
1898 – Customs of Aragon.
1904 – The Blue Room.
1906 – Gertrude Stein.
1906 – Les Demoiselles d'Avignon.
1937 – Guernica.
1953 – Stalin.

PABLO PICASSO WAS born in Malaga, Andalucia, on 23 October, 1881. His father was an artist and Professor at the Academy of Fine Arts in Barcelona. The young Pablo naturally had his first lessons in art from his father. At the age of 14 he entered the academy at Barcelona. Two years later he transferred to Madrid for advanced training. He quickly became a master of the traditional techniques of painting. His early work shows him as a talented illustrator, though in rather sentimental style, and this sentimentality can still be seen later, for example in his blue period paintings. In 1898 he won a gold medal for his painting *Customs of Aragon*, which was exhibited in his home town.

In 1901, Picasso set up a Paris studio in what is now Place Emile-Goudeau in Montmartre, and though he was a Catalan by birth he made France his home for the rest of his life. Paris was the natural haven for artists at that time. He quickly absorbed the Neo-Impressionist influences of the Paris school, as seen in the work of Toulouse-Lautrec, Degas and Vuillard, painting works such as *The Blue Room* (1904). In his blue period, 1902–4, Picasso painted a series of haunting but depressing interiors. In the pink period that followed, 1904–6, he produced a contrasting series of harlequins and acrobats. Toulouse-Lautrec had painted the bars and the music halls, Degas had painted the ballet, now Picasso was painting the circus.

But Picasso never stayed long in the same waters, and he moved on to explore what African art could teach him. He was fascinated by the simplified, reductive forms of African sculpture in particular. This preoccupation produced the transitional *Two Nudes* (1906), which heralded a major break with traditional styles, and a breakthrough into a series of '20th-century' styles. The landmark work was *Les Demoiselles d'Avignon* of 1906, the first full-blown Cubist painting.

The principle of Cubism was to render three-dimensional objects on canvas without resorting to perspective. Instead of describing objects, the new style allowed the artist to analyze them and present what he regarded as their key features; facets as seen from several different vantage points might be re-assembled in the painting to create an entirely new and perhaps unrecognizable form. It was in its way more like music than the 19th century concept of visual art, though it was still not quite fully abstract. It was certainly a more thoughtful and thought-provoking approach to visual art than people were used to seeing. Many people hated it and ridiculed Picasso for being incapable of drawing 'properly'. This perception, and the rift that it created between serious artists and the general public, was to prove a problem for many decades. Ordinary people were still ridiculing Picasso long after his death.

Georges Braque was at the same time experimenting with strong colours, with a group calling themselves Les Fauves, but from 1909 until 1914 he joined forces with Picasso in exploring the possibilities of Cubism. Picasso and Braque experimented with collage and mixed media techniques, including incorporating bits of wood and wire in the composition.

From 1917, Picasso became associated with Diaghilev's Russian Ballet, designing costumes and sets for *Parade, Pulcinella* and *Le Train Bleu*. For these, he used both Cubist and Neo-Classical styles, which was a clever way of making Cubism more accessible to the public. *Three Dancers* (1925) contains grotesque distortions of the human body, following Cubist principles, and prepared the way for the grotesqueness of what has become Picasso's most famous piece of work, *Guernica*.

Guernica was painted in 1937. It is a huge canvas, on which Picasso expresses his horror at the bombing of a Basque town during the Spanish Civil War, and of the horrors of war in general. It has become a classic art work, with the same status as Leonardo's *Mona Lisa*, Michelangelo's *David* or Constable's *The Hay Wain;* it is recognized as great art. Picasso became director of the Prado Gallery in Madrid in 1936, but during the Second World War, in spite of being stoutly anti-Nazi, he spent most of his time in occupied Paris. He took a risk in staying there during the German occupation; he just carried on as usual, like Archimedes in Syracuse.

After the war he became a communist, but neither the visual nightmare *Guernica* nor his portrait of Stalin painted in 1953 endeared him to the Communist Party. His was not the art of the people, by a long way. But the 1949 Paris Communist World Peace Conference used the dove of peace that he painted as its logo.

Picasso designed more stage sets, illustrated translations of classical texts, tried his hand at sculpture and in later years simply-painted ceramics. He was one of the most fluent, versatile and eclectic painters who ever lived. He was also extremely accessible and uninhibited. Unlike most artists, he was ready to let film-makers come into his studio and film him at work. He made it difficult for Picasso-enthusiasts to keep up with him, as he was always innovating. In a very real sense, his artistic career reflected the turmoil and swiftness of change that characterized every aspect of life in the 20th century – that speeding-up process that was initiated by Trevithick, Brunel, Dunlop, Benz, Daimler, Marconi and Edison.

Everything Picasso did was widely imitated and copied by his thousands of followers and admirers, assimilated into other arts and every aspect of design, including the architecture of Frank Lloyd Wright and Le Corbusier. It is easy to see the influence of Picasso's Cubist paintings in the mid-20th century sculptures of Henry Moore and Barbara Hepworth. Picasso was the paramount influence on 20th century art.

JAMES JOYCE

Born in Dublin 1882, died 1941.

ACHIEVEMENTS:
*Elaborated the interior monologue in the light of modern
    psychology.*
Invented the stream-of-consciousness novel.
Provoked debate on what a 20th-century novel could attempt.
1914 – Dubliners.
1918 – Exiles.
1922 – Ulysses.
1939 – Finnegan's Wake
1944 – Stephen Hero.

JAMES AUGUSTINE ALOYSIUS Joyce was born at Rathgar in Dublin on 2 February 1882. His father was John Joyce, a wit from Cork, and his mother was Mary Murray. Joyce spent relatively little of his life in Dublin, yet it remained the setting for most of his writing. He was educated by Jesuits at Clongowes Wood and Belvedere Colleges, and then went to University College, Dublin.

Joyce was a voracious reader as well as a linguist. He corresponded with the playwright Ibsen, who was one influence on Joyce's work. Other influences included Dante, George Moore and Yeats. Joyce started off as a devout Catholic, but became disturbed by the bigotry of the Catholics who surrounded him in Dublin, and consequently became increasingly anti-Catholic. He felt he needed to escape, and went to Paris for a year in 1902. There, free but in poverty, he wrote poetry. He might have stayed there, but his mother's death drew him back to Ireland, where he stayed for a time in the Martello Tower that is featured in the early part of Ulysses.

He then left Ireland permanently, in 1904, taking with him Nora Barnacle, who was to be his partner for the rest of his life. Even though he had abandoned Ireland as his home, he still inhabited it in his imagination. His idea was to work out his destiny as a writer without interference from family, country or religion. He would wander Europe, scratching a living in any way he could. He would be the classic artist in exile. He taught English in Trieste for a while, but found that this did not give him enough to live on.

Joyce's frame of reference was unusually broad. Literature was very important to him, naturally, but he was also a modern languages specialist. He was a gifted tenor and through his singing he acquired an encyclopaedic knowledge of music. For a time he studied medicine. He considered founding an Irish daily newspaper. He opened a cinema in Dublin. In Zurich he involved himself in the theatre. It was an extraordinary range of serious interests, and it helps to explain the virtuosic handling of knowledge, language and style in his writing.

During the First World War, Joyce and Barnacle spent most of their time in Switzerland. After the war they settled in Paris. By this stage, Joyce had completed two books, *Chamber Music* and *Dubliners*, a collection of short stories. The publication of *Dubliners* was delayed until 1914, because Joyce's text was too candid for the publishers. Joyce said of the fifteen stories:

> *My intention was to write a chapter of the moral history of my country and I chose Dublin for the scene because that city seemed to me the centre of paralysis. I have tried to present it to the indifferent public under four of its aspects; childhood, adolescence, maturity and public life. I have written it for the most part in a style of scrupulous meanness.*

In spite of this author's anti-blurb the stories were very well received, and Joyce was from then on championed by the poet Ezra Pound. *A Portrait of the Artist as a Young Man* came out in instalments in *The Egoist* during the war years. It represents the first work of Joyce's in stream-of-consciousness style.

Yeats and Pound together petitioned the Royal Literary Fund for a grant on his behalf, which came through in 1915. The Civil List followed suit. Joyce was in severe difficulties now. His health was breaking up, his eyesight was deteriorating and he was profoundly disturbed by his daughter's mental illness. There was no public interest in his writing, yet Joyce had unbounded confidence that what he was doing was leading somewhere, that it would be seen as worthwhile in time.

In 1918, Joyce wrote *Exiles*, a play that owed much to Ibsen. The following year he had the opportunity to be analyzed by Jung. Jung was very keen to analyze Joyce, but Joyce declined. One of Joyce's weird utterances may throw light; 'We grisly old Sykos who have done our unsmiling bit on alices when they were easily freudened . . . the law of the jungerl.' In fact Jung thought that Joyce was a charlatan, and maybe Joyce sensed that he would be found out. Jung persuaded Edith McCormick to stop giving Joyce money. In spite of the resulting friction, Joyce did eventually approach Jung, not for himself but to treat his schizophrenic daughter. It was in 1934, and Joyce was angry when Jung wrote off his daughter as incurable.

James Joyce's landmark year was 1922. It was in 1922, on 2 February, that *Ulysses* was published in Paris. It was an extremely innovative book, written in an entirely new style, and it provoked very strong reactions. It describes, at enormous length and in enormous detail, a day in the lives of Stephen Dedalus, Leopold Bloom and his wife Molly – in Dublin. Joyce uses the device of extended interior monologues by each of the main characters. The technique was borrowed from Edouard Dujardin's *Les Lauriers sont Coupes*, published in 1887, but developed considerably in the light of intervening developments in psychology. Dujardin plus Freud plus Jung. *Ulysses* is now seen as an epoch-making book, a great leap forward for fiction, or at any rate a great leap outward. *Ulysses* was not published in Britain until 1936. Another book, Stephen Hero, was not published until 1944, after Joyce's death.

Joyce's eyesight worsened – he suffered from glaucoma – but he pressed ahead with another mammoth book, *Finnegan's Wake*, which was published in 1939. The book reflects Joyce's incredible breadth of reading in its thousands of side references and word-plays, many of them very obscure indeed. Joyce became a major literary cult figure who had an ever-widening influence on his contemporaries. The internal monologue device seemed particularly apt for reflecting the fragmentation of the modern mind, the atomization of thoughts and sense impressions. It was a technique akin to the invention of Cubism by Picasso and twelve-note music by Schoenberg, and it was probably no coincidence that the three phenomena erupted at about the same time. *Finnegan's Wake* bewildered even its supporters with its complexity and its barrages of references – but even a partial understanding of what Joyce was up to made a deep impression. Joyce's opponents were hostile to the experiment, just as Picasso's and Schoenberg's critics were hostile, and the three great creative forces were jointly responsible for alienating many ordinary people from high art; they were in a very real sense responsible for provoking 20th-century philistinism. Joyce's style is challenging, but much of the writing is incredibly funny, in places its outlandish Irish humour anticipating Monty Python. T. S Eliot said that Joyce was the greatest master of the English language since John Milton. Certainly James Joyce's work represented a huge breakthrough in the scope and sheer ambition of the novel – in any language.

D. H. LAWRENCE

Born at Eastwood 1885, died at Vence 1930.

ACHIEVEMENTS:
Included explicit sex scenes in novels.
Explored the psychology of sex in novels.
1911 – The White Peacock.
1912 – The Trespasser.
1913 – Sons and Lovers.
1916 – Twilight in Italy.
1920 – The Lost Girl.
1921 – Women in Love.
1922 – Aaron's Rod.
1923 – Kangaroo.
1926 – The Plumed Serpent.
1928 – Lady Chatterley's Lover.
1928 – Collected Poems.

DAVID HERBERT LAWRENCE was born at Eastwood in Nottinghamshire on 11 September, 1885, the son of a miner. He went to Nottingham High School and then University College, Nottingham. His scholarly and literary side was nurtured by his mother, and it was through her that he became a schoolteacher and writer. Edward Garnett and Ford Madox Ford noticed and praised his work, which encouraged him.

In 1911, after the success of his first novel, *The White Peacock*, Lawrence decided to try to make his living by writing. It was already obvious to some critics that a young writer of great force and originality had arrived. The following year he eloped with Frieda von Richthofen, who was a cousin of the German flying ace Baron von Richthofen; she was, more to the point, the wife of Ernest Weekley, a professor at Nottingham University. The runaways toured Germany, Austria and Italy for a year and then, after Frieda's divorce, married in 1914. By this time, Lawrence had made quite a reputation for himself with his second novel, *Sons and Lovers*. The couple returned to England just as the First World War broke out. They lived in a cottage in Cornwall, surrounded by suspicion. The German woman was regarded with fear and hatred.

In 1915, Lawrence published *The Rainbow*, and was surprised and alarmed to find himself the target of a prosecution for obscenity. This brush with the law stopped Lawrence in his creative tracks for a while. When the war ended, he left England for Italy, where he wrote some travel impressions, *Twilight in Italy*, and another novel which adventurously explored sex and marriage, *Women in Love*.

Then he went to Mexico, settling there until the worsening of his tuberculosis drove him to return to Europe. His novel *Lady Chatterley's Lover*, covering the same controversial territory as before, was published privately in Florence in 1928. Once again he was prosecuted for obscenity. Lawrence was by all accounts a very bad painter, but in the maelstrom that was modern art in the first two decades of the 20th century it was difficult for many to tell the difference between good art and bad. Lawrence mounted an exhibition of his sexually explicit paintings in London in 1929, and was apparently surprised to be accused once again of obscenity. *Lady Chatterley's Lover* was not published in Britain until after a landmark obscenity trial in 1961. He died of tuberculosis at Vence near Nice on 2 March, 1930.

Few doubt that the paintings are bad, and only hold any interest because it was Lawrence who painted them, but readers and literary critics are still divided about the worth of Lawrence's novels. Some of his writing, especially the descriptive passages, are wonderful. But he lacked a sense of humour and the sense of proportion that normally goes with humour; as a result he seems to have been unaware that some of the narrative and some of the dialogue is absurd – there are episodes that are unintentionally comical. The poetry generally escapes this major flaw, containing beautiful observation of natural scenery. His collected poems were published in 1928. The novels nevertheless have a certain raw strength that derives from well-observed background, and from autobiographical strands.

Lawrence finds his way into this book because of his profound influence on other writers of his own and the following generation. It was Lawrence who opened the marital bedroom door and made it permissible for novelists to explore what happened behind it. He also challenged other writers to deal more honestly and less sentimentally about sexual feelings and emotions, about the emotional differences between men and women, about the sexual problems that result from those differences, about the emotional strains that exist between the generations within families. Above all Lawrence expressed and analyzed sex as a motive force for human action. Lawrence's novels were a natural outcome of Freud's revelations. The lid was off sexuality.

Lawrence was above all challenging and controversial. Some hated what he was doing, some idolized him for it. He was one of the most powerful and distinctive modern English novelists.

LE CORBUSIER

Born at La Chaux-de-Fonds 1887, died 1965.
Swiss-born French architect.

ACHIEVEMENTS:
Pioneered clean-lined modern architecture.
Invented the piloti.
Pioneered the use of tubular steel for furniture.
Pioneered the designing of towns as integrated wholes.
1923 – Vers une Architecture.
1925 – Pavillon de l'Esprit Nouveau, Paris.
1945 – Unite d'habitation, Marseilles.
1948 – Le Modulor.
1950 – United Nations Building, New York.
1955 – Le Modulor 2.

CHARLES EDOUARD JEANNERET was born at La Chaux-de-Fonds near
Neuchatel in 1887. He designed his first house at the early age of 17, then
studied for a short time in Paris with the architect Auguste Perret, who was
a pioneer in the use of reinforced concrete for building construction. After
that, in 1910, he went to work with Peter Behrens in Germany. In 1916,
Jeanneret settled in Paris, where for some years he worked at industrial
research and as a painter; some of his architecture shows the influence of
the Cubist style invented by Picasso.

In 1919 he published, jointly with Amedee Ozenfant, the Purist manifesto. Charles Jeanneret, who adopted the pseudonym of Le Corbusier,
started to work on a new theory of architecture. In this he tried to establish
the relationships between machine forms and the techniques and shapes of

modern architecture. He affirmed engineer-building as the only approach appropriate, spiritually and economically, to the 20th century. 'Style is a lie.' 'The house is a habitable machine.' He had become not just a great practitioner of architecture, but a great doctrinaire theorist too. He held up the exact engineering fitness of the steamship's shape to its function as a perfect model for the land architect. The simple lines and shapes that came with reinforced concrete perfectly expressed a building's function. His buildings would always look stripped, minimalist, windswept and rather bleak. It is a style that lends itself to the strong lights and sharply defined shadows of the Mediterranean, and it looks far less pleasant in the greyer lights of northern Europe. It is low-latitude architecture.

In 1923, he published his book *Vers une Architecture,* where he outlined his architectural theories. This book and two others produced later, *Le Modulor* in 1948 and *Le Modulor 2* in 1955, had a worldwide impact on both building design and city design in the 20th century. The Modulor was a system using units of standard size, the proportions of which depend on the proportions of the human figure. He was concentrating on the means of building construction, which needed to be on an industrial scale, hence the use of mass-produced modules. Even window frames and built-in furniture were to be mass-produced.

The first building Le Corbusier designed using his Modulor system was the Unite d'habitation in Marseilles, a huge housing unit designed as a self-contained community in 1945–50. This complex was conceived as a cluster of tall buildings. When the overall scheme, the Radial City, was built the cluster of tall blocks would form a pattern sticking up from a carpet of low-rise buildings and open spaces. That was the vision.

This arrangement was Le Corbusier's favourite town-planning concept. He used it again in his design for Chandigarh, the new capital city of the Punjab.

One of Le Corbusier's best-known buildings is the Pavillon de l'Esprit Nouveau, designed for the Paris Exhibition of 1925. He was also a member of the ten-man team responsible for designing the United Nations Building in New York in 1950.

Le Corbusier liked to give his buildings flat roofs. This was partly to give them a clean, cubic (Cubist?) appearance, and partly to enable him to install a roof garden – a feature he particularly loved. Thick concrete flags laid on sand, with open, grass-sown joints, insulate the house beneath and reduce the reaction of the concrete structure to varying weather conditions.

Another distinctive feature of Le Corbusier's buildings is his use of pilotis, reinforced concrete stilts or pillars raising the building up from the ground so that people or vehicles can pass underneath. Le Corbusier invented the *piloti* and used it first in his design for the Cité Universitaire in Paris. Now, of course, we see them everywhere; Le Corbusier has legions of imitators. He believed in designing not just buildings, but entire cities for them to stand in. He similarly believed in designing furniture that would harmonize with the new designs for buildings. In the 1920s, he designed furniture – chairs especially – in collaboration with Charlotte Perriand. He used tubular metal in their construction, which was another major innovation.

Many of the features of modern furniture, modern buildings and modern cities that we take for granted were originally devised by Le Corbusier. And he has had thousands of imitators, including the mediocre British architect Basil Spence. The negative side of Le Corbusier's legacy was his idea of the 'city in the sky', which hovered in the minds of many post-war European architects when they designed housing to replace the buildings destroyed in the Second World War. High-rise apartment blocks were seen as the way forward. Built too cheaply and shoddily in the 1950s and 1960s, they became a nightmare for those who had to live in them. They were not designed by Le Corbusier, but by those who had been seduced by his vision of the cities of the future.

IRVING BERLIN

Born at Temun 1888, died in New York 1989.
Siberian-born American song-writer.

ACHIEVEMENTS:
Pioneered ragtime music.
Pioneered jazz.
Set the standard for popular song in the first half
of the 20th century.

IRVING BERLIN, WHOSE real name was Israel Baline, was born in the village of Temun in Siberia on 11 May 1888. In 1893, at the age of four, he was taken to America when the family emigrated. As so often happened with migrants with foreign names, he adopted a name that would be easier for other Americans to spell and pronounce – Irving Berlin.

He left home at the age of 14 to earn his living. He worked for a time as a singing waiter in various Chinatown and Bowery beerhalls and cabarets in New York. While he was doing this work, he began writing song lyrics and composing melodies to go with them. He was soon introducing some of his own songs, such as *Alexander's Ragtime Band* and *Everybody's Doin' It*, both written in 1911. These won him instant and international recognition as a songwriter and pioneer of ragtime music. The evolution of ragtime into jazz owes a lot to Berlin's own innovations, introducing more complex rhythms and more intricate and inventive melodic lines in songs like *Everybody Step* and *Pack Up Your Sins*, written in 1921 and 1922.

The increasing popularity of his songs enabled him to open his own music publishing business in 1919. Berlin mounted a 'soldier show' in 1918 and this led on naturally to musical comedy and films in the 1920s and 1930s.

He was very soon writing music that seemed to have a truly universal appeal. He left ragtime and jazz behind, found an idiom that belonged to Western mid-culture and occupied the centre of the world's sound stage. His songs were emotionally direct yet musically sophisticated; he had a particular gift for writing a middle section that was a genuine development section, and therefore musically satisfying. The harmonies too were often rich and adventurous. He was writing songs such as *Always, All Alone, Remember* and *What'll I Do?* By the 1940s, Irving Berlin as at the peak of his career. He wrote the music for the hit musical *Annie Get Your Gun* in 1946 and *Call Me Madam* in 1950. He wrote *Anything You Can Do, There's No Business Like Show Business, Doin' What Comes Naturally, We're a Couple of Swells* and *White Christmas*. In 1939 he wrote *God Bless America*, which became an unofficial second national anthem.

In 1954, Irving Berlin was awarded a special citation from the President of the USA as a composer of patriotic songs.

Irving Berlin retired from show business in 1962 at the age of 74. After that he led a reclusive life in Manhattan, dying there in 1989 aged over 100. His versatility and fluency were remarkable. Most song composers depend on a lyricist to write their words for them. Irving Berlin was unusual in being able to write words as well as music – a very rare accomplishment. In a long and successful career, he wrote the words and music for over 900 songs. He seemed able to produce an endless stream of likeable and instantly memorable songs – songs that are sung all round the world and have remained at the centre of mainstream modern culture. Irving Berlin not only wrote many of the hit songs of the first half of the 20th century, but set the standard for popular song in the West for the rest of the century.

LUDWIG WITTGENSTEIN

Born in Vienna 1889, died in Cambridge 1951.
Austrian-born British philosopher.

ACHIEVEMENTS:
Had a profound effect on 20th century philosophy.
Took two conflicting complementary approaches to language.
1922 – Tractatus Logico-Philosophicus.
1953 – Philosophical Investigations.

LUDWIG WITTGENSTEIN WAS born in Vienna in 1889. His family was wealthy, the money coming from industry, yet also cultivated. He was educated at home until he was 14, before spending three years in an Austrian school. He studied mechanical engineering at Berlin (1906–08) and Manchester (1908–11). He did some research on aeronautics and designed a reaction jet propeller. His work led him deeper into mathematics, and then on to the foundations of mathematics.

In 1911, Wittgenstein gave up his engineering research to study mathematical logic at Cambridge under Bertrand Russell. Russell was profoundly impressed by the intensity with which Wittgenstein studied and commented, 'he soon knew all that I had to teach'.

In the First World War, Wittgenstein fought in the Austrian army as an artillery officer, and was taken prisoner on the Italian front in 1918. He did not allow the war to interrupt his mathematical thought process, carrying his notebooks with him in his rucksack. While a prisoner of war at Monte Cassino he completed his first work, which turned out to be the only one published during his lifetime. The book was published in 1922 as *Tractatus Logico-Philosophicus,* with a preface by Russell. It was presented in a highly original way, as a series of numbered and portentous remarks about the nature and limits of language. He argued that meaningful language consisted of propositions that are pictures of facts. A lot of human discourse must therefore be discarded as meaningless because, for example, it contains value judgements. The limits of language are the limits of thought. 'Whereof one cannot speak, thereof one must be silent.'

Wittgenstein turned away from philosophy to look for another vocation, working as a junior school teacher in rural Austria from 1920–26, then as a gardener's assistant in a monastery and as an amateur architect for one of his sisters.

Meanwhile, the effects of *Tractatus* were rippling through the world of philosophy, and various philosophers inspired by it tracked him down, especially the logical positivists of the Vienna Circle. This revived his interest in philosophy and in 1929 he went back to Cambridge as a research fellow at Trinity College, and later as Professor of Philosophy (1939–47). During the war he characteristically did war service as a hospital porter.

At Cambridge his philosophy began to take a new direction. He attracted a group of committed disciples and through them he came to exert an enormous influence on the post-war generation. Wittgenstein's second-period ideas are summarized in his *Philosophical Investigations,* published in 1953, after his death. This puzzling work rejects much of what he wrote in *Tractatus.* He had become more lenient in his treatment of language, now pointing to the variety and open-endedness of everyday language. He explored the communicative and social functions of different modes of speech. He moved away from logic, now seeing language as a toolkit.

Wittgenstein died of cancer in Cambridge in 1951, but in the years after his death there was a steady stream of posthumously edited publications based on his many notebooks. Wittgenstein had a profound effect on philosophy because of his two contradictory, and therefore complementary, approaches to language. He drew attention to the fundamental importance of language in constructing, analyzing and evaluating thought. In *Tractatus* he wrote, 'The limits of my language mean the limits of my world.'

ADOLF HITLER

Born at Braunau 1889, died in Berlin 1945.
German dictator.

ACHIEVEMENTS:
Caused the Second World War.
Lost the Second World War.
Caused 50 million deaths.
Prompted the Allied deal with Stalin, which led to the partition
of Europe.
Indirectly brought about the European Union.

ADOLF HITLER WAS born in the Austrian town of Braunau, close to the Bavarian border, on 20 April, 1889. His father, Alois Hitler, was a lower-middle class customs official, a hard disciplinarian, and the young Adolf had little affection for him. There was a great deal of tension between Adolf and his father. Adolf thought his father boorish and unkind to his mother, to whom he was very protective. Adolf had to help his father home after late-night drinking bouts, then hear him abusing his mother. Alois in his turn had no time for his son's high-flown ambitions. He had after all failed twice to get into the high school at Linz.

In 1903, when Adolf was 14 his father died and the family moved to Linz. He decided to become an artist. In 1907, when he was 18, he went to Vienna on a generous allowance from his mother. He approached the Vienna Academy of Art, but was rejected when a sample of his artwork was viewed. He was turned away by the Academy of Architecture, who told him he had not pursued his school studies at Linz to a high enough level. He was thwarted in the great ambition of his life.

His mother's death from cancer in 1908 left him with an inheritance, which included the proceeds of the sale of her house in Linz. Hitler also claimed part of his mother's pension on the grounds that he was a full-time student, which he certainly was not. The lies, the deception, the myth-making had begun. What Hitler was actually doing was sitting about in cafés, joining in heated arguments about philosophy and politics, going to the opera, writing a play, painting pictures of street scenes and grand buildings. He earned a little money as an illustrator.

At this stage, Hitler had no close friends, and it may be that the peculiarly unsatisfactory relationship he had with his parents played a part in this. What he did acquire, though, was a relentless hatred of Jews. Anti-semitism was widespread at all levels of society in Germany and Austria, especially in the Catholic south German culture, but with Hitler it was to reach an alarmingly destructive pitch. He was, after all, to become directly responsible for the deaths of millions of Jews. The Jews were a common scapegoat at the time, as large numbers of them were driven west out of Russia and the rest of eastern Europe by persecutions there. It was easy, for Hitler and for others like him, to blame these poor dispossessed people for taking jobs from more deserving local people. Migrants have always had to bear this Cross. It was at this time, too, that the ranting tirades started, possibly born out of his frustration at being unable to pursue his chosen career.

In 1912, Hitler's legacy ran out. He had to work on a building site during the day and sleep in a doss-house at night. He made the decision to move in 1913 to Munich. He alleged it was because he wanted to live in the Fatherland; in fact it was to avoid conscription by the Austrian Imperial Army. Hitler was a draft-dodger. The Munich police caught him, returned him to the Austrian authorities. Hitler pleaded to be excused military service, but he was in any case rejected as unfit.

Oddly, when war broke out in 1914, Hitler saw (as Churchill had already seen) that the way forward might be to become a war hero and he succeeded in joining a Bavarian infantry regiment. He was sent to the front and given a dangerous job as a company runner. This exposed him continually to cross-fire in no-man's land. He showed surprising courage and acquired a reputation as a man immune to bullets. He was awarded the Iron Cross, first class.

Hitler avoided bullets, but not mustard gas. While he was recovering in hospital, news of Germany's surrender came through. Like most of the rest of Germany, Hitler could not believe it. In military terms, Germany seemed to be winning the war. Hitler blamed the surrender on a Jewish-Communist conspiracy. Certified disabled through gassing, Hitler returned to Munich, where he became the fifth member of the new German Workers Party. He threw himself into the task of recruiting for this new cause, and changed the name of the party to the National Socialist German Workers Party. Hitler discovered a hitherto unknown gift for oratory, though often it was a rant against Jews, Communists or Slavs, and a gift for inspiring personal loyalty. It was a remarkable transformation that had taken place, and some have explained it in terms of the psychiatric support he was given to help him overcome the profound depression he felt when in hospital – excessive psychiatric support that gave him excessive self-confidence.

Hitler emerged from the First World a German patriot, even though he was not actually a German, and he continued to believe that Germany had not really been defeated. Early followers included Rudolf Hess, Hermann Goering, Ernst Röhm and Field-Marshal Erich Lödendorff. Hitler used Lödendorff as a front in an absurd attempt to seize power on 8 November 1923. In this 'Beer Hall Putsch', the Nazis marched from a beer hall to the Bavarian War Ministry, with the intention of overthrowing the Bavarian government, and then marching on Berlin. They were quickly dispersed by soldiers and Hitler was arrested and tried for treason.

In April 1924 he was sentenced to five years in prison, where he dictated *Mein Kampf* to the loyal Hess. This rambling autobiography contains Hitler's views on race, history and Jews, and includes threats against his enemies if he should win power. It was published in two volumes (1925 and 1926). No-one took much notice, of course, at the time. Considered a harmless crank, Hitler was released early.

Hitler was able to build on a sense of injured national pride, caused by the Treaty of Versailles imposed on Germany. Huge reparations were exacted from Germany to pay for the war. Most Germans bitterly resented having to pay, particularly since they did not consider that they had lost. The second turning point in Hitler's career came when the Depression hit

Germany in 1930. The traditional parties were unable to deal with the unprecedented shock of the Depression, and in the September 1930 elections the Nazis won 107 seats in the Reichstag, becoming the second largest party. In the July 1932 elections they won 230 seats, making them the largest party. Behind the scenes, conspirators persuaded Hindenburg to appoint Hitler Chancellor.

Using the pretext of the Reichstag fire, which may have been started by Nazis themselves, Hitler issued a Decree suppressing civil rights in the interests of national security. The Communist leaders and other opponents of Hitler's regime found themselves in prison.

In the space of a few months, Hitler had achieved authoritarian control over Germany by more or less legal means and without suspending the Weimar constitution. But democracy in Germany was over and the escalation of evil had begun. With Goebbels as his propaganda chief, Hitler was able to persuade most Germans that he was their saviour. Those who were not persuaded were rounded up by the SA, the SS and the Gestapo, the Secret State Police. Thousands were to disappear into concentration camps. Thousands more, including half of Germany's Jewish population, emigrated in order to escape the Holocaust that was clearly coming. Those Jews who had not emigrated soon regretted their decision to stay. Under Hitler's 1935 Nuremberg Laws, they lost their status as citizens and were thrown out of all government employment, the professions and many other jobs too. From 1941 Jews were subjected to the further humiliation of wearing a yellow star in public places. Hitler was the evil behind this, but the Christian Churches, riddled as they were with anti-semitism, stayed silent.

Hitler's foreign policy was to prove astonishingly aggressive. He violated the Versailles Treaty in 1936 by re-occupying the demilitarized Rhineland. Britain and France did nothing. Emboldened by the lack of response, Hitler sent troops to assist Franco in Spain. It was the Luftwaffe that destroyed the town of Guernica in 1937. In 1938, Austria was annexed to Germany (the Anschluss), and Hitler entered Vienna in a triumph that must have had a keen personal edge to it. Vienna after all was the scene of several early humiliations. Hitler's army invaded Czechoslovakia in 1939. At last Britain and France decided to call a halt, but were unable to reach an agreement with Russia to stop Hitler. Hitler managed to outflank them by concluding his own agreement with Stalin, the Molotov-Ribbentrop Pact. After the long period of inaction, Hitler was startled and surprised when Britain and France declared war on him for invading Poland. He had miscalculated.

Even so, Hitler had a run of military successes, invading Denmark, Norway, Holland, Belgium, Luxembourg and France, closely followed by Yugoslavia and Greece. The only major setback was his failure to invade Britain. The Battle of Britain failed because he was unable to use his blitzkrieg technique, which involved sending tanks in as well as planes; Britain was saved from the tanks by the Channel.

The power-crazed land-grabbing went on successfully until Hitler opened up a second front, in the east. The invasion of the Soviet Union (1941–42), was Hitler's undoing. He was trying to reach the oilfields on the Caspian Sea, but his army was heavily defeated at the Battle of Stalingrad – the first and most decisive major defeat. Then the British army, led by Montgomery, defeated the German army in North Africa at the Battle of El Alamein, which prevented Hitler from reaching the Suez Canal and the oilfields of the Middle East.

A second motive for invading the Soviet Union was to reach the second largest Jewish population in Europe, after Poland. His mad intention was to clear eastern Europe of Jews and Slavs, to make room for German settlers. The murder of Jews was going on during and in the wake of each invasion; probably two million Jews were killed as the Germans swept through the newly occupied territories. Then there was the question of disposing of the millions of Jews in Poland. In 1941 Hitler decided on mass murder as the solution, and he must have explicitly ordered Himmler to initiate the Holocaust. The infamous Wannsee Conference held near Berlin in January 1942 was a discussion of the Final Solution, a formal procedure for the Holocaust. Huge numbers of Jews were to die as were large numbers of other minority groups, including homosexuals, Gypsies, socialists, communists and others regarded by Hitler as his enemies. The Wannsee Conference was led by Heydrich and Eichmann, but there can be no doubt that they were working under Hitler's direct orders.

Hitler was unnerved by his defeat at Stalingrad. After that his military decisions became more erratic. Those close to Hitler knew that he was in serious need of psychiatric help. They approached Jung, asking him to come to Berlin to analyze Hitler. Jung was so full of hatred and contempt for Hitler that he refused, but he must later have regretted missing this extraordinary opportunity. The British considered a plan to assassinate Hitler, but by this stage in the war, he was making such poor decisions that it was better to leave him in charge – the war would be over sooner – and the assassination plan was dropped. The entry of the Americans into the war in 1941 was another major turning-point; now that the British Empire, the Soviet Union and the United States were gathered into a huge coalition against Hitler many German officers could see that Germany must be defeated. This led some courageous officers to try to remove Hitler and bring the war to a quick end. The July 20th Plot of von Stauffenberg almost succeeded in killing Hitler, but not quite; he survived. Hitler responded with characteristic savagery and resistance was stamped out. Mussolini was deposed in 1943, and the Soviet army gradually pushed in from the east.

On 6 June, 1944 (D-Day) Allied armies landed in France; within six months they reached the Rhine. Hitler launched a final offensive in the Ardennes, but the Allies were now unstoppable. Early in 1945 they crossed the Rhine and marched towards Berlin.

At the same time Russia troops were advancing on Berlin from the east, arriving on the outskirts of the city in April. Hitler's advisers wanted him to escape and make a last stand at the Eagle's Nest in Bavaria, but he was set on dying in Berlin. He married Eva Braun, shot her, then shot himself. In his will he ordered that his body should be taken outside and burned, and that Admiral Doenitz should be the new Fuhrer, Goebbels the new Chancellor. Hitler's plans came to nothing. Doenitz was Fuhrer for a week, and Goebbels glumly bore the burden of the Chancellorship for only a day before killing his entire family and then killing himself. In early May, 1945 Germany surrendered.

The Second World War had only been started because of Adolf Hitler's megalomania. It was only drawn out for a final unnecessary year because he had lost touch with reality. The cost in human misery and human life was incalculable. The Second World War was in large part due to the actions of this one man, and that war is estimated to have cost 50 million lives. The only comparable blood-letting in the past century has been Mao Zedong's regime in China, which cost 48 million lives.

There were other consequeneces to Hitler's career. In order to defeat Hitler, the American and British leaders had to buy Stalin's support. The direct result of that bargaining was the partition of Berlin, the partition of Germany, and indeed the partition of Europe. The map of Europe during the Cold War was the legacy of Hitler. The determination of France and Germany not to let a European war break out again fuelled the political drive to create a European Union, which haunts us still. The influence of Adolf Hitler on European history has proved to be very far-reaching.

CHARLIE CHAPLIN

Born in London 1889, died 1977.
Silent film comedian, cinema actor and director.

ACHIEVEMENTS:
Pioneered silent film comedy.
Created the irrepressible underdog persona.
1915 – The Champion.
1920 – The Kid.
1925 – The Gold Rush.
1926 – The Circus.
1940 – The Great Dictator.
1957 – A King in New York.

CHARLIE CHAPLIN (CHARLES Spencer Chaplin) was born on 16 April at Kennington in London. His parents were in show business as music hall performers. At an early age, Charlie performed on stage with his father and brother Sydney. His father died when Charlie was still a child, leaving the family poor. The hard times he experienced as a boy were often mirrored in the early films he made, where the impoverished and threadbare little tramp battled optimistically on against adversity in scenes that are often poignant as well as funny. Chaplin's down-at-heel tramp was not just poor, he was also fastidious and genteel, and therein lay the poignancy. He was a self-improving underdog with whom many people in the great underclass in the West could identify.

By the age of eight, Charlie Chaplin was already a seasoned stage performer. He spent some time in the legitimate theatre before returning to vaudeville. His skill as a comedian developed under the guidance of Fred

Karno. As a member of Fred Karno's vaudeville company, Chaplin went to America in 1910. He was to be the leading comedian in Karno's production *A Night in an English Music Hall.*

It was while performing in this production that Chaplin was noticed by Joseph M. Schenck, and on his recommendation Chaplin was taken on by Mack Sennett to make films with the Keystone Comedy Company in Hollywood.

It was an incredible success story. Within a very short time, Charlie Chaplin had gone from being a music hall turn to playing the lead in an American production, to acting in film – an experimental medium then still in its infancy. Chaplin went into the motion picture business, making 35 films in his first year alone. It was in these early films that he adopted the bowler hat, baggy trousers, out-turned feet, moustache and walking-cane that became his trademark image. He was immediately identifiable in this clowning down-at-heel persona in one film after another.

In 1918, Chaplin formed his own company, and produced the series of films that put him and his little tramp into the front rank of American artists. Chaplin made *A Dog's Life* and *Shoulder Arms* in 1918, *The Kid* and *The Idle Class* in 1920, *The Gold Rush* in 1925 and *The Circus* in 1926. In all of these films, Chaplin's little tramp was the central figure.

Chaplin's style was eminently suited to the silent film. He realized this, and when sound arrived he experimented with music, in *City Lights* (1931), and scripts that were partly spoken, partly mimed, in *Modern Times* (1936).

He entered the orthodox sound world of the talkies in *The Great Dictator* (1940), in which he carried off a brilliant lampoon of Adolf Hitler as a thinly disguised 'Kid'. It was a major contribution to the Allied war effort.

In 1952, Chaplin acted, directed and composed the music for *Limelight*. Chaplin's strong left-wing sympathies inevitably got him into trouble with the rabid anti-Communist factions in Cold War America. This trouble caused him to emigrate to Switzerland. He got his own back in a biting satire on the American way of life in *A King in New York* (1957). Chaplin was belatedly knighted in 1975.

Chaplin was the greatest pioneer of silent film comedy, and perhaps the first great international comedian. His little tramp persona, with the bowler hat and cane, was iconic, one of the enduring comic creations of the 20th century.

JOMO KENYATTA

Born at Mitumi 1889, died 1978.
Kenyan politician.

ACHIEVEMENTS:
Organized Mau Mau terrorist attacks on the British.
Campaigned for and achieved the independence of Kenya.
First President of the Republic of Kenya.

JOMO KENYATTA WAS born at Mitumi in Kenya. Orphaned when very young, Kenyatta was educated at a Scots mission school before beginning work as a herdboy. In 1922 he joined the Kikuyu Central Association and became its president.

Kenyatta visited Britain in 1929 and stayed in Britain from 1931–44, during which time he studied for one year at London University under Malinowski. It was Malinowski who wrote the preface to Kenyatta's 1938 book, Facing Mount Kenya.

Kenyatta visited Russia three times and became president of the Pan African Federation, with Kwame Nkrumah (later President of Ghana) as his Secretary. During the Second World War Kenyatta was in Britain, working on the land and in 1942 he married an Englishwoman.

When the Second World War ended, Kenyatta returned to Kenya, where his Kenya African Union advocated extreme nationalism. It was Jomo Kenyatta who led the notorious Mau Mau guerrilla group, which carried out many atrocities against Europeans in Kenya. In 1952, Kenyatta was sentenced to seven years' hard labour for his part in the Mau Mau attacks. He was released in 1958, but exiled to a remote northern area, then to his native village.

Kenyatta was elected president of the dominant KANU party and became an MP in 1961. He became Prime Minister of Kenya when the country became internally self-governing in June 1963 and kept the post after Kenya became fully independent in December that year. He was instantly embroiled in problems in the north, where there were cross-border attacks by Somali bandits. He then became President of the Republic of Kenya in 1964. Until his death in 1978, Kenyatta was Africa's black elder statesman, and he became a familiar and respected figure at conferences and other ceremonial occasions, wielding his fly-whisk as if it was a pharaoh's flail of office.

Jomo Kenyatta was the leader of a generation of black African political activists who campaigned for – and won – independence for their countries. Kenyatta worked, as a politician and as a terrorist, to get Kenya back under the control of the Kenyans. It meant overturning British imperial rule, and he believed that was achievable. Kenyatta was one of those spirited men of iron who stubbornly resist when others give in; like Gandhi, he went on campaigning until his country was free of imperial rule.

JAWAHARLAL NEHRU

Born in Allahabad 1889, died in New Delhi 1964.
Indian statesman.

ACHIEVEMENTS:
President of the Indian National Congress.
Worked to achieve independence for India.
Became the first Prime Minister of India.
Initiated an industrialization programme in India.
Created India's foreign policy in the 1950s.
Initiated the policy of Cold War non-alignment.
Mediated between great powers in the Cold War.
Campaigned for the recognition of Communist China.

JAWAHARLAL NEHRU WAS born in Allahabad on 14 November, 1889, the son of Motilal Nehru, the Indian nationalist leader who was a follower of Gandhi. By caste, he was a Kashmiri brahmin. In 1905, the young Nehru was taken to England, where he went to Harrow School and Trinity College, Cambridge. He took a degree in Natural Sciences at Cambridge. Then he took up law at the Inner Temple (1912), before returning to India to serve in the high court of Allahabad. The Nehrus were a strongly Anglophile family, and with his English education, Jawaharlal Nehru was now thoroughly at home in an English milieu, and at ease in conversing with the English, whether civil servants, diplomats or politicians. This served him in good stead later on. He developed a distinguished style of written English and knew a lot about European literature and history.

Nehru nevertheless had a persistent vision of himself as a freedom fighter, an Indian version of Garibaldi. It was this self-image that made him join the still-moderate Indian Congress Committee in 1918. By this stage he had already met Gandhi (in 1916), who was later, prophetically, to name him as his successor and heir.

The Amritsar massacre of 1919 changed the Nehru family's attitude radically, made them more determined that India should be free of British rule. Jawaharlal Nehru abandoned his law practice and became a conspicuous follower of Gandhi, eventually emerging as second in rank to him. Because of his scientific training, Nehru nevertheless maintained some reservations about Gandhi's teachings. Instead of following Gandhi's traditionalist views, Nehru studied Marxism and Taoism, visiting both Russia and China. The Nehru-Gandhi family seems to have seen itself as having a dynastic destiny.

Following Gandhi's non-co-operation demonstrations, Nehru quickly became known nationally. He was sent to prison in 1921 and spent 18 of the next 25 years in prison. In 1928 Nehru was elected President of the Indian National Congress, an office he held intermittently and frequently. He was the acknowledged leader of the movement's socialist wing. In the 1930s, while in prison, Nehru wrote two books, Glimpses of World History and Autobiography. In 1936, the year of his wife's death, Nehru was re-elected President of Congress. He himself organized the campaign that swept Congress to power in most of the provinces of India in the new elections.

Nehru was sympathetic to the British cause in the Second World War, but along with other Congress leaders he refused to co-operate with the British while they withheld independence from India. When Stafford Cripps, for the British government, made his offer of dominion status in 1942, Nehru turned it down.

On 15 August, 1947, when India achieved full independence, Nehru was sworn in as the first Prime Minister of India. Nehru was at the helm during the two-way migrations that took place on partition. Nehru felt Gandhi's assassination in 1948 as a great personal blow. In one of the most moving speeches he ever made, Nehru referred to 'the light that has gone out of our lives.' Nehru himself died on 27 May, 1964, in New Delhi. He was cremated according to the Hindu rite, in Delhi, next to the place where Gandhi had been cremated 16 years before. .

Nehru had the distinction of being the first democratically elected leader of the first republic to exist in the Commonwealth. As a colony,

India had not needed a foreign policy; now that the country was independent, it was free to pursue any foreign policy it likes. Nehru created India's foreign policy himself, from scratch, and it was both inspired and progressive. He followed a policy of studied and statesman-like neutrality through the Cold War, often acting as a go-between among the leaders of the great powers. He pursued a global campaign against colonialism, which meant that the British Empire or Commonwealth was under constant attack from him, and ensuring that other colonies would one by one be granted independence.

It was Nehru who initiated the policy of non-alignment, refusing to side with the West or with the Soviet Union. To compensate for the attitudes of the West, Nehru campaigned for China to be given its place in world councils. Nehru committed India to a programme of industrialization, which may have been a mistake, and also to a reorganization of its states on a linguistic basis. He championed India's claim to the state of Kashmir, but adroitly managed to bring this major dispute with Pakistan to a peaceful conclusion. Nehru, with Gandhi, was the architect of India's independence. He also shaped India's non-aligned place in the post-war, post-independence world.

MAO ZEDONG

Born at Shao Shan 1893, died 1976.
Chinese dictator.

ACHIEVEMENTS:
1949 – Set up the People's Republic of China.
Forced the programme of collectivization on China.
Forced the Great Leap Forward on China.
Organized the Cultural Revolution in order to retain power.
Responsible for the deaths of millions of Chinese.

MAO WAS BORN on 26 December, 1893 in the village of Shao Shan in Xiangtan County. The eldest of four children, he was the son of a peasant farmer. In his youth he served in the Hunan provincial army, afterwards returning to school, where he became very keen on physical fitness and collective action. In 1918, Mao graduated from Hunan Normal School, travelling to Beijing with his teacher and future father-in-law Professor Yang Changjin. This was during the May Fourth Movement, when Yang was lecturing at Peking University. On Yang's recommendation, Mao worked under the head of the university library. He also married Yang Kaihui, a Peking University student. When Mao was 14, his father had arranged a marriage for him with a girl in the same village, Lo-Shi, but Mao never accepted this marriage.

Mao spent the early 1920s travelling round China, eventually returning to Hunan, where he took the lead in promoting worker's rights and collective action. In 1921, when he was 27, Mao attended the First Congress of the Communist Party of China in Shanghai, and two years after that he was elected to the Party's Central Committee, and then became director of the Peasant Training Institute. In 1927 he was sent to Hunan province to report on recent peasant risings; his report is regarded as the first important statement of Maoist theory. It was at this time that Mao developed many of his political theories, the most important one being that peasants are the source of revolution. The traditional thinking of Marx and Lenin held that it was urban workers who led the way to revolution, but Mao argued that in China it would be the rural peasants. He also developed a three-stage theory of guerrilla warfare and a concept of a 'people's democratic dictatorship'.

The first attempt at revolution was a failure. He led the Autumn Harvest Rising at Changsa in Hunan in 1927, and was lucky to survive. He was being led to execution when he managed to escape from his guards. Together with a band of guerrillas, he took refuge in the Jinggang Mountains in south-east China. There, between 1931 and 1934, he helped set up the Chinese Soviet Republic and was elected its chairman.

Mao's first wife was killed by KMT (enemy) forces, and he married He Zizhen. By now Chiang Kai-shek, who had assumed partial control of China, was determined to eradicate the Communists. To avoid being encircled by Chiang Kai-shek's KMT forces, the Communists set off on 'The Long March', which was in effect a retreat from Jiangxi in south-east China to Shaanxi in the north-west. It was during this arduous journey, almost 10,000 km long, that Mao emerged as the natural leader. Mao divorced He Zizhen and misguidedly married the actress Jiang Qing.

After China defeated Japan, the country disintegrated into civil war, in which the Communists defeated the Kuomintang. And set up the People's Republic of China in October 1949. It had taken Mao and the Communist Party 20 years to achieve it. Mao became Chairman of the new republic. His main programme now was a phase of fast, forced collectivization, which went on until 1958. Mao also indicated that he was willing to consider different views about the way China should be ruled. Given this opportunity, many Chinese people voiced their doubts about the dogmas of the Communist Party. Mao reversed his policy and rounded up his critics in an Anti-Rightist Movement.

Then came Mao's Great Leap Forward, which was supposed to be a programme of economic growth based on different principles from the

Soviet model, which had depended on the development of heavy industry. True to his initial beliefs, Mao based his Great Leap on agricultural growth and the development of small-scale industry. In the midst of this, Khrushchev withdrew the technical support that the Soviet Union had been supplying, because Mao was too aggressive in his demands to precipitate world-wide Communist revolution. Mao was in still greater difficulties because of droughts. The Great Leap came to an end in 1960. Both Chinese and outside observers now see the Great Leap Forward as a fiasco that led to millions of deaths. A fundamental difference of view led to a distinct cooling of relations between Russia and China in the 1960s.

In the light of all of these economic, social and political failures, other Communist Party members decided that Mao should relinquish power; they included Liu Shaoqi and Deng Xiaoping. Instead of ousting him altogether, they wanted to keep him as a figurehead, but take away his authority. Mao's response to this palace coup was to try to rally the Chinese people in a quite extraordinary way. In his Cultural Revolution, power was given directly to the Red Guards, groups of young people who set up their own tribunals. The Cultural Revolution was an even bigger catastrophe than the Great Leap Forward. It led to the destruction of much of China's heritage, the pointless imprisonment of huge numbers of Chinese academics, and general social chaos.

In 1969, Mao declared that the Cultural Revolution was over. The last years of his life were marked by declining health and the onset of Parkinson's disease, while various factions within the Communist Party squabbled over the succession, jockeying for position in anticipation of Mao's death. Curiously, it was in this final, pathetic decade of disempowerment that Mao created a personality cult in which his image was displayed everywhere and quotations from his writings were included in bold or in red in every conceivable kind of text.

The legacy of Mao is complex. The Great Leap was a terrible economic and social failure. The Cultural Revolution was an even bigger failure. Huge numbers of people died in the aftermath of the Chinese civil war. On the other hand, the numbers of deaths were small compared with those resulting from famine, anarchy and foreign invasion in the period before the Communists took over, and Mao did give China a period free of foreign domination, which it had not enjoyed for a very long time. During Mao's time literacy rates rose from 20–93% and life expectancy had risen to over 70 years.

The improvement in life expectancy may not have been due to Communism, though; there were similar improvements in Taiwan, which was ruled by Mao's political enemies. Mao has been denounced for failing to promote birth control; this failure led to a rapid and unmanageable population increase which forced later Chinese leaders to adopt the over-strenuous one-child policy. Another harmful effect of Mao's life has been the imitation of Maoism in communist countries around the world, spawning aggressive revolutionary movements such as the Shining Path in Peru and the Khmer Rouge in Cambodia. While other less economically developed countries have been busily (and often very destructively) imitating Mao and trying to follow his principles, China itself has moved sharply away from Maoism.

In China the official view of Mao Zedong is that he was a great revolutionary leader who made serious mistakes in his later life. The cult of personality in particular is deplored. He is widely regarded as an heroic figure in the first half of his life and an evil egotistical monster once he gained power. He was 'the Four Greats': 'Great Teacher, Great Leader, Great Supreme Commander, Great Helmsman.' One curious thing about Mao is that, in spite of the apparent radicalism of his political theory, he actually turned into something remarkably close to an ancient Chinese emperor once he was in power – autocratic, self-obsessed, dictatorial, cruel and heedless of the needs of his people. It is as if China has been unable to escape its own past. Even the most radical political thinker and activist imaginable ended up turning into something very like the Qin Emperor.

WALT DISNEY

Born in Chicago 1901, died 1966.
Pioneer of cartoon films and children's mass entertainment.

ACHIEVEMENTS:
Made the first full-length animated cartoon films.
Raised cartoon films to an art form.
Created Mickey Mouse and Donald Duck.
1937 – Snow White and the Seven Dwarfs.
1940 – Pinocchio.
1941 – Dumbo.
1942 – Bambi.
1951 – Alice in Wonderland.
1952 – Robin Hood.
1954 – 20,000 Leagues Under the Sea
1955 – Lady and the Tramp.
1959 – Sleeping Beauty.

WALTER ELIAS DISNEY was born in Chicago, Illinois, on 5 December 1901. He went to school in Kansas City and Chicago and at the young age of 17 became an ambulance driver for the Red Cross with the American troops in France in 1918. After the war he worked as a commercial artist for a couple of years, before becoming a cartoonist for the Kansas City *Film Advertizing* from 1920 to 1922. Walt Disney experimented with a number of animated cartoon films in Hollywood, creating the Alice comedies. He created and produced the first *Oswald the Rabbit* cartoons in 1926. Disney created his first successful sound picture, *Steamboat Willie*, in 1928. From then on his creations Mickey Mouse and Donald Duck became firm favourites. Disney's short *Silly Symphony* cartoons in colour were, in their day, the most popular entertainment on the screen.

Disney broke new ground with his full-length colour cartoon films. They required enormous numbers of hand-drawn images, and this work was shared among a team of dedicated artists. Disney was a hard task-master and demanded incredibly high standards from his staff. The first of these very ambitious projects was *Snow White and the Seven Dwarfs*, which was first shown in 1937. The film was – and still is – very popular. The reception of this film encouraged Disney to go on to make more feature-length cartoon films: *Pinocchio, Dumbo, Bambi, Lady and the Tramp* and *Sleeping Beauty*. All became 20th century classics.

Fantasia was a different experiment. Disney took an orchestral score, conducted by Leopold Stokowski, and made an animated animal cartoon film to synchronize with the music. Many of the effects were surreal, and as a piece of craftsmanship it is an outstanding piece of work, but *Fantasia* lacks a story line and has never had the same popular following as *Snow White*.

In 1948, Walt Disney embarked on a new venture, a series of documentary nature films, which included *The Living Desert*, made in 1953. He also produced and directed several swashbuckling adventure films for children, including *Treasure Island, Robin Hood, 20,000 Leagues Under the Sea* and *Davy Crockett*. Major features of these films were the high quality of production, artwork, scenery, music score – and a certain naïve zest. The films had a great appeal to children.

After the war, Disney resumed full-length cartoon films, with two more huge successes: *Cinderella* in 1950 and *Alice in Wonderland* in 1951.

Another major feature of Walt Disney's activity was his strong and voracious business sense. He was intent on making as much money as possible out of each project, and there were always tie-in books, toys and other merchandize that developed into as big a business as the films.

The most spectacular tie-in projects were the theme parks: the Disneyland amusement park built in California in 1955, and its spin-off theme parks in Florida and Paris.

Disney transformed a very minor art form, the black and white short cartoon film of the early 1920s, into a major art form that became large-scale mass entertainment. He revolutionized popular entertainment. He introduced a range of cartoon characters that have become icons of 20th century popular culture – Mickey Mouse, Donald Duck and Goofy. The art is marred by a tendency to fall back on sentimental stereotypes and rather folksy American values. It could be argued that narratives that are self-limited in this way are short-changing generations of children.

RICHARD RODGERS

Born in New York 1902, died 1979.
American composer.

Achievements:
Wrote songs that have become popular music classics.
Set the standard and style for popular song writing in the 20th
   century.
1925 – The Garrick Gaieties.
1938 – The Boys from Syracuse.
1943 – Oklahoma!
1949 – South Pacific.
1959 – The Sound of Music.

Richard Rodgers was born in New York in 1902. He first collaborated with Lorenz Hart, writing the music scores for a number of musicals such as *The Garrick Gaieties* in 1925. *Babes in Arms* (1937) included the song *The Lady is a Tramp*. *The Boys from Syracuse*, written in 1938, included the song *Falling in Love with Love*. *Pal Joey*, written in 1940, included *Bewitched, Bothered and Bewildered*.

Rodgers and Hart had a gift for writing great show songs that had the capacity to stand on their own, long after the musical itself closed and was forgotten. Many of their best songs became standards that are still sung and enjoyed over half a century later.

When Lorenz Hart died in 1943, Richard Rodgers needed a new collaborator, and he found an excellent lyricist in Oscar Hammerstein II. Together they wrote a spectacular series of commercially successful musicals. *Oklahoma!* (1943) won the Pulitzer Prize. *Carousel* quickly followed in 1945, then *South Pacific* in 1949 and *The King and I* in 1951. There was a creative falling off in *Flower Drum Song* (1958) and *The Sound of Music* (1959), but no decline in commercial success. Hammerstein lacked Hart's flair for manipulating the English language, but certainly sensed what was commercial. Rodgers very rarely misjudged when writing a string of songs for a musical, but there was a certain limpness in the music he wrote, ironically, for *The Sound of Music*. Perhaps it was one musical too many. Rodgers died in 1979.

Richard Rodgers composed a great many songs that have remained in the popular repertoire, and his long working life with his collaborators Lorenz Hart and Oscar Hammerstein II meant that his music dominated the popular music scene from 1925 until 1955 – until the eruption of what might be called the 'youth music' of the rock era. Richard Rodgers and Irving Berlin between them set the standards for melodic and harmonic invention in popular song.

GREGORY PINCUS

Born at Woodbine 1903, died 1967.
Experimental biologist.

ACHIEVEMENTS:
Invented the contraceptive pill.
Empowered women by giving them choice regarding birth control.
Freed women to have careers.
Reduced family size and birth rates in many countries.
Averted the 'population explosion' predicted in the 1960s.

GREGORY GODWIN PINCUS was born at Woodbine, New Jersey in 1903. He was educated at Cornell, Harvard, Cambridge and Berlin. After that he set up his own consultancy in experimental biology at Shrewsbury in Massachusetts.

In 1951, he was persuaded by the birth control campaigner Margaret Sanger to focus his work on reproductive biology. Pincus worked with M. C. Chang and John Rock; together they studied the negative effect of steroid hormones on the fertility of mammals. Synthetic hormones became available during the 1950s, and Pincus organized some field trials of the effect on human fertility of doses of these hormones. The trials, conducted in Haiti and Puerto Rico in 1954, were overwhelmingly successful.

Since then, oral contraceptives – generally referred to as 'The Pill' – have gone into general use in all the more economically developed countries of the world. There have been some concerns about the side effects of taking the pill, especially for many years at a time, but the popularity of oral contraception as the major birth control technique is undiminished. The success of oral contraception is a pharmaceutical rarity. It is very uncommon for synthetic chemical agents to have a near 100% effectiveness in controlling human physiology.

The sociological effects have been phenomenal. The main birth control technique until the arrival of the pill was the condom; it was worn by men, so whether it was worn was a decision made by men. The oral contraceptive, taken discreetly by women, was something about which women could make their own decisions. For the first time in human history, women could decided when, or whether, they became pregnant. As a result, women have been freed to work, to have professional careers, and families have become smaller, enabling parents to give more care and attention to each child. The effects of this social, economic and demographic revolution have spread out first through the richer countries, and now through the poorer countries too. Many human geographers see this process, of reducing the birth rate, as one major way of improving the quality of life for women and children throughout the world. Gregory Pincus changed the world on a very large scale, by averting the 'population explosion' that pessimists were predicting in the 1960s.

ROBERT OPPENHEIMER

Born in New York 1904, died 1967.
American nuclear physicist.

ACHIEVEMENTS:
Directed the research team that produced the first atom bombs.
Helped to end the Second World War.
Worked on peaceful applications of atomic energy.
Tried to stop the US government developing the hydrogen
  bomb.

JULIUS ROBERT OPPENHEIMER was born in New York. He studied at Harvard, Cambridge, Gottingen, Leiden and Zurich, before becoming Assistant Professor of Physics at the California Institute of Technology.

He researched electron-positron pairs, cosmic ray theory and deuteron reactions. In 1942 he joined the atom bomb project set up by President Roosevelt at Einstein's suggestion. In 1943, Oppenheimer became Director of the Los Alamos laboratory. He was now in effect leading the atomic bomb project, with the responsibility for bringing together a formidable team of scientists to design and build the first atom bombs. Oppenheimer therefore carries a heavy responsibility for the havoc caused at Hiroshima and Nagasaki and for creating the weapons that sustained the Cold War.

Robert Oppenheimer resigned as Director of Los Alamos in 1945, arguing for joint control of the future development of atomic energy with the Soviet Union.

He was chairman of the Advisory Committee to the US Atomic Energy Commission from 1946–52, and in 1947 he became director and Professor of Physics at the Institute for Advanced Study at Princeton. In these post-war roles, Oppenheimer did his utmost to promote peaceful uses of atomic energy. He bitterly opposed the further research which led to the development of the hydrogen bomb as a weapon that America could use to threaten the Soviet bloc.

In 1953, his views came home to roost, and he was suspended from further secret nuclear research by a security review board. He was believed to have left-wing sympathies, which in the Cold War was sufficient to remove him from any position where he would have access to sensitive information. Robert Oppenheimer had many supporters who believed that the charges brought against him were absurd. In the same year, he was invited by the BBC to deliver the Reith Lectures. He received the Enrico Fermi Award in 1963.

Robert Oppenheimer was responsible for directing the research team that produced the atom bombs used against Japan to end the Second World War in 1945. He worked on peaceful applications of atomic energy for electricity generation. He also worked to try to persuade the US government to stop developing the hydrogen bomb.

MOTHER TERESA

Born at Skopje 1910, died in Calcutta 1997.

ACHIEVEMENTS:
Highlighted the need for direct action to help the needy.
Became a focus for advocates of 'alternative' aid.
1950 – Founded the Order of the Missionaries of Charity.
1952 – Opened her House for the Dying in Calcutta.
1956 – Founded a leper colony.

MOTHER TERESA WAS born in 1910 in Yugoslavia of Albanian parents. As a child she lived at Skopje in Macedonia.

Mother Teresa went to India in 1928, where she joined a religious community, the Irish order of Sisters of Loretto. Initially she taught at a convent school in Calcutta, taking her final vows in 1937. She then became the school's principal.

In 1948, deeply conscious of the poverty all around her in Calcutta, she felt an irresistible call to help the poor. She left the convent to work alone in the slums, taking a one-week course in basic nursing at Patna in Bihar. Gradually she was joined in the slums by other nuns. She opened her House for the Dying in 1952; it was a shelter for the homeless, offering them a final refuge to save them from the indignity of dying on the streets.

Mother Teresa founded her own sisterhood, the Order of the Missionaries of Charity, in 1950. She and her order became directly responsible to the Pope in 1956. In 1956, Mother Teresa started working with lepers, setting up a leper colony which she called Chanti Nagar, Town of Peace, near Asansoi in West Bengal. Her congregation now has 2,000 sisters and 200 branch houses in several different countries.

Mother Teresa became internationally known for her unstinting and selfless charitable works, and she was able to exploit this status to bring pressure to bear on politicians of many countries to do something about the situation in the poorer countries. Mother Teresa was very direct and unsparing in her comments, and did not go out of her way to appear to be saintly. Many have nevertheless come to see her as a saint, and there is a movement under way to have her canonized. When she died in 1997 the news of her death was eclipsed in the world media by that of Princess Diana, a very different sort of woman. Mother Teresa did much to highlight the need for direct action to help the needy, cutting across all the high-flown talk of politicians about aid and economic development. What she saw was that people in Calcutta were dying in the streets – and needed help and shelter. In 1971, she said, 'The biggest disease today is not leprosy or tuberculosis, but rather the feeling of being unwanted.'

JESSE OWENS

Born at Danville 1913, died 1980.
Record-breaking American athlete.

ACHIEVEMENTS:
Won four gold medals at the 1936 Berlin Olympics.
Annoyed Hitler by being a winning black athlete.

JESSE JAMES CLEVELAND Owens was born at Danville in Alabama. He was a great black athlete, and in particular a great sprinter. When he competed for the Ohio State University team in May 1935, he set three new world records and equalled a fourth, all within the space of an hour. His long jump record stood for the next 25 years.

At the 1936 Olympics in Berlin, Jesse Owens won four gold medals: long jump, 100 metres, 200 metres, 4 x 100 metres relay. Adolf Hitler watched Owens winning these races and then promptly left the stadium in order to avoid having to congratulate a very obviously non-Aryan athlete. It was a kind of moral victory for Jesse Owens, for the opponents of Hitler and for black people. The incident was caught on film and caused a sensation in the world press.

Yet, perhaps surprisingly, when Owens returned to the USA he gained no recognition for his remarkable feat at the Olympic Games. He was reduced to running races against horses and dogs, in effect turning himself into a freak show. Later he was given an executive position with the Illinois Athletic Commission. He also attended the 1956 Olympics as President Eisenhower's personal representative. In 1976, Owens was awarded the Presidential Medal of Freedom. He died in 1980.

JOAN LITTLEWOOD

Born 1914, died 2002.
English stage director.

ACHIEVEMENTS:
Founded Theatre Workshop.
Staged plays dealing with current social issues.
Introduced 'kitchen-sink' drama.
Pioneered satire.

JOAN LITTLEWOOD WAS born in 1914, the illegitimate daughter of a Cockney maid. She trained at RADA, and in 1935 she founded Theatre Union, an experimental theatre company in Manchester. This was re-formed in 1945 as Theatre Workshop. It opened in London, at the Theatre Royal, Stratford East, with Shakespeare's *Twelfth Night*. It was a strange choice, scarcely an experimental play, but the group quickly won good reviews. Theatre Workshop was invited to represent Britain at the Theatre des Nations in Paris in 1955 and 1956.

Joan Littlewood directed the first British production of Brecht's *Mother Courage*. This was premiered in Barnstaple, with Littlewood herself in the title role.

The ideology of Theatre Workshop was aggressively left-wing. Its artistic policy revolved round a fresh, politically committed interpretation of well-established plays and the production of new plays on working-class themes. Joan Littlewood was responsible for staging *The Quare Fellow* by Brendan Behan in 1956 and *A Taste of Honey* by Shelagh Delaney in 1958. In 1959 she produced *Fings Ain't What They Used T'Be*.

One of her most memorable Theatre Workshop creations was the revue, *Oh, What a Lovely War!* This was a biting satire, not just on the First World War, but on war in general and the role of the feckless upper classes in causing it. It was a huge success. *Oh, What a Lovely War!* was not just good entertainment; it was good art too, as Richard Attenborough's later film showed. In 1975, Joan Littlewood went abroad to work.

Joan Littlewood revolutionized British theatre by introducing social and political commitment. She staged plays that dealt head-on with current social issues, and in particular with issues that affected the working class. This marked the advent of what was sometimes disparagingly called 'kitchen-sink' drama. She was also at the spearhead of another new movement in British entertainment – satire.

FRANCIS CRICK

Born 1916, died 2004.
Molecular biologist.

ACHIEVEMENTS:
Discovered the molecular structure of DNA.
Discovered the genetic code contained in DNA.

FRANCIS HARRY COMPTON Crick was educated at Mill Hill School, London University and Cambridge. From 1949 onwards he carried out research into molecular biology at the Cavendish Laboratory.

In 1953, in collaboration with James D. Watson, a young American biologist who joined the laboratory two years earlier at the age of only 23, he constructed a molecular model of the extremely complex genetic material known as DNA (deoxyribonucleic acid). The molecular model was in the form of a double helix. Later he went on to research the nucleic acids, making far-reaching discoveries about the genetic code they contain. When Crick died in 2004, James Watson said, 'I will always remember Francis for his extraordinary focused intelligence. He treated me as though I were a member of his family. I always looked forward to being with him and speaking to him.'

Crick was awarded the Nobel Prize for medicine and physiology in 1962, jointly with James Watson and Maurice Wilkins, his co-workers. James Watson returned to America, where he became director of the Cold Spring Biological Laboratories in New York.

The discovery of the structure of DNA and its significance was one of the great scientific breakthroughs of the second half of the 20th century. It was a discovery with lots of ramifications. When it emerged that everyone has different DNA, the possibility of using it for identification presented itself. DNA analysis has since become a major forensic tool. A criminal has now to leave only a few traces of human tissue at the scene of a crime, and he or she can be identified. This new technique has made it possible to solve some crimes committed decades ago and also, disturbingly, prove that some people serving very long prison sentences really did not commit the crimes for which they were convicted. At least DNA has ensured their release.

Family members have related DNA, so DNA analysis can establish kinship links; this was how the remains of Tsar Nicholas II and his family were identified. This kinship feature can also help to resolve cases of disputed paternity. Since DNA can survive for a long time after death, it has also proved invaluable to historians, archaeologists and anthropologists in establishing kinship groups. DNA has opened many doors.

JOHN F. KENNEDY

Born at Brookline 1917, died in Dallas 1963.

ACHIEVEMENTS:
1956 – Profiles of Courage.
Youngest US President.
First Catholic US President.
Supported black civil rights.
*Worked hard to end racial segregation in US schools and
colleges.*
Failed to invade Cuba.
Risked inter-continental nuclear war over Cuban missiles.

JOHN FITZGERALD KENNEDY was born at Brookline, Massachusetts in 1917.
He was the son of Joseph Kennedy, a wealthy financier and former US
ambassador to Britain. John F. Kennedy studied at Harvard and under Laski
in London. He served for a time in the American Embassy in London in
1938, writing a thesis on Britain's unpreparedness for war. His account of the
rise of Fascism in Europe, published as *Why England Slept*, was a best-seller.

During the Second World War, Kennedy served as a torpedo boat
commander. In September 1943 his boat was sunk under him and he
managed to save his crew. He was awarded the Navy Medal and the Purple
Heart. After the war, in 1946, Kennedy went straight into politics, the
family's chosen career, becoming an elected Democrat representative in
1947. He became senator for Massachusetts in 1952. In 1953 he married
Jacqueline Bouvier, a photographer for the *Washington Times-Herald*. She
would later be criticized for her extravagance at the White House, but
there were those who liked the way she transformed the First Family of
America into a kind of old-style European royalty.

In June 1956, Kennedy launched a campaign to win the vice-presidential nomination. In 1960 came his opportunity to become president. In the run-up to this, he and Richard Nixon took part in the first television debate between candidates. Afterwards, voters said that the televised debate made no difference to the way they voted, but it was clear that Kennedy looked better than Nixon, who appeared unshaven and shifty. From that moment, television took on a more significant role in world politics, and Kennedy in particular exploited the media. Kennedy narrowly won the election in 1960. He was the first Catholic and the youngest person to be elected President of the USA.

The conservatism of Congress blocked Kennedy's programme, a 'new frontier' in social legislation. Kennedy supported federal desegregation policies in schools and universities, partly through his brother, Robert Kennedy. He prepared civil rights legislation.

In foreign policy, Kennedy was firm and intolerant. He took the view that the Caribbean was America's backyard, and that it was America's right to police it. Along with a great many other Americans, Kennedy hated the presence of a Marxist regime in Cuba, under Fidel Castro. In 1961 Kennedy's 'Bay of Pigs' invasion of Fidel Castro's Cuba was a complete fiasco. Kennedy seemed to learn little from this mistake. In October 1962 he risked nuclear war with the Soviet Union by insisting that the Soviets withdraw missiles from Cuba. He was lucky – and so was the rest of the world – that the Soviet leader, Khrushchev, backed down. In 1963, he followed this by negotiating a partial nuclear test ban treaty with the Soviet Union.

On 22 November 1963 President Kennedy was assassinated as he was driven in an open car through the streets of Dallas in Texas. A sniper, Lee Harvey Oswald, fired several shots from the window of a bookstore overlooking Dealey Plaza. He was an assassin with no particular purpose beyond grabbing a place in history, just like Herostratus long before.

John F. Kennedy's reputation remained high partly because of his assassination. Had he lived, the inadequacy of some of his policies and strategies might have been seen and the reputation tarnished. Cut off in his prime, he seemed to have infinite promise. The foreign policy was disastrous, and the Cuban missile crisis could have ended in a catastrophe of global proportions; no president should take such risks. He did much to support the cause of black civil rights, actually travelling to Alabama to show his personal support for Martin Luther King, and worked hard to end racial segregation in schools and colleges. He went so far as to intervene by taking over the Alabama state militia to ensure that racial integration went ahead at a high school.

SPIKE MILLIGAN

Born at Ahmadnagar 1918, died 2002.
English surreal comedian.

ACHIEVEMENTS:
Invented zany madcap surreal humour.
1951–59 – The Goon Show
1963 – Puckoon.
1971 – Adolf Hitler, My Part in His Downfall.
1985 – Where Have All the Bullets Gone?
1987 – The Looney: An Irish Fantasy.

TERENCE ALAN MILLIGAN was born at Ahmadnagar in India in 1918. It was while 'Spike' Milligan was a singer and trumpeter doing his war service in 1949 that he made his radio debut in the talent show *Opportunity Knocks*. From 1951 onwards he co-wrote and performed in *The Goon Show* with Peter Sellers, Harry Secombe and Michael Bentine. *The Goon Show*, a weekly half hour radio show, went on for eight years. It proved to be not only ground-breaking as entertainment but a highly original brand of humour. Often it seemed child-like in its humour, but there was a strong vein of adult mischief at work, like the well-observed crooked army officer, Major Bloodnok, and the word-games that somehow got past the producer, like the name of the minor character Hugh Jampton.

The Goon Show scripts owed much to the vocal characters the four actors were able to conjure up. The vocal characters seemed to invent their own narrative. But much of that narrative invention was Spike Milligan's.

On stage, Milligan appeared in *Treasure Island* in the 1960s and 1970s. He also appeared in the play *The Bed-Sitting Room*, of which he was the co-author. He also went on to make several experimental comedy programmes for television, though none were as successful as *The Goon Show*.

Spike Milligan also wrote children's books, poetry and comic novels including *Puckoon, Adolf Hitler, My Part in His Downfall, Where Have All the Bullets Gone?* and *The Looney: An Irish Fantasy*.

Spike Milligan died in 2002 at the age of 83.

Milligan had an irrepressible sense of the ridiculous and the surreal, and his manic humour drove the performances along with pace and style. His sense of humour had an ancestry, of course, and it is possible to see it as part of an English tradition that goes back through Kingsley Amis, Evelyn Waugh and P. G. Wodehouse to Laurence Sterne. What Spike Milligan introduced was what he himself called 'zany madcap humour': a new kind of comedy that was less rational than anything that had gone before, a kind of absurdist frenzy. It was in fact not far from madness, and Spike Milligan suffered bouts of real mental illness requiring treatment. Spike Milligan's major contribution to comedy was *The Goon Show*, which was a powerful influence on a whole generation of younger listeners, sowing the seeds of future developments like *Monty Python's Flying Circus*, which can be seen as a direct descendant of *The Goon Show*.

BILLY GRAHAM

Born in Charlotte 1918.
American evangelist.

ACHIEVEMENTS:
Caused millions to review their lives in an age of materialism.
Spawned copy-cat evangelists who seek to make money.

WILLIAM FRANKLIN GRAHAM was born in Charlotte, North Carolina, in 1918. He studied at the Florida Bible Institute, later called Trinity College, from 1938 to 1940, before being ordained as a Minister of the Southern Baptist Church in 1940.

In 1943, Billy Graham graduated in anthropology from Wheaton College, Illinois. He also got married that year, to Ruth Bell. He launched his first high-profile preaching crusade in 1949 in Los Angeles. He went on from this to organize and lead similar crusades in one country after another all round the world, including the Communist countries of Eastern Europe during the Cold War, and even the Soviet Union itself.

Billy Graham relied heavily on mass hysteria to convey his message. He was an imposing-looking man with a big square jaw, flashing eyes and a ready smile. He assembled huge crowds in sports stadia, addressed them in a highly emotional rhetorical style, and persuaded them that they had been converted to the way of life of Jesus Christ. Graham's supporters claimed that millions of converts were made in this way, though it is not known how many of those conversions were lasting or meaningful. Certainly Graham's preaching caused millions to review their lives in an age of secular materialism. He was much admired by those who were already 'low church' believers. He reassured them and reinforced their faith.

The touring crusades were backed up by TV and radio broadcasts and publications. Billy Graham was undoubtedly a charismatic preacher who influenced huge numbers of people. Even those not persuaded by his message were impressed by the apparent sincerity and power of the man. He became the friend and counsellor of many Americans holding high office, including President Nixon.

Investigative journalists naturally poked, pried and researched, trying to find a hint of corruption or abuse, but they were never able to discover anything against him; he seems to have been a man of the very highest integrity as well as sincerity. His Billy Graham Evangelistic Association is thought of as a model of financial accountability. Unfortunately, his model has not been followed with such scrupulousness by others. Other evangelists have copied his crusading strategy, but with a more sinister motive – the creation of personal fortunes.

NELSON MANDELA

Born in the Transkei 1918.
South African nationalist leader.

ACHIEVEMENTS:
Set up the first black legal practice in South Africa.
Played an active role in the ANC campaign against apartheid.
Political prisoner, symbolizing the subjugation of black South
  Africans.
Became the first black President of South Africa.
Ensured the peaceful transition to black majority rule.

NELSON ROLIHLAHLA MANDELA was born in the Transkei, South Africa. He was a member of the royal family of the Tembu tribe. He became a successful lawyer in Johannesburg, where he set up the first black legal practice in South Africa. Then his political career began when, in 1944, he joined the African National Congress (ANC).

For the next 20 years, Mandela directed a campaign of defiance against the government of South Africa, in protest against its aggressive racist policies. In May 1961, he organized a three-day national strike. The police tried to head it off by carrying out mass arrests of black activists; in all nearly 10,000 black people were detained. The police tried to arrest Mandela too, but when they called at his home in Orlando, near Johannesburg, he was out. His wife Winnie answered the door. They wanted to search the house. Winnie asked them for their search warrant. They had to go back for one. They searched the house and found nothing, and he became known as the Black Pimpernel for his skill at evading arrest. But he was eventually arrested and brought to trial on 22 October 1962.

He was accused specifically of being the mastermind behind the call for a national strike. He pleaded not guilty. A few weeks later he was found guilty and imprisoned for five years for incitement.

When the strike failed, Nelson Mandela despaired of using non-violent means of overturning the racist regime; he turned instead to violence and helped to found the Spear of the Nation movement.

Inevitably, the South African authorities retaliated, re-arresting Mandela and putting him on trial for more serious political offences. While he was in prison, the police raided the ANC's underground headquarters, where they found Mandela's diaries, which contained notes on guerrilla warfare. In April 1964 he went on trial for treason. He was accused of sabotage and trying to overthrow the South African government by revolution. Mandela bravely told the court in Pretoria that his purpose was to rid the country of white domination. 'I do not deny that I planned sabotage. We had either to accept inferiority or fight against it by violence.'

With his law training behind him, Mandela was able to put up a spirited and coherent defence. His memorable defence speech, given in June, lasted four hours. But in spite of this eloquence, he was sentenced to life imprisonment. The police tried to smuggle Mandela and the other eight men convicted with him out of the courthouse without anyone noticing. The crowd nevertheless spotted Mandela and ran along shouting, 'We have the strength!' He was flown from Pretoria to Cape Town, and then taken by boat out to the penal colony on Robben Island. This has a strong current of cold Antarctic water sweeping past it, and escape was reckoned to be impossible.

Nelson Mandela continued to be a political force while in prison. In fact he became a potent symbol of the subjugation of the black population of South Africa, a rallying point. The symbolism of Mandela's captivity became a worldwide phenomenon, and a co-ordinated international campaign for his release was launched. His captivity became an increasing political embarrassment to the government of South Africa. When thousands of cards flooded in to mark Mandela's 60th birthday, the authorities refused to let him have them, but the point had been very effectively made; the world had not forgotten Nelson Mandela.

Mandela's controversial wife, Winnie, was also frequently subjected to restrictions, so that her freedom of action was curtailed. On 6 May 1987, she was invited to speak on her husband's behalf by the liberal white students of Witwatersrand University at Johannesburg. The police moved in to stop the speech, resorting to whips, tear gas and 120 arrests in order to silence her.

Side by side with the campaign to release Mandela, there was a worldwide campaign for the South African government to end its system of apartheid, the anti-black racial discrimination that saturated every aspect of South African life. Economic sanctions were applied, with many countries refusing to trade with South Africa. For a long time these sanctions had little effect, and the white South Africans seemed set to maintain their privileged position for ever, but suddenly in the 1980s sanctions began to bite.

President F. W. de Klerk took office in 1989, and introduced liberalizing measures that started the process of dismantling apartheid. Within months of his election, President de Klerk visited Mandela in prison, preparing him for freedom and the new role he was about to play. The ban on the ANC was lifted, restrictions on political meetings were removed.

In February 1990, on de Klerk's orders, Nelson Mandela was released. There was worldwide rejoicing. At the age of 71, Mandela was free. At the same time the white supremacy within the South African government crumbled, and the whole country was on the threshhold of a massive political and cultural transformation. Mandela was made president of the ANC, and he opened negotiations with de Klerk about the country's future. He pressed the governments of other countries to continue applying pressure; apartheid had to be abolished completely. In 1993, Mandela and de Klerk were jointly awarded the Nobel Peace Prize for their work on the process of reform, and the following year Mandela became the first black President of South Africa.

Some anticipated a bloodbath, in which many old scores against the white community would be settled by the newly-empowered blacks. Mandela was the natural figurehead for the newly emergent black South Africa, and it would have been understandable if he had used his new-found power to punish, humiliate or even destroy his ex-jailers. In fact Mandela showed incredible restraint and magnanimity, encouraging people to confess and come to terms with the bad events of the past, but without undue recrimination, without revenge.

Nelson Mandela won the respect of the whole world for the statesman-like – even saintly – way in which he accepted and wielded political power in the new South Africa. Thanks to his leadership, there were no revenge killings, there was no bloodbath. Against all expectations, the liberation of black South Africa proved to be a happy rite of passage.

LEONARD BERNSTEIN

Born 1918, died 1990.
American conductor, pianist, composer.

ACHIEVEMENTS:
Successfully combined popular and classical music.
Showed that music does not have to be either popular or serious.
1942 – Jeremiah.
1949 – The Age of Anxiety.
1956 – Candide.
1957 – West Side Story.
1963 – Kaddish.
1971 – Mass.

LEONARD BERNSTEIN WAS born at Lawrence, Massachusetts, of a Russian Jewish family. He was educated at Harvard and the Curtis Institute of Music; from very early on he showed prodigious ability. He became famous overnight in 1943, when the distinguished guest conductor, Bruno Walter, was too ill to conduct the New York Philharmonic. The 25 year old trainee conductor, with no rehearsal and no preparation time, stepped onto the podium at the last minute and conducted the concert brilliantly. The concert was broadcast live and hailed as a triumph. For the first time there was a native-born American among the elite group of international conductors.

Bernstein was in great demand for conducting, but that excluded composing, and in later life he regretted that he only managed to compose three symphonies. But the symphonies were not enough for him anyway. He discovered Broadway. The main catalytic agent here was Jerome Robbins, a gifted young choreographer who proposed that they create a modern ballet.

This led to *Fancy Free,* a ballet about three sailors on shore leave. It was very successful, so Bernstein expanded it into a musical; it became Bernstein's hit musical, *On the Town,* which included the song *New York, New York.*

Now Bernstein was in demand for Broadway shows, which worried Bernstein's classical following, who now considered him success-hungry and shallow. Then Bernstein tried to re-establish himself as a serious classical conductor, which he did very successfully at La Scala, Milan, conducting *Verdi.*

In 1953 he started work on a pastiche comic opera based on Voltaire's *Candide.* Bernstein tilted the 18th satire at the McCarthy witch-hunt, but the technique did not work well. Then he tried applying grand opera techniques to the modern world, and that worked far better. In 1949 he started planning a modern *Romeo and Juliet,* which was eventually finished in 1957 as *West Side Story.* It was a long time evolving, and turned out to have many similarities to Bizet's *Carmen,* the opera he had loved most as a boy, and his new musical/opera was to have the same enormous popular appeal. This was the moment, mid-century, when popular and serious music collided and merged.

By the 1960s, Leonard Bernstein was a well established figure at the centre of the musical world. But he reflected ruefully that the music then being composed by serious composers interested nobody any more – not even musicians. His *Third Symphony* was full of disillusionment, and includes a speaker who sounds as if he is angry with God.

The 20th century saw a widening gap between popular music and classical music. Popular music won ever-bigger audiences as classical composers moved further from popular taste. Bernstein's achievement was to walk the tightrope between the two. All the currents of 20th century converged and fermented in Bernstein, who was a composer, conductor, concert pianist, TV personality, educationist and visionary. His 40-year career integrated jazz, classical, sacred music from Christian and Jewish traditions, and European and Latin American dance rhythms. His career was a journey towards a musical fusion – though a fusion that went several steps too far.

The *Mass,* commissioned by Jackie Kennedy from Bernstein for the opening of the Centre of the Performing Arts, was to be in memory of her husband, John F. Kennedy. This *Mass*, first performed in 1971, included so many disparate elements that it fell apart. Interestingly, a British cross-over piece written at almost exactly the same time was an enormous success, both artistically and commercially – Andrew Lloyd Webber's *Jesus Christ Superstar*. But it was Bernstein's magnificent example, *West Side Story*, that had made it possible.

EDMUND HILLARY

Born in Auckland 1919.
Mountaineer, 'conqueror' of Everest.

ACHIEVEMENTS:
First to climb Mt Everest.
First to climb Mt Herschel.
Deputy leader of British Commonwealth Antarctic Expedition.
First to reach South Pole on a tracked vehicle.
Raised funds for development in Nepal.

EDMUND PERCIVAL HILLARY was born in Auckland, New Zealand, and educated at Auckland Grammar School. He was a bee-keeper by profession and mountaineering was his hobby. He climbed both in New Zealand and in the Himalayas.

The high point in his life came when he joined the Everest expedition organized by John Hunt. Together with the Sherpa Tenzing Norgay, Hillary became the first person to reach the summit of Everest on 29 May, 1953. From below, all that could be seen of the summit led the team to expect a jagged rock pinnacle. Hillary described it to them when he returned as 'a symmetrical beautiful snow-cone summit.' Hillary was knighted for his achievement. Tenzing was not.

During the International Geophysical Year (1957–58), Hillary acted as deputy leader, under Vivian Fuchs, on the British Commonwealth Antarctic Expedition. On this expedition, Hillary took part in the first journey overland to the South Pole using tracked vehicles.

In the 1960s, Edmund Hillary made further expeditions to the Everest area, during which he became increasingly interested in offering help to the people of the area. In 1967 he led a geological expedition to Antarctica, and during this expedition he made the first ascent of Mount Herschel.

Hillary was appointed New Zealand High Commissioner to India in the 1980s, and he raised funds in New Zealand to provide hospitals and schools in the Himalayas. Edmund Hillary's extraordinary contributions to geographical exploration were finally acknowledged when he was made a Garter Knight.

The ascent of Everest was a landmark event in that the last conspicuous wilderness had been visited. The long centuries of exploration and discovery were over. In fact there were a few areas still unvisited, like the interior of Tierra del Fuego, but these would shortly be recorded on satellite images. Hillary's ascent of Everest marked a watershed in our relationship with the planet. After that, we had to start worrying about losing it; the age of discovery was over and the age of environmentalism began.

POPE JOHN PAUL II

Born 1920, died 2005.
Controversial charismatic pope.

ACHIEVEMENTS:
Became the first non-Italian pope for 450 years.
Travelled widely and became a kind of superstar.
Made global outreach the main feature of his papacy.
Helped Poland achieve independence.
Refused to relax the Catholic Church's ruling on birth control.
Tried to alleviate poverty and environmental stress in the
Third World.

KAROL JOZEF WOJTYLA was born at Wadowice in Poland, the son of an army NCO. Karol Wojtyla was ordained in 1946 and became Professor of Moral Theology at the Universities of Lublin and Cracow. As a young man he was interested in drama and poetry; his *Collected Poems* were published in 1982.

In 1964 he became Archbishop of Cracow, and was made a cardinal in 1967. In 1978 he became the first non-Italian pope for 450 years. After eight ballots, his election was a victory for the Third World cardinals who wanted a non-Italian pope. He had no expectation of becoming pope, and had actually taken some reading matter into the secret conclave gathering to choose the new pope; he had not anticipated any personal involvement in the process. He was very surprised by his own election. The thousands of Italians waiting for the result in St Peter's Square were also surprised, and for some time they were stunned by the news. But when the new Pope addressed them, he spoke to them in Italian, not the customary Latin. He understood – and they cheered him for it. He was Pope at 58, the youngest for a long time, and it meant that he would be Pope for a long time to come.

A few months later, in June 1979, he made his visit 'home', to Poland. It was an historic visit in that it was the first time a pope had visited a Communist country. When he stepped onto the Warsaw airport tarmac, he knelt and kissed it. 'I have kissed the ground of Poland on which I grew up and the land from which, through the inscrutable design of Providence, God called me to the chair of Peter in Rome.' This tarmac-kissing ritual was to be repeated in each country he visited subsequently. Later he told journalists in Poland, 'Communism and capitalism are realities, but underneath stand the people. This is a human reality.'

In May 1980, Pope John Paul arrived in Zaire (now Congo) on the first leg of an African tour. He was well aware, because of the circumstances of his election, that the Catholic congregations round the world were alienated, feeling that the Vatican was 'too Italian' and inward-looking, and he made global outreach the outstanding feature of his papacy. He wanted people everywhere to know that he was their Pope, not just Italy's Pope. Later that year the Queen met him on the first state visit to the Vatican by a British monarch.

In May 1981 he was shot while being driven in a white open-topped jeep through a crowd of 20,000 people in St Peter's Square. The Pope was hit by four bullets, two of which lodged in his intestines; he was incredibly lucky to survive this attack, which was meant to kill him. He was seriously wounded but after a five-hour operation he made a full recovery. The would-be assassin was a Turk called Mehemet Ali Agca, and it is possible that he was a hitman hired by Bulgarians. In his boarding house close to the Vatican Agca left a letter, in which he wrote that he wanted 'to demonstrate to the world the imperialistic crimes of the Soviet Union and the United States.' Whatever view one takes of John Paul, it is hard to see how he could be held responsible for any crimes perpetrated by the Great Powers. It was a peculiar reason for killing him and some other motive must really have lain behind Agca's assassination attempt. The Turkish authorities had warned Interpol about Agca, but he had slipped into Italy disguised as a student.

As Pope John Paul II, he was the most energetic pope in memory, just as he had been an energetic cardinal. Some of his colleagues told him that it was inappropriate for a cardinal to ski; he replied that it was in-appropriate for a cardinal to ski badly. As pope he travelled to many foreign countries, preaching wherever he went, and becoming a kind of superstar. He championed economic justice and was an outspoken defender of the Church in Communist countries; in this he was of course speaking from his own bitter experience as a Christian priest in an Eastern European Communist state – Poland. In 1981 he declared his hand; 'Trade unions are indispensable in the struggle for social justice.' He repeated this two years later when he visited Poland, and held meetings with Lech Walesa, the leader of Solidarity. He said that people had the right to belong to trade unions. 'This right is not given to us by the State. It is a right given by the Creator.' He also held meetings with Mikhail Gorbachev, the Soviet leader. By these startlingly direct interventions, John Paul greatly assisted the trade union movement in general, Solidarity in particular, and promoted Polish independence, which was achieved in 1989. He went even further than this, though, making a huge sum of money available for Solidarity. It may be questioned whether this Vatican wealth was allocated legitimately and fairly. In becoming Pope, Karol Wojtyla did not set aside his Polish nationality or his Polish nationalism; did he perhaps abuse his position to further a private interest? Could the funds that he took for Poland have been used more effectively in alleviating suffering in Third World countries?

His political stance was unequivocal. When he visited Nicaragua in March 1983, he attacked the Sandanistas and the People's Church, saying, 'There is only one Church.'

He was unswervingly opposed to artificial methods of birth control, and there were many who thought this an unenlightened position, in view of the situation in many Third World countries. It is curious that Italy, the 'most Catholic' country in Europe, also has the lowest birth rate; many Italian Catholic couples must be making their own private decision about limiting their family size. With higher economic development comes education; with education and literacy, especially female literacy, comes a fall in the birth rate. Many human geographers believe that Pope John Paul could have done much to improve living conditions, and reduced the pressure on the environment, in less developed countries, by relaxing the Catholic Church's ruling on birth control. But he never did.

In 1995, Pope John Paul II took part in some historic meetings that discussed the relationship between the Orthodox and Roman Catholic Churches.

From 1996 onwards, John Paul's health declined intermittently. In his last few years he found it increasingly difficult to carry out ceremonial duties, yet continued to do so in spite of extreme frailty. His last appearances were pitiful, and there were many in the Vatican hierarchy who thought that abdication would have been a better option. His death in 2005 prompted eulogies from every quarter of the world. His funeral brought together heads of state and other representatives of every country together in St Peter's Square, and created some bizarre moments, such as the one when Robert Mugabe held out his hand and Prince Charles felt he could not avoid shaking it.

ROBERT MAXWELL

Born 1923, died 1991.
Publisher, fraudster.

ACHIEVEMENTS:
Founded Pergamon Press.
Bought Mirror Group Newspapers.
Abused, disempowered and robbed those around him.
Stole hundreds of millions of pounds from employees' pension
* funds.*

ROBERT MAXWELL COMES from a long line of migrant serial criminals who change their identity as they move from one field of operation to another and pose as respectable and trustworthy high-powered businessmen; they go on to commit large-scale white-collar crimes such as embezzlement. It is a fascinating personality type, brilliantly explored by Anthony Trollope in his 1875 novel *The Way We Live Now*, in the semi-fictional character Sebastian Melmot. Though they may not kill, they steal, cheat, defraud, bully and disempower the people round them: they ruin countless lives in countless ways in their self-seeking greed. With Maxwell the chief crime, but only one of many, was robbing people of their pensions.

Robert Maxwell was not what he seemed in any way. Even his name was false. He was born in 1923 with the name Jan Ludwig (or Ludvic) Hoch, one of seven siblings, in a village called Slatinske Doly in the province of Ruthenia; at the time of Hoch's birth the village was in Czechoslovakia, but after 1945 it was in the Ukraine. His parents, Mechel and Hannah, were Orthodox Jews. Mechel made a poor living as a cattle dealer, woodcutter and farm labourer.

During the Second World War, Hoch allegedly joined the Czech Resistance, and he certainly made his way to France to escape from the Nazis. His parents were Nazi victims. Exactly which parts of Maxwell's life story are true and which he invented it is still difficult to tell. He later claimed the classic self-made man's 'rags to riches' story, going so far as to say that he did not have a pair of shoes until he was seven.

In May 1940 Hoch arrived in England. Here he assumed the name Leslie Du Maurier and joined the North Staffordshire Regiment. Later he transferred to the Fifth Battalion of the West Surrey Regiment, stationed in Belgium, and changed his name again, to Ian Robert Maxwell.

On 29 January 1945 he was leading a platoon of soldiers towards Paarlo when he captured a machine-gun post. For this he was awarded the Military Cross and was promoted to Captain. After this he married a French girl, Elisabeth Meynard, in Paris. They had four sons and five daughters; one son and one daughter died in childhood.

It was at the end of the war that Hoch/Du Maurier/Maxwell went into business, publishing academic textbooks and scientific journals and in 1949 founded Pergamon Press. He was keen to be accepted as English but also wanted to become part of the English establishment. He was eventually to set himself up in a manor house. In 1959, as a next step in this direction, he stood for Parliament as Labour candidate for Buckingham. He was defeated, but won the seat in 1964 and kept it in 1966, losing it again in the 1970 election; he failed to regain it in both the elections in 1974. Being an MP no longer looked like an option.

Meanwhile, in 1971, an American entrepreneur called Saul Steinberg showed interest in buying a subsidiary of Pergamon Press dealing in encyclopaedias. Maxwell inflated the share price to make it appear more profitable by using transactions between Pergamon and his family companies. When Steinberg discovered that he was being tricked in this way he understandably withdrew from the deal. A Department of Trade investigation into the matter resulted in the following damning verdict; 'Notwithstanding Mr Maxwell's acknowledged abilities and energy, he is not in our opinion a person who can be relied upon to exercise proper stewardship of a publicly quoted company.'

Maxwell was very lucky that the Director of Public Prosecutions decided not to press charges, so he was allowed to recover from this particular scandal. Even so, it is incredible that any businessman could recover a career in business after such comments had been publicly made, yet he did.

Though heavily in debt he was able to buy back Pergamon in 1974. In this way he earned the press nickname 'the Bouncing Czech'. By the time he came to take over the troubled British Printing Corporation in 1980, renaming it Maxwell Communications Corporation, most people had had time to forget the DTI's warning about him. Maxwell had long hoped to be able to take over one of the national newspapers in Britain, but twice lost out to Rupert Murdoch, who successfully took over the *Sun* and the *News of the World*. He then got a chance to gain control of the Mirror Group. He borrowed heavily in order to buy Mirror Group Newspapers from Reed International for £113 million in 1984 and later in the 1980s he bought the American publishing house Macmillan. These business ventures were extravagantly over-ambitious, and Maxwell pushed himself deep into debt. As a result in 1991 he floated Mirror Group Newspapers as a public company as a desperate measure to raise cash; the idea was to save the rest of his business empire, which was drifting towards bankruptcy. Maxwell's debts had reached over two billion pounds.

Maxwell's business practices were often questionable, though rarely questioned openly in the press. He was very quick to sue for libel. When the whole story, or what we now think of as the whole story, eventually came out after his death, it became very obvious why he had to silence investigative journalists who wanted to expose his goings-on. Anyone who implied that he was dishonest was sued. A high-profile victim of this aggression was the public-spirited satirical magazine *Private Eye*, whose writers seemed to know far more about Maxwell than they were allowed to print.

On 5 November 1991, just as his empire was on the point of collapse, Maxwell went missing under very mysterious circumstances from his yacht off the Canary Islands. His body was found floating in the North Atlantic shortly afterwards and taken for burial on the Mount of Olives in Jerusalem. It has never been established whether Robert Maxwell accidentally fell off his yacht, committed suicide or was murdered.

Immediately following Maxwell's death there were eulogies for his business achievements. But just a few days after the funeral, it emerged that in order to keep his companies solvent and to subsidize his own extravagant lifestyle he had stolen hundreds of millions of pounds from his employees' pension funds. Obviously Maxwell himself was unaccountable for this crime, and it is probable that this is why he took his life. His sons Kevin and Ian were tried for the misuse of Maxwell Group pension fund stocks to assist a faltering Maxwell company and risking pension fund shares to secure a loan for another Maxwell company. This was one of the largest fraud cases in Britain; Maxwell's two sons were both acquitted in 1996.

Once the true state of Maxwell's business empire became known, his long-silent critics gained courage, and his memory was damned by press and public alike for the unscrupulous way in which he had run his businesses. Commentators speculated that his extraordinary behaviour might be partly explained by the extreme deprivation of his childhood.

British intelligence officers had for a long time suspected that Maxwell was a rogue and possibly a traitor. One theory was that he was a Soviet agent. One report submitted to the Information Research Department, a covert Foreign Office unit, described Maxwell as 'a thoroughly bad character and almost certainly financed by Russia.' The report remained secret until its release in 2003. Another theory is that Maxwell was a secret Israeli agent. The generally shady dealings in the east suggest a figure not unlike Harry Lime, the shadowy anti-hero in the novel and film *The Third Man*, who traded across the Cold War iron curtain. But, ultimately, it is as the destroyer of people's pensions that he will be remembered, and hated for, most.

PETER SELLERS

Born in Southsea 1925, died 1980.
English comedian.

ACHIEVEMENTS:
Co-creator of The Goon Show.
Pioneer of surreal comedy.
1955 – The Ladykillers.
1959 – I'm Alright Jack.
1963 – Dr Strangelove.
1963 – The Pink Panther.

PETER SELLERS WAS born in Southsea in 1925. His career in comedy began with a spell as a stand-up comic and impressionist with the Entertainments National Services Association, invariably known by its acronym ENSA, which some of its employees mischievously said stood for 'Every Night Something Atrocious'. Along with many other comics before him, Peter Sellers learned his trade working with ENSA. Then he went to the Windmill Theatre in London before moving into radio.

Then Peter Sellers met Spike Milligan, and that encounter sparked off the creation of *The Goon Show*. This highly original and innovative half-hour radio programme was a major landmark in the development of comedy. It was Milligan's mad, anarchic plotting that made the scripts so distinctive. Peter Sellers supplied many of the remarkable character voices that carried Milligan's mad narrative along. Harry Secombe and Michael Bentine supplied some of the voices, but neither of them had the extraordinary vocal versatility or character sense that Sellers had. He was a great mimic, and a great collector of voices. He told a story about a scout master who called on Spike Milligan hoping to recruit him for a charity event. Spike told him he was a genius and that although he couldn't help he must go and call on Peter Sellers. When he knocked on Peter Sellers' door, Peter knew at once why Spike had sent him. It was a brand-new comic voice, the one Peter Sellers borrowed for the character Bluebottle.

His gift for character acting, regional and national accents, funny voices, funny faces and slapstick comedy suited him ideally to a career in comedy films. Ironically his main problem in life was taking himself too seriously. His film debut was in *Penny Points to Paradise* in 1951, and he became a well-known face (and voice) in British comedy films in the 1950s and 1960s. He played a spiv in *The Ladykillers* in 1955, a self-important union leader in *I'm Alright Jack* in 1959 and a Welsh librarian in *Only Two Can Play* in 1962.

In 1963, he played three roles in Stanley Kubrick's film *Dr Strangelove*, which established his reputation internationally. But, next to his radio performances in *The Goon Show*, it was for his role as Inspector Clouseau in the Pink Panther films that Peter Sellers was most loved. Sellers refused heart surgery and died in 1980 at only 55. At his funeral, he asked for a particular record to be played. It was Glenn Miller's *In the Mood*. The bewildered priest taking the service speculated that the piece must have held some special significance for Sellers. It was in fact the music Peter Sellers hated most; he thought it was utterly inane. Only those who knew him well understood what Sellers was doing. Spike Milligan got the final joke, chuckled and thought, 'God bless you, Peter Sellers.'

MARILYN MONROE

Born in Los Angeles 1926, died 1962.
American film star, undomestic goddess.

ACHIEVEMENTS:
Became the definitive female sex symbol.
1953 – Gentlemen Prefer Blondes.
1955 – The Seven Year Itch.
1959 – Some Like it Hot.
1961 – The Misfits.

NORMA JEAN BAKER was born in Los Angeles. She had a disturbed childhood, spent mainly in foster homes because of her mother's mental illness. She was an incredibly beautiful young woman, and she got work as a photographer's model in 1946. She turned out to be not only beautiful but extremely photogenic.

It was not long before she was getting offers of small parts in films. The film studio realised the potential of her screen image, and mounted a high-powered publicity campaign to turn her into a star. It worked. She took leading roles in many highly successful films as the stereotype dumb blonde. In 1953, she appeared in both *How to Marry a Millionaire* and *Gentlemen Prefer Blondes*. Though not a great actress, she turned out to have a gift for light comedy, which was used to good effect in *The Seven Year Itch* in 1955 and *Some Like it Hot* in 1959.

Unfortunately, Norma Jean, now the great film star Marilyn Monroe, started to take her acting career seriously. She wanted more serious acting roles. She took acting lessons at Lee Strasberg's Actors' Studio and surprised everybody by being able to carry off more serious roles in *Bus Stop* in 1956 and *The Misfits* in 1961. *The Misfits* was specifically written for her by her third husband, the playwright Arthur Miller.

Marilyn travelled to London to make *The Prince and the Showgirl* with Laurence Olivier in 1957. Two years later she returned to Hollywood, divorcing Arthur Miller in 1961. By this stage she was disintegrating psychologically, unable to manage her life or her career. She had affairs with both President Kennedy and his brother Bobby and there were persistent rumours that her eventual death might have been connected with these affairs. Had Marilyn become a security risk? She became increasingly unstable, perhaps a legacy of her insecure childhood, perhaps an inheritance from her mother. Perhaps she was apprehensive about middle age, when she would no longer be able to dazzle men and audiences with her beauty. She became dependent on sleeping pills, and died by taking an overdose in 1962.

Marilyn Monroe became a symbol of Hollywood's unscrupulous and relentless exploitation of beauty and youth, but she was something more important than that. She – or at least her public persona – was the epitome of a 20th century ideal of womanhood. She represented the dream-come-true girlfriend, shapely, full-lipped, sensual, willing. The negative side was the lack of intelligence, the scattiness, the impracticality; she was a dumb blonde, a bimbo, an air-head. She represented the beautiful possession, the female sex toy that most men wanted to dominate. Other actresses have projected this image too, such as the young Goldie Hawn (who, as many of us suspected, turned out to be far more intelligent than she appeared to be in *The Rowan and Martin's Laugh-In*), but none have projected it so completely, so effectively. Marilyn was what Jung called an archetype – and we all recognize an archetype when we see one. Marilyn presented 'real' women, off-stage women, with a serious problem. Many tried to imitate her. Many tried to be that kind of woman for their men, and it rarely worked, not least because the attributes of a Marilyn Monroe are not the attributes of a good mother or house-keeper; nor are they likely to lead to psychological well-being – as Marilyn herself found out at a terrible cost.

BILL HALEY

Born at Highland 1927, died 1981.
American rock and roll singer.

ACHIEVEMENTS:
Pioneered rock and roll music.
Pioneered 'extreme' band behaviour on stage.
Provoked hysteria among young audiences.

JOHN CLIFTON HALEY (his original name) was born on 6 July 1927 at Highland, Michigan. He started his career as a country music singer. He grew up near Wilmington, listening to the cowboy acts, and learned to play the guitar at the age of only eight. He was playing in public from early on and joined a group in Indiana. Yodelling was one of his specialities.

With his band, The Comets, Bill Haley had a worldwide hit with *Rock Around the Clock* in 1955. His previous record, *Crazy, Man, Crazy,* was very similar indeed rhythmically and melodically, yet only made it as high as number 14 in the pop music charts. There was nothing very special about the music or the melody of *Rock Around the Clock* – both were poor, in fact. The main reason why the number was successful was that it was featured in the 1955 film *The Blackboard Jungle.* The film was about teenage rebellion, and regardless of its inherent quality the song acquired the connotation of gritty rebelliousness; it became iconic by association, rather than because of its content. The song has words that are trite and almost meaningless, and the musical texture is coarse and crude. The dominant feature is the driving rhythm-and-blues dance beat.

The next year a film featuring Bill Haley and the Comets in performance was shown in British cinemas, and the rebellion message was already imprinted. The young audiences, sang, shouted, clapped and danced during showings of the film; boys jived in the aisles. Police had to be called into cinemas to quell the riotous behaviour. It was the beginning of a new, more uninhibited, era of rock concerts – and of freer youth behaviour generally.

From that moment on, Bill Haley has been associated with the beginning of rock and roll music. Other Bill Haley songs include *Shake, Rattle and Roll* and *See You Later, Alligator*. This catch-phrase and its answer, In a while, crocodile, became popular in Princess Margaret's set.

In February 1957, Bill Haley and the Comets in person arrived in England. They disembarked from the Queen Elizabeth and gave performances of *Rock Around the Clock, Rip It Up, Rockin' Through the Rye* and *Don't Knock the Rock*. The new performance style included a saxophonist playing while kneeling and a double bass playing straddling his instrument. The band wore incredibly loud tartan jackets. It was a foreshadowing of what was to come in pop music.

Bill Haley was approaching 30 when he had his great hit. He actually looked nearer 50. He was rather puffy and overweight, and the famous 'kiss curl' on his forehead looked as if might have been stuck on or, worse still, be part of a toupee. Haley died in February 1981 at the aged of 54.

The song that started all the fuss had a strange pedigree. On the face of it, Bill Haley was performing *Rock Around the Clock,* the song written and published by Max Freedman in 1952. But the sheet music of the song is rather more conventional than the piece Haley actually performed. Interestingly the melody that Haley sang was plagiarized from *Move It On Over* by Hank Williams. Haley had had a lengthy career in country music before he reached this strange turning-point. His speciality was what was called 'cowboy swing'. What was peculiar about the music Haley concoted to make his final breakthrough was that it was thoroughly urban in character – as far from the wide open spaces of country music as you could get.

FIDEL CASTRO

Born 1927.
Cuban revolutionary, head of state.

ACHIEVEMENTS:
Organized two revolutions in Cuba.
Overthrew the Batista regime.
Reorganized the Cuban economy along Marxist–Leninist lines.
Repulsed the Bay of Pigs invasion by the Americans.
Staved off American intervention.
Survived numerous attempts by America to remove him.

FIDEL CASTRO WAS born in 1927, the son of a successful sugar planter. He studied law and practised as a lawyer in Havana. He specialized in cases that involved fighting on behalf of poor people, against official corruption under the oppressive rule of President Batista.

In July 1953, Fidel and his brother Raul led a revolution against Batista. It was unsuccessful and Castro was sentenced to 15 years in prison. Under an amnesty, he was free within the year and he took refuge in the United States. Then he went on to Mexico, organizing anti-Batista activities there.

In 1956, Castro and a small band of revolutionaries landed in Cuba, but they were betrayed, ambushed and barely escaped into the mountains. From there he waged an ongoing guerrilla warfare campaign. As Cuba degenerated into a police state, more and more young men drifted over to the revolutionary cause. In December 1958, Castro was able to mount a full-scale attack that was strong enough to force Batista to flee. He was assisted by Che Guevara.

In February 1959 Fidel Castro became Prime Minister of Cuba, announcing a Marxist-Leninist programme adapted to suit Cuba's needs.

He initiated sweeping reforms in agriculture, education and industry. These were not all successful, but enough of his reforms worked for his new regime to gain support. He managed to overthrow the dominance of the USA in the Cuban economy. The American response to the Communist regime in its backyard was an invasion. Luckily for Castro, the Bay of Pigs invasion in April 1961 was a high-profile disaster for the Americans and a propaganda victory for Castro.

Following the Bay of Pigs, Castro depended on Soviet support against the ever-present threat from America. This led directly to confrontation between the super-powers and the near-catastrophe of the Cuban missile crisis of 1962.

Castro has had ongoing problems in managing the Cuban economy. Sugar and tobacco production have not proved reliable. In spite of many problems, Fidel Castro's personal popularity remained high.

There have been many attempts by the Americans, both open and covert, to get rid of Castro, but all have failed. It is not known how many attempts the Americans made to assassinate Castro, but in 1975 a committee set up by the US Senate to investigate the CIA, found documentary proof that the CIA had planned to assassinate Castro. Given the power and wealth of the USA, and given how much the US authorities have hated having him as a next-door neighbour, his survival is in itself a remarkable achievement. Castro has denied any involvement in the assassination of President John F. Kennedy, and there is no reason to doubt his denial. Castro succeeded, against huge odds, in overthrowing the Batista regime, in reorganizing the Cuban economy along Marxist-Leninist lines, and in staving off American intervention. His actions led indirectly to the Cuban missile crisis, but the principal blame for that must rest with Kennedy.

CHE GUEVARA

Born in Buenos Aires 1928, died at Villa Grande, Bolivia,
  1967.
Argentinian Communist revolutionary leader.

ACHIEVEMENTS:
Second-in-command to Castro in the Cuban revolution.
Set up guerrilla groups in other Latin American states.
Inspired a generation of young people with the hope of change.
1961 – Guerrilla Warfare.
1968 – Reminiscences of the Cuban Revolutionary War.

ERNESTO GUEVARA DE la Serna was born in Buenos Aires on 14 June
1928. He studied medicine, graduating from the University of Buenos
Aires in 1953.

Two years later, Guevara joined Fidel Castro's revolutionary movement
in Mexico and he played an important role in leading the Cuban revolution
from 1956 to 1959. On 17 September 1958, six columns of insurgents left
Castro's mountain fortress in western Cuba intent on destroying the
Batista regime. Two of these columns marched on central Cuba; one was
led by Fidel Castro's brother Raul, the other by Ernesto, now 'Che',
Guevara. After Castro's installation as head of state, Major Guevara held
various posts in the Cuban government under Castro's leadership. He was
for a time head of the Cuban National Bank.

What was remarkable about Che Guevara was that he was not content
to overturn one corrupt and oppressive government; he wanted to go on
and topple more. In this respect he was like La Fayette or Bolivar. In
October 1965, Castro announced that Che Guevara had left Cuba to

become a revolutionary and guerrilla leader in South America, as Castro put it, 'to fight imperialism abroad.'

He was eventually hunted down by government troops while attempting to stir up revolution in Bolivia. Guevara's movements for the previous two years had been uncertain. There were unreliable reports of sightings, even reports of his death. Eventually Bolivian government troops found him at Villa Grande in Bolivia. He was ambushed, caught and summarily shot along with 6 other guerrillas on 10 October 1967. He was 39 years old.

What Che Guevara actually did was not particularly glamorous, praiseworthy or constructive, but he had a strong appeal to young people in the 1960s and 1970s as a symbol of endeavour, of fighting tyranny and injustice. Che Guevara would not accept that ordinary people had to put up with the status quo. If governments were unsatisfactory, oppressive or tyrannical, people should believe in the possibility of getting rid of them. He was a symbol of striving, of rebellion, of the hope of freedom. One photograph of Guevara in particular, with beret, long hair, moustache and beard, became a poster icon that was seen everywhere in students' lodgings. It was a zeitgeist icon that gave hope for change. There are other photographs of Guevara that show him as strikingly ordinary in appearance. One, of the adolescent Ernesto lying flat on his back on a balcony in Buenos Aires, shows a boy who looks too idle to achieve anything at all. But the poster icon is the archetypal revolutionary. Many young people in the 1960s and 1970s wanted to be like Guevara. The young are idealistic. They want to change the world, and Che Guevara seemed to be the ultimate world-changer.

MARTIN LUTHER KING

Born in Atlanta 1929, died in Memphis 1968.
Black American civil rights leader.

ACHIEVEMENTS:
Campaigned vigorously for the civil rights of black people in
America.
Succeeded in maintaining non-violent protests in spite of
provocation.
Responsible for the Civil Rights Act of 1964.
Martyred for the cause of human rights.

MARTIN LUTHER KING was born in Atlanta, Georgia, in 1929. He was the son of a Baptist minister, and went on to study theology at the Crozier Theological Seminary at Chester, Pennsylvania, then Boston University. It was while at college that King became a disciple of Gandhi, who was assassinated at that time, and became committed to Gandhi's doctrine of non-violence.

King set up the first black ministry at Montgomery, Alabama, in 1955. Segregation – the separation of blacks and whites – still prevailed in the state of Alabama. Martin Luther King first became widely known as a black activist and anti-segregationist when he led the Alabama bus boycott. The University of Alabama defied the federal court by admitting their first black student. The Supreme Court ruled that its outlawing of segregation in state schools extended to independent colleges; this ruling was aimed at the University of North Carolina, which had turned away three students just because they were black. President Eisenhower gave weak support to the civil rights movement with the words, 'It is incumbent on all the South to show some progress toward racial integration.' It was not enough.

Martin Luther King founded the Southern Christian Leadership Conference in 1957, which set up civil rights activities throughout the country. King was therefore responsible for galvanizing both the black and white populations of the United States into confronting the unfair treatment of black people. He was the central figure.

He became a natural target for discrimination. In 1958 he was arrested 'for loitering' and beaten up by the police. Two years later he was arrested for falsifying his income tax return, but later acquitted.

Martin Luther King was a powerful orator, with a big preacher's voice and an ear for telling and memorable phrases. Using his powers of oratory, King addressed public meetings and energized the civil rights movement, which was firmly based on non-violent principles. The movement led to the great march through Washington in 1963, attended by over 200,000 black and white demonstrators, among them Marlon Brando, Judy Garland, Bob Dylan and Burt Lancaster. At this, the biggest demonstration for civil rights, King asked people not to 'drink from the cup of hatred and bitterness'. He told them:

> *I still have a dream. It is a dream chiefly rooted in the American dream. I have a dream that one day this nation will rise up and live out the true meaning of its creed: 'We hold these truths to be self-evident, that all men are created equal.'*

In April 1963, three days after John F. Kennedy awarded Winston Churchill honorary US citizenship, King was arrested for leading another civil rights march in Alabama. Shortly afterwards, 1,000 black people were arrested on another march, prompting President Kennedy to visit the South in person and praise the work of the demonstrators. But in September Governor Wallace of Alabama ordered his state troops to halt integration at a high school. A week later, the president took control of the Alabama state militia in order to allow integration to proceed. There were shootings. King pleaded with demonstrators 'to remain non-violent in the face of extreme provocation.'

But in 1964 he saw success on a grand scale. Martin Luther King was there to shake hands with President Johnson after Johnson signed the Civil Rights Act, which enshrined in law all the things for which King had been campaigning. Kennedy had been preparing the legislation as the time of his own assassination approached. Johnson saw it through, ensuring that the US Congress did not weaken it. Johnson called on Americans to 'eliminate the last vestiges of injustice in America.' That year, King was given an honorary doctorate by Yale University, the Kennedy Peace Prize and the Nobel Peace Prize.

The struggle was not over. Early in 1965 King led yet another march in Montgomery to protest about bombs found on the premises of various black organizations.

Martin Luther King's career came to an abrupt end in 1968, when he was assassinated in Memphis, Tennessee, where he had gone to lead a dustmen's strike. He stepped out onto the balcony outside his motel room, and leant over the rail to speak to his friend, Revd Jesse Jackson. His last words were, 'Be sure to sing *Precious Lord* tonight, and sing it well!' He was shot dead by a sniper in a nearby building. His alleged assassin, a white man called James Earl Ray, escaped from the country and was arrested in London. Ray was found guilty and sentenced to 99 years in prison. It is still unclear whether Ray acted alone, or even whether he was involved at all.

Martin Luther King's widow, Coretta King, continued his civil rights work through the Martin Luther King Jr Centre for Social Changes which was set up in Alabama. The third Monday in each January has been established in America as Martin Luther King Day.

MIKHAIL GORBACHEV

> *Born at Privolnoye 1931.*
>
> ACHIEVEMENTS:
> *Launched* glasnost *(openness) and* perestroika *(restructuring)*
>   *in the USSR.*
> *Initiated the Nuclear Forces abolition treaty with USA.*
> *Ended the Cold War.*
> *Ended the power of the Communist Party in the Soviet Union.*
> *Brought about the disintegration of the Soviet Union.*

MIKHAIL GORBACHEV WAS born at Privolnoye in the Caucasus in 1931. His father was an agricultural mechanic. Gorbachev studied law at Moscow University, starting his course in 1950. It was while at university that he met and married Raisa Titorenko, a philosophy student.

He joined the Communist Party in 1952, worked actively for it, introducing reforms and becoming local party leader in 1970. He was admitted to the CPSU secretariat as Agriculture Secretary in 1978 and became a member of the Politburo in 1980. During the brief Chernenko administration of 1984–85, he emerged as second-in-command, becoming party general secretary on Chernenko's death. At 54, Gorbachev was the youngest member of the ruling Politburo, and he represented a new generation who wanted change. In an early speech he talked of wanting better relations with the West and a reduction in weapons stockpiles. It turned out that these were not empty words. As early as April 1985 he announced a 10-month freeze in the deployment of missiles aimed at Western Europe.

As party leader, he soon forced the retirement of obstructive colleagues and brought in a younger generation of technocrats who were interested in reform, which is what Gorbachev had in view. In 1985 he launched a campaign against alcoholism and corruption, quickly followed by a large programme of liberalizing reforms under the general slogans of *glasnost* (openness) and *perestroika* (restructuring). A major test of Gorbachev's openness was the Chernobyl nuclear disaster of 1986; information about the disaster was made freely available not only within the Soviet Union but abroad. The openness extended to releasing at least some political dissidents. Gorbachev telephoned Dr Andrei Sakharov, a high-profile dissident who had been exiled to Gorky, that his exile was over. Sakharov took the opportunity to ask Gorbachev to release all the other political dissidents still languishing in prisons and labour camps.

In foreign policy, Gorbachev was just as radical. He held out the hand of friendship to President Reagan, meeting him several times. He had his first meeting with the American president in November 1985, when the two men agreed to work towards halving their strategic weapons stockpiles. Before he returned to Moscow, Gorbachev held an unprece- dented 95 minute press conference. His message was, 'The world has become a safer place.' The October 1986 summit in Reykjavik was less successful. It emerged that Reagan was not prepared to give up his planned outer-space defence shield (known as Star Wars) and the meeting ended without agreement – except to meet again. In April 1987, Gorbachev offered to remove all the Soviet short-range missiles from Europe; this unexpected offer took the Americans completely by surprise and led to the historic Nuclear Forces abolition treaty signed on 8 December 1987. It marked the end of the Cold War. In a similar spirit, Gorbachev ordered the withdrawal of Soviet troops from Afghanistan in 1989 and a gradual disengagement from the Communist countries of Eastern Europe. What was under way was far more radical, and far more historic than any Western observers expected – or indeed thought possible.

Gorbachev became an executive president with enhanced powers in 1990. His thrust towards the creation of a 'socialist pluralist' democracy met with a lot of opposition from conservatives within the Communist party, especially in Russia; the Russian empire seemed to be disintegrating and the hegemony of Russia was no longer guaranteed. The Baltic republics claimed their independence from the Soviet Union. Gorbachev attempted to stop or delay this in order to avoid further internal trouble, but the disintegration of the Soviet Union was under way.

In 1990 Gorbachev was awarded the Nobel Peace Prize, in recognition of his role in improving East-West relations – in effect bringing the Cold War to an unexpected end.

Dissidents within were a constant threat. In November 1987, Gorbachev made the mistake of sacking Boris Yeltsin, who was the Moscow Communist Party boss, for criticizing him – he had said that Gorbachev was too slow to make reforms. Yeltsin was an enthusiastic supporter of glasnost and perestroika, but impatient for change. From that time on, opposition to Gorbachev was increasingly led by Boris Yeltsin, apparently out of revenge. Gorbachev's resignation was forced in 1991. He fell from power at a critical moment when the power of the Communist Party collapsed and the Soviet Union was abolished.

ELVIS PRESLEY

Born at Tupelo 1935, died at Graceland 16 August 1977.

ACHIEVEMENTS:
Combined country and western music and rhythm and blues.
Used an overtly sexual performance style.
Encouraged audience hysteria as part of the performance.
Pioneered a new, raw, youth-driven popular music.

ELVIS AARON PRESLEY was born on 8 January, 1935 at Tupelo, Mississippi. He was brought up in a religious family, and was singing from an early age in the local church choir. Like many other boys, he taught himself how to play guitar. In 1953, while he was still driving trucks in Memphis, he was discovered by Sam Phillips, who was president of Sun Records. He heard a record Presley had made privately for his mother. It was the ultimate lucky break, the chance encounter that makes the difference between success and failure, between fame and obscurity. Elvis Presley's first single, *That's All Right Mama,* was released on 19 July, 1954.

By 1956, just three years after he was discovered, Elvis Presley was the most popular performer in the USA. At 21 he was already a millionaire. Within another year he was known all over the world. It was an incredibly rapid rise to fame. His most popular records were *Blue Suede Shoes, Heartbreak Hotel, Hound Dog, Love Me Tender, All Shook Up* and *It's Now or Never.* He performed on Ed Sullivan's television show in September 1956 and was watched by 50 million Americans. The *New York Times* commented that his 'singing was singularly distasteful'. His provocative gyrations and animal grunts sent the girls wild. There were demands that in future TV appearances, Presley was to be shown from the waist up only. But all this official disapproval only enhanced his popularity with the young.

His particular contribution to popular music was the way he combined two very different types of music: white country and western music and rhythm and blues. Presley's music bridged two sub-cultures – and two races. This in itself made an interesting new sound. His performance style was also extremely provocative. Bill Haley's band got down on their knees and straddled their instruments. Elvis Presley used an earthy, sensual style that suggested that he was in the grip of sexual passion. It was a consummate stage act that was a terrific success with teenage girls. They yelled, they screamed, they fainted. In fact the audience response became part of the act. That in itself was something new.

Sex had found its way into popular music before. *Bewitched, Bothered and Bewildered* and a whole string of other steamy romantic numbers had been written long before Presley arrived on the scene. Sex was an integral part of the music-hall tradition too – George Formby's *My Little Stick of Blackpool Rock*, for instance. What was different here was that Presley was not trying to make his audiences laugh at sex, nor was he crooning. He was, or was pretending to be, in the grip of sexual ecstasy.

This not only attracted a committed female following – it also attracted a lot of criticism and therefore press coverage. Controversy raged over Elvis Presley, nicknamed Elvis the Pelvis after his thrusting hips. People either loved him or hated him. Moralists accused him of obscenity. Blacks also accused him of pilfering black music.

The other thing that was new was that Presley's music was unequivocally the music of teenagers. For the first time popular music was about the young, by the young, for the young – or so it seemed. It was a breaking loose from the older generation, along the same lines as Bill Haley.

Presley's career was broken, in more ways than one, by his period of national service. He received his call-up papers in December 1957 and the following March he reported for duty at a Memphis Draft Board to begin his two-year stint. The loss of earnings was considerable, but he dutifully commented, 'I think it will be a great experience for me.' After the national service, though, his songs were weaker, limper, more pedestrian. Had he run out of ideas? Or had army life made him more ordinary?

After the army, Presley's appearances were mainly in a sequence of poor films which were the idea of his forceful manager, Colonel Parker, who had once been a carnival huckster. The films include *Loving You*, made in 1957, *GI Blues*, made in 1960, and *That's the Way It Is* in 1971. In the 1970s, Presley launched into a new career phase, performing in a nightclub in Las Vegas. His act consisted of rather short-winded and poor performances of his early hit numbers and weepy ballads. He looked puffy, overweight, sweaty and unfit.

In his final years Presley suffered poor health through drug-taking and obesity. His death at Graceland, his Memphis mansion, on 16 August, 1977 nevertheless came as a great shock to his fans. Some of them refused to believe that he really was dead. For many years afterwards there were repeated 'Elvis sightings'.

GERMAINE GREER

> *Born 1939.*
> *Australian feminist author, academic and lecturer.*
>
> ACHIEVEMENTS:
> *Launched the feminist movement.*
> *Helped to bring about an equalization of the sexes.*
> *Became a role model for the New Woman.*
> *1970* – The Female Eunuch.
> *1984* – Sex and Destiny.

GERMAINE GREER WAS born in 1939. She attended the universities of Melbourne, Sydney and Cambridge, where she was awarded her doctorate. Then, in 1968, she became a lecturer in English at the University of Warwick, where she remained until 1973.

Germaine Greer made her name in 1970 when she published her book, *The Female Eunuch*. In this strong and very effective polemic, Dr Greer portrayed marriage as a legalized form of slavery for women. She also vehemently attacked the systematic denial and misrepresentation of female sexuality by a society whose values were set and maintained by men. The book made a huge impact. It was the greatest single landmark in the emancipation of women since the invention of the contraceptive pill by Gregory Pincus, and it marked the beginning of a new wave of militant feminism. Women took up the cause of female emancipation in a way that paralleled the behaviour of another generation earlier in the 20th century over votes for women.

In the wake of this movement came legislation ensuring equal treatment for men and women in the workplace, improved protection of women's property rights while going through divorce, and a range of other measures.

Germaine Greer has continued to be a regular contributor to periodicals and magazines, and a frequent television panellist and reviewer. Her face and voice are internationally known.

Germaine Greer has been a great activist, in setting in motion a whole series of changes that have empowered women. She has also become an icon of another kind of woman. Marilyn Monroe is the icon of the ideal women in the traditional Western male-dominated society. Germaine Greer has become the icon of the 'New Woman', fully empowered, outspoken, challenging, setting her own values and not accepting those dished out to her by men. This too has empowered many women – by showing them another role model, an alternative to Marilyn.

JOHN LENNON AND PAUL McCARTNEY

John Lennon: born in Liverpool 1940, died in New York 1980.
  Paul McCartney: born in Liverpool 1942.
Pop musicians.

ACHIEVEMENTS:
Closed the widening gap between serious and popular music.
Greatly enriched the language of popular music.
Set new standards for popular music.
1963 – From Me To You.
1964 – A Hard Day's Night.
1967 – Sergeant Pepper's Lonely Hearts Club Band.
1969 – Abbey Road.
1970 – Let It Be.

JOHN LENNON AND Paul McCartney were the two leading members of the Beatles. This was a British pop group formed in Liverpool in 1960, learning its trade in a relentless series of engagements at The Cavern Club in Liverpool and at venues in Hamburg. Skilfully managed by Brian Epstein, they produced a series of highly successful records. In 1964 *She Loves You* and *I Want to Hold Your Hand* were released in the USA, and Beatlemania instantly spread round the world like a bush fire.

The Beatles split up in 1970, yet their influence continues many years later. They had great admiration for the pop singers of the previous generation, and some of their own generation – they revered Elvis Presley and Chuck Berry, for instance – but they outstripped all of them.

One curious feature of the Beatles was the rate at which their musical style developed. Songs they were writing in the early 1960s were still in the bland, perky style of the 1950s. *From Me To You,* written in 1963, was still in the mainstream of 1950s pop. It was a good enough song, with a well-written middle section, but it did not stand out as any kind of breakthrough. By the time *Strawberry Fields* came out a new, exotic sound had been created that was both musically and emotionally more complex, and that was only four years later.

The classical tradition in Western music developed through the 18th and 19th centuries by a process of evolution, using well-tried melodic and harmonic procedures. In the 20th century, many serious composers felt that this was all rather tired and predictable and that a new musical language was needed. Schoenberg led the way. Writing music in keys was abandoned, and in some cases even writing for recognized musical instruments was abandoned. The result was a period of alienation. Avant-garde composers wrote music that interested themselves and each other, and they lost their mass audiences. By the middle of the 20th century, very few people in the West were listening to contemporary 'serious' music; most were listening to popular music, which had kept to the conventions of 19th century music. Most pop songs were written in ABA, or ABABA, form, and always in an identifiable key, always on traditional instruments. There was a dangerous division between the two musical worlds. This was paralleled in the art world, where abstract artists had left most of the art lovers, who liked figurative art, way behind.

The Beatles, and their composers in particular, John Lennon and Paul McCartney, did much to close the rift. They did it by drawing on more of the melodic and harmonic devices from the classical vocabulary than any popular musicians had previously done. Nearly all pop songs in the 1940s and 1950s depended on just three chords. The early Beatles songs did the same. In 1962 they used four. By 1967 they were up to 16. In the song *I am the Walrus* a strange monotonous melody line is given an eerie slithering character by the shifting, gliding sequence of chords underneath it.

The Beatles' technique of plundering the 18th and 19th centuries for tricks and effects that would add interest to their songs extended to keys as well as chords. In classical music, excitement is often produced by a key change, as in the climax of Beethoven's *Egmont Overture*. McCartney was fascinated by this effect and used seven key changes in his song *Penny Lane*. He took the melody line up for the chorus or refrain, which is a traditional song-writing technique, as it creates a sense of moving forwards, often a sense of optimism. But he also took the underpinning chords down, which took the emotional charge down to something less positive. The overall effect was to express ambivalent feelings about the past, about a Liverpudlian boyhood in particular. This put *Penny Lane* right into English nostalgia, a major tradition in English art, and one that is found in works as different as Elgar's *Introduction and Allegro*, Belloc's *Halnaker Mill* and Britten's *Serenade*.

In 1966, Lennon and McCartney wrote *Eleanor Rigby*. This very moving piece, a cleverly and wittily orchestrated urban folk ballad, is quite different from contemporary pop songs. It is in an unusual key, for a start. It is in E minor in the Dorian mode, like *Scarborough Fair*, and it may well be that Paul McCartney used *Scarborough Fair* as his starting point.

Then came the Indian influence. The Beatles became interested in the teachings of Indian mysticism, and through that Indian music. George Harrison, another member of the group, learned to play the sitar. From there it was a short step to using Indian instruments to create extra layers of colour in their music. John Lennon's melodic writing was less adventurous than Paul McCartney's, but the rivalry between the two men pushed him into trying new things. In *Jealous Guy*, Lennon used the pentatonic scale characteristic of Indian music.

Then came the recording studio influence. McCartney attended performances of works by avant-garde composers like Berio and Stockhausen and became interested in their use of prepared tapes, adopting them as, in effect, additional instruments. Tape loops became part of the musical texture. Soon the group was producing soundscapes that sounded hallucinogenic. In *Tomorow Never Knows*, Lennon set out to create the effect of the drug LSD. At every stage, the music developed by a process of inclusion, embracing new and old techniques, and enriching the language of music. The great landmark was the *Sergeant Pepper* album, which showed them at the peak of their ability as creators and performers, and showed what might be achieved in popular music. It was felt as such by many of us who were young at the time, and it has certainly been recognized subsequently as a landmark in music.

The avant-garde composers' insistence on atonality and other innovations was profoundly destructive. It took the Beatles working in the world of popular music and Michael Tippett working in the world of classical music to make good the damage, to show how the Western tradition could be rescued. With the Beatles, the process of healing began. After the Beatles, it was all right to compose in keys or modes. It was all right to express emotion through harmonies and chord progressions.

How untrained musicians like Paul McCartney and John Lennon could have achieved this is something of a mystery. Part of the explanation lies in their early experiences in Hamburg, when they had to slog their way through a large repertoire of popular music in seven-hour sessions. This ordeal gave them range, variety, facility and versatility to write almost anything. In the technical achievement of the sounds they wanted, they were helped enormously by the ingenuity of George Martin, the unseen 'Fifth Beatle', who was their producer and arranger.

BOB GELDOF

Born in Dublin 1951.
Pop singer, charity fundraiser, controversialist.

ACHIEVEMENTS:
Organized fund-raising record (Do they know it's
  Christmas?)
Organized the first Live Aid *concert.*
Organized the Sport Aid *event.*
Organized the Live8 *concerts.*
Raised public awareness of poverty in Africa.
1986 – Is That It? *(autobiography)*

BOB GELDOF WAS born in Dublin on 5 October, 1951, and educated at
Black Rock College. He had a career in journalism, writing for the *New
Musical Express* and *Melody Maker*. In 1975 he became the lead singer in a
rock band called the Boomtown Rats. On the strength of his rock band
profile, Geldof was given some roles in films, such as *Pink Floyd – The Wall*
and *Number One*.

  Some observers in the music business saw him then as a singer with
little future, but something happened in 1985 that changed the direction
of his life. Like thousands of other people he watched a powerful TV news
report by Michael Buerk – himself a major influencer – on the famine in
Ethiopia. He was moved by the plight of starving Africans and struck by
his own relative comfort. Geldof decided to make a record as a means of
raising money to relieve the famine. Some of the artists and bands he
approached were understandably suspicious of his motives, but Geldof was
on a mission. He tried persuasion, he resorted to abuse, until people went

along with his plan. Michael Jackson and other black singers were approached, but ironically – given that the cause was starving black people – they all declined.

The result was a record entitled *Do they know it's Christmas?* with its chorus 'Feed the World'. It was a great success, raising £8 million to alleviate the famine in Ethiopia. Other charities saw Geldof's initiative as a threat, so his associates persuaded Geldof to go to Africa to make sure the aid reached the needy. He was unwilling to do this for a variety of reasons. Not least, he did not want to be filmed with starving children, knowing that this would be seen as milking the charity image. He still had a living to make as a musician and did not want to damage his music career. Naturally, the press photographers who accompanied him wanted exactly that sort of picture story from him. He did however manage to meet the Ethiopian head of state and tell him what he thought of him, although the translator stopped translating at that point. Later, when he met Margaret Thatcher, there was no need for a translator.

The success of the British aid record prompted an American copy-cat record, called *We are the World*. This featured a host of American black singers, including Michael Jackson.

Geldof went on to organize a massive fund-raising event, the *Live Aid* concert. Many pop musicians offered their services free in order to mount the concert at Wembley on 13 July 1985, which featured 25 bands on stage. A parallel and simultaneous event was mounted across the Atlantic in Philadelphia, and a total of 58 bands played live. Many critics predicted that it would be chaotic, but it was a huge success. A huge sum was raised – £50 million – and this was distributed in Africa to alleviate distress. In 1986 he organized a similar *Sport Aid* event, which raised a further £50 million.

Many people admire Bob Geldof for his determination to help the needy, and for his success in raising huge sums of money for worthy causes. He has been given the UN World Hunger Award, the FAO Medal, the EEC Gold Medal, the Irish Peace Prize, the Order of Two Niles (Sudan) and been made a Cavalier of the Order of Leopold II of Belgium.

Geldof has been criticized by the major aid organizations. While he has succeeded in raising huge sums of money as gifts from the general public, these 'one-off' charities have resulted in a reduction in the income of organizations such as Oxfam and Christian Aid, who have long-term aid programmes organized. There is also a danger that emotional appeals made through TV and the press in the wake of a particularly 'photogenic' emergency may produce a lop-sided financial response. This seems to have been the case with the Boxing Day tsunami disaster in 2004, when the global response to an appeal for financial aid was overwhelming and excessive – in relation to the hundreds of smaller tragedies unfolding round the world all the time.

Bob Geldof staged another event 20 years later, *Live8*, to coincide with a G8 meeting of politicians from eight rich countries in July 2005. The *Live8* campaign was dogged by problems, including Geldof's questionable appeal for a Dunkirk-style squadron of supporters to come to Britain across the Channel. He was widely criticized for this. There is also the huge cost of the concerts and the cost of travelling to attend them.

A further criticism coming from experts is that aid beyond a certain level is unhelpful. Gandhi did not approve of giving hand-outs to beggars. Some countries have become aid-dependent, waiting for the next hand-out from the rich countries instead of seeking radical self-help solutions within their own frontiers. There is also the thought that there is an air of patronage and condescension about giving money to the poor; it is a piece of cultural chauvinism. The best way to deal with a beggar is not to give him food but to show him how to produce his own food; then he can be permanently self-sufficient.

Any effort to alleviate the destitution of Africa must be welcomed, and Geldof's initiatives are certainly a positive effort in that direction. Geldof is also conscious that it is essential to use non-violent means, and he specifically cites Gandhi and Martin Luther King as successful precedents. But populist initiatives such as *Live Aid* and *Live8* do nothing to address the main problems that bedevil the continent. One is what journalist Basildon Peta describes as the 'criminal incompetence of Africa's post-colonial black elites.' It is this more than anything else that prevents the poor countries of Africa from lifting themselves out of poverty in the way that their Asian equivalents have done. South Korea was a much poorer country than Senegal or Ghana back in 1964, yet it is now 40 times richer than both of those countries put together, both in total GDP and in per capita income. In a similar way, Thailand has become richer than most African countries, simply as a result of good government. The key to development is not aid from rich outsiders but systematic spending on education. High spending on education helps the poor to make the most of their abilities; it also leads to the evolution of a middle class, and African countries lack middle classes. The leaders of South Korea realised they had to invest in their people, educated them, and the country as a whole has reaped the benefits, in both social and economic development. The political elites in the poorer countries in Africa have shown no interest in helping their people to better themselves – only in enriching themselves and remaining in power as long as possible in order to do so.

One newspaper commented that *Live8* was 'old white guys singing the wrong song.'

Even so, Bob Geldof has empowered many ordinary people, and made them feel that they can directly improve the lives of other people less fortunate than themselves. He has also had the courage to confront high-ranking politicians and ask them uncomfortable questions about their actions. Any activity that discomposes politicians and makes them more accountable to their electors has to be a good thing.

BILL GATES

Born in Seattle 1955.
American software designer, computer programmer,
  philanthropist.

ACHIEVEMENTS:
Founded Microsoft Corporation.
Developed BASIC, the language for the first microcomputer.
Pioneered personal computers for home and office.
Created MS-DOS, then Microsoft Windows.
Controls the internet.
Founded the Bill and Melinda Gates Foundation.
Helped to establish English as the international language of
  computing.
Helped to establish English as the global language.
1999 – Business @ the Speed of Thought.

WILLIAM HENRY GATES was born in Seattle, Washington on 28 October, 1955. His father, William H. Gates Senior, was a Seattle attorney. His mother Mary was a schoolteacher. Bill Gates developed an early obsession with computers. It was while he was at the private Lakeside School that he first discovered his interest, and he was programming computers by the age of 13.

He entered Harvard University as a freshman in 1973, where he lived not far from Steve Ballmer, who later was to become Microsoft's chief executive officer. While he was still at Harvard, which he left without graduating, Bill Gates developed a version of the programming language BASIC, which was to be used for the very first microcomputer, the MITS Altair. He worked on BASIC with Paul Allen, a friend since childhood.

In 1975, at the age of only 19, Bill Gates founded Microsoft Corporation in collaboration with Paul Allen. Five years later, they licensed a computer operating system to IBM (International Business Machines) to use in the personal computer industry which was then just getting started. With the advent of the microchip it was suddenly possible to manufacture computers that were small enough to install in people's homes and offices. The computer system that Bill Gates and Paul Allen created, MS-DOS (Microsoft Disk Operating System), and all the applications systems that dovetail into it have been a phenomenal success.

From the early days onward, Gates and Allen have been motivated by the belief that the computer would be a valuable tool in every office and home. The Microsoft mission is to improve software continually, to make it easier, more cost-effective, and to make it more enjoyable for people to use computers. And the mission is successful. Through his Microsoft firm, Gates had been able to maintain his remarkable dominance in the personal computer industry by producing repeated updates that are hugely successful in meeting customer needs – such as Windows 95, Windows 98 and Windows XP 2005. Microsoft became the world's largest producer of microcomputer software.

Microsoft is now a huge multinational enterprise. It brought in revenues of almost 37 billion dollars in one year recently, and it employs 55,000 people in 85 countries. Adaptation to rapid change and keeping ahead of possible competitors are very important, and the level of investment is very high – over 6 billion dollars in one year.

Bill Gates has made aggressive attempts to expand his business into new markets. One of these initiatives was his purchase in 1995 of the Bettmann Archives. This enabled him to transform historic photographs into digital images for use on-line as part of his Corbis resource, which is one of the largest resources of visual images in the world. In 1996 he made efforts to gain a big stake in the Internet market.

By 1986, Bill Gates was a billionaire. He is undoubtedly one of the richest people in the world. He is also, because he in effect controls the internet, one of the most powerful people in the world. He uses his money intelligently and thoughtfully. With his wife he set up the Bill and Melinda Gates Foundation, which has supported global health and learning to the tune of 27 billion dollars.

Bill Gates compiled a list of tips to help the young. One was that it was a bad idea to pick on the nerd in your class; one day he might be your boss.

TIM BERNERS-LEE

Born in London 1955.
British software designer.

ACHIEVEMENTS:
Invented the World Wide Web.
Designed the URL (universal resource locator) or web address.
Invented HTML, the hypertext markup language.
Helped to establish English as the international language of
*   computing.*
Helped to establish English as the global language.
2000 – Weaving the Web.

TIM BERNERS-LEE was born in London on 8 June, 1955. He was educated at Emanuel School, London, and Queen's College, Oxford, where he graduated in 1976.

Berners-Lee worked for Plessey Telecommunications Ltd as a software engineer for two years, then as an industrial consultant to D. G. Nash Ltd for a further two years. At this time, while he was a software consultant, he designed an unpublished programme which he called Enquire. This was the forerunner of the World Wide Web.

He then became the founding director responsible for technical design at Image Computer Systems Ltd (1981–84). Then for ten years he worked at CERN in Geneva. From 1989 onwards he worked on his highly ambitious global hypertext project, which became known as the World Wide Web in 1990, and was available on the internet from 1991. Tim Berners-Lee joined the Laboratory for Computer Science at the Massachusetts Institute of Technology in 1994.

The World Wide Web is the great invention of our age, and the biggest advance in communications since the invention of television. It is an easy, point-and-click way of navigating and sorting the data stored on the internet. It has turned the information stored on the internet into a colossal, but very accessible, magazine. Addresses on the World Wide Web are instantly recognizable by their opening formula – www, for World Wide Web – such as www.rodneycastleden.co.uk. The web has proved to be such an easy, cheap and flexible platform for communication that it has sparked an explosion of publishing, both professional and amateur. As a result of its popularity, it contains a colossal amount of information and spans a huge range of topics. The lack of editorial control is both its strength and its weakness; the web is all-inclusive, a noisy babbling marketplace where the mad, the wicked and the ignorant take their place alongside the sane, the virtuous and the well-informed.

As if devising the World Wide Web were not a great enough achievement, Tim Berners-Lee designed the URL (universal resource locator) that we are all familiar with – the web address. He also invented HTML, the hypertext markup language. Thanks to Tim Berners-Lee, we have a global communications system – open to us all.

OSAMA BIN LADEN

Born in Saudi Arabia 1957.
Islamic terrorist leader, leader of the terrorist organization Al
  Qaeda.

ACHIEVEMENTS:
Declared a new kind of war to replace the Cold War.
1993 – Responsible for ordering the first attack on the World
  Trade Centre.
1998 – Issued a fatwa against all American citizens and their
  allies.
2001 – Responsible for ordering the 9/11 attack on the World
  Trade Centre.
2004 – Responsible for ordering the Madrid train bombings.

OSAMA BIN LADEN was born in Saudi Arabia in 1957. For some years past now, he has figured in the FBI's list of Ten Most Wanted Fugitives, and it is revealing to see bin Laden through the eyes of the FBI. He is wanted for 'murder of US nationals outside the United States; conspiracy to murder US nationals outside the United States; attack on a federal facility resulting in death'. The FBI give his details as follows:

Height: 6ft 4ins to 6ft 6ins; Weight: approximately 160 pounds; Build: Thin; Occupation: Unknown; Hair: Brown; Eyes: Brown; Complexion: Olive; Sex: Male; Nationality: Saudi Arabian; remarks: Bin Laden is the leader of a terrorist organization known as Al-Qaeda, 'The Base'. He is left-handed and walks with a cane. Osama bin Laden is wanted in connection with the August 7 1998 bombings of the United States embassies in Dar es Salaam, Tanzania and Nairobi, Kenya. These attacks *killed over 200 people. In addition, bin Laden is a suspect in other terrorist attacks throughout the world. Considered armed and extremely dangerous. The US Department of State is offering a reward of up to $25 million for information leading directly to the apprehension or conviction of Osama bin Laden.*

This sum of $25 million would not be easy money, though.

Osama bin Laden is a remarkable, ascetic-looking Islamic fundamentalist. He was a Saudi millionaire, and is now an Islamic terrorist leader. He has been known to the US authorities ever since the days when he was fighting with the CIA against the Soviet army in Afghanistan. Now he is US public enemy number one. He was born on 30 July, 1957, the 17th of 20 sons of a Saudi construction magnate of Yemeni origin. He took a degree in public administration in 1981 in Jeddah. Bin Laden came to prominence in the Afghan war of independence against the Soviet Union. In 1989, when the war was over, he returned to Saudi Arabia to work in the family firm, the Bin Laden Construction Group.

As a result of his radical Islamic contacts and opposition to the ruling Al Saud family, the Saudi government revoked his citizenship in 1994 and his family disowned him. In 1996, in response to US and Egyptian pressure, Sudan expelled him too and he returned to Afghanistan, where he has lived ever since under the protection of the Taliban. He has put himself in the unusual position of being an incredibly wealthy outcast, rich but dispossessed. His already distorted vision of the world has become yet more distorted. America has become the evil empire, the corrupter of Islamic cultures, the supporter of a Zionist Israel against the Muslim Palestinians, and the source of all the evils of the Near and Middle East; America is the enemy.

In February 1998, bin Laden issued a fatwa against all American citizens – military and civilian:

'The ruling to kill the Americans and their allies –civilian and military – is an individual duty for every Muslim who can do it in any country in which it is possible to do it, in order to liberate the al-Asqua Mosque (Jerusalem) an the holy mosque (Mecca) from their grip, and in order for

their armies to move out of all lands of Islam, defeated and unable to threaten any Muslim.'

In June 1999 bin Laden was added to the FBI's Ten Most Wanted List and a $5 million reward was offered.

Bin Laden has extraordinary mobility. During his time in Afghanistan, bin Laden was able to disguise his movements from the 50 US special officers who worked full-time on tracing his movements by regularly varying his style of movement. He varied the number of vehicles in his convoy, and varied the type of vehicle. Sometimes he gave his entourage hours of notice, sometimes only minutes. Since September 11, when US officials are more determined to find him, far less has been known. It is thought that only 20 dedicated guards know exactly where he is and that they are pledged to die rather than reveal where he is.

During the war in Afghanistan it seemed impossible that he could survive the systematic ambush in the Tora Bora hills, yet he escaped. Today, no-one knows for sure where he is. The last time he was heard of for sure was close to the Pakistan border. Most analysts think he is now in Pakistan. Bin Laden used to communicate with his organization, and the outside world generally, by satellite phone. Unfortunately, the US leaked that they were not only listening in but using the calls to locate him. Since then, he has naturally taken to using other methods – e-mail or couriers. The couriers carry computer discs with encrypted messages, which are carried from country to country and only de-encrypted in the destination country. Bin Laden is often referred to by aliases, such as the Sheikh, Hajj, Abu Abdullah, the Director. Multiple aliases are the hallmark of Al-Qaeda chiefs. Ramzi Yousef, who masterminded the World Trade Centre attack, used 15 different identities and 11 passports.

Bin Laden is the undisputed leader of Al Qaeda. He is called 'emir' or 'prince' by his followers, who have to swear an oath of personal allegiance to him, and violation of that oath is punishable by death. Under bin Laden is a consultative council. His two aides are Egyptian, Ayman al-Zawahiri, a doctor and leader of al-Jihad, and Muhammed Atef, his military commander who also served in al-Jihad. It was al-Jihad that was responsible for the massacre of tourists at Luxor in 1995. Then there is a fatwah committee of the council which makes the decisions to carry out terrorist attacks. Al-Qaeda is a transnational organization with operations in sixty countries and active cells in 20 of those. It is believed to operate training centres in Sudan and Afghanistan. There are active cells in Pakistan, Afhanistan, Kosovo, Chechnya, Philippines, Egypt, Tunisia and the USA.

Bin Laden's organization is meticulous in its organizational methods. Operations are planned months and even years ahead. Sites are often carefully researched using fieldwork. The 1995 assassination attempt against the President of Egypt, Hosni Mubarak, in Addis Ababa was based on surveillance of Mubarak's security arrangements in Ethiopia two years earlier. The East African embassy bombers phoned in credible but hoax threats to the embassies and then observed the embassy response; this was an operation that was planned over the course of five years.

Responsibilities for each operation are clearly divided, with a planning cell that mulls over and researches every aspect of the attack for months or years beforehand, and an execution cell that is brought in at the last moment, in some cases only a few weeks before the attack.

A surprising feature of the terrorist attacks is that they are relatively cheap. It has been estimated that the 1993 World Trade Centre attack cost Al-Qaeda $18,000 altogether, excluding $6,000 in unpaid phone bills. It was once assumed that bin Laden's huge personal fortune enabled him to finance these lavish projects, but it is not so. His personal fortune is not as great as was once thought, though still tens of millions of dollars, and his operations are relatively inexpensive.

The Americans are naturally disappointed not to have apprehended or killed bin Laden, but several senior Al-Qaeda officials have been eliminated, imprisoned or detained. There were also some successes in foiling several planned attacks, but pride in those successes diminished considerably after the September 11th catastrophe in 2001. The more recent train bombings in Madrid in March 2004, when 199 people were killed and the train, bus and tube bombings in London in July 2005, when 56 were killed, are grim reminders that bin Laden is still a force to be reckoned with.

The thing that will never be forgotten about this misguided man is that he bears the ultimate responsibility for the attacks on the World Trade Centre and the Pentagon on 11 September, 2001. Attacks in which over 3,000 people died unnecessarily.

Osama bin Laden's health is poor and he is regularly attended by a doctor. It has also emerged that he is dependent on kidney dialysis. Inevitably all sorts of stories and rumours circulate round such a figure. The only certainty is that the world has been changed by having Osama bin Laden in it. It has become a much more dangerous, frightening and uncertain place for the rest of us to live in.

INDEX
OF NAMES